HOW TO

JOB

IN

Atlanta

Robert Sanborn with A. Tariq Shakoor and Rosita Jackson

The Insider's
Guide Series

SURREY BOOKS
CHICAGO

HOW TO GET A JOB IN ATLANTA

Published by Surrey Books, Inc., 230 E. Ohio St., Suite 120, Chicago, IL 60611.

This book is manufactured in the United States of America.

4th Edition.   1   2   3   4   5

Library of Congress Cataloging-in-Publication data:
Sanborn, Robert, 1959-
    How to get a job in Atlanta—4th ed./ Robert Sanborn, A. Tariq Shakoor, and Rosita Jackson.
        p.   cm.
    Includes bibliographical references and index.
    ISBN 0-940625-60-1
        1. Job hunting—Georgia—Atlanta. 2. Job vacancies—Georgia—Atlanta.
3. Professions—Georgia—Atlanta. 4. Occupations—Georgia—Atlanta. 5. Industries—
Georgia—Atlanta—Directories. 6. Business enterprises—Georgia—Atlanta—Directories.
I. Shakoor, A. Tariq. II. Jackson, Rosita. How to get a job in Atlanta. IV. Title.
HF5382.75.U62G43   1997   96-39378
650.14'09758'231—dc21   CIP

AVAILABLE TITLES IN THIS SERIES — $16.95

How To Get a Job in Atlanta
How To Get a Job in Chicago
How To Get a Job in The New York Metropolitan Area
How To Get a Job in The San Francisco Bay Area
How To Get a Job in Seattle/Portland
How To Get a Job in Southern California

Single copies may be ordered directly from the publisher. Send check or money order for book price plus $4.00 for first book and $1.50 for each additional book to cover insurance, shipping, and handling to Surrey Books at the above address. For quantity discounts, please contact the publisher.

Editorial production by Bookcrafters, Inc., Chicago.
Cover and book design by Joan Sommers Design, Chicago.
Illustrations by Mona Daly.
Typesetting by On Track Graphics, Inc., Chicago.
"How To Get a Job Series" is distributed to the trade by Publishers Group West.

Acknowledgments

Robert Sanborn wishes to thank his personal support system: Ellen Sanborn and Virginia Elisabet, wife and daughter respectively. Tariq Shakoor also wishes to thank his wife, Elease, for her support, and he and Rosita Jackson wish to acknowledge researcher Flora Hammond and the Emory University Career Center staff for their contributions to this book. The authors also are indebted to Kim Lila for her editorial research and production assistance.

We also wish to acknowledge the seminal contributions of Thomas M. Camden, Editor Emeritus.

NAMES AND ADDRESSES CAN CHANGE

The authors and editors have made every effort to supply you with the most useful, up-to-date information available to help you find the job you want. Each name, address, and phone number has been verified by our staff of fact checkers. But offices move and people change jobs, so we urge you to check before you write or visit. And if you think we should include information on companies, organizations, or people that we've missed, please let us know.

The publisher, authors, and editors make no guarantee that the employers listed in this book have jobs available.

DROP US A LINE

Among the new features in this edition are "Dear Dr. Bob" letters—short notes from job seekers or workers like yourself, recounting their experiences. For this feature to be a success, we need your input. So if you have any interesting stories to share with your fellow job hunters, write to us in care of Surrey Books. We cannot guarantee publication, and letters will not be returned. Send your letters to:

> Dear Dr. Bob, Job Hunting Stories
> c/o Surrey Books
> 230 E. Ohio St., Suite 120
> Chicago, IL 60611

JOB HUNTING?

These books, covering 6 major markets, can help you achieve a successful career

HOW... to get the job you want: Each book gives you more than 1,500 major employers, numbers to call, and people to contact.

WHERE... to get the job you want: How to research the local job market and meet the people who hire.

PLUS... how to use the World Wide Web, local networks and professional organizations; how to choose a career; advice on employment services; how to sell yourself in the interview; writing power resumes and cover letters; hundreds of names and numbers, many available nowhere else!

Contents

one

So You Want To Get a Job in Atlanta

You've decided to get a job in one of the great cities of the world. Atlanta and the surrounding areas provide numerous opportunities for job seekers. Whether you want to work in the communications industry, a summer job in the north Georgia mountains, or a position working in an international trade firm in the New South, the Atlanta area can be exciting and rewarding. This book will help you find the job you're looking for.

How This Book Can Help

There are, of course, other books about finding jobs and about aspects of the job search such as resume writing and interviewing. This book is a little different. We have taken an approach that will make your Atlanta job search easier and, hopefully, successful.

How is this book any different from the rest? First, we are local. This book focuses on Atlanta. We have inside information on the job market and things unique to the job search here. Second, this book combines job-search information from the World Wide Web with conventional information on how to conduct a job search. Once you have access to the Internet, you will see how your search for a career can be made easier with a wealth of information at your fingertips. Finally, this Insider's Guide is coauthored by an expert on the local job market and a national career guru; the information you'll get is cutting edge and proven effective. This book is designed to help you find *and land* the best job in Atlanta.

Before You Arrive

Preparation is a key to any job search, and this is especially true if you are relocating from another city. If you're from out of town, you'll want to learn as much about the Atlanta Metropolitan area as possible. This will help ease the transition to your new home and allow you to concentrate on your job search. This chapter will give you a head start on learning about the area and its job market.

Much of this chapter is devoted to surveying the vast array of media sources that can help you gain a better knowledge of the region. But for some readers, the first step in the job search might be to figure out their best career options. In other words, you might need to revisit the old "what do I want to do when I grow up?" question. Choosing a career direction early on will help you focus on which industries to target. Chapter 2 will help you get that part of your search behind you.

The Atlanta Area Job Search

As unique as the area is, it is no different from any other place in the world when it comes down to finding a job. It takes work and perseverance. Chapter 4 outlines the ten steps toward seeking and securing a job. From networking to interviewing, all steps in the process are important. Chapter 5 highlights one of the most important and proven activities of the search for a career: networking. Chapter 6 will help you get your resume in shape, and Chapter 7 gets you ready to give that prospective employer the "killer" interview. Chapter 8 will help if you are looking for a summer or temporary job. And Chapter 10 is our exclusive listing of major employers in the Atlanta area, complete with addresses, phone numbers, and other information.

Going to a new city to look for a job is much different from being a tourist. You'll face not only the challenges of getting to know a new place but you'll face the task of carving a niche for yourself as well. Getting a head start on researching the city and employers will make your search much easier.

Using Local Newspapers

Learning more about the area and all it has to offer should be one of the more interesting and enjoyable parts of your preparation. The Atlanta area has a number of local publications that can help you learn more about the city and the local job markets.

Local newspapers are an excellent place to begin. As you start your job search, it is important to read the want ads for more than job vacancies. The classifieds can give you an idea of who the key employers are in your field and which ones are growing.

MAJOR NEWSPAPERS IN THE ATLANTA AREA

Atlanta Constitution
Atlanta Journal
72 Marietta St.
Atlanta, Georgia 30303
(404) 526-5151
http://www.ping.com/ajc/ajchome.html
The *Atlanta Constitution* is Atlanta's daily morning paper; the *Journal* comes out in the afternoon and is Atlanta's largest newspaper. Both have business sections that track local developments. The two papers publish together on Sundays and include an extensive business section. The following are some additional local newspapers with business information and limited classified job ads.

Atlanta Tribune
875 Old Roswell Road
Roswell, Georgia 30076
(770) 587-0501

Atlanta Jewish Times
1575 Northside Drive, N.W., Suite 470
Atlanta, Georgia 30318
(404) 352-2400

Korean Journal—Atlanta Edition
5455 Buford Highway
Doraville, Georgia 30340
(404) 451-6946

World Journal
5150 Buford Highway
Doraville, Georgia 30340
(770) 451-4509

Mundo Hispanico
1929 Piedmont Circle, N.E.
Atlanta, Georgia 30324
(404) 881-0441

Clayton News Daily
138 Church St.
Jonesboro, Georgia 30236
(770) 478-5753

DeKalb Neighbor
3060 Mercer University Drive
Chamblee, Georgia 30341
(770) 454-9388

Douglas County Sentinel
P.O. Box 1568
6405 Fairburn Road
Douglasville, Georgia 30133
(770) 942-6571

Marietta Daily Journal
580 Fairground St., S.E.
Marietta, Georgia 30061
(770) 795-3000

Rockdale Citizen
969 S. Main St.
Conyers, Georgia 30207
(770) 483-7108

The Big Picture: Business Magazines and Newspapers

The general business climate affects the local job market no matter what career field you are in. You should keep abreast of changing trends in the economy, both regional and national. The following publications can help.

The Wall Street Journal
Atlanta Bureau
11 Piedmont Center

Atlanta, GA 30305
(404) 233-2544
http://www.wsj.com
The *Journal* is the nation's leading business newspaper, covering everything
from national and international business trends to personnel changes in major
corporations. Its classified section usually carries ads for mid- to upper-level
management positions. Special issues to look for are: Black Entrepreneur
(February), Executive Pay (April), Technology (May and November), Education
(September), and Small Business (October).

Business Week
1221 Avenue of the Americas
New York, NY 10020
(212) 997-1221
Published weekly, this magazine will keep you informed as to key happenings in
the business world. Special issues include: Industry Outlook (24 key industries;
January), Corporate Scoreboard (ranks companies in selected industries;
March), Hot Growth Companies/Best Small Companies (May), and Best
Business Schools (October).

Atlanta Business Chronicle
1801 Peachtree St.
Atlanta, GA 30309
(404) 249-1048
Weekly
The premier source of Atlanta business news (no classified section); reports on
"real estate, advertising, technology, small businesses, retailing, etc." A MUST read!

Forbes
60 5th Ave.
New York, NY 10011
(212) 620-2200
Publishes 26 issues/year. Special issues include: The Annual Report on
American Industry (January), Top 500 U.S. Companies (April), International
500 (July), 800 Top U.S. Corporate Executives (personal and compensation
information; May), 200 Best Small U.S. Companies (November), and 400
Largest Private Companies in the U.S. (December).

Fortune
Time-Life Building
1271 Avenue of the Americas
New York, NY 10020-1301
(212) 586-1212
http://www.uophx.edu/lrc2.html#Business
Publishes 27 issues/year. Special issues include: 18-Month Economic Forecast
(January and July), America's Most Admired Corporations (February), U.S.
Business Hall of Fame (profiles selected business leaders; March), Fortune 500:

Largest U.S. Industrial Corporations (April), Service 500 (June), Global 500: U.S. and Foreign Corporations (July), Fastest Growing 100 Public Companies (October), Pacific Rim Survey (October), and Best Cities for Business (November).

Inc.
38 Commercial Wharf
Boston, MA 02110
(617) 248-8000
Published monthly. Special issues include: Best Cities for Starting a Business (April), 100 Fastest Growing Public Companies (May), and 500 Fastest Growing Private Companies (October).

Money
Time-Life Building
1271 Avenue of the Americas
New York, NY 10020-1301
(212) 522-1212
Published monthly. Annual September issue (Best Places to Live) is especially insightful for those thinking of relocating.

Fulton County Daily Report
190 Pryor St., S. W.
Atlanta, GA 30303
(404) 521-1227
The official daily court newspaper.

Black Enterprise
130 5th Ave.
New York, NY 10011
(212) 242-8000
Monthly business magazine highlighting minority-owned businesses and articles on business-related topics.

Working Woman
342 Madison Ave.
New York, NY 10173-0008
(212) 309-9800
This monthly publication is a great resource for professional women. Special issues include: Salary Survey (January), Top 50 Women in Business (May), Top 25 Careers for Women (July), and Ten Women to Watch (November).

The spirit of volunteerism: Get involved
As a newcomer to the area, you should know that Atlantans have a tremendous spirit of volunteerism. While conducting your employment search, consider volunteering with one of the numerous arts, recreational, or not-for-profit

organizations. This is an excellent way to make new
friends and business contacts, while becoming better
acquainted with your new home and making a difference
in your community. Contact the United Way of Metropolitan
Atlanta at (404) 527-7200 or read the Saturday "Leisure"
section of the *Atlanta Journal Constitution* for a listing of
volunteer opportunities.

The Internet

One of the key features of this book is the inclusion of numerous World Wide
Web (WWW) addresses to help you learn about the local area and jump-start
your job search. If you have never used cyberspace or the WWW, don't worry. In
most cases it's as simple as point and click. Surfing the Internet is an excellent way
to stay up-to-date on career opportunities and techniques. The Internet provides
access to volumes of information and numerous contacts, all without leaving
your desk.

To get started you'll need a computer, modem, and software to give you
Internet access. You'll probably find it most convenient to have your own computer, but if you don't, fear not. Friends, universities, and cybercafes can provide
you access to the Internet so you can join the millions now "on-line."

The "information superhighway" is really a worldwide link-up of computers
and computer networks. Most WWW addresses start with the letters http:// .
Following this will usually be a long string of characters—often words or abbre-
viations—with no spaces in between. When you type that "address" into the Web
browser on your computer (Netscape, Mosaic, or something similar), you will be
linked with the organization listed.

There are many articles and books about the Web and how to access it. We
will let you explore those on your own. However, we would like to give you an
idea of the type of information the Web addresses provide. For example, there are
places to get career counseling, learn about careers, post your resume, find information on companies, and view the types of positions they have open. You should
note the cost of each Internet-access service (America On-Line, Prodigy, or others) and other charges before signing up for any service. In addition, there are
career services on the Net that will offer you some free service with hopes that you
will buy others. Keep in mind that many of the best sites and homepages are free.

Let's get you started with some WWW addresses that can provide information first about Atlanta itself and next about careers and the job search.

CYBERINFO ABOUT THE ATLANTA AREA

Bus Information—Atlanta
http://www.itsmarta.com

City Net—Atlanta
http://www.city.net/countries/united_states/georgia/atlanta /
Provides city guides, general information on libraries, events, news, and transportation.

Business and Leisure Information
http://www.acme-atlanta.com/
General information about Atlanta including transportation, education, weather, etc.

Atlanta Government
http://www.acme-atlanta.com/gover.html
Telephone listing of federal, state, and local government agencies in the metro Atlanta area; includes key government offices.

City of Atlanta Home Page
http://www.Atlanta.com/city/cityinfo.html
General information about Atlanta.

CYBERRESOURCES FOR YOUR JOB SEARCH—NATIONAL

Try a few of these sites on the World Wide Web to get an overview of the job search and how the Internet might help. Many of these sites will give you a multitude of other links to continue honing your job-hunt skills.

Career Action Center
http://www.GATENET.com/cac/
A good page with links to other career-related resources. Also includes job listings, resource library, employer forums, job-search information, and local business trends.

The Career Channel
http://riceinfo.rice.edu:80/projects/careers/
A lot of links to other career sites, as well as material on all aspects of careers and the job search, from Rice University's Career Center.

Career Magazine
http://www.careermag.com/careermag/
Internet links and career information.

Career Mosaic
http://www.careermosaic.com/cm/
Includes information on hot companies, new products and technology, benefits and employee programs, and sites and lifestyles around the world.

CareerNet—Career Resource Center
http://www.careers.org
Thousands of job, employer, and career-reference Web links. Database includes employers, professional associations, career counselors, educational and self-employment resources. Also government jobs access and employer homepages.

The Catapult
http://www.wm.edu/catapult/catapult.html
An excellent page with links to almost all other good career-related Internet resources, run by the College of William and Mary Career Center. Many links to other college career centers.

Employment Opportunities and Job Resources (Margaret Riley)
http://www.wpi.edu/~mfriley/jobguide.html
One of the most highly respected collections of career resource links, with extensive advice on using the Internet's resources in the career-search process.

Interactive Employment Network
http://www.espan.com
Provides current resources for the job seeker: salary guides, advice from career specialists, and job listings (mostly in technical fields).

JobHunt (Dane Spearing at Stanford University)
http://rescomp.stanford.edu/jobs.html
A well-organized list of major Internet career resource links.

Job Listings Available via Dial-Up on BBS's (Harold Lemon)
http://rescomp.stanford.edu/jobs-bbs.html
A very large list of BBS systems nationwide, available by "dial-up" modem with no Internet connection.

Online Career Center
http://www.occ.com
A highly respected Internet jobs resource. Online Career Center is a non-profit employer association that provides a database, job and resume files, company information and profiles, and on-line search software to assist both employers and applicants in using the Internet in their career search.

Rennsselaer Polytechnic Institute (Career Resource Homepage)
http://www.rpi.edu/dept/cdc
An excellent collection of career resource links maintained by the R.P.I. Career Development Center.

Stanford University Yahoo Guide
http://akebono.stanford.edu/yahoo/
Links to several job-listing databases, as well as resume services and positions available on campus.

CYBERRESOURCES FOR YOUR JOB SEARCH—ATLANTA

Metroscope—Atlanta, Georgia
http://metroscope.com/atlanta.html
Listing of selected Atlanta area businesses and professional organizations.

Yahoo Regional Information on Atlanta
http://www.yahoo.com/Regional/U_S__States/Georgia/Cities/Atlanta/Business/
Employment
This WWW site will link you to many others with information on business,
professional organizations, educational institutions, real estate, and much more.

RECOMMENDED BOOKS FOR THE ON-LINE JOB SEARCH

Gonyea, James C. *The On-line Job Search Companion.* McGraw-Hill, New York,
NY, 1994. A complete guide to hundreds of career-planning and job-hunting
resources available via your computer.

Hahn, Harley, and Rick Stout. *The Internet Yellow Pages.* Osborne McGraw-Hill,
Berkeley, CA, 1994. Provides listing of where to search for ads or post your
resume.

Kennedy, Joyce Lain, and Thomas J. Morrow. *Electronic Resume Revolution.* John
Wiley & Sons, New York, NY, 1994. Provides resume information and
resources via the Internet.

Kennedy, Joyce Lain. *Hook Up, Get Hired!* John Wiley & Sons, New York, NY,
1995. Provides job-search information via the Internet.

Rittner, Don. *The Whole Earth On-line Almanac: Info from A to Z.* Brady
Publishing, New York, NY, 1993. Describes bulletin boards and on-line services along with phone numbers.

Business Trends in the Atlanta Area

Atlanta is the state capital of Georgia and the seat of Fulton County. The city
population as of the mid-1990s was approximately 415,000, but the metropolitan
area had approximately 3,512,000 inhabitants. The Atlanta metropolitan area
includes 18 counties that cover approximately 5,147 square miles. It is one of the
fastest growing regions in the United States.

According to DRI/McGraw-Hill, Inc., a Boston-based economic consulting
firm, Atlanta's metro area is expected to lead the nation's major metropolitan
areas in job creation between 1995 and 2000, with 267,600 of them in Atlanta. In
addition, the area is expected to benefit from the upgrading of Hartsfield
International Airport, the area's proximity to markets in the Midwest and Latin
America, an increasingly educated workforce, and a large presence of corporate
headquarters and distribution centers.

Atlanta's history is full of stories that attest to its toughness and "can do" spirit—from its resurgence after its burning during the Civil War to its winning the bid to host the 1996 Summer Olympic Games. Although it is well known as the home of the world's most popular soft drink and CNN, Atlanta's economic base is diverse. Based upon our research and reports from the local media, Atlanta is fast becoming the software development center of the Southeast. On the other hand, there are also a number of businesses related to health care—either delivery of services or product development.

Great opportunities have also been identified in the manufacturing of transportation equipment, printing and publishing, food, telecommunications, and information system processing. A growing number of software developers are calling Atlanta home and there's plenty of business to keep the software developers busy!

A shift is expected to occur from manufacturing to the service industry—a broad category that ranges from fast food to software development. DRI/McGraw Hill also expects 50,000 new jobs to be added by the trade and export-related employment. The largest percentage of Atlanta area residents are currently in the services or trade industries, followed by government, manufacturing, financial, transportation, utilities, and construction. Expect technology also to have an impact on how business is done, even with government regulation.

United Parcel Service is the largest private company in the metropolitan Atlanta area. Other well-known, major employers include Delta Air Lines, BellSouth Corporation, the Southern Company, the Kroger Company, SunTrust Banks, AT&T, Lockheed Martin, NationsBank Corporation, Home Depot, and the Coca-Cola Company. Metro Atlanta is also home to 18 Fortune 500 companies, including (again) BellSouth, Coca-Cola, Georgia-Pacific, Home Depot, Delta Air Lines, the Southern Company, AFLAC, Coca-Cola Enterprises, Genuine Parts, SunTrust Banks, Turner Broadcasting System, Shaw Industries, Alumax, and First Financial Management.

On the other hand, remember to consider Atlanta's smaller employers during your job search. National census data indicate that the country's smallest companies created nearly all of the 2.6 million new positions between 1989 and 1991. Networking meetings and articles in local periodicals are just two of the ways to uncover these employers. Other great sources of employment are the not-for-profit agencies, which can be identified through the *United Way Help Book* and similiar publications. Post-secondary schools, and local, state, and federal governments also employ a signficant number of Atlantans.

16 Best Places to Work in the Atlanta Area

Based upon local interviews, media coverage, annual surveys, and words from our working friends, we came up with a list of some of the best places to work in the Atlanta area. While most of these companies are growing, growth was only one factor in our selection process. Rather, we chose these employee-friendly companies based on the quality of their corporate culture. In other words, people like working at these places for many reasons besides business growth.

Our picks for the 16 best places to work in Atlanta are, in alphabetical order:

AT&T Corporation
1200 Peachtree St.
Atlanta, GA 30309
(404) 853-2900
(telecommunications)
http://www.att.com

BellSouth Corporation
1155 Peachtree St., N.E.
Atlanta, GA 30367
(404) 329-9455
(regional telecommunications)
http:www.bellsouth.com

The Coca-Cola Company
1 Coca-Cola Plaza, N.W.
Atlanta, GA 30339
(404) 676-2121
(soft drink producer)
http://cocacola.com

Cox Enterprises
1400 Lake Hearn Drive, N.E.
Atlanta, GA 30319
(404) 843-5000
(media)
http://www.ajc.com/cox/coxlst.htm

Delta Airlines
1050 Delta Blvd.
Atlanta, GA 30320
(404) 715-2501
(airline)
http://www.delta-air.com

The Home Depot
2727 Paces Ferry Road
Atlanta, GA 30339

(770) 433-8211
(building materials retailer)
http://homedepot.com

IBM Corporation
4111 Northside Parkway
Atlanta, GA 30327
(404) 814-0683
(computers and information technology)
http://www.ibm.com

The Kroger Company
2175 Parklake Drive
Atlanta, GA 30345
(770) 496-7400
(grocery store chain)
http://www.krogerusa.com

Lockheed Martin
86 S. Cobb Drive
Marietta, GA 30063
(770) 494-5052
(diversified services; aircraft production)
http://lmco.com/new

McMaster-Carr Supply Company
6100 Fulton Industrial Blvd., S.W.
Atlanta, GA 30336
(404) 349-9700
(product distributor for manufacturers)
http:www.mcmaster.com

NationsBank Corporation
600 Peachtree St., N.E.
Atlanta, GA 30308
(770) 969-0550
(consumer/commercial financial services)
http://ww.nationsbank.com

Scientific-Atlanta
1 Technology Parkway
Norcross, GA 30092
(770) 903-5000
(manufacturer of communications products)
http://www.sa.com

The Southern Company
64 Perimeter Center East
Atlanta, GA 30346

(770) 668-3464
(operates electric utilities)
http://www.southernco.com

Southwire Company
1 Southwire Drive
Carrollton, GA 30119
(770) 832-4242
(manufacturer of wire and cable for the electric industry)
http://www.southwire.com

United Parcel Service
55 Glenlake Parkway, N.E.
Atlanta, GA 30328
(770) 432-9494
(worldwide delivery service)
http:www.ups.com

United Way of Metropolitan Area
100 Edgewood Ave.
Atlanta, GA 30303
(404) 527-7200
(social service organization)

10 Fast-Growing Companies in the Atlanta Area

Based upon our research and reports from the local media, some of the fastest growing companies in the Atlanta area are, in alphabetical order:

Bruder Healthcare Company
1395 S. Marietta Parkway
Marietta, GA 30067
(770) 422-5994
Bruder manufactures and markets health care products.

Checkmate Electronics
1011 Mansell Road, Suite C
Roswell, GA 30076
(770) 594-6000
This growing company designs, manufactures, and markets point-of-service payment systems.

Corporate Environments
1636 Northeast Expressway
Atlanta, GA 30329
(404) 679-8999
Handles design services and provides office furniture for industry.

Firearms Training Systems
7340 McGinnis Ferry Road
Suwanee, GA 30174
(770) 813-0180
One of the most unusual businesses in Atlanta. This company manufactures simulators for firearms training.

IQ Software Corporation
3295 River Exchange Drive, Suite 550
Norcross, GA 30092
(770) 446-8880
http://www.iqsc.com
This corporation sells and supports computer systems.

Jenny Pruitt & Associates
990 Hammond Drive, Suite 1035
Atlanta, GA 30328
(770) 393-5400
http://www.jennypruitt.com
This real estate company is becoming well known throughout the Atlanta metropolitan area. Focus is on residential real estate services.

Mikart Inc.
1750 Chattahoochee Ave.
Atlanta, GA 30318
(404) 351-4510
Another growing major player in the health care industry. This company manufactures pharmaceuticals.

Retirement Care Associates
6000 Lake Forest Drive, Suite 200
Atlanta, GA 30328
(404) 255-7500
A major employer in the health care industry. Owns and operates nursing homes.

Softsense
115 Hammond Drive, Suite E-5200
Atlanta, GA 30328
(770) 399-0991
This organization is part of the growing computer-related industry in Atlanta. It develops, sells, and supports computer systems.

XcelleNet Inc.
5 Concourse Parkway, Suite 200
Atlanta, GA 30328
(770) 804-8100
http://www.xcellenet.com
Another organization that is a part of the growing computer-related industry in Atlanta. It develops, markets, and supports computer systems.

10 Largest Private Sector Employers in the Atlanta Area

Based upon our research and reports from the local media, the largest employers, by number of employees, in the Atlanta area are, in alphabetical order:

America's Favorite Chicken Company
6 Concourse Parkway, Suite 1700
Atlanta, GA 30328
(770) 353-3000
http://afc-online.com
Employees worldwide: 13,435; Atlanta area: 1,296
Parent company of Popeye's Chicken and Church's Chicken.

Cox Enterprises
1400 Lake Hearn Drive
Atlanta, GA 30319
(404) 843-5000
http://ajc.com/cox/coxlst.htm
Employees worldwide: 21,954; Atlanta area: 3,822
Media.

Gold Kist
244 Perimeter Center Parkway
Atlanta, GA 30346
(770) 393-5000
http://goldkist.com
Employees worldwide: 15,000; Atlanta area: 550
Poultry processing.

Johnson, W.B. , Properties
3414 Peachtree Road, N.E., Suite 300
Tucker, GA 30326
(404) 237-5500
Employees worldwide: 19,500; Atlanta area: 1,300
Owner of Ritz-Carlton hotels; franchisor of Waffle House restaurants.

Law Companies Group
1000 Abernathy Road, N.E.
Atlanta, GA 30328
(770) 396-8000
http://www.lawco.com
Employees worldwide: 4,500; Atlanta area: 782
Engineering and environmental consulting.

RTM Restaurant Group
5995 Barfield Road
Atlanta, GA 30328
(404) 256-4900
Employees worldwide: 12,000; Atlanta area: 4,000
Restaurant franchise owner.

Southwire Company
1 Southwire Drive
Carrollton, GA 30119
(770) 832-4242
http://www.southwire.com
Employees worldwide: 4,531; Atlanta area: 2,258
Manufacturer of wire for industry.

United Parcel Service
55 Glenlake Parkway, N.E.
Atlanta, GA 30328
(770) 828-6000
http://www.ups.com
Employees: worldwide: 315,000; Atlanta area: 7,800
Delivery service.

Watkins Associated Industries
1958 Monroe Drive
Atlanta, GA 30324
(404) 872-8666
Employees worldwide: 5,780; Atlanta area: 625
Diversified services.

Worldspan Travel Information Services
300 Galleria Parkway
Atlanta, GA 30339
(770) 563-7400
http://www.worldspan.com
Employees worldwide: 2,800; Atlanta area: 1,650
Transaction processing services for the travel industry.

Using Chambers of Commerce

Most chambers of commerce publish material that is helpful to newcomers or anyone who wants to be better informed about a community, and the Atlanta area chambers of commerce are no exception. They provide brochures and maps available free or for a nominal charge and provide much of what you'll want to know about area businesses, city services, transportation, public schools, utilities, and entertainment. Additionally, many chambers publish lists of professional organizations and other networking options within their city. The following chambers provide information and publications:

Atlanta Chamber of Commerce
235 International Blvd., N.W.
Atlanta, GA 30303
(404) 880-9000

Clayton County Chamber of Commerce
8712 Tara Blvd.
Jonesboro, GA 30236
(770) 478-6549

Cobb Chamber of Commerce
250 Interstate North Parkway, N.W.
Atlanta, GA 30339
(770) 980-2000

DeKalb Chamber of Commerce
750 Commerce Drive
Decatur, GA 30030
(404) 378-8000
Excellent source of networking events related to international business.

Gwinnett Chamber of Commerce
1230 Atkinson Road, N.W.
Lawrenceville, GA 30246
(770) 513-3000

South Fulton Chamber of Commerce
6400 Shannon Parkway
Union City, GA 30291
(770) 964-1984

Choosing a Career

Choosing a career or making a decision about which direction you wish to take in the world of jobs is certainly important, but it also can be one of the most difficult processes we go through in life. Ever since we learned to speak as two-year-olds, aunts, uncles, and other assorted adults have asked us, "What do you want to be when you grow up?" Now we ask ourselves that same question. So how do we choose that career, anyhow?

The first step in choosing a career is to learn who you are and what you want. In other words, start with self-assessment. We've outlined a few tools for you to use in assessing yourself and your abilities. It is important to remember that it is very difficult to get a job if you do not know what you want to do. Self-assessment will enable you to start with a goal in mind. After you figure out who you are, it is much easier to find a compatible career.

A Few Facts about Career Decision Making

According to a recent Gallup poll, most people don't have goals when starting to think about the job search. No real planning goes into what is arguably the most important decision of their lives. The poll shows that:

- 59% of us work in an area or career in which we never planned to work.
- 29% of us are influenced by another person to go into a career. It's like the advice given to Dustin Hoffman in *The Graduate*. Someone says, "Plastics—that's where you should be. Try working in plastics." So we consider plastics.
- 18% of us fall into jobs by chance. You're looking for a job in banking and someone mentions that they know of a job in consulting. Sure you're willing to look at it. Next thing you know, you're a consultant.
- 12% of us took the job because it was available. You're walking by the local GAP store and see a "management trainee" sign. You take it!

This same Gallup poll indicated that we fail to properly assess ourselves and our career options. If we had to do it over, the poll indicates, 65% of the American public would get additional information on career options early on. Other polls show that up to 80% of the working public is dissatisfied with one or more aspects of their career and have seriously considered changing.

All of these facts and figures certainly bode poorly for those who jump into a career haphazardly. And, conversely, the statistics bode well for those who delve into a little career exploration before taking the plunge. This is especially true in light of the fact that the average American emigrates through seven to ten jobs and three to four careers in a lifetime. Thus, we will probably need to assess ourselves more than once as our own life changes with the changing job market. Self-assessment is a tool we will use throughout our professional lives.

Strategies in Self-Exploration

Practically everyone wants a job that provides personal satisfaction, growth, good salary and benefits, a certain level of prestige, and a desirable location. But unless you have a more specific idea of the kind of work you want, you probably won't find it. You wouldn't take off on your big annual vacation without some kind of destination in mind. Given that your job will take up much more of your time than your vacation, a little planning is certainly in order.

There are several strategies that can help you learn who you are. Among them are talking with friends and family, self-assessing, and getting help from a career professional.

Friends and family sometimes know you better than you think. They can also provide great support throughout the job search. Try the self-assessment exercises in this chapter, then discuss your results with those who know you best. They may have some insight that you overlooked. However, it is important to follow your own desires and not the dreams of family and friends when choosing a career.

Everyone can benefit from a thorough self-appraisal. The insight gained from self-appraisal is valuable not only in deciding on a career but also in articulating this knowledge in the resume and interviewing process. Perhaps you want to be a little more scientific in your appraisal of yourself. Try career testing. Professionals in vocational planning have literally dozens of tests at their disposal designed to assess personality and aptitude for particular careers.

Getting Started with Self-Assessment

What follows is a list of highly personal questions designed to provide you with insights you may never have considered and to help you answer the Big Question, "What do I want to do?"

To get the most from this exercise, write out your answers. This will take some time, but it will force you to give each question careful thought. The more effort you put into this exercise, the better prepared you'll be for the tough questions you'll be asked in any job interview. The exercise also can be the basis for constructing a winning resume—a subject we'll discuss in more detail in Chapter 6.

QUESTIONS ABOUT ME

Here are some questions to get you started. The answers will indicate what kind of person you are. Be honest. Take as much time as necessary.

1. Describe yourself in less than 500 words. Address these questions: Do you prefer to spend time alone or with other people? How well disciplined are you? Are you quick-tempered? Easygoing? Do you prefer to give orders or take orders? Do you tend to take a conventional, practical approach to problems? Or are you imaginative and experimental? How sensitive are you to others?
2. What accomplishment are you most proud of?
3. What are the most important things you wish to accomplish?
4. What role does your job play in those achievements?
5. Why do you (or don't you) want your career to be the most important thing in your life?
6. What impact do you have on other people?
7. Describe the kind of person others think you are.
8. What role does money play in your standard of values?
9. What do you enjoy most/dislike most?
10. What do you want your life to be like in 5 years?
11. What are your main interests?

What Job Attributes Do You Value Most?

After answering the above questions, it is important to match the job attributes you value to your career. Job burnout usually happens when people are in jobs that don't allow them to do and get the activities and rewards they want. But job satisfaction will occur if a person follows his or her motivations into a career. The following ranking will assist you in beginning to match the job attributes you value with careers that are in step with them.

Rank the following in order of importance to you:

- Leadership
- Creativity
- High Salary
- Helping Others
- Variety
- Physical Activity
- Self-development
- Recognition

- Job Security
- Competition
- Taking Risk

- Working with My Mind
- Prestige
- Independence

Once you've ranked the above, you should begin to get an idea of what's important to you. Compare your priorities to those of the workplace in your potential career/job. Values of the workplace can be determined in several ways. One method is to interview current employees of the company. Another is to research the company through articles and publications to determine its values and beliefs.

QUESTIONS ABOUT MY JOB

Questions about your job can also help in your self-assessment.

1. Describe *in detail* each job you have had. Begin with your most recent employment and work back toward graduation. Include your title, company name, responsibilities, salary, achievements and successes, failures, and reason for leaving. If you're a recent college graduate and have little or no career-related work experience, you may find it helpful to consider your collegiate experience, both curricular and extracurricular, as your work history for questions 1, 2, 3, 7, 8, 9, and 10.
2. What would you change in your past, if you could?
3. In your career thus far, what responsibilities have you enjoyed most? Least? Why?
4. How hard are you prepared to work?
5. What jobs would allow you to use your talents and interests?
6. What have your subordinates thought about you as a boss? As a person?
7. What have your superiors thought about you as an employee? As a person?
8. If you have been fired from any job, what was the reason?
9. Does your work make you happy? Should it?
10. What do you want to achieve by the time you retire?

Answering these questions will help clarify who you are, what you want, and what you realistically have to offer. They should also reveal what you don't want and what you can't do. It's important to evaluate any objective you're considering in light of your answers to these questions. If a prospective employer knew nothing about you except your answers to these questions, would he think your career objectives were realistic?

One way to match who you are with a specific career is to refer to the *Dictionary of Occupational Titles (DOT)*. The *DOT* is an encyclopedia of careers, covering hundreds of occupations and industries. For the computer buff, *The Perfect Career* by James Gonyea (3444 Dundee Rd., Northbrook, IL 60062) has a database of over 600 occupations for IBM and compatibles.

Professional Testing

As mentioned earlier, professionals in career counseling (see list below) have literally dozens of tests at their disposal designed to assess personality and aptitude for particular careers. Here are a few of the most commonly used career tests.

Strong Interest Inventory

This test looks at a person's interests to see if they parallel the interests of people already employed in specific occupations. It is used chiefly as an aid in making academic choices and career decisions. It continues to be one of the most researched and highly respected counseling tools in use.

Myers-Briggs Type Indicator

This test is based on Carl Jung's theory of perception and judgment and is a widely used measure of personality dispositions and preferences. Used in career counseling, it helps to identify compatible work settings, relate career opportunities and demands to preferences in perception and judgment, and gain insight into personality dimensions, all of which provide the opportunity for greater decision-making ability.

16 PF (Personality Factor) Questionnaire

This test measures 32 personality traits of a normal adult personality along 16 dimensions. Used frequently in counseling, the computerized printout and narrative report show how personality traits may fit into various career fields.

Career Counseling

Although the terms are often used synonymously, there is a difference between a career counselor and consultant. Most professionals use the title "counselor" if they have an advanced degree in psychology, counseling, social work, or marriage, family, and child counseling and are licensed by the state.

Need a list of certified counselors?
The National Board for Certified Counselors provides a list of professional "certified career counselors" in local areas. Certification requires a master's degree and three years of supervised counseling experience. For further information call (800) 398-5389.

Professionals who are not licensed often call themselves "career consultants." This field attracts people from a variety of backgrounds, education, and levels of competency. It's important, then, to talk to others who have used a given service before committing yourself.

Because most career counseling and consulting firms are private, for-profit businesses with high overhead costs, they usually charge more for testing than local colleges or social service agencies, which are listed later in this chapter.

What can you expect from a career counselor? For one thing, counselors offer an objective viewpoint. One licensed professional career counselor puts it this way: "You may not be able to discuss everything with family, friends, and especially coworkers if you happen still to be working. A trained professional can serve as a sounding board and offer strategies and information that you can't get elsewhere. We can essentially help a person become more resourceful."

This particular career counselor usually spends four sessions with individuals who want to establish a sense of direction for their careers. Here's what sessions cover:

- Exploring problems that have blocked progress and considering solutions.
- Establishing career objectives and determining strengths and areas to work on.
- Writing a career plan that outlines a strategy to achieve goals.
- Preparing an ongoing, self-directed plan to explore career goals.

"A counselor should help people develop methods and a framework on which to base continual exploration about what they want from a career, even after they are employed," our counselor friend says.

All too often people look for "quick fixes" in order to get back to work, she says. "In haste, they may not take time to reflect on where their career is going, to make sure they look for a job that will be challenging and satisfying."

What follows are some local area counselors and consultants who may be able to help you in your job search. Keep in mind, though, that a listing in this book does not constitute an endorsement of any consulting firm or testing service. Before embarking on a lengthy or expensive series of tests, try to get the opinion of one or more persons who have already used the service you're considering. To check out a particular practitioner, you can contact the following:

- Better Business Bureau of Metropolitan Atlanta (404) 688-4910
- State of Georgia Human Resources Department (404) 656-9358
- Office of the Secretary of State, Professional Examining Boards (404) 656-3900
- Attorney General's Office, Consumer Protection (404) 656-3790
- Office of Consumer Affairs, Complaint Intake Center (404) 651-8600

ATLANTA AREA CAREER COUNSELORS AND CONSULTANTS

APRS Career & Resume Services
1155 Hammond Drive, N.E.
Atlanta, GA 30328
(770) 393-3554
Offers variety of services. Free initial consultation.

Atlanta Counseling and Career Services
2531 Briarcliff Road, N.E.
Atlanta, GA 30329
(770) 633-6826
Offers a variety of career and personal counseling services. Flexible hours and fee schedule.

Atlanta Psychological & Vocational Center
4684 Roswell Road, N.W.
Atlanta, GA 30342
(404) 256-7998
Provides both personal and career counseling on a sliding scale.

Ballew Consultation Services
1447 Peachtree St., S.E.
Atlanta, GA 30342
(404) 874-8536
Contact John Ballew. Testing available. Counseling $60.00 an hour.

Career Assessment Atlanta
1651 Mt. Vernon Road
Dunwoody, GA 30338
(404) 257-9353
Career testing and counseling. Contact: Jeanette Nicholson.

Center for Professional & Personal Growth, The
3475 Lenox Road, N.E.
Atlanta, GA 30326
(404) 261-9200
Offers a wide range of career planning and personal growth services.

Haddle, Harold, Ph.D.
1649 Tullie Circle, N. E., Suite 112
Atlanta, GA 30329
(404) 634-1213
Emphasizes testing and self-assessment through counseling. No job search or placement.

Highlands Program, The
999 Peachtree St., N.E.
Atlanta, GA 30309

(404) 872-9974
An integrated program designed to help you figure out what to do with your life. It is a 35-hour process involving ability testing, self-discovery, and planning seminars. Specially designed programs for adults and students.

Johnson O'Connor Research Foundation
3400 Peachtree Road, N.E. , Suite 1023
Atlanta, GA 30326
A non-profit agency, specializing in measuring innate abilities by means of apparatus tests. $480 fee for 3 half-day testing sessions and interpretation.

McTier, Alan, and Associates
2001 Montreal Road, N.E.
Tucker, GA 30084
(770) 939-5722
Provides a variety of services including career testing and counseling and seminars to assist with job search.

Career Assistance at Local Colleges and Universities

Students and recent graduates often don't realize how much help is available through college and university career services offices. Career Services offices provide assistance in choosing a program of study as well as career testing to current students. After graduation, many colleges and universities continue to work with alumni through their career centers. Most colleges and universities offer some form of reciprocal services for students and graduates from other schools. Check with your undergraduate school to find out what's available and who is eligible for assistance.

While most colleges and universities don't permit the general public to use their counseling and placement services, some will offer programs to the public for a fee. The extent of assistance varies from campus to campus. The services offered at colleges and universities is generally of good quality and affordable.

Some colleges and universities offer non-credit and credit courses as well as special lectures and seminars to help individuals prepare for the job hunt and explore options in the work world. In recent years, schools also have offered more practical courses that are designed to help individuals acquire job skills or brush up on skills they already have.

Try on a career with an internship
Internships are more popular today than ever before—with both new grads and seasoned workers interested in changing careers. Internships are a form of on-the-job training that lets both you and your employer determine your potential in a specific work environment.

If you're about to graduate, check the career services office at your college, where lists of available internships usually abound. If you're already in the workforce, get in touch with the same office at the college you attended or try the career offices at local colleges and universities listed in this chapter. When applying for an internship, be sure to stress what you can offer an organization and express your enthusiasm for the field.

For more information, look into these resources:

America's Top 100 Internships, Mark Oldman and Samer Hamadeh (Princeton Review).

Internships 1996 (Peterson's Guides, Princeton, NJ).

Internships Leading to Careers (The Graduate Group, West Hartford, CT).

Job Finder series, Daniel Lauber (Planning/Communications Publishers, River Forest, IL).

National Association for Interpretation (Ft. Collins, CO), call (303) 491-6784 for free Dial-an-Intern service.

National Directory of Internships (National Society for Experiential Education, Raleigh, NC).

ATLANTA AREA COLLEGES OFFERING CAREER GUIDANCE

DeKalb College
Career Directions
North Campus
2101 Womack Road
Atlanta, GA 30338

South Campus
3251 Panthersville Road
Decatur, GA 30034
(770) 551-3062
An ongoing program that includes a complete series of career assessments and a private session with a career counselor. Registration required. Fee: $169.00.

Emory University
New Visions for Career Success
1784 N. Decatur Road, Suite 200
Decatur, GA 30033
(404) 727-6211
Program provides career assessment, resume critique, and assistance with developing a career plan and job search. Participants receive weekly job-listing newsletter. Registration required. Fee: $165.00.

Emory University
Evening at Emory
1799-X Briarcliff Road
Decatur, GA 30306
(404) 874-0999
The Continuing Education Program of Emory University offers classes and
workshops that provide the job seeker with career assessments and other job-
search help. Registration required. Fees: vary.

Georgia State University
Division of Continuing Education
P.O. Box 4044
Atlanta, GA
(404) 651-3456
Georgia State University's continuing education program offers a variety of
programs that assist job seekers with the job search, from assessment to inter-
viewing skills.

Georgia State University
Project Explore
Career Development Center
University Plaza
Atlanta, GA 30303-3083
(404) 651-2215
An ongoing comprehensive career development program, including three tests,
workshops, and individual sessions with career counselors. Fee: $135
By appointment only.

Oglethorpe University
Career Assessment and Planning
4484 Peachtree Road, N.E.
Atlanta, GA 30319
(404) 364-8383
Program provides assessments and individual counseling. Registration required.
Fee: $165.00

Social Service Agencies Offering Career Assistance

Unlike independent career counselors and consultants, social service agencies are
not-for-profit. They offer a wide range of services, from counseling and vocational training to job placement and follow-up—and their services are either low
cost or free. Again, keep in mind, that a listing in this book does not constitute an
endorsement of any agency.

Agencia Latina Americana
2785 Clairmont Road, N.E.
Decatur, GA 30033

(404) 636-9496
This organization provides assistance to Spanish-speaking people seeking employment, training, and social assistance.

Atlanta Urban League
100 Edgewood Ave., N.E.
Atlanta, GA 30303
(404) 659-1150
Offers job training, counseling to clients seeking employment; referrals to prospective employers. All services are free.

Employment Resource Center for Mature Workers
957 N. Highland Ave., N.E.
Atlanta, GA 30306
(404) 872-2231
This non-profit center offers services to men and women age 45 and older. Operates a job bank, offers counseling, job-search assistance, and business contacts to semi-skilled, skilled, and professional people who are not eligible for government-assisted programs.

Georgia Veteran's Assistance
722 W. College Ave.
Decatur, GA 30330
(404) 371-0566
Provides veterans with assistance in a variety of areas including benefits, training, employment assistance, and counseling.

Jewish Vocational Service
4549 Chamblee-Dunwoody Road
Dunwoody, GA 30338-6210
(770) 677-9440
Provides vocational counseling, employment assistance, and self-development seminars.

Nonprofit Resource Center
50 Hurt Plaza, Suite 220
Atlanta, GA 30303
(404) 688-4845
Provides non-profit management training and workshops, as well as management consulting to non-profit organizations; bi-weekly publication listing employment opportunities in the non-profit area; volunteer opportunities and resume listing service available.

Veterans Employment and Training Service
U.S. Department of Labor
148 International Blvd., N.E., Room 504
Atlanta, GA 30303
(404) 656-3127
Assists veterans with employment and training opportunities.

Career Change: Reality Bites

One morning you wake up, put on your $200 sunglasses, and head to work in your new Lexus. When you get to the office the doors are locked. To your surprise a sign on the door says "Filed for Bankruptcy." At this point you are probably saying, "I must be dreaming." Well, in today's work world, downsizing, mergers, and cost-cutting are all real—and sometimes reality bites!

Dramatic setbacks can often be your best opportunity for considering a career change. However, most people changing careers tend to believe they lack the skills for another career field. Maybe and maybe not. Self-assessment, defining your aptitudes and values, and possibly vocational testing can assist you in deciding on a career change.

There are three main reasons why people change careers:

1. A desire for a better fit among occupation, interests, and values is the primary reason that managers and professionals change careers. People want more career satisfaction and are usually willing to change careers to get it. Those who were coerced into that first career either by parents, misguided ambition, or lack of career information are highly likely to be dissatisfied. In time, they seek change.

2. Job loss. People that are laid off or fired make up a significant portion of those deciding to change careers rather than just replace the job that was lost. Appropriately, it is these people who may experience depression in their search because they feel they have been forced into the change.

3. A smaller group of career changers comprise those who at mid-career decide to turn a passion or hobby into an occupation.

The ability to transfer your skills is crucial in a career change. Many people feel their experience is only relevant to the previous job. In reality, most skills may be applied to a wide variety of jobs. Below are a number of commonly transferable skills. How many do you have?

administering	operating
analyzing	organizing
assisting	persuading
calculating	planning
creating	problem-solving
distributing	recommending
editing	researching
gathering	speaking
instructing	supervising
monitoring	trouble-shooting
motivating	writing

From customer service to fund-raising

After working for a year in customer service for a large retail chain, Sharon decided to make a career change when the company was faced with financial difficulties and had to downsize. Having been a music major in college, Sharon was not sure if she had acquired enough useful job skills to transfer into a new career. She became interested in a fund-raising job at a local university when one of her business contacts mentioned an opening in the development office.

"I volunteered for the annual tele-fund-raising campaign at the university to find out if I could handle development activities. I discovered that I really enjoyed the work. Best of all, many of my skills from my previous job, especially in communication, writing, and computer literacy, were well suited for it. I interviewed for the job and got it, with the additional help of a recommendation from my business contact."

Starting Your Own Business

Perhaps your self-assessment results lead you away from employment altogether and toward starting your own business. If so, a wealth of information is provided through the **U.S. Small Business Administration,** which provides free information on a variety of topics, including loan programs, tax preparation, government contracts, and management techniques. Although simple questions can be answered by telephone, you'll learn a lot more by dropping by one of the main offices to meet with staff members or volunteers from SCORE (Service Corps of Retired Executives). You might be matched with a retired professional in your field who could share information that will help you get started.

In addition, members of ACE (Active Corps of Executives), a volunteer group of working professionals, are on hand to offer assistance. These volunteers conduct free seminars covering major topics of interest to new business owners. Programs are scheduled regularly at the main offices; others are held at local colleges and elsewhere in the community.

SMALL BUSINESS CENTERS IN METRO ATLANTA

These centers provide technical assistance to entrepreneurs in such areas as developing business plans, market research, and financing. Most seminars and other assistance are free.

Small Business Development Center
Clayton State College
P.O. Box 285
Morrow, GA 30260
(770) 961-3440

Small Business Development Center
1770 Indian Trail Road
Norcross, GA 30393
(770) 806-2124

Small Business Development Center
1 Park Place South
Atlanta, GA 30349
(404) 651-3550

Small Business Development Center—DeKalb
750 Commerce Drive
Decatur, GA 30030
(404) 378-8000

Small Business Institute of Georgia
1827 Powers Ferry Road, S.E.
Marietta, GA 30339
(770) 955-5980

U. S. Small Business Administration, Atlanta District
1720 Peachtree Road, 6th Floor
Atlanta, GA 30309
(404) 347-2441

OTHER SMALL BUSINESS SERVICES AVAILABLE

Small Business Services
881 Ponce De Leon Ave. N.E.
Atlanta, GA 30306
(404) 873-0470
Provides services to small and mid-size businesses in the area of taxes, book-keeping, accounting, incorporation, and loan packaging. A fee-based service.

Small Business Accounting and Income Tax Service
1229 Salem Gate Drive
Conyers, GA 30208
(770) 860-1321

Small Business Computer Consulting
148 Basil Court, N.E.
Lawrenceville, GA 30243
(770) 995-3360

Women's Web sites

http://www.sbaonline.sba.gov/womeninbusiness/
is the SBA's homepage for women in business. Links are
provided to the National Women's Business Council and
other related sites.

http://www.intac.com/~kgs/bbpw/meta.html
lists sites related to businesswomen's issues and
organizations, employment, and more.

http://www.igc.apc.org/womensnet/
links you to services and resources for women.

Business Resources for Women

The following resources for women may also be of help. Refer to the networking
organizations listed in Chapter 5 for additional support groups and information.

Women's Entrepreneurial Center
1614 Pinehurst Drive, N.W.
Atlanta, GA 30310
(404) 752-5720

Women Of Distinction
5540 Old National Highway
College Park, GA 30349
(404) 767-3889

Women's Center For Self Development
1014 Canton St.
Atlanta, GA 30075
(770) 993-2676

Women's Chamber of Commerce of Atlanta
1447 Peachtree St., N.E.
Atlanta, GA 30309
(404) 892-0538

Women's Commerce Club
1195 Dunbrooke Lane
Dunwoody, GA 30338
(770) 395-1582

Women's Economic Development Agency
127 Peachtree St., N.E.
Atlanta, GA 30303
(404) 659-5003

Women's Information Center
957 N. Highland Ave., N.E.
Atlanta, GA 30307
(404) 892-3476

Women's Information Service And Exchange/WISE
125 5th St., N.E.
Atlanta, GA 30308
(404) 817-3441

Great Books to Help You Figure Out Your Life

People who are entering the job market for the first time, those who have been working for one company for many years, and those who are considering a career change can usually use a little more help than we have supplied here, and certainly the more help the better. To get that little extra boost, we can refer you to some excellent books. If you have access to college resources, be sure to take advantage of the career libraries as well as the counseling and career planning services that are available on most campuses.

CAREER STRATEGY BOOKS

Baldwin, Eleanor. *300 Ways to Get a Better Job.* Holbrook, MA: Adams
   Publishing, 1991.
Beatty, Richard H. *Get the Right Job in 60 Days or Less.* New York: John Wiley &
   Sons, 1991.
Bolles, Richard N. *The Three Boxes of Life and How to Get Out of Them.*
   Berkeley, CA: Ten Speed Press, 1981
Bolles, Richard N. *What Color Is Your Parachute?* Berkeley, CA: Ten Speed Press.
   The bible for job hunters and career changers, this book is revised every
   year and is widely regarded as one of the most useful and creative manuals
   on the market.
Clawson, James G., et al. *Self Assessment and Career Development.* Englewood
   Cliffs, NJ: Prentice-Hall, 1991. A very thorough guide with self-assessment
   worksheets and a good bibliography.
Dubin, Judith A., and Melonie R. Keveles. *Fired for Success.* New York: Warner
   Books, 1990.
Harkavy, Michael. *One Hundred One Careers: A Guide to the Fastest Growing
   Opportunities.* New York: John Wiley & Sons, 1990.
Jackson, Tom. *Guerrilla Tactics in the Job Market.* New York: Bantam Books,
   1991. Filled with unconventional but effective suggestions.
Krannich, Ronald L. *Change Your Job, Change Your Life: High Impact Strategies
   for Finding Great Jobs in the 90's.* Manassas, VA: Impact Publications, 1994.

Levinson, Harry. *Designing and Managing Your Career*. Boston: Harvard University Press, 1989.

Morin, William J., and Colvena, James C. *Parting Company: How to Survive the Loss of a Job and Find Another Successfully*. San Diego, CA: HBJ, 1991.

Munschauer, John L. *Jobs for English Majors and Other Smart People*. Princeton, NJ: Peterson's Guides, 1991.

Petras, Kathryn and Ross. *The Only Job Hunting Guide You'll Ever Need*. New York: Fireside, 1995.

Roper, David H. *Getting The Job You Want...Now!* New York: Warner Books, 1994.

Washington, Tom. *Complete Book to Effective Job Finding*. Bellevue, WA: Mount Vernon Press, 1992.

Weinstein, Bob. *Resumes Don't Get Jobs: The Realities and Myths of Job Hunting*. New York: McGraw-Hill Inc., 1993.

Yate, Martin. *Knock 'Em Dead*. Holbrook, MA: Adams Publishing, 1995.

If you're **still in college or have recently graduated,** the following books will be of particular interest:

Briggs, James I. *The Berkeley Guide to Employment for New College Graduates*. Berkeley, CA: Ten Speed Press, 1984.

Holton, Ed. *The M.B.A.'s Guide to Career Planning*. Princeton, NJ: Peterson's Guides, 1989.

La Fevre, John L. *How You Really Get Hired: The Inside Story from a College Recruiter*. New York: Prentice-Hall, 1993.

Richardson, Bradley G. *Jobsmarts for Twentysomethings*. New York: Vintage Books, 1995.

Steele, John, and Marilyn Morgan. *Career Planning & Development for College Students and Recent Graduates*. Lincolnwood, IL: National Textbook Co., 1991.

Tener, Elizabeth. *Smith College Guide: How to Find and Manage Your First Job*. New York: Pflume, 1991.

For those involved in a **mid-life career change,** here are some books that might prove helpful:

Anderson, Nancy. *Work With Passion: How to Do What You Love for a Living*. Rafeal, CA: New World Library, 1995.

Birsner, E. Patricia. *The Forty-Plus Job Hunting Guide: Official Handbook of the 40-Plus Club*. New York: Facts on File, 1990.

Byron, William J. *Finding Work Without Losing Heart: Bouncing Back from Mid-Career Job Loss*. Holbrook, MA: Adams Publishing, 1995.

Holloway, Diane, and Nancy Bishop. *Before You Say "I Quit": A Guide to Making Successful Job Transitions.* New York: Collier Books, 1990.

Logue, Charles H. *Outplace Yourself: Secrets of an Executive Outplacement Counselor.* Holbrook, MA: Adams Publishing, 1995.

Stevens, Paul. *Beating Job Burnout: How to Turn Your Work into Your Passion.* Lincolnwood, IL: VGM Career Horizons, 1995.

For workers who are **nearing retirement age** or have already reached it, here are some books that might be useful:

Kerr, Judy. *The Senior Citizen's Guide to Starting a Part-Time, Home-Based Business.* New York: Pilot Industries, 1992.

Morgan, John S. *Getting a Job After Fifty.* Blue Ridge Summit, PA: TAB Books, 1990.

Ray, Samuel. *Job Hunting After 50: Strategies for Success.* New York: John Wiley & Sons, 1991.

Strasser, Stephen, and John Sena. *Transitions: Successful Strategies from Mid-Career to Retirement.* Hawthorne, NJ: Career Press, 1990.

And for people with **disabilities,** these titles could prove helpful:

Rabbi, Rami, and Diane Croft. *Take Charge: A Strategic Guide for Blind Job Seekers.* Boston: National Braille Press, 1990.

Pocket Guide to Federal Help for Individuals with Disabilities. Clearinghouse on the Handicapped, Washington, DC: U.S. Department of Education, 1989. Discusses the many types of federal help for disabled job seekers. Useful and concise, only $1.

For **women and minority groups** in the workforce, these titles will be of interest:

Berryman, Sue E. *Routes Into the Mainstream: Career Choices of Women & Minorities.* Columbus, OH: Continuing Educational Training Employment, 1988.

Betz, Nancy E., and Louise Fitzgerald. *The Career Psychology of Women.* Orlando: Academic Press, 1987.

Lunnenborg, Patricia. *Women Changing Work.* New York: Bergin & Garvey Publishers, 1990.

Nivens, Beatrice. *The Black Woman's Career Guide.* New York: Anchor Books, 1987.

Thompson, Charlotte E. *Single Solutions—An Essential Guide for the Single Career Woman.* Brookline Village, MA: Branden Publishing, 1990.

three

If I Can't Find a Job, Should I Go Back to School?

"**I**'m having a real hard time finding a job. Maybe I'll just go back to school." The rationale seems logical; more school should get you a job. The facts, however, don't always show the "more schooling" route to be the best one, as we will discuss below. Sometimes, however, getting another degree or a bit more education can make the difference between a job and a great career.

When To Go Back to School

Admittedly, additional education can enhance your marketability. But as you weigh the pros and cons of committing time and money to the classroom, you should never consider additional education a panacea for all of your career woes.

A myth people want to believe is that an advanced degree, a different degree, or even a bit more education will automatically translate into a better job. People considering law school or an MBA frequently fall prey to this myth. The reality is that the job market is very tight, especially for lawyers, and employers are resistant to hire people who may have entered a particular field on a whim and don't have any real long-term commitment to the profession. It is less risky for employers to hire someone with a proven track record than someone with a new advanced degree. Those pursuing graduate work in the liberal arts, and not wishing to teach, are also in for a big surprise when they realize that they often end up in the same predicament they were in upon graduating with a B.A.: undecided upon a career and having very few options.

Despite the negatives, though, there are several good reasons for returning to school for additional education. These include:

To Acquire Additional Skills

If you find that your skills are not keeping pace with the demands of your career, you may consider returning to school. Learning accounting, computer systems, or a foreign language, for example, may be the boost your career needs.

To Prepare for a Career Change.

Frequently, job changers will realize that they want to leave their current field altogether. If after talking with a career counselor, assessing your goals, and weighing your options, you decide that a career change is the right choice, additional education—a different degree—may be a requirement.

To Advance in Your Career.

For certain fields, such as investment banking, an MBA is necessary to advance. In other fields, the standards for additional education may be more subtle. Another degree or merely additional coursework toward a degree may translate into a salary increase or consideration for a promotion.

Some people may be intimidated at the thought of acquiring additional education because they associate it with spent time and money. In reality, professional education can take many forms and carry a wide range of price tags. Other options to graduate school with varying cost-benefit trade-offs include community college courses, evening classes at a university, professional training for certification, or even executive education programs offered by many business schools. The bottom line is that when you consider additional education, do not limit your thinking only to formal degree programs at a university.

Tips on Considering Additional Schooling

There are many issues to consider before returning to school. First, determine how an additional degree or professional training will fit into your long-term goals. As you prepare to invest money, time, and energy on education, it is essential to know how you will benefit one year, five years, or even ten years later. Additionally, in order to select your best educational alternative, you must be able to articulate what benefit it will offer your career.

Second, many graduate schools require work experience before you can apply. For example, top business schools require two years of work experience. Thus, it is important to be familiar with the requirements of your proposed field of study.

Third, ask yourself whether you've really done your homework when weighing alternatives. Your watchword should be research. If you are changing career fields, avoid any post-degree surprises by researching the market, employment trends, and major employers. When evaluating professional training programs, be sure you have researched the schools to know who is offering accredited and respected courses. Make your decisions based on facts and figures and not on the suggestions of well-meaning friends and family members—and certainly not on the advice of admission representatives from graduate schools.

Finally, the biggest obstacle to returning for more education may be yourself. Saying that you're too old, you don't want to invest the money, or you don't want to take time off from your current job may merely be excuses to justify your refusal to take the plunge. Alternatively, you may have valid reasons for staying put for the time being. Be honest with yourself; only you can decide.

Law school at sixty—you're never too old!
One of our favorite stories is about a man who decided at the age of 60 to go to law school. "That will take three years," his friends and family moaned. "You'll be 63!" "So what?" Ed replied. "If I don't go to law school, in three years I'll still be 63." In Ed's way of thinking, he couldn't put three years to better use than to accomplish a lifelong goal.

In considering additional education, ask yourself, "If I do not choose to pursue additional education now, will I be satisfied with my career progress in a year?…five years?" This may be the best measure of how you might benefit from additional education.

Education and Income

Most of us have heard of the guy down the street who flunked out of college or failed to complete high school and is now a millionaire. *Forbes* magazine listed Bill Gates, a Harvard dropout, the founder of Microsoft computers, as the world's richest individual in 1995. Howard Hughes flunked out of Rice University and still managed to gain genius status and amass an empire. The fact is that there are many such success stories among the not-so-educated.

What we don't hear are stories about the many failures. According to the Bureau of the Census, when salaries of all working people over the age of 25 were examined, on average those with the most education had the highest annual incomes. People who failed to enter high school averaged a salary of $15,223 a year. These figures include those with large amounts of experience. Those with less than a high school diploma but with some high school education increased on average to $18,012 per year, and high school graduates earned $23,410 per year.

In terms of income, even some college education is better than none. Americans who have completed some college average incomes of $27,705. Those completing a bachelor's or four-year degree earn an average of $35,900 per year, some $12,000 higher per year than the high school graduate.

Finally, there are those that strive for more than a bachelor's degree. For those who complete graduate, professional, or other college work beyond the bachelor's, the extra education will garner them an average of $43,032 per year. This will, of course, vary with the type of graduate study pursued. Law or medical school will almost certainly give you a higher income than one year of graduate study in a less marketable area.

Dear Dr. Bob

I recently heard that a doctor who is a general practitioner makes on average $117,000 a year and that internal medicine specialists make $181,000 a year. Should I change careers to become a doctor? Signed, Curious Career Changer

Dear Curious Career Changer
Certainly, becoming a doctor can seem like a wonderful choice. The drama of the emergency room, a good salary, knowing that you're making a difference in people's lives. However, you should consider the hard work, high cost, and many years it takes to become a doctor. Since there are three times as many applicants as there are slots for med school, I recommend exploring all your options in the medical field.

First, make sure that the health field is the field you are most interested in, then look into all the options. Options such as medical physics, physicians' assistants, pharmacy, and occupational and physical therapy are a few alternatives in the health field that may be a good fit and more time and cost effective for you.

However, don't do anything drastic! Being in medicine isn't exactly what you see on TV. You ought to talk to a few real health professionals or a career counselor before leaping into anything.

Getting Organized for Graduate School

If you decide that graduate or professional school is definitely what you need in your life and you've weighed the pros and cons, then get ready for the graduate school application process, which can be "The Nightmare on Elm Street." However, organization can make your life much easier and good preparation can eventually land you in the school of your choice. Here are some tips to help you:

- Request application materials around September of the year prior to the year you want to enroll.
- Know each school's application timeline (exam results, application due date, etc.).
- Establish a time frame for yourself, setting goals to complete tests and prepare paperwork and other relevant information well before the actual due date.
- Take practice tests, and learn what to expect on the tests, how answers are scored, whether you lose points for wrong answers, and so on.
- Take the actual tests.
- Forward exam results to selected schools.
- Get transcripts from schools attended.
- Obtain letters of recommendation.
- Write essays.
- Use certified mail, U.P.S., or a courier service to deliver materials to schools. This ensures you a receipt for the materials you send to the school.
- Visit schools you are interested in attending, if possible.

Preparing for graduate school admissions tests

Graduate schools, law schools, and medical schools all require test scores before admitting anyone. The standardized tests include the GMAT (Graduate Management Admission Test), LSAT (Law School Admission Test), and MCAT (Medical College Admission Test). Prep courses can help ready you for these tests. Such courses help familiarize you with the contents of the tests and question types. They also offer strategies of test taking to help you improve your scores. Below are two services that provide test preparation courses.

Kaplan (1-800-KAP-TEST)
Princeton Review (1-800-2-REVIEW)

Selecting a Graduate School

Selecting a graduate school requires much consideration before committing money and two to three years of your life. The task of making the best selection in a graduate school is one that will have a significant impact on subsequent job placement, starting salary, and career potential. Here are some criteria to help in evaluating potential graduate schools: the school's reputation, both academically and among the employment community; curriculum, specialization(s), geographic location, department size, selectivity of admissions, faculty reputations and areas of expertise, and level of financial aid/support for students.

CYBERTIPS ON GRADUATE SCHOOLS

The Career Channel
http://riceinfo.rice.edu:80/projects/careers/
Provides information on graduate school application deadlines; rankings of top professional, medical, and graduate schools; test prep courses; and test examples.

Jobtrak
http://www.jobtrak.com/gradschool_docs/gradschool.html
Offers advice on grad school: applying, testing, and financing; also has links to grad school sites by topic.

National Association of Graduate and Professional Students
gopher://accgopher.georgetown.edu/11gopher_root%3a%5bnagps%5d

Graduate & Professional Schools from the University of Virginia
http://minerva.acc.virginia.edu/~career/grdsch.html

Peterson's Guide to Graduate and Professional Study
http://www.petersons.com:8080/gsector.html
Links to over 1,500 universities on the Net that offer grad programs.

Educational Testing Service
http://hub.terc.edu/ra/ets.html
Provides test dates.

The Best Graduate Programs for Your Success

There are many resources to help you select graduate programs such as *Peterson's Guides* and *Barron's Guide, Gorman's, Business Week's* annual "Best B Schools" edition and the follow-up book, and *U.S. News and World Reports'* issue on best graduate schools. All of these give some type of information on graduate schools.

We encourage you to look at all these sources. However, we have compiled a list, along with Web addresses, of programs from around the country that consistently show up at the top of national rankings. Additional lists outline local programs in the professional, trade, and continuing studies areas available in this city and its environs.

TOP BUSINESS SCHOOLS

The WWW addresses for business and law schools listed below will provide information on each university listed, its faculty and students, admission requirements, financial assistance, and general information about its graduate school. Entries are listed alphabetically and are not intended to imply any ranking.

Harvard University
http://www.hbs.harvard.edu/

Massachusetts Institute of Technology (Sloan)
http://www-sloan.mit.edu/

Northwestern University
http://www.nwu.edu/graduate/

Stanford University
http://www-gsb.stanford.edu/home.html

University of Pennsylvania (Wharton)
http://www.wharton.upeen.edu/

TOP LAW SCHOOLS

Columbia University (NY)
http://www.janus.columbia.edu/

Harvard University
http://www.harvard.edu/

Stanford University
http://www-leland.stanford.edu/group/

University of California at Berkeley
gopher://law164.law.berkeley.edu:70/1

Yale University
http://www.yale.edu/

STATE AND LOCAL BUSINESS SCHOOLS:

Clark Atlanta University
111 James P. Brawley Drive, S.W.
Atlanta, GA 30314
(404) 577-0306
http://galaxy.cau.edu

Emory University
Goizueta School of Business
1602 Mizell Drive
Atlanta, GA 30322
(404) 727-8099
http://www.emory.edu/

Georgia Institute of Technology
Dupree School of Management
225 North Ave., N.W.
Atlanta, GA 30332
(404) 894-2604
http://www.gatech.edu

Georgia State University
College of Business
35 Broad St.
Atlanta, GA 30303
(404) 651-1913
http://www.gsu.edu/

Kennesaw State University
Michael J. Cole School of Business
1000 Chastain Road
Kennesaw, GA 30144-5591
(770) 423-6087
http://www.coles.kennesaw.edu/

Oglethorpe University
4484 Peachtree Road, N.E.
Atlanta, GA 30319
(404) 261-1441
http://www.oglethorpe.edu/

Southern Polytechnic State University
1100 S. Marietta Parkway
Marietta, GA 30060-2896
(770) 528-7440
http://www.sct.edu/sct

University of Georgia
Terry College of Business
217 Brooks Hall
Athens, GA 30602
(706) 542-5671
http://www.uga.edu/

LOCAL LAW SCHOOLS

Emory University Law School
1301 Clifton Road
215 Gambrell Hall
Atlanta, GA 30322
(404) 727-6801
http://www.emory.law.edu/

Georgia State University
College of Law
P. O. Box 4049
Atlanta, GA 30302-4049
(404) 651-2048
http://www.gsu.law.edu/

John Marshall Law School
805 Peachtree St., N.E.
Atlanta, GA 30308
(404) 872-3593
http://www.jmls.edu.html

University of Georgia
School of Law
Athens, GA 30602
(706) 542-7541
http://www.uga.edu/

Business and Vocational Colleges

There are numerous business and vocational schools in the Atlanta metro area that can meet your needs for upgrading your skills and education. Some of these are listed here to offer you a starting point. Many of these are private schools that offer specialized training in a variety of career paths.

It is recommended that if you have any questions or concerns about any of the schools listed in this section, you call the Consumer Tips Hotline. For free information call: (404) 633-3336, and enter the code of your choice:

9950 Careers With A Future.
9951 Choosing The Right School For You.
9952 Getting Financial Aid.
9953 Job Placement Services.

American Institute for Paralegal Studies
1 Dunwoody Park
Atlanta, GA 30338
(800) 624-3933

Asher School of Business
100 Pinnacle Way
Norcross, GA 30071
(770) 368-0800

Atlanta Metropolitan College
1630 Stewart Ave., S.W.
Atlanta, GA 30310
(404) 756-4000

Bauder College
3500 Peachtree Road, N.E.
Atlanta, GA 30326
(404) 237-7573

Brown College of Court Reporting
& Medical Transcription
1100 Spring St., N.W.
Atlanta, GA 30309
(404) 876-1227

Capelli Learning Center
2581 Piedmont Road, N.E.
Atlanta, GA 30324
(404) 261-5271

Center for Continuing Education
Pre-License and Continuing
Education
1465 Northside Drive, N.W.
Atlanta, GA 30318
(404) 355-1921
Insurance education.

DeKalb Technical Institute
495 N. Indian Creek Drive
Clarkston, GA 30021
(404) 297-9522

Devry Institute of Technology
250 N. Arcadia Ave.
Decatur, GA 30030
(404) 292-2645

Draughons College
1430 W. Peachtree St.
Atlanta, GA 30309
(404) 892-0814

Georgia Institute of Real Estate
5784 Lake Forrest Drive, N.W.
Atlanta, GA 30342
(404) 252-6768

Georgia Medical Institute
40 Marietta St., N.W.
Atlanta, GA 30303
(404) 525-3272

Gupton-Jones College of Funeral
Services
5141 Snapfinger Woods Drive
Decatur, GA 30035
(770) 593-2257

Gwinnet College of Business
4230 Highway 29
Lilburn, GA 30247
(770) 381-7200

Gwinnet Technical Institute
1250 Atkinson Road, N.W.
Lawrenceville, GA 30243
(770) 962-7580

Massey College of Business and
Technology
3355 Lenox Road, N.E.
Atlanta, GA 30326
(404) 816-4533

National Business Institute
243 W. Ponce De Leon Ave.
Decatur, GA 30030
(404) 377-0500

North Metro Technical Institute
5198 Ross Road, N.W.
Acworth, GA 30102
(770) 975-4000

Paralegal Training,
National Center for
3414 Peachtree Road, N.E.
Atlanta, GA 30326
(404) 266-1060

Software IQ
1117 Perimeter Center West, N.E.
Atlanta, GA 30303
(770) 698-0800

Southern College of Technology
1100 South Marietta Parkway
Marietta, GA 30060
(770) 528-7200

Superior Court Reporting School
770 Old Roswell Road
Roswell, GA 30076
(770) 642-0551

Tuskegee University School of Nursing
100 Edgewood Ave.
Atlanta, GA 30303
(404) 523-0262

Ultrasound Diagnostic School
1 Corporate Blvd., N.E.
Atlanta, GA 30329
(770) 248-9070

On-line Education

No need to pack those bags or leave your job and friends to head off for school. Today's technology brings the teachers, ideas, books, and dialogue to the student electronically. The advantages are that correspondence study is dependable, low cost, and can be done anywhere. Still it is important to check out what credits, degree, or credentials you may receive. Additionally, consider all costs associated with on-line education and don't forget to inquire about financial aid.

Although on-line education is convenient, some people may not do well outside a typical classroom environment where you see the teacher and take part in dialogue. Think about the kind of study environment that works best for you. It is also important to note that the field of on-line education is constantly changing, and new possibilities certainly will pop up after the publication of this book.

If you would like to learn more about on-line or long-distance learning programs, the following books and organizations can assist you:

- The National University Continuing Education Association (NUCEA) provides comprehensive guides to long-distance learning, ranging from correspondence programs to programs delivered through various electronic media. These guides are:

- *Peterson's Guide to Independent Study.* Princeton, NJ: Peterson's Guides, 1992.

- *The Electronic University: A Guide to Long-distance Learning Programs.* Princeton, NJ: Peterson's Guides, 1993.

Did you know that you can also take courses offered by certified teachers and professional experts on-line? Typical courses offered include: History, English, Sociology, Languages, Math, Science, the Arts, and Computer Science. However, no college credit or certificates are awarded for these courses. For further information contact The Electronic University Network (Sarah Blackmun, Director of Instruction, 1977 Colestin Road, Hornbrook, CA 96044, (415) 221-7061). This network consists of organizations that work with groups of colleges to provide long-distance learning programs.

The 10-Step Job Search

Almost everything can be broken down into steps. The job search is no different. If you take the process one step at a time and follow our basic rules, you are more likely to find a job. As you begin, it is important to remember that you are in control, and in the end it is you who must land the job. To get there you need to be proactive; companies will not come looking for you. Rather, you have to search out the companies, the jobs, and the people that are in a position to hire.

The 10-Step Job Search

1. Know Thyself—Where Are You Going?
2. Research the Job Market.
3. Organize Your Search.
4. Network.
5. Persistence and Follow-Up.
6. Prepare Your Resume.
7. Mail Your Resume.
8. Use Your Career Resources.
9. The Killer Interview.
10. Make Sure This Is the Job for You.

Step 1: Know Thyself—Where Are You Going?

Hopefully, Chapter 2 has set you on the right path to choosing a career. To get somewhere you need to decide where it is you are going, what you want to do, and what you are capable of doing. Other items to assess include the characteristics of your ideal work environment, the type of experience you wish to gain from the job, and how much money you intend to make. To a large extent, your happiness with your job coincides with how closely it meets your needs and motivates you.

Once you've answered these questions you will be able to articulate why you are interviewing for a particular position and why you are right for that position.

Step 2: Research the Job Market

The alarm clock rings, and you slowly get out of bed and head downstairs for your morning jolt of java along with the want ads from the daily paper. Tempted to read the comics, you resist the urge and resume your job search with the want ads. After all, this is how people find jobs. Wrong! According to *Forbes* magazine, only about 10 percent of professional and technical people find their jobs through want ads.

Your best bet is *not* to send a resume to every ad in the paper. Instead, try to identify who's hiring and where the opportunities may be. How do you learn these things? Research.

Libraries

Libraries provide vast amounts of resources for job searching, ranging from company information (ranking, annual sales, product information, number of employees, who's running the show) to resume writing guides, business newspapers and magazines, salary statistics, and, of course, directories such as *Standard and Poor's Register of Corporations, Directors, and Executives.* To save precious time in your research, the reference desk is invaluable in locating materials for your job search.

Local university and community college libraries may also offer resources for job seekers. Many local schools have reference libraries that are well equipped with career resource information and job directories that you can use even if you are not an alumnus. Some libraries also offer vocational testing and career guidance, often in conjunction with the school's career planning office.

TOP ATLANTA AREA LIBRARIES

The four most useful libraries, each housing a wealth of information on business and career resources, are:

Atlanta-Fulton Public Library
1 Margaret Mitchell Square
Atlanta, GA 30303
(404) 730-1700
The Atlanta-Fulton Public Library includes 32 branches throughout the county. The larger branches maintain an extensive collection of resources related to busi-

ness but the branch at Margaret Mitchell Square is especially complete. It is considered THE best source of business information resources and resources related to the not-for-profit sector. In addition to the widely known directories mentioned in this chapter, the library also maintains a broad selection of directories, periodicals, and other sources that target the Atlanta business and economic market.

The librarians at this branch have compiled several free handouts to assist you in researching employers and other business-related topics. These publications can be found on the 2nd floor and include: "Finding Information About Companies," "Finding Information About Industries," "Finding Information in Directories," "Finding Demographic Information," and "Sources of Information on Local Organizations."

The Atlanta-Fulton Public Library also has an information line that is staffed with librarians to assist you in retrieving difficult to find information. The telephone number is (404) 730-4636.

Business Newsbank is located on the 4th floor of the Atlanta Fulton Public Library. It provides local and regional business news articles on CD Rom. It also provides company and industry news (public and private companies) from business journals, newspapers, and wire services.

See the Blue Pages of the telephone directory or call the main number above for more information and to find the branch nearest you.

Cobb County Central Library
266 Roswell St., N.E.
Marietta, GA 30060
(404) 528-2320
The Cobb County library system includes 15 branches throughout the county. This is the central branch and it has the best collection of resources related to business. It houses the standard directories, books, databases, and periodicals that cover business and related topics.

DeKalb County Public Library
215 Sycamore St.
Decatur, GA 30030
(404) 370-3070
The DeKalb County library system includes 23 branches throughout the county. This is the central branch and it houses the best collection of business resources. One floor is devoted to reference materials including directories and other resources to assist you in researching companies and job-search-related topics.

Gwinett County Public Library
5570 Spalding Drive, N.W.
Norcross, GA 30341
(770) 513-5911
The Gwinett County Public Library system includes 9 branches throughout the county. This is the central branch and an excellent source of business informa-

tion. The branch also includes the Business Information Center, which houses a broad collection of directories, periodicals, and databases related to business topics. Call (770) 729-1028 to reach the Business Information Center.

Directories

Directories provide you with corporate structures, company financial figures, company rankings, best companies to work for, best places to live, who's making what salary, and top careers. When you're beginning your homework, whether you're researching an entire industry or a specific company, there are four major directories with which you should be familiar.

OUR FOUR FAVORITE DIRECTORIES

The **Directory of Corporate Affiliations** (National Register Publishing, New Providence, NJ) is an organized business reference tool covering public and private businesses in the U.S. and throughout the world. This six-volume directory allows the user to examine the parent company and all subsidiaries of the parent company, categorized by geographic area or S.I.C. (Standard Industrial Classification) codes that identify the company's product or service. If you want to know the corporate reporting structure, the company's subsidiaries, or the company's banking, legal, or outside service firms, this is the directory to use.

    Standard and Poor's Register of Corporations, Directors, and Executives (Standard and Poor's Publishing, 25 Broadway, New York, NY 10004) is billed as the "foremost guide to the business community and the executives who run it." This three-volume directory lists more than 50,000 corporations and 70,000 officers, directors, trustees, and other bigwigs.

    Each business is assigned an S.I.C. number. Listings are indexed by geographic area and also by S.I.C. number, so it's easy to find all the companies that produce, say, industrial inorganic chemicals.

    You can also look up a particular company to verify its correct address and phone number, its chief officers (that is, the people you might want to contact for an interview), its products, and, in many cases, its annual sales and number of employees. If you have an appointment with the president of XYZ Corporation, you can consult *Standard and Poor's* to find out where he or she was born and went to college—information that's sure to come in handy in an employment interview. Supplements are published in April, July, and October.

    Ward's Business Directory of U.S. Private and Public Companies (Gale Research Inc., New York, NY) is the leading source for hard-to-find information on private companies. This six-volume publication lists more than 142,000 companies in alphabetic, geographic, and industry arrangements. It also provides rankings and analyses of the industry activity of leading companies. If you want to determine parent/subsidiary relationships, merger and acquisition positions, or general information on private and public companies, this is the directory to use.

The **Million Dollar Directory** (Dun & Bradstreet, 3 Century Drive, Parsippany, NJ 07054) is a three-volume listing of approximately 160,000 U.S. businesses with a net worth of more than half a million dollars. Listings appear alphabetically, geographically, and by product classification and include key personnel. Professional and consulting organizations such as hospitals and engineering services, credit agencies, and financial institutions other than banks and trust companies are not generally included.

So much for our favorite directories. The following listings contain additional directories and guides, most with a local focus, that may come in handy. Many of these, as well as other directories, are available at area libraries.

ATLANTA AREA DIRECTORIES

Asia Business and Community Directory of Georgia
4621 Buford Highway, Suite 2
Atlanta, GA 30341
A publication that includes consumer information targeting Asian Americans with a "Yellow Pages" of Asian-owned businesses.

Atlanta Area Hospitals
Atlanta Chamber of Commerce
235 International Blvd., N.W.
Atlanta, GA 30303
Listing of health-care facilities in the Atlanta area and area health-care associations.

Atlanta International
Atlanta Chamber of Commerce
235 International Blvd.
Atlanta, GA 30303
Listing of firms in Atlanta engaged in international commerce and trade.

Atlanta Operations—The Fortune 500 and Fortune Service 500 Companies
Atlanta Chamber of Commerce
235 International Blvd., N.W.
Atlanta, GA 30303

Book of Lists
Atlanta Business Chronicle
1801 Peachtree St.
Atlanta, GA 30309
Annual compilation of the region's top companies, individuals, and organizations in various groupings. Includes over 50 lists; for example, the top 20 banks, top 20 retailers, and top 50 employers. Also includes an alphabetical directory covering approximately 850 businesses, medical and educational institutions, government and social agencies with over 100 employees. Entries include company name, address, phone, name of principal officer, annual sales, number of employees.

Business Wise
6190 Powers Ferry Road, #190
Atlanta, GA 30339
Major source of Atlanta area employers. Indexed by company name, S.I.C. codes, and zip code; also includes a directory of area business buildings and tips on target marketing.

Dun's Market Identifiers (DMI) Series
3 Sylvan Way
Parsippany, NJ 07054
(800) 526-0651

Atlanta Companies—Sales

Atlanta Companies—Employee Totals

Atlanta Companies—Zip Codes

Atlanta Companies—S.I.C. Codes

All of these volumes include business name, address, telephone number, line of business, sales figures, and total number of employees.

Georgia International Facilities
Georgia Department of Industry, Trade and Tourism
285 Peachtree Center Ave., Suite 1100
Atlanta, GA 30301
Directory of Georgia facilities wholly or partly owned by foreign countries. Table of contents arranged by country while indexes list companies in alphabetical order.

The Help Book 1996
United Way of Metropolitan Atlanta
100 Edgewood Ave., Suite 303
Atlanta, GA 30303
A comprehensive directory of human-service organizations in the metropolitan Atlanta area.

Major Atlanta Headquartered Firms
Atlanta Chamber of Commerce
235 International Blvd., N.W.
Atlanta, GA 30303
A listing of the largest Atlanta-headquartered firms by net worth and number of employees.

Manufacturing Directory
Atlanta Chamber of Commerce
235 International Blvd., N.W.
Atlanta, GA 30303
A guide to manufacturing firms in the metropolitan Atlanta area.

Metropolitan Atlanta Larger Employers
Atlanta Chamber of Commerce

235 International Blvd., N.W.
Atlanta, GA 30303
A listing of employers in Atlanta with more than 300 employees.

Metropolitan Atlanta Utilities
Atlanta Chamber of Commerce
235 International Blvd., N.W.
Atlanta, GA 30303
Sorts utilities by industry and includes brief company information.

Trade Magazines

Every industry or service business has its trade press—that is, editors, reporters, and photographers whose job it is to cover an industry or trade. You should become familiar with the magazines of the industries or professions that interest you, especially if you're in the interviewing stage of your job search. Your prospective employers are reading the trade magazines; you should too.

Many of the magazines we've included are available at the libraries listed earlier in this chapter. Most of the following magazines have editorial offices in the region, reporting area news about the people and businesses in their industry. Some carry local want ads and personnel changes. Additional trade magazines are listed in Chapter 10 under specific career categories. For a complete listing of the trade press, consult the *Gale Directory of Publications* at the library.

ATLANTA AREA TRADE MAGAZINES

Adhesives Age Magazine
6151 Powers Ferry Road
Atlanta, GA 30359
(770) 955-2500
Monthly magazine of news and technology for those engaged in the manufacture, application, research and/or marketing of adhesives, sealants, and related products.

AdWeek Magazine
3525 Piedmont Road
Atlanta, GA 30305
(404) 841-3333
Weekly advertising and marketing magazine.

American City and County Magazine
6151 Powers Ferry Road
Atlanta, GA 30339
(404) 955-2500
Monthly municipal and county administration magazine.

American Health Consultants
Department BCI
P.O. Box 740056
Atlanta, GA 30074
(404) 262-7436
Publishes newsletters on topics in the health-care field.

American Papermaker Magazine
Roger's American Papermaker
57 Executive Park South, Suite 310
Atlanta, GA 30329
(770) 325-9153
Monthly magazine on manufacturing and converting paper.

Apparel Industry Magazine
6255 Barfield Road, Suite 200
Atlanta, GA 30328
(404) 252-8831
Trade publication for U.S. apparel manufacturers.

ASHRAE Journal
American Society of Heating,
Refrigerating and Air Conditioning
Engineers
1791 Tullier Circle, N.E.
Atlanta, GA 30329
(404) 636-8400
Professional publication for people in
this profession.

Container News/Magazine
Intermodalism
6151 Powers Ferry Road
Atlanta, GA 30339
(770) 955-2500
Monthly trade magazine, covering
intermodal transportation and con-
tainerized shipping.

Display and Design Ideas
Shore Communications
6255 Barfield Road, N.E.
Atlanta, GA 30331
(404) 252-8831
Magazine for visual merchandisers
and store designers.

Dixie Contractor
Associated Construction Publications
209-A Swanton Way
Decatur, GA 30091
(404) 377-2683
Bi-weekly magazine for Southeastern
construction industry.

Economic Review
Federal Reserve Bank of Atlanta
Public Information Department
104 Marietta St., N.W.
Atlanta, GA 30303
(404) 521-8788
Bi-monthly journal, presenting
research and educational articles on
macroeconomic and international
issues, as well as the economy of the
Southeast.

Economics Update
Federal Reserve Bank of Atlanta
Public Information Department
104 Marietta St., N.W.
Atlanta, GA 30303
(404) 521-8788
Monthly newsletter, covering econom-
ic trends, policy problems, and recent
Atlanta-based federal research on eco-
nomics.

EMC Test & Design
Argus Business/Magazine Publishing
6151 Powers Ferry Road
Atlanta, GA 30339-2941
(770) 955-2500
Professional magazine for engineers,
focusing on electromagnetic
compatibility.

Employee Health and Fitness
American Health Consultants
P.O. Box 740056
Atlanta, GA 30374
Monthly newsletter covering corpo-
rate health promotion and the fitness
industry.

Energy Engineering
700 Indian Trail-Lilburn Road
Lilburn, GA 30247
(770) 925-9388
Bi-monthly trade journal, featuring
energy use in building new sources
of energy.

Georgia Food Industrial Association
Georgia Grocers Association
3200 Highland Parkway, S.E., Suite 210
Atlanta, GA 30345
(770) 438-7744
Quarterly trade magazine serving
independent retail grocers and
suppliers.

Georgia Press Association
3066 Mercer University Drive
Atlanta, GA 30341-4137
(770) 454-6776
Bi-monthly journalism publication.

Georgia Professional Engineer
McRae Communications
105 Commerce Drive
Fayetteville, GA 30214-1376
(770) 460-7277
Professional publication targeted
toward professional (registered)
engineers.

Georgia State Bar Journal
50 Hurt Plaza
Atlanta, GA 30303
(404) 527-8700
Quarterly law journal.

Georgia Technology Sourcebook
Jaye Communications
2841 Akers Mill Road, N.W.
Atlanta, GA 30339
(770) 984-9444
Excellent publication covering
Georgia's high technology firms.

Industrial Engineering
Institute of Industrial Engineers
25 Technology Park/Atlanta
Norcross, GA 30092
(404) 449-0460
Monthly magazine covering information systems, production, and related
topics in industrial engineering.

The Journal of Film and Video
Georgia State University
Department of Communication
University Plaza
Atlanta, GA 30303
(404) 651-3200
Film and video journal.

**Journal of the Medical Association of
Georgia**
938 Peachtree St., N.E.

Atlanta, GA 30309
(404) 876-7535
Monthly medical journal.

LOMA Resource
Life Office Management Assn.
5770 Powers Ferry Road
Atlanta, GA 30327
(770) 951-1770
Bi-monthly life insurance-industry
management magazine.

Management of World Wastes
6151 Powers Ferry Road
Atlanta, GA 30339
(404) 955-2500
Monthly waste removal and disposal
magazine.

National Real Estate Investor
6151 Powers Ferry Road
Atlanta, GA 30339
(770) 955-2500
Monthly magazine on real estate
investment and development.

Robotics World
6151 Powers Ferry Road
Atlanta, GA 30339
(770) 955-2500
Monthly publication focusing on the
use of industrial robots.

Shopping Center World
6151 Powers Ferry Road
Atlanta, GA 30339
(770) 955-2500
Shopping center and commercial real
estate magazine published 13 times a
year.

Southeast Food Service News
3678 Stewart Road
Doraville, GA 30340
(770) 452-1807
Monthly magazine covering
commercial and industrial real estate
transactions.

Southeast Real Estate News
6151 Powers Ferry Road
Atlanta, GA 30339
(770) 955-2500
Monthly magazine covering commercial and industrial real estate transactions.

Sports Trend
6255 Barfield Road, Suite 200
Atlanta, GA 30328-4300
(404) 252-8831
Monthly magazine serving sporting goods retailers.

TAPPI Journal
Technology Park/Atlanta
P.O. Box 105113
Atlanta, GA 30348
(404) 446-1400
Magazine on textiles and man-made fiber products.

Tech Notes
Jaye Communications
2841 Akers Mill Road, N.W.
Atlanta, GA 30339
(770) 984-9444
Publication that includes a calendar of high-technology events.

Technology South
Jaye Communications
2841 Akers Mill Road, N.W.
Atlanta, GA 30339
(770) 984-9444
Technology and business publication for the Southeast.

Textile World
Maclean Hunter Publishing Company
4170 Ashford Dunwoody Road, Suite 420
Atlanta, GA 30319
(404) 847-2770
Magazine on textile manufacturing and man-made fiber products.

Job Listings

Cover all your bases and respond to promising job advertisements in your field. The following resources contain only job listings and job-related information and advice. Also see "Internet Job Listings" later in this chapter.

AAR/EEO Affirmative Action Register
8356 Olive Blvd.
St. Louis, MO 63132
(314) 991-1335
"The only national equal employment opportunity recruitment publication directed to females, minorities, veterans, and the handicapped." Monthly magazine consists totally of job listings.

Black Employment & Education
2625 Piedmont Road, 56-282
Atlanta, GA 30324
(404) 469-5891
Magazine lists career opportunities nationwide. Your resume may be placed on their database for employer access.

Career Pilot
Future Aviation Professionals of America
4959 Massachusetts Blvd.
Atlanta, GA 30337
(409) 997-8097
Monthly magazine outlines employment opportunities for career pilots.

Federal Jobs Digest
Breakthrough Publications
310 N. Highland Ave.
Ossining, NY 10562
Elaborate listing of job opportunities with the federal government.

National and Federal Legal Employment Report
Federal Reports
1010 Vermont Ave., N.W.
Washington, DC 20005
(202) 393-3311
Monthly in-depth listings of attorney and law-related jobs in federal government and with other public and private employers throughout the U.S.

Opportunity NOCs (Nonprofit Organizations Classifieds)
Nonprofit Resource Center
50 Hurt Plaza, Suite 220
Atlanta, GA 30303
(404) 688-4845
Twice monthly publication of the Nonprofit Resource Center. Contains listings of positions in the Atlanta area with not-for-profit agencies.

Voice-Based Job Hot Lines

"Let your fingers do the walking!" Just dial any one of the numerous telephone job banks listed below and listen to recordings that describe available positions and how to apply. Many are available at no charge other than the cost of the telephone call.

Agnes Scott College
(404) 638-6383

AT&T
(404) 810-7001

Atlanta (City of)
(404) 330-6456

Atlanta Gas Light Company
(404) 584-4705

Attachmate Corporation
(770) 442-4010

BellSouth Advertising and Publishing Corporation
(770) 491-1747

BellSouth Corporation
(404) 329-9455

BellSouth Management Employment Center
(800) 407-0281

Centers for Disease Control & Prevention
(404) 332-4577

Cigna Health Care of Georgia
(404) 681-7799

Clayton County
(770) 473-5800

Cobb County
(770) 528-2555

DeKalb County
(404) 371-2331

Douglas County
(770) 920-7363

Environmental Protection Agency
Region 4
(800) 833-8130

Equifax Inc.
(404) 885-8550

Equifax Information Services Center
(770) 612-2558

Federal Home Loan Bank of Atlanta
(404) 888-5331

Federal National Mortgage
Association (Fannie Mae)
(404) 398-6242

Federal Reserve Bank of Georgia
(404) 521-8767

First Union National Bank of
Georgia
(404) 827-7150

Fulton County
(404) 730-5627

Geological Survey
United States Department of the
Interior
(404) 448-5320

Georgia Department of Natural
Resources
(404) 656-2695
(404) 656-7567

Georgia Institute of Technology
(Georgia Tech)
(404) 894-4592

Georgia State University
(404) 651-4270

Grady Health System
(404) 616-5627

Gwinnett County
(770) 822-7930

HBO & Company
(770) 393-6015

Hitachi Home Electronics
(770) 279-5600 x865

Internal Revenue Service
United States Department of the
Treasury
(770) 455-2455

Lockheed Martin Aeronautical
Systems
(770) 494-5000

Marietta (City of)
(770) 528-0593

MARTA (Metropolitan Atlanta Rapid
Transit Authority)
(404) 848-5231

Maxell Corporation of America
(770) 922-1000 X235

MCI Business Markets
(800) 274-5758

National Data Corporation
(404) 728-2030

NationsBank of Georgia NA
(404) 491-4530

Oglethorpe Power
(770) 270-7939

Oki Telecom
(770) 822-2701

Promina Northwest Health Systems
(770) 793-7070, then press 2

Prudential Bank
(770) 604-7070 X1

Rockdale County
(770) 929-4157

Rollins, Inc.
(404) 888-2125

Safeco Insurance Company
(770) 498-3142

SmithKline Beecham Clinical
Laboratories
(770) 621-7450

Smyrna City Government	**United Parcel Service**
(770) 431-2811	(770) 828-6800
Spelman College	**U.S. Federal Job Information Center**
(770) 223-5627	(404) 331-4315
State of Georgia Merit System	**Wachovia Bank of Georgia**
(404) 656-2724	(404) 841-7050

Internet Job Listings

Use the Net as another source for career research and job listings. Below are a few places to begin; you can surf the Net and find many others.

WORLD WIDE WEB JOB-SEARCH SOURCES

American Employment Weekly
http://branch.com/aew/aew.html
Contains help-wanted ads, ranging from data processing to medical positions from over 50 leading newspapers.

America's Job Bank
http://www.ajb.dni.us/
A federal program that may eventually include the jobs posted with state unemployment offices (Job Service, Employment Security, etc.) nationwide.

Career Channel
http://riceinfo.rice.edu:80/projects/careers/
Rice University lists jobs, links, and a wealth of other job-search information.

Career Connections
http://www.employmentedge.com/employment.edge/
Specializes in professional career placement throughout the U.S.

Career Magazine
http://www.careermag.com/careermag/
A comprehensive resource that includes job-opening database, employer profiles, articles, and news to assist in the career search and career forums.

CareerNet
http://www.careers.org/
A good source, with links to many other job-listing and job-resources organizations.

CareerWeb
http://www.cweb.com/
Job seekers can browse worldwide career opportunities, including the *Wall Street Journal National Business Employment Weekly.*

Catapult
http://www.wm.edu/catapult
Serves as a starting point for career service practitioners and students, covering topics from resumes to job listings.

Contract Employment Weekly
http://www.ceweekly.
Furnishes job openings throughout U.S. and overseas.

Easynet Job-Centre
http://www.easynet.co.uk/
Here you can peruse the jobs on offer, and look for people to employ you.

Employment Opportunities and Resume Postings—EINet
http://galaxy.einet.net/
A guide to worldwide information and services.

Entry Level Job Seeker Assistant
http://www.utsi.edu:70/students
Ideal for people who have never held a full-time, permanent job in their field or who have less than a year of non-academic experience.

E-Span
http://www.espan.com/
Provides a searchable database of high-tech job openings as well as a wide variety of resources for the job seeker.

Help Wanted
http://www.webcom.com/
On-line employment services.

JobCenter
http://www.jobcenter.com
Matches job searcher's skills with employer's needs.

Job Junction
http://www.iquest.net/iq/jobjunction
Contains career information, reference material, and on-line job database.

JobWeb
http://www.renzema.org
National Association of Colleges and Employers. Primarily targeted at college students, JobWeb offers career planning and employment information, job-search articles, and job listings.

MedSearch America
http://www.medsearch.com/
This Washington-based firm maintains an extensive health-jobs database nationwide.

Monster Board
http://www.monster.com/
Companies around the country list jobs along with employer profiles. Search for jobs by location, industry, company, and discipline.

Online Career Center
http://www.occ.com/
Includes job listings from over 300 U.S. companies. Browse by job title, company name, or geographic region.

PursuitNet Jobs
http://www.tiac.net/users/job
Job-search service matches skills and desires with compatible jobs in the U.S.

Recruiters Online Network
http://www.onramp.net
Recruiters, employment agencies, search firms, and employment professionals share business opportunities and job postings.

Today's Classifieds
http://www.nando.net/classads/
Internet users can search classifieds by career field.

RECOMMENDED READING

Dixon, Pam, and Sylvia Tiersten. *Be Your Own Headhunter Online.* New York: Random House, 1995.
Kennedy, Joyce Lain. *Hook Up, Get Hired! The Internet Job Search Revolution.* New York: John Wiley & Sons, 1995.

Small Companies

Today's job market has changed. Big business is no longer the biggest employer. Today, 80% of new jobs created in the United States are by small and medium-sized firms that are four or five years old.

Small and medium-sized businesses, those that employ less than 500 people, are good bets for employment opportunities. These companies are expected to expand. Small businesses employ 48% of the American workforce. Two-thirds of all first jobs come from these growing businesses. The big boys of business may still provide better benefits and pay to their employees, but they only manage to provide 11% of the jobs sought by first-time job seekers.

Searching for jobs with small businesses is not, however, as easy as the traditional job search at the large corporation. Small business is less likely to advertise for a position, use an agency, or post a listing at a local college. They generally use the networking method of knowing someone who knows someone. Thus, you may need to be creative when searching out small companies. Use your resources, such as Chambers of Commerce and Small Business Centers (see Chapter 2) to help you in your search.

RECOMMENDED READING

Colton, Kitty, and Michele Fetterolf. *1995: A Job Seeker's Guide to America's 2000 Little-known, Fastest-Growing High-Tech Companies.* Princeton, NJ: Peterson's Guides, 1994.

Step 3: Organize Your Search

The most difficult part of any job search is getting started. The next most difficult is staying organized. Preparing a resume, sending it out, scheduling interviews, and returning phone calls is enough to cause anyone to grab for the extra-strength aspirin! Organize your job search and you'll have fewer headaches.

Don't Get Caught Without Your Daily Planner

Have you ever noticed how many people carry around those little black "Daily Planners"? In this case, what's good for the crowd is also good for you, the job searcher. You need to keep a written record of every person you contact in your job search and the results of each contact. This will prevent a job lead from falling through the cracks. It may even come in handy for future job searches.

Your Daily Planner should serve as a way of organizing your efforts for greatest efficiency. Much of your job search will be spent developing your network of contacts. Still, you should allocate a portion of each week for doing research on companies that interest you and for pursuing other means of contacting employers.

As you go through your contacts and begin to research the job market, you'll begin to identify certain employers in whom you're interested. Keep a list of them. For each one that looks promising, start a file that contains articles on the company, its annual report, product brochures, company profile, and any other interesting information. Every so often, check your "potential companies" list against your planner to ensure that you stay in contact with them.

Step 4: Network

While Chapter 5 will give you the essentials of networking, it is important to remember that it's "who you know" that gets you ahead in the job search. Professional organizations are a great source for networking and gleaning vital information about employment. Get involved in organizations in your field of interest to keep abreast of opportunities as they become available. And don't forget to stay abreast of the business world in general through business magazines and newspapers (see Chapter 1 for listings).

If you are just starting your network, use the information interview (see Chapter 5) to find out more about a particular career field and to acquaint yourself with professionals in that field. People like to hire individuals they know, so the more potential employers you meet, the better your odds for landing a job.

Dear Dr. Bob

Is there job-search etiquette I should know about?—Proper Etiquette Job Searcher

Dear Proper Etiquette Job Searcher

As everywhere else, there exists proper etiquette in the job search. For example, the telephone is a wonderful tool by which an assertive job seeker can make contact with employers and follow-up on job applications and leads. However, reminding the employer of your interest in a position is not tantamount to badgering him or her into interviewing you. Follow every letter you mail with a phone call, but allow ample time for the employer to receive and review your credentials. One to two weeks is the usual rule of thumb.

Manic Monday mornings are a particularly unpleasant time for employers to receive phone calls. A better time is between 10 a.m. and 2 p.m. Tuesdays, Wednesdays, or Thursdays. And always check to see if you have called at a convenient time.

The fax machine can be a dangerous beast and should be used cautiously by the job searcher. Certainly it does offer instant communication with an employer. But unsolicited faxes are annoying to employers. Not only does it tie up the fax line and use expensive paper but it is likely that the hiring authority will not even see it. However, my advice is to fax only when requested to do so by a hiring authority.

Finally, treat the potential employer with the utmost respect. Be sure to keep meetings at the time you both agreed on. Follow up with a thank-you letter, reiterating your qualifications and thanking your host for his time. Try to keep everyone in your network informed of your status in the job search.

Step 5: Persistence and Follow-Up

Persistence is one of the key strategies in the job search. Whether you are pursuing job leads, sending out resumes, scheduling interviews, or contacting a hiring authority, you need to be persistent. The passive job searcher relies upon the want ads as his or her only source of job leads. The persistent job searcher is proactive, using resources such as networking groups, newspapers, professional organizations, and directories. The passive job searcher will accept "no" without questioning or pursuing the hiring authority. The persistent job searcher will make a few more calls. Being persistent can help you accomplish the ultimate goal—landing the job.

Persistence is also a state of mind. It's important to remain enthusiastic, to keep going, and to make calls. It is only too easy for the job searcher to lose energy and conveniently forget to make those important follow-up calls. Remember you most likely are just one of many applicants for a job, and persistence is the key to success. Plenty of rejection will probably come your way. It is up to you to keep going and put rejection behind you.

Follow-up all promising contacts with calls and letters. Whether you're networking or actually talking with someone in a position to hire you, it is important to stay in touch with whomever can assist you in your job search. If someone takes the time to give you a lead, it is only proper for you to inform the individual of the outcome.

Follow-up resumes with a phone call to ensure that your resume was received. It is impossible to get an interview if your resume got lost in the mail. Likewise, a thank-you note after an interview will keep your name foremost with the interviewer and less likely to be lost in the shuffle.

Our "silent" president speaks

Nothing in this world can take the place of persistence. Talent will not; nothing is more common than unsuccessful men with great talent.

Genius will not; unrewarded genius is almost a proverb.

Education will not; the world is full of educated derelicts.

Persistence and determination alone are omnipotent.
— *Calvin Coolidge*

Step 6: Prepare Your Resume

Writing a good resume and a cover letter to accompany it is important in marketing yourself and lining up interviews. Chapter 6 goes into detail on resume writing. It is important to remember that this step can be crucial to your other steps.

Remember that most resumes get about 20 seconds of the employer's time. Therefore, it is vital to keep the resume to one page and skimmable enough to grab the reader's attention. The following guidelines should help you develop a well-written resume:

- Tailor your resume to the potential job as much as possible.
- Information should be easy to skim and locate.
- Length should be one page and no more than two.
- Proofread your final version; then have someone else proofread it.
- The overall appearance should be professional.
- Printing should be done on a laser printer.

A cover letter should always accompany your resume. The purpose of the cover letter is to persuade the employer to read your resume and invite you for an interview. The cover letter should be sent to a specific person. It should be brief but provide enough information to entice the employer. The following information should be in the cover letter:

- The first paragraph should identify who you are, whether you were referred by someone, and what your objective is.
- The second paragraph is your chance to sell yourself. It should tell the employer why you are good for the company and what you can offer. Use facts and figures to describe your qualifications.
- The last paragraph is where you request an interview and state how you will follow up with the employer.

The cover letter and the resume are often the *first impression the employer will have of you.* Do your best in preparing them!

Step 7: Mail Your Resume

When sending your resume out, the Personnel Department is probably not your best target since their job is to screen out rather than welcome applicants. Understand that Personnel or Human Resources can help your career once you're in the company. However, your best initial target is the decision-maker who is the "hiring authority."

Mass Mailing

A common job-search technique is to research a list of companies and send off as many resumes and cover letters as possible. Then you wait for your hard work and many dollars in postage to pay off with a call back and an interview. Sometimes mass mailings work, but mostly they don't. We recommend the targeted mailing technique.

Targeted Mailing

A targeted mailing is one that focuses only on companies with jobs you know you are qualified for and in which you have names of specific hiring authorities. Most importantly, in a targeted mailing you must be prepared to follow-up with phone calls.

In doing your research about prospective companies you have come up with the names of many that you are interested in working for. Prioritize these companies and target the top 15—those you are most interested in. Send these a resume and carefully written cover letter directed to the individual who can help or hire you. Follow-up with a phone call. When you take a company off your list, add a new one.

Various directories and networking contacts will help you come up with names of individuals who could be in a position to help or hire you. Or a phone call to the company can sometimes secure the name of the right person to mail to. Never be afraid to mail letters to more than one person at a firm, especially at some of the larger companies, where the more people who see your resume and are in a position to do something about it, the better.

A targeted mailing cannot work without follow-up phone calls. Let the employer know you will be calling so that the resume remains on his or her desk, and make sure you call within 10 to 14 days after you send the letter.

Although we make this sound easy, contacting the hiring authority could require talking with two or three people in order to determine who the decision-maker is. It could take many phone calls and much follow-up, but don't get discouraged. The important thing is to get your resume in front of the right person and away from the resume graveyard.

Treat the secretaries/assistants with all the respect possible since they are essentially gatekeepers. They often have the power to grant or deny you access to a hiring authority. Getting off on the right foot with the secretary enhances your chances of talking directly with the more influential person. Treating the secretary/assistant as a professional is crucial since he or she often knows everything going on in the office and can give you access to the boss.

Step 8: Use Your Career Resources

Finding a good job is difficult and today the traditional job search is insufficient. You need to use every resource available, including employment agencies, executive search firms, social service agencies, government agencies, career consultants, college career centers and career fairs. Let's examine these resources one by one. (Also see "Internet Job Listings" earlier in this chapter.)

Employment Agencies

Your first impulse may be to turn the job hunt over to a professional employment service. However, if you're a recent college graduate or offer no special or high-demand skills, employment agencies can be less than helpful. Those that specialize in temporary jobs are even less likely to lead you to your dream job. We recommend taking charge of your own job search since you know yourself and your goals better than anyone else. If you do decide to use employment services, become familiar with their operations and limitations. This will save you a lot of time, effort, and possibly money.

Employment agencies act as intermediaries in the job market between buyers (companies with jobs open) and sellers (people who want jobs). Agencies are paid either by the employer or the worker for placing people. Find out the total cost beforehand and how the fee is handled.

Employment agencies seldom place a candidate in a job that pays more than $50,000 a year. Most employment agencies concentrate on support jobs rather than middle or upper-management positions. A company will do a job search on their own or utilize an executive search firm to fill top management positions. However, if you are in the secretary/assistant field, it may be worth your while to look at employment agencies. To many companies, it's worth the agency fee to avoid the hassle of prescreening dozens, if not hundreds, of applicants.

If you decide to use an agency, be sure it's a reputable firm. Ask people in your field to recommend a quality agency, and consult the Better Business Bureau or another consumer watchdog agency to see if there have been any complaints about the agency you're considering. Most important, *read the contract thoroughly, including all the fine print, before signing anything.* Remember, the agency is loyal to its source of income—usually the company. Also remember that if a company has to pay a fee to hire you, you may be at a disadvantage over candidates not using an agency. Finally, the job-search strategies an agency provides are all outlined in this book and you can implement most of them yourself.

A listing in this book does not constitute an endorsement of any agencies or firms. Before using a service, try to get the opinion of one or more people who have already used the service you're considering. You can also contact the following: **Better Business Bureau of Metropolitan Atlanta** (404) 688-4910.

Below is a list of some local employment agencies, including their areas of specialty.

ATLANTA AREA EMPLOYMENT AGENCIES

Accountemps Division of Robert Half of Atlanta
1816 Independence Square
Dunwoody, GA 30338
(770) 392-0540
Permanent positions for CPAs and tax accountants, auditors, system analysts, financial analysts, and treasurers.

Adia Personnel Services
229 Peachtree St., N.E., Suite 1225
Atlanta, GA 30303
(404) 681-1180
Offices in several locations throughout the metropolitan Atlanta area.

Apple One
1375 Peachtree St., N.E., Suite 125
Atlanta, GA 30309
(404) 815-9393
Diverse positions including but not limited to accounting, clerical support, engineering, manufacturing and litigation support.

Bell Oaks Company
3390 Peachtree Road, N.E., Suite 924
Atlanta, GA 30326
(404) 261-2170
Accounting and finance; engineering; manufacturing; insurance; computer science and data processing.

Caldwell
200 Galleria Parkway, Suite 1280
Atlanta, GA 30339
(770) 955-0112
Office support. Several locations.

Dunhill Professional Search
3340 Peachtree Road, N.E. , Suite 2570
Atlanta, GA 30326
(404) 261-3751

Howie & Associates
875 Old Roswell Road, Bldg. F,
Suite 100
Roswell, GA 30076
(404) 998-0099
Data processing, accounting, finance,
sales, and technical writers.

Hudson Personnel/Search
7001 Peachtree Industrial Blvd.
Norcross, GA 30092
(770) 825-8046
Sales and marketing, including middle management and executive levels.

International Insurance Personnel
300 W Wiecua Road, N.E.
Atlanta, GA 30342
(404) 255-9710
Insurance personnel.

Jobbank USA
3232 Cobb Parkway, Suite 611
Atlanta, GA 30339
(770) 971-1971
www.jobbankusa.com
Search and placement information
technologies; employment information services via Internet.

King Personnel Consultants
3390 Peachtree Road, N.E., Suite 304
Atlanta, GA 30326
(404) 266-1800
Fast food management; mortgage
loan program; telecommunications
and sales.

Lawstaf
1201 W. Peachtree St., Suite 4610
Atlanta, GA 30309
(404) 872-6672
Legal staffing.

Medpro Personnel
1955 Cliff Valley Way
Atlanta, GA 30329
RNs, LPNs, PAs, X-ray and lab tech-
nicians, medical office managers.

Office Mates 5
5901C Peachtree Dunwoody Road,
Suite 350
Atlanta, GA 30328
(770) 394-1700
Diverse areas including administrative, clerical, data entry, and
accounting.

Perimeter Placement
24 Perimeter Center East, Suite 2417
Atlanta, GA 30346
(770) 393-0000
Office support.

Romac International
3 Ravinia Drive, N.E., Suite 1460
Atlanta, GA 30346
(770) 604-3880
Accounting and information systems.

Snelling and Snelling
1309 Powers Ferry Road, S.E.
Marietta, GA 30067
(770) 952-0909
Sales and marketing, banking,
engineering/technical, hospitality,
medical, accounting, retail, and
management.

Software Search
2163 Northlake Parkway, Bldg. 1,
Suite 100
Tucker, GA 30084
(404) 934-5138
Business and scientific applications;
software development.

Talent Tree Staffing Services
2 Ravinia Drive, N.E., Suite 320
Atlanta, GA 30346
(770) 396-5767

OTHER CAREER-SEARCH RESOURCES

In addition to the above listings, there are a number of other services available throughout the Atlanta Metro area. Many of these are free and open to the public. A few of these services are listed here:

Atlanta Transplants
219 Hermer Circle, N.W.
Atlanta, GA 30311
(404) 505-7800
This is a relocation service which welcomes newcomers to Atlanta from across the country and around the world. They host newcomers' job expos annually in the fall and spring.

Career Quest
4905 Roswell Road, N.E.
Marietta, GA 30342
(770) 552-6402
Job-search workshops include creative tools and practical courses for employees at risk and anyone requiring job-search assistance.
Free. Adult Education Center, Catholic Church of St. Ann.

Career Support Groups
Ongoing meetings are available throughout the metropolitan area for anyone between jobs and needing the emotional support of others. Meetings provide interaction, reinforcement, encouragement, candid appraisal, and individual and group accountability. Free. Times and locations determined by participation.
(404) 303-5959

Career Transition Ministry
3098 Northside Parkway
Atlanta, GA 30327
(404) 237-5589
Workshops cover career focusing, resume writing, marketing strategies, and interviewing skills. Free. St. Anne's Episcopal Church.

Job Network (Atlanta)
3434 Roswell Road, N.W.
Atlanta, GA 30305
(404) 842-3147
Free. 7-10 p.m. Thursdays. Peachtree Presbyterian Church, Room 221.

Job Network (Gwinnett)
1400 Killian Hill Road
Lilburn, GA 30247
(770) 921-7434
Free. 7:30-10:00 p.m. Thursdays. Good Shepherd Presbyterian Church.

Job Search Assistance
Institute of the Christian World
201 Ashby St., N.W.
Atlanta, GA 30314
(404) 522-5934
Sharing, training, and assistance for the unemployed and the underemployed.
7-9 p.m. Tuesdays. Free.

Media Group
176 W. Wieuca Road N.E., Suite B-13
Atlanta, GA 30346
(404) 851-1763 or (770) 671-1176

Recent Grads, New in the Workforce
Roswell United Methodist Church
814 Mimosa Blvd., Building B, Room 236
Roswell, GA 30375
(770) 642-7943
Networking seminars for job seekers who need help making cold calls, writing
business letters, or interviewing. Will include sessions on resume/cover letter
writing, focusing, and networking. Free.

S.A.M.S.
Roswell United Methodist Church
814 Mimosa Blvd., Building B, Room 236
Roswell, GA 30375
(770) 642-7943
Sales and Marketing Seekers offers networking and job-hunting assistance for
people in sales and marketing, though any discipline is welcome. 7-9 a.m.
Mondays. Free.

Executive Search Firms

Executive search firms are paid by companies to locate people with specific qualifications to meet a precisely defined employment need. Most reputable executive
search firms belong to an organization called the Association of Executive
Recruiting Consultants (AERC). A search firm never works on a contingency
basis. Only employment agencies do that. Because the company has to pay a large
fee, they may opt to forgo using an executive search firm during hard times.

Yet, if you choose to use an executive search firm, as specialists who know the
market they can be very helpful in providing advice and leads. Keep in mind that
you are only useful to the search firm if there is an assignment that matches your
background and qualifications exactly.

Dear Dr. Bob

I have recently graduated and was considering using an executive search firm to simplify my job search. What do you recommend?—Recently Confused Graduate

Dear Recently Confused Graduate

Unless you are middle to upper management, the search firm will not be interested in helping you. Since the search firm looks for candidates with highly developed skills in a particular area, your experience may seem inadequate compared to the candidate with 15 years of work history. For the present time, try the techniques in this book to land a job on your own.

Below is a selected list of local executive search firms, including their areas of specialty.

ATLANTA AREA EXECUTIVE SEARCH FIRMS

Ashford Management Group
2295 Parkway Place, S.E.
Marietta, GA 30067
(770) 938-6260

Bradshaw Management Search
1850 Parkway Place, S.E.
Marietta, GA 30067
(770) 426-5600
Most fields.

Bridgers, Goeltz and Associates
5335 Triangle Parkway, Suite 510
Norcross, GA 30092
(770) 368-9835
Insurance search specialists.

Cooper, David C., and Associates
400 Perimeter Center Terrace, N.E.
Atlanta, GA 30346
(770) 395-0014
Financial specialists.

Engineering Group
3000-7000 Langford Road
Norcross, GA 30071
(770) 441-2729

Executive Resource Group
2470 Windy Hill Road, S.E., Suite 300
Marietta, GA 30067
(770) 955-1811
Senior and middle management for manufacturing field.

Fox-Morris Associates Inc. of Atlanta
9000 Central Park West, N.E., Suite 150
Atlanta, GA 30328
(770) 399-4497
Upper middle-managment positions and above.

Handler, W.L., & Associates
100 Cumberland Circle, Suite 1290
Atlanta, GA 30339
(770) 850-6220
Generalist firm.

Hospitality Resources
131 Roswell Road
Alpharetta, GA 30239
(770) 664-5354
Hospitality industry.

Maddox & Associates, Bob
3134 W. Roxboro Road, N.E.
Atlanta, GA 30326
(404) 231-0558
Sales professionals and marketing
professionals.

Management Recruiters—
Atlanta/Buckhead
1776 Peachtree St., Suite 770
Atlanta, GA 30303
(404) 874-3636
Health-care specialists at above loca-
tion; several offices throughout
Atlanta.

McHale & Associates
5064 Roswell Road, N.W., Bldg. D-301
Atlanta, GA 30342
(404) 252-9020
Sales and management; engineering;
manufacturing.

Omega Executive Search
2033 Monroe Drive, N.E.
Atlanta, GA 30324
(404) 873-2000
Hospitality industry.

The Packaged Solution
3 Piedmont Center, Suite 300
Atlanta, GA 30305
(770) 671-1107
Software; information technology.

Social Service Agencies with Job Resources

Unlike professional employment agencies, career consultants (see below), and
executive search firms, social service agencies are not-for-profit. They offer a wide
range of services, from counseling and vocational testing to job placement and
follow-up—and their services are either low cost or free. Below is a list of social
service agencies in the Atlanta Area.

ATLANTA AREA SOCIAL SERVICE AGENCIES

AARP—Senior Community Service Employment Program
1776 Peachtree St., N.W.
Atlanta, GA 30308
AARP program to provide employment assistance to persons 55 and older.

Atlanta Urban League
100 Edgewood Ave., Suite 600
Atlanta, GA 30303
(404) 659-1150
Free employment referral program; includes training and referrals.

Employment Resource Center for Mature Workers
957 N. Highland Ave., N.E.
Atlanta, GA 30306
(404) 872-2231
Employment assistance to persons 50 and older.

Jewish Vocational Service
4549 Chamblee Dunwoody Road
Atlanta, GA 30338-6210
(770) 677-9440
JVS offers employment counseling and assistance. Nominal fee is charged for
services.

Veterans Employment and Training Service
148 International Blvd., Suite 504
Atlanta, GA 30303
(404) 656-3127

Government Agencies with Job Resources

Most job seekers do not take advantage of the free job listings available through the city, county, and state because the caliber of jobs is often disappointing. However, the services of these government agencies are usually free. You may as well stop in and see what is available.

ATLANTA AREA GOVERNMENT EMPLOYMENT AGENCIES

North Metro/Taco Hills
2943 N. Druid Hills Road
Atlanta, GA 30329
(404) 679-5200

South Metro
2636 Martin Luther King Jr. Drive
Atlanta, GA 30314
(404) 699-6900

DeKalb County/Pendley Hills
3879 Covington Highway
Decatur, GA 30209
(404) 298-3970

Smyrna/Cobb County
2972 Ask Kay Drive, S.E.
Smyrna, GA 30082
(770) 319-3960

Clayton County/Lake City
1193 Forest Parkway
Lake City, GA 30525
(404) 363-7643

Gwinett County/Lawrenceville
1535 Atkinson Road
Lawrenceville, GA 30243
(770) 995-6913

Georgia State Government
Merit System of Personnel
200 Piedmont Ave.
Atlanta, GA 30303
(404) 656-2724
Employment with the state.

Career Consultants

Career consultants vary greatly in the kind and quality of the services they provide. Some may offer a single service, such as vocational testing or preparing resumes. Others coach every aspect of the job search and stay with you until you accept an offer. The fees vary just as broadly and range from $100 to several thousand dollars. You, not your potential employer, pay the fee.

A qualified career consultant can be an asset to your job search. But no consultant can get you a job. A consultant can help you focus on an objective, develop a resume, teach you to research the job market, decide on a strategy, and provide interviewing techniques. But in the end, the consultant can't interview for you. You are responsible.

The only time you should consider a consultant is after you've exhausted all the other resources we've suggested here and still feel you need expert and personalized help with one or more aspects of the job search. The key to choosing a career consultant is knowing what you need and verifying that the consultant can provide it.

Check references. A reputable firm will gladly provide them. Check the Better Business Bureau and get referrals from friends who have used a consultant. Before signing anything, ask to meet the consultant who will actually provide the services you want. What are their credentials? How long have they been practicing? What does the consultant promise? What is required from you? How long can you use the consultant's services? Be sure to shop around before selecting a consultant. Refer to Chapter 2 for a list of possible counselors.

College Career Centers

If you are in college and are not acquainted with your school's career center, make a point to stop by and check out the services available. Colleges and universities usually provide services to their alumni and members of the local community also.

There is more to a college career center than just job postings. It's a great resource for building your network, researching the job market, and seeking counseling to establish a career strategy. And most colleges and universities also offer services such as vocational testing and interpretation and the use of the resource library to the general public. Refer to Chapter 2 for a listing of local colleges and universities and the career services provided to students, alumni, and the general public.

Career Fairs

Another job-search resource that can help is the ubiquitous career fair. Career fairs are the shopping malls for job searchers. Employers line up to market their companies and job opportunities. Job searchers browse the aisles, often stopping when a particularly glitzy brochure or big company name catches their eye. And like the shopping mall, employers want to sell, sell, sell their opportunities while job searchers want to snatch up great deals.

Career fairs are a job shopper's delight. The large number of employers in one place makes it easy to research many companies. Additionally, career fairs afford the job searcher a chance to meet face to face with company representatives, often an advantage for people who make a better impression in person than on paper. Finally, at some career fairs candidates can actually interview for jobs with prospective employers during the event.

Career fairs are most often advertised in the classified section of the newspaper. Professional associations will also frequently receive announcements. Colleges and universities often sponsor career fairs and post announcements of these and other events. Some coordinators of career fairs will even put up billboards and advertise on television.

As more and more employers rely on career fairs to meet qualified applicants, the savvy job searcher must be comfortable attending these events. These few tips will help you more effectively use a career fair.

- Prior to the fair, get a list of the companies attending in order to begin researching potential employers. Knowing what a company does allows you to use the precious few minutes you will have with a company representative to sell yourself rather than ask basic questions about the company's products.
- Plan a strategy. Use your research to prioritize the companies you want to talk with. Sequence the companies according to which companies you must, without a doubt, talk with before the end of the fair.
- Arrive early the day of the fair in order to scope out the facilities and meet with company representatives before lines get too long. Familiarize yourself with the location of employers, the flow of traffic, and the layout of the building.
- Avoid wasting time in long lines to talk to big-name employers, even if they have great company give-away goodies. Smaller employers and their representatives will have less traffic, which means that you may be able to spend more time talking with him or her and making a positive impression.
- Take the initiative in approaching employers. Prepare a short two-to-three-minute "infomercial" about yourself so that you can quickly acquaint employers with your background. Have a list of questions ready for employers so that you don't have to suffer angst while trying to decide what to say to him or her.
- Bring lots of resumes and be prepared to leave them with any employer who interests you. Before leaving the career fair, revisit your favorite employers and leave your resume with them again to make sure your name does not get lost in the pile.

The shopping mall was created as a convenience to vendors who want lots of consumers and consumers who want lots of vendors in one easy place; the career fair provides the same convenience to job searchers and employers. A successful strategy will help you avoid lost time and hopefully get you inside the company for a proper interview later.

CAREER FAIR ORGANIZATIONS

Van Treadaway Associates
4665 Lower Roswell Road, #142
Marietta, GA 30068
(770) 908-0929
The only locally managed high-tech career fair in the Atlanta area. Fairs occur twice a year—in March and September with approximately 50 hires per fair.

http: //www.espan.com/js/jobfair.html
Lists career fairs geographically.

Step 9: The Killer Interview

The killer interview consists of three parts; preparation, success during the interview, and follow-up. We'll highlight key aspects of this process. However, Chapter 7 discusses the interview in greater detail.

Preparation

Before any interview, you need to prepare and practice in order to do the best job possible in selling yourself to the employer. Follow this procedure for best results:

- Identify your strengths, skills, goals, and personal qualities. Self-assessment is crucial to knowing what you have to offer an employer and to conveying it effectively. Try to come up with five unique strengths. Have examples of how you have used them professionally.
- Research the company in order to ask intelligent questions. An interview is supposed to be a dialogue; you want to learn about them just as they want to learn about you.
- Rehearse what you plan to say during the interview. Practice answers to commonly asked questions and determine how you will emphasize your strengths and skills.
- Dress professionally and conservatively. If you make a negative first impression, you may not be fairly considered for the job. Refer to Chapter 7 for dressing tips in the interview.

Success During the Interview

Chapter 7 covers what interviewers are looking for. Below are some additional tips to help you succeed in your interview.

- Arrive on time or ten minutes early. This will ensure you the full amount of time allotted and show that you are enthusiastic about the position.
- The first five minutes of the interview can be extremely important. To start your interview off right, offer a firm handshake and smile, make good eye contact, and say something to break the ice. "Nice to meet you," or something of that sort, should clear your throat nicely and prepare you for more substantive conversation.
- As you begin the interview, be aware of non-verbal behavior. Wait to sit until you are offered a chair. Look alert, speak in a clear, strong voice, try to stay relaxed, avoid nervous mannerisms, and try to be a good listener as well as a good talker.
- Be specific, concrete, and detailed in your answers. The more information you volunteer, the better the employer gets to know you and thereby is able to make a wise hiring decision. But *don't* be longwinded.
- Always have questions for the interviewer.
- Don't mention salary in a first interview unless the employer does. If asked, give a realistic range and add that opportunity is the most important factor for you.

- Offer examples of your work and references that will document your best qualities.
- Answer questions as truthfully as possible. Never appear to be "glossing over" anything. If the interviewer ventures into ticklish political or social questions, answer honestly but try not to say more than is necessary.
- Never make derogatory remarks about present or former employers or companies. Make sure you look very positive in the interviewer's eyes.

Follow-Up

The following suggestions will help you survive the "awful waiting" time after the interview.

- Don't get discouraged if no definite offer is made or specific salary discussed.
- If you feel the interview isn't going well, don't let your discouragement show. Occasionally an interviewer who is genuinely interested in you may seem to discourage you to test your reaction.
- At the end of the interview, ask when a hiring decision will be made. This is important not only because it reconfirms your interest in the position but also so you'll know when to expect a response.
- Send a thank-you letter to the interviewer: thank him or her for the time and effort; reiterate your skills and qualifications for the position; and make clear your interest in the job.
- Make notes on what you feel you could improve upon for your next interview and on what you feel went particularly well. After all, experience is only valuable to the extent that you're willing to learn from it.
- If offered the position, up to two weeks is a reasonable amount of time to make your decision. All employment offers deserve a written reply, whether or not you accept them.

You will learn a great deal about patience during the waiting period that follows an interview. The important point to remember during this time is that all your hopes shouldn't be dependent on one or two interviews. The job search is continuous and shouldn't stop until you have accepted an offer. Keeping all your options open is the best possible course.

Keep in contact with the company if they haven't responded by the date they indicated in the interview. Asking the status of your application is a legitimate question. This inquiry should be stated in a manner that is not pushy but shows your continued interest in the company.

Step 10: Make Sure This Is the Job for You

Start celebrating! You have received a job offer after working so diligently on the job search. But before you accept or decline, consider the offer carefully. Make sure the details of the offer are clear; preferably, get them in writing. Details should include starting date, salary and benefits, location, job description and responsibilities, and the date by which you must respond. Evaluating a job offer can be both exciting and difficult. We have provided the following information to assist you in making a job decision.

Negotiating Salary

Be aware of what other people in similar positions are making before accepting any offer. The *Occupational Outlook Handbook,* put out by the U.S. Department of Labor every two years, cites salary statistics by field. Another good source of information is *The American Almanac of Jobs and Salaries* by John Wright, published by Avon. Professional societies and associations frequently provide this sort of information too. It's one more good reason to belong to one.

When negotiating salary, proceed with care to prevent jeopardizing a positive relationship with your new employer. Here are some points in negotiating salaries:

- Be prepared with salary research before discussing any figures.
- Approach the session with trust and a willingness to compromise.
- Know when to stop. Don't push your luck.
- Be open to substituting other benefits in exchange for a higher salary.

The end result should be that both parties are happy with the outcome. For advice on how to get the salary you want, we recommend these books:

BOOKS ON SALARY NEGOTIATION

Chapman, Jack. *How to Make $1000 a Minute.* Berkeley, CA: Ten Speed Press, 1987.

Chastain, Sherry. *Winning the Salary Game: Salary Negotiation For Women.* New York: John Wiley & Sons, 1980.

Fisher, Roger, and William Levy. *Getting to Yes: Negotiating Agreement Without Giving In.* New York: Penguin Books, 1992.

Kennedy, Marilyn Moats. *Getting the Job You Want & The Money You're Worth.* American College of Executives, 1987.

Krannich, Ronald L., and Rae. *Salary Success: Know What You're Worth and Get It.* Woodbridge, VA: Impact Publications, 1990.

Compare the Offers on Paper

Don't blindly accept the first offer you receive. You've put a great deal of effort in the job search, so spend a little more time in comparing the relative merits of each offer. Below is a sample checklist to assist you in this endeavor. The idea is to list the factors that you consider important in any job, and then assign a rating for how well each offer fills the bill in each particular area.

We've listed some factors that should be considered before accepting any offer. Some may not be relevant to your situation. Others that we've left out may be of great importance to you. So feel free to make any additions, deletions, or changes you want. Assign a rating (1 being the lowest and 5 the highest) for each factor under each offer. Then total the scores.

The offer with the most points is not necessarily the one to accept. The chart doesn't take into account the fact that "responsibilities" may be more important to you than "career path," or that you promised yourself you'd never punch a time clock again. Nevertheless, looking at the pros and cons of each offer in black and white should help you make a much more methodical and logical decision.

Factor	Offer A	Offer B
Responsibilities	_____	_____
Company reputation	_____	_____
Salary	_____	_____
Vacation leave	_____	_____
Insurance/Pension	_____	_____
Profit sharing	_____	_____
Tuition reimbursement	_____	_____
On-the-job training	_____	_____
Career path advancement	_____	_____
Company future	_____	_____
Product/service quality	_____	_____
Location (housing market, schools, transportation)	_____	_____
Boss(es)	_____	_____
Co-workers	_____	_____
Travel	_____	_____
Overtime	_____	_____
Other	_____	_____
_____	_____	_____
TOTAL POINTS	_____	_____

Evaluating Job Offers

A job involves more than a title and salary. Before you accept any offer, be sure you understand what your responsibilities will be, what benefits you'll receive besides salary (insurance, profit sharing, vacation, tuition reimbursement, etc.), how much overtime is required (and whether you'll be paid for it), how much travel is involved in the job, who your supervisor will be, how many people you'll supervise, and where the position could lead (do people in this position get promoted?). In short, find out anything and everything you can to evaluate the offer.

The cost of living is essential in comparing job offers in different cities. The difference in the cost of living can mean living like royalty in Houston or struggling in New York, even if the salaries offered seem relatively close. To compare cost of living, check the Consumer Price Indexes provided by the Bureau of Labor Statistics.

It seems obvious that it's unwise to choose a job solely on the basis of salary. Consider all the factors, such as your boss and colleagues and the type of work you'll be doing, before making any final decision.

Corporate Cultures

Every company has a different corporate culture (philosophies and management style) and some fit better with your own personality than others. Thus it is important to research the company's culture in your career search. Specific companies are discussed in the following books:

BOOKS ON CORPORATE CULTURE

Kanter, Rosabeth Moss, and Barry A. Stein. *Life in Organizations.* New York: Basic Books, 1979.

Levering, Robert, and Milton Moskowitz. *The 100 Best Companies To Work For In America.* New York: Doubleday, 1993.

Peters, Thomas J., and Robert H. Waterman, Jr. *In Search of Excellence.* New York: Warner Books, 1982.

Peters, Thomas J., and Nancy Austin. *Passion for Excellence.* New York: Random House, 1985.

Plunkett, Jack. *The Almanac of American Employers.* Boerne, TX: Corporate Jobs Outlook, 1994.

It is also possible to decipher a company's culture during the interview. The following are factors worth examining:

- What is the environment like? Look at the appearance of the office, the company newsletter, brochures, and bulletin boards.
- Who is on board? How does the company greet strangers, what kind of people work for them, and why is the company a success (or failure)?
- How are employees rewarded? Look at the benefits, awards, compensation, and recognition given to employees.
- What is the fashion statement? Look at the dress code. Are there different dress styles for levels of employment?
- How do people spend their time? Look at the ambience of the workplace and what an average day is like.
- How do managers behave? Look at the history of the company, how things get done, and the management style.

Is the Job a Dream or a Nightmare?

Dream jobs sometimes do turn into nightmare employment. It happens all the time. How do you avoid this possibility? Look for the eight danger signs of the "job from hell."

Financial problems and corporate turmoil. Prospective employees rarely do financial or management research on a company in which they are interested. It will behoove you to find out if the firm is financially sound and if there has been much turmoil within the company.

Layoffs indicate danger. Many companies try to convince new employees that recent layoffs will have no effect on their position. Don't believe it! A good indication of a job about to go bad is that mass layoffs have recently occurred.

Recent mergers or acquisitions can be another danger signal. Companies that have bought or merged with another company are usually trying to reduce expenses. And the easiest way for the corporate world to reduce expenses is to cut employees and reorganize. The chances of you working in the position you interviewed for will diminish with reorganization. Being new, you may also be one of the first to be laid off or transferred.

Word on the street. What is the informal word about your new potential workplace? Word of mouth is often a good source of inside information about the reality of working for a particular company. Try to eliminate gossip and scuttlebutt from those who are naturally and overly negative. But if a general consensus exists that a company is not good to its employees or that people are unusually unhappy, carefully weigh your decision.

Turnover within your position. How many people have worked in your new position during the last couple of years? Is your particular job one that experiences a great deal of turnover? High turnover should alert you to the possibility that either the job is horrible and no one can stand it or that no one is really capable of doing this job, including you. Percentages show that those who take jobs with high turnover rates are very likely to become a statistic as well.

Elusive or vague job description. A key danger signal is the absence of or vagueness in your job description. Look for a job where the duties are known up front. It's fine for some things about a job to be determined later, and you certainly want your responsibilities to be increased, but don't take a job in which you are not sure what your primary duties will be or to whom you will report.

"Bad boss" potential. Don't discount the boss's influence on your job performance or your satisfaction within a job. Most employees spend more waking time with a boss than with their spouse. Try to meet your boss before you accept the job and ask yourself if you are ready to live with him or her on a daily basis. As we have mentioned before, your boss should be a role model. He or she should help you grow and develop in your career. If you have doubts about your boss, you should have doubts about the job.

That gut feeling. Finally, you can never discount that deep-down feeling you get about your job offer. Even when the pay and benefits are great, you still might have mixed emotions about a particular job. Explore those emotions and find out why they are "mixed." They may be more than a premonition.

Even if a job looks like a winner, if you see one or more of these danger signs, do a little more research before you accept. Don't wind up a major loser.

five

Network, Network, Network: The Best Job-Search Technique

What's the difference between knowing a lot of people and having an influential network? If you're a smart job searcher, you will realize that knowing a lot of people is just the start. It is the process of staying in touch with people and building strong connections that creates an influential and powerful network. While the old axiom "it's not what you know but who you know" may be an overstatement, savvy job seekers use who they know to help them find jobs in which they can use what they know. Atlanta is a city where personal relationships are highly valued. So who you know and who knows you is very important.

For many people, networking has a negative connotation. It implies cocktail parties, insincere conversation, and golf games with people you don't really like. In reality, however, job networking is simply asking people for information about careers and employment. You may already be networking and not know it!

The Six Myths of Networking

In order to encourage more networking, let's start by debunking some common myths.

MYTH #1: People get jobs through ads and other formal announcements. The truth is that fewer than 20 percent of available jobs are ever advertised. The majority of jobs are in the "hidden job market." Mark S. Granovetter, a Harvard sociologist, reported to *Forbes* magazine that informal contacts, or networks, account for almost 75 percent of successful job searches. Agencies find about 9 percent of new jobs for professional and technical people, and ads yield about another 10 percent.

If those figures don't convince you to begin networking, how about these. A recent study found that employers preferred using networks to hire new employees because it reduced recruiting costs and decreased the risks associated with hiring a new, unknown employee. Furthermore, people who use networking are generally more satisfied with the job they land and tend to have higher incomes.

MYTH #2: *Networking is so effective, you can ignore more traditional means of job searching, such as responding to ads.* This is simply not true. As important as networking is to your job search, you will shorten the time you spend looking for a job if you use more methods. The average job seeker only uses a few of the available job-search techniques. No wonder job searches take so long! Networking complements your other techniques, not replaces them. Don't put all your eggs in one basket; use as many options as possible.

MYTH #3: *Networking is only effective for people who are very assertive.* If you were asking people for jobs, this might be true. However, networking is just asking people for information for your job search, which requires you to be polite but not overly assertive.

If you are uncomfortable contacting people, start your network with people you know well or with whom you have some connection: you go to the same church, you are both members of the same alumni association, etc. Talking with friends and family is less intimidating than approaching strangers. Networking in friendly territory will help you develop confidence in your approach and know what questions to ask.

MYTH #4: *The job hunter's most important networking contacts within a company are in the HR department.* If you limit your network to human resources personnel, you will be waiting a long time for a job. Only one person in four gets their job by relying strictly on personnel offices. Human resources people are there to help others hire. Find those "others."

The purpose of networking is to talk to as many people as possible. Sometimes people only tangentially related to the hiring process can provide you with valuable information about your industry, tips on companies that may be hiring, or names of other contacts.

MYTH #5: *No one knows enough people to network effectively.* Most people know an average of 200 people. Even if only 20 people you know can help you with your job search, those 20 can refer you to 400 additional people, and your network has taken off.

Certainly if you're moving to a new town, your list of contacts will be small. You must act to develop it. Find out about your local alumni association, join a church, join professional associations, and attend as many social functions as possible. Meet people!

MYTH #6: Once you've found a job, there is no need to keep up with your network. Absolutely false. Write a thank-you note immediately after meeting with someone who was helpful with your job search. Once you've landed a job, let your network know and periodically touch base with them.

Networking as a waiter

Eric, a recent college graduate, was interested in getting a job in the very competitive field of advertising. While waiting for interviews to roll in, he waited tables at a local pub in order to pay the bills.

One night, several months and part-time jobs after graduation, Eric struck up a conversation with a group of people that had stopped by after work. After learning that they worked for a large advertising agency, Eric told them about his job search, collected their business cards, and contacted the office the following week. Eric's personality, resume, and samples impressed the office staff so much that they invited him for an interview. He got the job.

Step-by-Step Guide to Networking

To begin the networking process, draw up a list of all the people you know who might help you gain access to someone who can hire you for the job you want. Naturally, the first sources, the ones at the top of your list, will be people you know personally: friends, colleagues, former clients, relatives, acquaintances, customers, and club or church members. Just about everyone you know, whether or not he or she is employed, can generate contacts for you.

Don't forget to talk with your banker, lawyer, insurance agent, dentist, and other people who provide you with services. It is the nature of their business to know lots of people who might help you in your search. Leave no stone unturned in your search for contacts. Go through your holiday-card list, college yearbook, club membership directories, and any other list you can think of.

The next step is to expand your network to include new people who can help you. The easiest way to do this is to ask each of the people you do know for the names of two or three other people who might be helpful in your job search.

Professional organizations are another resource. If you are changing careers, you should view professional organizations as essential to your job search. Most groups meet on a regular basis and are an excellent way to contact other people in your field. Some professional associations offer placement services to members. Many chambers of commerce publish directories of the professional and trade associations that meet in your area. Local business magazines and newspapers also publish times and locations for meetings of professional associations.

Your college alumni association is another resource to expand your network. Alumni club meetings provide opportunities to catch up on happenings with your alma mater and meet other professionals in your area. Additionally, some schools maintain alumni databases for the express purpose of networking. This is a valuable resource for both seasoned professionals and recent college grads looking for a job lead and a friendly face. Still other alumni associations offer resume referral services that you can join for a small fee.

The Information Interview

There are situations, however, when your existing network simply won't be adequate. If you're changing careers, you may not know enough people in your new field to help you. If you've just moved to a new area, your network may still be elsewhere. Your situation may require you to creatively build a new network. One of the best techniques for doing this is the "information interview."

Information interviewing is a technique for developing contacts by interviewing people for job-search information. This technique acknowledges that names of contacts are easy to find but relationships that can help you find a job require additional action on your part.

First, telephone or write to possible contacts whom you've identified through lists of acquaintances, professional associations, your alumni organization, or simply a cold call. Explain that you are very interested in his or her field, and arrange a twenty-minute appointment. Be very clear that you are not asking him or her for a job but only for information. Also, never ask new people out to lunch. It is too time consuming and lunch isn't as important to the business person as it may be to the job searcher. Don't give someone a reason to turn you down. Twenty minutes is enough time for you to get information without imposing on your host.

The information interview is the time to ask your contact questions about the field, the job market, and job-hunting tips. Ask your contact to review your resume and make recommendations about how to present yourself or fill in gaps in your experience. Most importantly, ask your contact for the names of two or three other people to talk with, thus expanding your network. And always follow up with a thank-you letter.

QUESTIONS TO ASK IN AN INFORMATION INTERVIEW

Job Function Questions

What do people with a job like yours do?

What does your typical day consist of?

What do you like/dislike about your work?

Who are the key people in your field?

What skills are necessary for your position?

Company Questions

What has been the major achievement of this organization?

How often do you interact with top management?

What trends do you foresee for this organization and in the field?

What is the company's corporate culture like?

Who are your major competitors?

Career Field Questions

What is the growth potential in your field for the next five years?

What journals or magazines should I read?

What professional organizations do you recommend?

Who else would you recommend that I talk with?

Information interviews not only help build your network but they can identify career paths, potential employers, worthwhile professional associations, and weaknesses in your work or educational background. Most importantly, learning to glean information is a skill that will serve you throughout your life.

Example of an Information Interview Letter

Jack Smith
6613 Barron Drive
Atlanta, GA 30030
(404) 555-3367

April 11, 1997

Dr. David Hart
President
Environmental Research

Dear Dr. Hart:

Dr. Young, with whom I have studied these past two years, suggested that you might be able to advise me of opportunities in the environmental engineering field in Atlanta.

I am about to graduate from Georgia Tech with a B.S. in civil engineering, and I am a member of Phi Beta Kappa. For two of the last three summers, I have worked as an intern with the Air Pollution Control Association.

I am eager to begin work and would appreciate a few minutes of your time to discuss trends in environmental research and, as a newcomer, gain the benefit of your advice regarding a career. Exams are finished on June 6, and I would like to arrange a meeting with you shortly thereafter. I look forward to hearing from you and in any case will be in touch with your office next week.

Sincerely,

Jack Smith

Information interview letter tips:
- Keep it short and direct.
- Tell enough about yourself to demonstrate that you are sincere and qualified.
- Always conclude with a date when you'll call, and always call if they haven't called you by that date.

Admittedly, networking will not work in every situation. No amount of networking will help you land a job for which you do not have the minimum qualifications. Nor will networking work if you try to meet with people at a much higher professional level than your own. A CEO will likely be unwilling to help someone looking for an entry-level position. You can also make people unwilling to help you by being pushy and demanding. But if you avoid these pitfalls, you should develop a great network.

Do You Know Your Networking Net Worth?

To determine the net worth of your networking ability, take the following quiz to assess how you approach people at professional meetings, social events, and community functions. For each statement, circle Y for yes or N for no.

Y   N   1. I belong to at least one professional or trade association in which I can meet people in my field.

Y   N   2. In the past year, I have used my contacts to help at least two people meet someone of importance to them.

Y   N   3. In the last month, I have attended at least two functions in order to meet people who are potential professional contacts.

Y   N   4. When I meet new professional contacts, I ask them for a business card and make notes on the back about our conversation.

Y   N   5. When asked, "What kind of job are you looking for?" I can answer in two sentences or less.

Y   N   6. I keep in touch with former classmates and workmates.

Y   N   7. I have given colleagues information to help them solve a problem.

Y   N   8. I always know at least 25 professionals in my field well enough to call and say, "Hi, this is (my name)," and they know who I am.

Y   N   9. When attending professional or social functions, I introduce myself to new people and show interest in their careers.

Y   N   10. I am involved in at least one community or social organization outside work or school.

Count how many times you circled Y, then analyze your score:

0-4   You can make your job search easier by learning the basics of networking.

5-8   You can give and get even more out of your professional networks.

9-10   You're well on your way to feeling the power of networking in your job search!

Networking Etiquette

There are, of course, many ways in which to network, and for each method you must know the rules, or the etiquette, of networking.

On the Telephone. Since the purpose of networking is to establish a personal relationship with people who can help you with your job search, you will find that the telephone is more effective than letters to contact people. When calling, clearly state the purpose of your call and explain how you found the person's name and telephone number. Be sensitive about the time you call. In one study, employers indicated that Monday mornings and Friday afternoons were the worst times to try to reach them, for obvious reasons. The best times to call business people, this same survey said, are Tuesdays, Wednesdays, and Thursdays between 9:00 a.m. and 11:00 a.m.

The Twenty-Minute Meeting. When you make an appointment to meet with someone for information, many of the same rules apply as when interviewing for a job. Arrive a few minutes early; bring a copy of your resume; and be prepared with questions to ask. It is best not to ask to meet someone for the first time over lunch.

Thank-You Notes. The thank-you note is more than just a polite gesture. A well-written thank-you note enhances your credibility with your interviewee. In your thank-you note, reiterate key points of your conversation and explain how you intend to act on your contact's advice. Include a copy of your resume for his or her files. Make sure that your contact has your correct phone number and address so that he or she can contact you with additional information.

Networking On-line. On-line computer services can help you expand your network to mind-boggling numbers. Many of the main on-line services such as CompuServe and America On-line have discussion groups that can be useful for job searchers. Prodigy offers a careers bulletin board that is another way to do information interviews.

One caution, however, about using these services. Be careful about providing too much personal information such as your address, phone number, social security number, and so on, because you never know who is lurking on the Net. Additionally, people can easily misrepresent themselves, and you may not be corresponding with whom you think you are.

E-mail has become commonplace in the corporate world and presents another way to make networking contacts. "Netiquette," or etiquette on the Net, however, suggests that this is not always the best way to conduct informational exchanges. It is, however, a great way to confirm appointments and send thank-you notes.

CYBERTIPS ON NETWORKING

A few sources for networking on the Net include:

Interactive Employment Network http://www.espan.com
Provides networking advice.

Forty Plus Club http://www.sirius.com/40plus/
Not-for-profit organization of skilled and experienced job-searching executives, managers, and professionals who share their knowledge and skills with each other. A great networking source.

Professional Organization Homepages. Many local and national professional organizations are developing sites on the Internet for their members. Often these include times of meetings and information on job openings or careers in that particular field. Ask your contacts if such sites exist within your field and look them up.

List-Serves. Many professional organizations also maintain list-serves, or E-mail lists that members use to maintain on-going dialogues on issues within the field. This is an excellent way to get up-to-date information and to learn of people who can help you in your job search. Do not, however, ask people for jobs over the list-serve. Find their E-mail address and write to those you are interested in talking to individually.

NETWORKING HANGOUTS

When putting together your networking strategy don't underestimate the potential of some of Atlanta's famous watering holes. Any list that we offer here will understandably be incomplete and arbitrary, but you will at least have a starting point. Here are some of the best networking hangouts in the estimation of the authors: The bar at **Bone's** (3130 Piedmont Road) ranks high in overall networking potential with business professionals in Atlanta. You will find a great cross-section of professionals, including lawyers, stock brokers, and advertising execs.

Houston's and **Ruby Tuesdays** at Lenox are other hot spots for networking where you will find an assortment of techies, software developers, financial analysts, investment bankers, and stockbrokers.

The **Hotel Nikko** (3300 Peachtree Road) and Buckhead's **Peachtree Cafe,** both in the heart of Buckhead's financial district, are great gathering places. The **Beer Mug,** located between Midtown and Buckhead, is a long-time favorite spot for the young and upwardly mobile. In downtown Atlanta there are a number of spots that rate high on the networking scale: **Jock's and Jill's** at 1 CNN Center, **Club 191,** and the **Hard Rock Cafe** on Peachtree.

Hairston's (1273 S. Hairston Road) in Stone Mountain is the hottest spot for professionals in the African-American community, and their cajun hot wings are a real treat. And finally, the old standby, the granddaddy of all networking spots, **Manuel's Tavern,** located at the corner of North Ave. and North Highlands, is the favorite spot for the city's politicians, lawyers, and businessmen.

Networking After You Land the Job

Networking doesn't end when you land the job. Keep people who are part of your network informed about your job search, and let them know when you finally land a job. Periodically touch base and let them know how things are working out with the new job.

Maintaining your network requires that you contribute as much as you receive. After you find your job — or even while you are looking for it — remember that your ideas, information, and contacts can help other people in your network. Often we have to train ourselves to offer such information because we don't think of ourselves as resources.

Sometimes people seem to walk into successful jobs or successful career changes. If you asked them how they did it, they would probably say they were in the right place at the right time. No doubt, some people do just get lucky, but others have high career awareness, or an idea of what their next career move or career change might be. Developing high career awareness means knowing what your next move is, planning for it, knowing who might be involved in helping you, and positioning yourself for it.

In other words, networking should become a part of your life and a part of your plans for your next career move. Knowing people in all types of career areas allows you to keep up with the possibilities and helps you position yourself to take the next step up the career ladder.

The friendly networker

Steve, an electrical engineer, interviewed with NASA. He realized during the interview that the position was not something he was cut out for or interested in. However, it was just the sort of thing that a friend of his would be perfect for. He admitted to the interviewer that he was the wrong person for the job and spent the next ten minutes describing how perfect his friend would be for the position. The interviewer was so impressed at this act of altruism that he actually followed up and called the person. He eventually offered her the job. Steve didn't land a job for himself, but he did enhance his network relationships by demonstrating his own quick thinking, integrity, and team spirit—qualities any employer can appreciate.

BOOKS ON NETWORKING

Numerous books have been written on job searching and networking. Here are a few good ones.

Krannich, R.L. and C.R. *Network Your Way to Job and Career Success.* Manassas, VA: Impact Publications, 1989.

Petras, Kathryn and Ross. *The Only Job Hunting Guide You'll Ever Need.* New York: Fireside, 1995.

Stoodley, Martha. *Information Interviewing: What It Is and How to Use It In Your Career.* Deerfield Beach, FL: Garrett Publishing, 1990.

Networking Resources in the Atlanta Area

There follows a list of over 125 organized groups, ready-made for networking, forming relationships, and gathering inside information about business, commerce, and jobs in the Atlanta area. Contact names, of course, are subject to change.

SELECTED ATLANTA AREA PROFESSIONAL ORGANIZATIONS, TRADE GROUPS, NETWORKS, CLUBS, AND SOCIETIES

Ad2 Atlanta
P.O. Box 18829
Atlanta, GA 30326
(404) 264-6223
Contact: Maureen McMahon, President
The local affiliate of the American Advertising Federation. Membership is comprised of young advertising professionals under the age of 32. Meets monthly and publishes a monthly newsletter. Maintains career network for members that assists with job referrals. Ad agencies call for referrals when they have openings.

Administrative Management Society
3290 Northside Parkway
Atlanta, GA 30327
(404) 264-2548 or (404) 264-9000
Contact: Carl Stone
Association of managers of administrative operations and staffs.
Monthly meetings and newsletter. Organizes professional development workshops for managers.

American Academy of Psychotherapists
P.O. Box 607
Decatur, GA 30031
(404) 299-6336
Professional association for psychiatrists, psychologists, clinical social workers, and pastoral counselors. Publishes a quarterly journal and provides a forum for members. Referrals to local and national therapists.

American Association of Occupational Health Nurses
50 Lenox Point
Atlanta, GA 30324-3176
(404) 262-1162
Association for registered nurses working in industry. Monthly
newsletter and journal, as well as continuing education opportunities.

American Association of Osteopathic Specialists
804 Main St., Suite D
Forest Park, GA 30050
(404) 363-8263
National headquarters of the association for osteopathic physicians. Meets twice
a year; publishes a quarterly newsletter.

American Association of University Women
2914 Ridgemore Road, N.W.
P.O. Box 360365
Decatur, GA 30036
(404) 355-1861
Contact: Dr. Joyce Morley-Ball
Association for women with college degrees. Meets monthly, September
through May. Provides career networking opportunities.

American Hospital Association
1675 Terrell Mill Road, Suite 250
Marietta, GA 30067
(800) 999-1560
Advocacy group, providing education and information. Regional office.
Publishes a directory of local and national hospitals.

American Institute of Architects—Atlanta Chapter
Colony Square Retail Mall
Atlanta, GA 30309
(404) 222-0099
Contact: Dorothy Spence
Association for registered architects and those working toward certification.
Holds monthly meetings and publishes *INFO* magazine quarterly and
INFOmation newsletter monthly.

American Institute of Banking
50 Hurt Plaza, Suite 1050
Atlanta, GA 30303
(404) 524-6125
An educational association. Member of the American Bankers Association,
headquartered in Washington, DC.

American Institute of CPAs/Georgia Society of CPAs
3340 Peachtree Road, N.E., Suite 2750
Atlanta, GA 30326-1026

Several chapters throughout metro Atlanta. Each meets monthly and welcomes visitors. Maintains a job bank of resumes and positions available. Certification not required for membership. For further information, write to the address above.

American Management Association, Atlanta Chapter
1197 Peachtree St., N.E.
Atlanta, GA 30361
(404) 892-7599
A local training center for management professionals.

American Marketing Association
4500 Hugh Howell Road
Tucker, GA 30084
(770) 270-0619
Professional association for people with an interest in marketing. Monthly luncheon meetings with speakers. Eight special interest groups include "career development" and "young professional." Publishes a regular newsletter that includes classified ads for members.

American Production and Inventory Control Society
c/o Dunhill Professional Search
340 Interstate North, Suite 140
Atlanta, GA 30339
(770) 952-0009
Members are companies and individuals engaged in manufacturing, management, and inventory control. Meets monthly; publishes a monthly newsletter that lists job seekers and positions available. Maintains a resume file for members.

American Society of Civil Engineers
1900 Emery, N.W.
Atlanta, GA 30318
(404) 355-0177
www.asce.org
Contact: Maria Simon
Professional association of civil engineers. Meets monthly.

**American Society of Heating, Refrigerating & Air
Conditioning Engineers**
1791 Tullie Circle, N.E.
Atlanta, GA 30329
(404) 636-8400
Monthly meetings. National monthly magazine, *ASHRAE Insights.*
Monthly newsletter.

American Society of Interior Designers—Georgia Chapter
351 Peachtree Hills Ave., N.E., Suite 504-A
Atlanta, GA 30305
(404) 231-3938

Professional association for interior designers. Full membership requires passage of an examination. Also admits student and allied members. Monthly meetings. Monthly newsletter.

American Society of Landscape Architects
1454 Holly Lane, N.E.
Decatur, GA 30303
(404) 315-0504
Professional association for landscape architects. Maintains full, associate, and student memberships. Meets four times a year. Maintains a resume file.

American Society of Mechanical Engineers
5801 Peachtree Dunwoody Road, N.E.
Atlanta, GA 30342
(404) 847-0072
Association for mechanical engineers. Meets monthly September through May. Monthly local newsletter.

American Society for Training and Development
325 Hammond Drive, N.E., Suite 104
Atlanta, GA 30328-5026
(404) 845-0522
International organization of human resources professionals in training. Publishes a monthy newsletter. Holds monthly meetings. Holds joint meeting with the Society of Human Resource Management once a year.

Asian American Hotel Owners Association
3490 Piedmont Road, Suite 1218
Atlanta, GA 30305
(404) 816-5759
Contact: Executive Director, Fred Schwartz
A non-profit association that represents Asian American hotelers in the United States. Headquarters. Monthly magazine to members; provides educational programs and seminars; scholarships.

Association of Black Cardiologists
2045 Manchester St., N.E.
Atlanta, GA 30324
(404) 582-8777
Primarily a support group that offers educational and networking as opportunities for professionals in the field.

Association of Builders & Contractors of Georgia
1215-C Hightower Trail, Suite 2240
Atlanta, GA 30350
(404) 587-0955
Association for commercial builders, general contractors, subcontractors, suppliers, and professionals who work with them. Monthly meetings. Publishes local newsletter, *Focal Point*. Will circulate individual resumes to appropriate member companies.

Association for Convention Operations Management
1819 Peachtree Road, N.E., Suite 620
Atlanta, GA 30309
(404) 351-3220
National organization for persons employed by hotels and convention centers to work with meeting planners. Annual meeting; quarterly newsletter, *ACOM.*

Association of Energy Engineers
4025 Pleasantdale Road, Suite 420
Atlanta, GA 30340
(770) 447-5083
National association for architects, engineers, energy managers, maintenance personnel. Chapters throughout world meet annually in Atlanta for the World Energy Engineering Congress.

Association of Fund-Raisers and Direct Sellers
5775 Peachtree Dunwoody Road, N.E.
Atlanta, GA 30328
(404) 252-3663
Contact: Janet Gunn
Organization of professional fund-raisers.

Association of General Contractors
1745 Phoenix Blvd.
Atlanta, GA 30349-9338
(770) 907-4100
Contact: Mike Dunham
A trade association representing over 600 firms in Georgia. Members include subcontractors, material suppliers, and industry service providers. Monthly newsletter and annual magazine.

Association of Mechanical Contractors of Atlanta
1950 Century Blvd., N.E.
Atlanta, GA 30345
(404) 633-9811
Trade association for mechanical contractors.

Association of Medical Illustrators
1819 Peachtree Road, N.E., Suite 620
Atlanta, GA 30309
(404) 350-7900
Provides networking opportunities to professional illustrators; publishes a newsletter, *Source,* which allows members to advertise their work to nearly 6,000 art buyers. Annual meeting; educational seminars that provide continuing education opportunities.

Atlanta Advertising Club
3988 Flowers Road, Suite 650
Atlanta, GA 30360

(770) 458-3181

Open to anyone involved with the creation, use, and production of advertising or advertising services. Meets monthly except summers. Visitors are welcome to meetings. Monthly newsletter is *Adlines.*

Atlanta Association of Educators
1065 Ralph D. Abernathy Blvd., S.W.
Atlanta, GA 30310
(404) 758-9444
Professional organization for certified teachers and principals. Meets twice monthly. Publishes *Action Lion,* a monthly newsletter.

Atlanta Association of Life Underwriters
4340 Georgetown Square
Atlanta, GA 30338
(770) 457-0199
Association for members of insurance industry. Monthly meetings, newsletter, continuing education programs, information.

Atlanta Bar Association
100 Peachtree St., N.W., 2500 Equitable Bldg.
Atlanta, GA 30303
(404) 521-0781
Association for lawyers. Monthly newsletter. Continuing education, magazine, research, cultural and social events.

Atlanta Board of Realtors
5784 Lake Forest Drive, N.W.
Atlanta, GA 30309
(404) 250-0051
Association of licensed Atlanta real estate professionals.

Atlanta Builders Exchange
1575 Northside Drive, N.W.
Atlanta, GA 30318
(404) 355-1091

Atlanta Business League
127 Peachtree St., N.E.
Atlanta, GA 30303
(404) 584-8126
A support group for small and minority businesses. Has some information on job openings among their membership. Will make referrals to their membership. Monthly meetings, quarterly newsletter, and annual directory.

The Atlanta Exchange Foundation
c/o Ware and Associates
55 Marietta St., Suite 2000
Atlanta, GA 30303
(404) 523-0303
Contact: William Ware

An association of black business and professional organizations. Individual organizations meet regularly. Hosts quarterly networking parties for members and non-members.

Atlanta Federation of Teachers, Local 1565
1718 Peachtree St., N.W.
Atlanta, GA 30309
(404) 607-9801
Contact: Tedra Carter
A professional advocacy organization for the teaching profession.

Atlanta Jaycees
1401 Peachtree St., N.E.
Atlanta, GA 30309
(404) 881-1676
A professional organization that provides young business professionals networking as well as community service opportunities.

Atlanta Job Network
Federation of non-sectarian job-search groups that offers networking opportunities and free seminars on various aspects of the job search. All job seekers are welcome, regardless of background or experience. Groups meet at selected churches throughout the metro area. Among them:

> Catholic Church of St. Ann (Marietta)
> > Contact: Sue Deering at (770) 998-1373
> Christ Our Shepherd Lutheran Church (Peachtree City)
> > Contact: Dick Ronco at (770) 487-3454
> Corpus Christi Catholic Church (Stone Mountain)
> > Contact: John Humphries at (404) 294-8377
> Embry Hills United Methodist Church
> > Contact: Greg Felty at (404) 491-7679
> Peachtree Presbyterian Church (Buckhead)
> > Contact: Tim Lane at (404) 434-0471
> Riverdale Presbyterian Church (Riverdale)
> > Contact: Southern Crescent Job Network
> Roswell United Methodist Church (Roswell)
> > Contact church at (770) 993-6218 or information recording at (770) 642-7943
> St. Jude's Catholic Church (Sandy Springs)
> > Contact: Jim or Trudy Knocke at (770) 393-4578

Atlanta Macintosh Users Group
Information Line
(404) 727-2300
A non-profit educational organization open to anyone interested in computers and computer science. Publishes a monthly newsletter.

Atlanta Medical Association
720 Westview Drive, S.W.
Atlanta, GA 30310
(404) 752-1858

Atlanta Press Club, The
250 Spring St., S.W., Suite 4E-338
Atlanta, GA 30303
(404) 577-7377
A professional organization for those who work in the media. Provides networking and educational activities for members.

Atlanta Producers Association, The (TAPA)
1570 Northside Drive, N.W., Suite 240
Atlanta, GA 30318
(404) 350-9039
Contact: Jack English
Open to all film, TV, and AV production people in Georgia interested in industry growth in Atlanta and the state. Must be headquartered in Georgia. Meets monthly. No formal job referral service.

Atlanta Songwriters Association
3121 Maple Drive, N.E.
Atlanta, GA 30305
(404) 266-2666

Atlanta Women's Network
P.O. Box 54614, Civic Center Station
Atlanta, GA 30308
For information on the Women's Network, write to the address above.

Atlanta Writing Resource Center
750 Kalb St., S.E.
Atlanta, GA 30312
(404) 622-4152
Association to promote the literary arts. Classes, critique groups, monthly open readings. Bi-monthly newsletter sometimes lists employment opportunities.

Black Data Processing Association
(404) 681-6025
Call above number for meeting information.

Black Professional Secretaries Association
2985 Gordy Parkway, N.E.
Marietta, GA 30066
(770) 578-5005
Meets first Wednesday of every month at Morerhouse School of Medicine.

Buckhead Business Association
3565 Piedmont Road, N.E., Suite 140

Atlanta, GA 30305-9998
(404) 261-0221
Open to all living or working in Buckhead. Meets for breakfast each Thursday.

Coalition Of 100 Black Women
600 Peachtree St., Suite 3710
Atlanta, GA 30308
(404) 892-4008
Contact: Yvonne Wiltz
A civic non-profit organization. Will circulate resumes of members and non-members for job openings.

Cobb County Bar Association
444 Maget St., Suite 100
Marietta, GA 30060
(770) 424-7149
Association for attorneys practicing or living in Cobb County.

Cobb County Medical Society
P.O. Box 1208
Marietta, GA 30061
(770) 428-2812
Association for physicians practicing in Cobb County. Located in Kennestone Hospital Community Services Building.

Community Bankers Association of Georgia
3715 Northside Parkway, N.W.
Atlanta, GA 30327
(404) 261-8853
Contact: C.E.O. Julian C. Hester
An affiliate of the Independent Bankers Ass'n. of America. Established to preserve community banking in Georgia. Annual meetings; membership ranges from $250 to $1,000 a year.

Construction Suppliers Association
133 Carnegie Way, N.W., Suite 600
Atlanta, GA 30303
(404) 653-0178
Contact: Exec. V. President, Ervin W. Goodroe

Consulting Engineers Council of Georgia
250 Williams St., Suite 2112
Atlanta, GA 30303
(404) 521-2324
Contact: Exec. Director, Thomas C. Leslie
Membership of over 200 firms; publishes a monthly newslettter and a quarterly journal. Annual meeting held in March. A membership directory is also published annually.

Creative Club of Atlanta
P.O. Box 77244
Atlanta, GA 30309
(404) 881-9991
Contact: Sal Kibler, Managing Director
Meets monthly. Members are from advertising creative departments, art directors, designers, copywriters, illustrators, photographers, etc.

Decatur Business and Professional Women
290 Green Hill Road, N.E.
Atlanta, GA 30342
(404) 256-5749
A professional organization for women that promotes leadership and growth in the business world. Lectures and seminars available for members and non-members.

Decatur-DeKalb Bar Association
118 E. Trinity Place
Decatur, GA 30030
(404) 373-2580
Association of lawyers practicing or living in DeKalb County.

DeKalb Association of Educators
640 Indian Creek Lane
Clarkston, GA 30021
(404) 292-3508
A teachers' organization that serves teachers working in the DeKalb County school system. A professional advocacy group. Publishes a newsletter, *DAE Newsletter,* five or six times a year for members.

DeKalb Medical Society
4500 Hugh Howell Road, Suite 340
Tucker, GA 30084
(770) 270-1733
A professional organization for physicians. Provides opportunities for professional development with seminars and lectures. Monthly newsletter available to members.

Fayette Board of Realtors
P.O. Box 405
Fayetteville, GA 30214
(770) 461-2401
Association of Georgia-licensed sales agents and brokers working in Fayette County. Monthly meetings. Newsletter.

Fulton County Association of Educators
3401 Norman Berry Drive
East Point, GA 30344
(404) 762-5956
A professional organization for educators that provides professional development opportunities and advocacy.

Gate City Bar Association
(404) 249-8477
Contact: Patrice Perkins-Hooker
A professional association for African-American lawyers. For more information, contact person listed above.

Georgia Association of Broadcasters
8010 Roswell Road, Suite 260
Atlanta, GA 30305
(770) 395-7200
Contact: William G. Sanders
Holds semi-annual meetings and publishes a newsletter, *GABcast.*

Georgia Association of Criminal Defense Lawyers
P.O. Box 8506
Atlanta, GA 30306
(404) 876-0562
An affiliate of the National Ass'n. of Criminal Defense Lawyers (Washington, DC). Publications include a bi-monthly newletter, *The Georgia Defender,* and *What's the Decision,* which is published annually.

Georgia Association of Educational Leaders
P.O. Box 909
Dahlonega, GA 30533
A professional advocacy group for the state's educators. Meets semi-annually; publishes a monthly newsletter, *GAEL.*

Georgia Association of Educators
3951 Snapfinger Parkway
Decatur, GA 30035
(404) 289-5867
Contact: Dr. Andrew Griffin, Jr.
Provides opportunities for professional development and advocacy. Publications include a weekly newsletter, *Leaders Letter,* and a bi-monthly newsletter, *Update.*

Georgia Association of Home Health Agencies
320 Interstate N. Parkway, Suite 490
Atlanta, GA 30339
(770) 984-9704
Contact: Judy Adams
Trade association of Medicare-certified home health agencies.

Georgia Association of Legal Assistants
P.O. Box 1802
Atlanta, GA 30301
(770) 433-5252
Association for legal assistants and others interested in the paralegal profession. Publishes a bi-monthly newsletter that lists job openings. Operates a job bank for members. Meets monthly.

Georgia Association of Personnel Services
P.O. Box 500386
Marietta, GA 31150-0386
(770) 952-3178
Association for recruiting firms, independent consultants, and related business-es. Publishes newsletter. Monthly meetings.

Georgia Association of Physician Assistants
5300 Memorial Drive
Stone Mountain, GA 30083
(404) 508-1482
Provides professional development for members as well as networking opportu-nities.

Georgia Association of Realtors
3200 Presidential Drive
Atlanta, GA 30340
(770) 451-1831
Contact: Bob Hamilton
Association of Georgia licensed real estate professionals. Meets twice a year.
Publishes a magazine.

Georgia Automobile Dealers Association
2255 Cumberland Parkway, N.W.
Atlanta, GA 30339
(770) 432-1658
Contact: William Morie
Trade association of franchise automobile dealerships.

Georgia Bankers Association
50 Hurt Plaza, S.E. , Suite 1050
Atlanta, GA 30303
(404) 522-1501
Contact: Joe Branen
Trade association of commercial banks.

Georgia Chiropractors Association
142 Mitchell St., S.W. Suite LL1
Atlanta, GA 30303
(404) 688-3730
Contact: J. Michael Honea
A professional group of chiropractors and vendors in related industries.

Georgia Dental Association
2801 Buford Highway, Suite T-60
Atlanta, GA 30329-2137
(404) 636-7553
Contact: Martha Phillips
Professional association of dentists. Meets annually. Publishes a monthly magazine.

Georgia Federation of Teachers
1718 Peachtree St., N.W.
Atlanta, GA 30309
(404) 607-8595
An affiliate of the American Federation of Teachers. An advocacy organization for teachers. Publishes a quarterly newsletter, *Georgia Teacher.*

Georgia Freight Bureau
229 Peachtree St., N.W., Suite 401
Atlanta, GA 30304
(404) 524-7777
Contact: John Youngbeck
Shippers association serving the transportation community.

Georgia Hospitality & Travel Association
600 W. Peachtree St., N.W., Suite 1500
Atlanta, GA 30308
(404) 873-4482
A private trade association for any person or business involved in the hospitality industry. Quarterly meetings; publishes a quarterly newsletter, *Georgia Hospitality.* Membership is drawn from four areas: lodging, food services, travel, and allied services.

Georgia League of Savings Institutions
41 Marietta St., N.W., Suite 1740
Atlanta, GA 30303
(404) 577-7910
A trade group for Georgia savings and loan institutions. Publishes an annual comparison report that ranks members by assets, savings, mortgages, and loads. Maintains a file of resumes.

Georgia Manufactured Housing Association
1000 Circle 75 Parkway, N.W., Suite 60
Atlanta, GA 30339
(770) 955-4522
Contact: Charlotte Gattis, Executive Director
An association of mobile home dealers, suppliers, manufacturers, and parks. Provides a membership information packet. Publishes a directory.

Georgia Motor Trucking Association
1280 W. Peachtree St., N.W., Suite 300
Atlanta, GA 30309
(404) 876-4313
An association of owners of major trucking firms, private carriers, couriers, suppliers, and other interested persons. Annual convention, committee meetings, seminars. Monthly magazine, *Trucking South,* carries classified ads that may include positions available.

Georgia Municipal Association
201 Pryor St., N.W.
Atlanta, GA 30303
(404) 688-0472
Organization for persons working for Georgia municipalities.

Georgia Nurses Association
1362 W. Peachtree St., N.W.
Atlanta, GA 30309
(404) 876-4624
Contact: Chris Samuelson
Association of registered nurses. Meets annually. Newsletter published six times
a year.

Georgia Pharmaceutical Association
20 Lenox Pointe, N.E.
Atlanta, GA 30324
(770) 231-5074
Contact: Larry Braden
Professional association for registered pharmacists.

Georgia Plumbers Trade Association
3339 Forrest Hills Drive
Atlanta, GA 30354
(404) 767-7764
A trade association for professional plumbers.

Georgia Press Association
3066 Mercer University Drive, Suite 200
Atlanta, GA 30341
(770) 454-6776
Open to Georgia newspaper people and vendors throughout the state.
Associate membership is extended to corporate/organizational public relations
departments. Networking and educational opportunities are available. Annual
meeting. Publishes a monthly newsletter, *GPA Bulletin.*

Georgia Psychological Association
1800 Peachtree St., Suite 525
Atlanta, GA 30309
(404) 351-9555
Contact: Pat Gardner
Association for professionals in the mental health field. Meets twice a year.
Publishes a quarterly magazine.

Georgia Retail Association
100 Edgewood Ave., N.E., Suite 1804
Atlanta, GA 30303
(404) 577-3435
Contact: Bill McBrayer
Association of retailers and suppliers.

Georgia Securities Association
South Tower, 1st Floor
3333 Peachtree St.
Atlanta, GA 30305
(404) 261-3295

Georgia Society of Association Executives
4500 Hugh Howell Road, Suite 340
Tucker, GA 30084
(770) 986-0700
Organization for association executives. Holds monthly meetings and publishes a monthly newsletter.

Georgia Society of CPAs
3340 Peachtree Road, N.E., Suite 2750
Atlanta, GA 30326
(404) 231-8676
A professional organization for certified public accountants. Meets monthly and provides membership with professional development opportunities.

Georgia Society of Professional Engineers
1900 Emery St., N.W., Suite 226
Atlanta, GA 30318
(404) 355-0177
Contact: Charles M. Wilson
Organization of engineers with professional status. Publishes a monthly magazine.

Georgia State Association of Life Underwriters
4340 Georgetown Square, Suite 616
Dunwoody, GA 30338
(404) 455-4459
Contact: June Townsend
An association of licensed life underwriters in Georgia.

Georgia Textile Manufacturers Association
50 Hurt Plaza, S.E., Suite 985
Atlanta, GA 30303
(404) 688-0555
Contact: Roy Bowen

Georgia Water & Pollution Control Association
P.O. Box 6129
Marietta, GA 30065-0129
(770) 429-0187
Organization provides training and education for those dealing with water and/or waste water. Provides workshops, seminars, and trade shows for members. Monthly newsletter and quarterly magazine.

Gwinnett County Board of Realtors
1310 Atkinson Road
Lawrenceville, GA 30243
(770) 963-3253

Homebuilders Association of Georgia
3015 Camp Creek Parkway
Atlanta, GA 30344
(404) 763-2453
Contact: Mark Baldwin
Trade association of builders, developers, suppliers, and related businesses.
Quarterly meetings. Publishes a bi-monthly magazine.

Homebuilders Association of Metro Atlanta
1399 Montreal Road
Tucker, GA 30084
(770) 938-9900
Contact: Connie Burney
Open to persons in residential construction. Meets monthly and publishes a
monthly newsletter.

Institute of Electrical and Electronics Engineers
Georgia Institute of Technology
School of Electrical and Computing Engineering
Atlanta, GA 30322-0250
www.ieeatlanta.org
For information write to the address above.

Institute of Industrial Engineers
25 Technology Park
Norcross, GA 30092
(770) 449-0461
Contact: Dr. Woodrow Leake
www.iie.org
Professional association of industrial engineers. Meets quarterly.

Institute of Management Accountants
P.O. Box 18880
Atlanta, GA 30326
(404) 525-2774
Contact: Robert Coons

International Association for Financial Planning
5775 Glenridge Drive, N.E.
Atlanta, GA 30328-5364
(404) 845-0011
Contact: Janet McCallen
National headquarters for persons in the financial planning field.

International Association for Financial Planning—Atlanta Chapter
244 Roswell St., Suite 800

Marietta, GA 30060
(770) 427-1554

Lawyers Club of Atlanta
34 Broad St.
Atlanta, GA 30303-2337
(404) 688-9627
Contact: Mary Lamar Bowden Fidler, Executive Director

Medical Association of Atlanta
875 W. Peachtree St., N.W.
Atlanta, GA 30309
(404) 881-1714
Professional association for physicians.

Medical Association of Georgia
938 Peachtree St., N.E.
Atlanta, GA 30309
(404) 876-7535
Professional association for physicians.

National Association of Black Accountants
P.O. Box 1633
Atlanta, GA 30301
(404) 584-4082
Contact: Arlene Thomas
For information write to address above. Meets monthly; publishes a list of job openings for members only. Maintains a "Job Bank" of resumes. Publishes a monthly and quarterly newsletter.

National Association of Securities Dealers
3490 Piedmont Road, N.E., Suite 500
Atlanta, GA 30305
(404) 238-6100
Contact: Marilyn Davis
Self-regulatory organization for securities dealers.

National Association of Social Workers—Georgia Chapter
300 W. Weicua Road, N.E., Bldg. 1, Suite 310
Atlanta, GA 30342
(404) 255-6422
Contact: Jackie Pray
Professional association of social workers. Meets quarterly.
Bi-monthly newsletter includes employment listings.

National Black MBA Association
(404) 853-6807
Contact: Pamela Williams
Publishes a monthly newsletter which includes job vacancies. Meets fourth Monday of each month.

National Contract Management Association
c/o Scientific Atlanta
3845 Pleasantdale Road Mail Stop 11X
Atlanta, GA 30340
(404) 903-2204
Contact: George Miller
Association for persons in government or industry who manage government contracts. Holds monthly meetings.

Professional Association of Georgia Educators
3700 B Market St.
Clarkson, GA 30021
(404) 292-7243
An association for teachers and educators. Sponsors conferences and publishes a newsletter.

Public Relations Society of America—Georgia Chapter
5108 Victor Trail
Norcross, GA 30071
(770) 449-6369
Contact: Denise Grant
Association of persons employed in public relations. Publishes a newsletter that includes employment listings.

Society for Human Resource Management
P.O. Box 2995
Lilburn, GA 30226
(770) 886-1800
Contact: Linda LeFevre
Monthly dinner meetings. Employment listings made available to members.

Society for Marketing Professional Services
1777 Lee Road
Atlanta, GA 30349
(770) 948-3963
Members are those responsible for marketing services of companies in architecture, engineering, planning, and construction. Maintains a file of job openings and applicants. Monthly luncheon meetings.

Society for Technical Communication
Atlanta, GA
(770) 612-7463
Call number above for meeting information. Professional association for technical writers. Monthly meetings. Monthly newsletter includes employment listings.

Southeast Council of Foundations
50 Hurt Plaza, Suite 910
Atlanta, GA 30303
(404) 524-0911

Association of grant-making organizations covering 12 states. Will provide information about the field and maintains informal resume file.

Southeast Employment Network
P.O. Box 2404
Lilburn, GA 30247
(404) 921-0751
Contact: Barry Jones
Organization of persons employed in high-tech companies. Holds job fairs.

Southeast Tourism Society
455 Highbrook Drive, N.E.
Atlanta, GA 30342
(404) 524-0911
Contact: Bill Hardman
Trade association for persons in tourism-related businesses.

Southeastern Library Association
P.O. Box 987
Tucker, GA 30085
(770) 939-5080
Organization for professional librarians.

Southern Arts Federation
181 14th St., Suite 400
Atlanta, GA 30309
(404) 874-7244
Contact: Jeffery Kesper, Executive Director
Grant-making organization; provides resource information and informal networking and employment information.

Southern Decorating Products Association
2971 Flowers Road
Chamblee, GA 30341
(770) 455-4049
Association of independent retailers.

Technical Association of the Pulp and Paper Industry
15 Technology Parkway S.
Norcross, GA 30092
(770) 446-1400
International association of professionals in the pulp and paper industry. Publishes a monthly magazine that includes job openings.

Young Bucks
1 Buckhead Plaza Building
3060 Peachtree Road, N.W., Suite 1060
Atlanta, GA 30305-2228
(404) 838-4907
Open to all persons age 25-40 interested in the Buckhead area. Meets monthly.

Developing the Perfect Resume

I t seems almost impossible to write the *imperfect* resume, with over 125 books on the market today pertaining solely to resume writing. However, we still anguish over the process, believing it will secure us a job. Keep in mind that no one ever secured a job offer on the basis of a resume alone. The way to land a good position is to succeed in the interview. You have to convince a potential employer that you're the best person for the job. No piece of paper will ever do that for you—but having an excellent resume is a necessary first step.

The resume is an invitation enticing the employer to interview you. With a little success, and some luck, the employer will want to meet you after reading your resume. However, the most effective method of resume delivery is for you to first meet the employer in person; then provide your resume. We understand that this is not always possible.

The French word *résumé* means "a summing up." Thus the purpose of a resume is not to catalogue, in exact detail, your entire biography. You should be concise with your work experience, education, accomplishments, and affiliations. Your goal is to pique the employer's interest. A good rule of thumb is that the resume should be kept to one or at most two pages.

The Basics of a Good Resume

To develop a resume that entices a potential employer to want to meet you, we suggest the following tips:

1. *Tailor your resume to the potential job opening.* The astute job searcher should always research a potential employer and find out as much information as possible on the qualifications needed for a particular job and then tailor his

or her resume to match the qualifications. When listing your experience and education, concentrate on those items that demonstrate your ability to do the job you are applying for. Using a computer will facilitate this process of customizing each resume.

2. *Be concise.* Most employers don't have time to read a two-page resume and usually scan a resume within 10-20 seconds. Thus, you want to capture the reader's attention quickly. Only then will you get a more careful reading. This is not the time to demonstrate your impressive vocabulary. Instead, describe your experience in short, pithy phrases. Give figures and facts when describing your accomplishments. Your resume should read more like a chart than a chapter in a textbook. And it should look more like an ad than a legal document.

3. *Be honest.* Never lie, exaggerate, embellish, or deceive. Be honest about your education, accomplishments, and work experience. A deliberate lie can be grounds for termination and will likely turn up in a background search. If you have gaps between jobs, and gaps are not always as negative as some would have you believe, you may consider listing years worked rather than months.

4. *Have a professional presentation.* Today's high quality computers allow you to prepare your own resume with the same professional results as paid resume preparers. A good rule of thumb: make your resume professional enough to send out on the potential employer's letterhead. If it isn't, it's probably not sharp enough.

Your resume should cover your most current work experiences (three to four jobs), with the name, location, and dates of employment plus a summary of your responsibilities relevant to the qualifications of the job you are seeking. Be sure to state your accomplishments on each job. Present your work history chronologically. Begin with your present position and work backward to your earlier jobs. If you haven't had that many jobs, organize your resume to emphasize the skills you've acquired through experience.

There are no hard and fast rules on what to include in your resume besides work experience, education, and special skills pertinent to the job for which you are applying. Professional affiliations may also be of interest to the employer. Do not list anything personal (such as marital status, date of birth, etc.) that could potentially screen you out. Salary history and references should not be included in your resume; these should be discussed in person during the interview.

Keep in mind that a resume is a sales tool. Make sure that it illustrates your unique strengths in a style and format *you* can be proud of. Be brief, tailor your experiences to the job you are seeking, and provide figures and facts to support your accomplishments.

Elements of a Resume

Here are the five main elements of a resume, with a brief description of each. All need not appear in the same order in every resume, and sometimes one or two are combined or left out, as you'll see in the sample resumes that follow.

NAME
Address
City, State, Zip
Phone
E-Mail Address (optional)

Objective: Employers use this information as a screening device or to assess a job match. It should grab the reader's attention and motivate him or her to read further. Make this relevant to the job for which you are applying!

Experience: The more impressive your work history, the more prominently you should display it. Use facts and figures to support accomplishments and goals reached.

List employment in reverse chronological order, putting the most promotable facts—employer or job title—first.

Give functional description of job if work history is strong and supports job objective.

List dates of employment last. They are the least important of all your information.

Skills: You may want to embed these in the employment section. Or, for career changers, list the skills section first. Highlight skills that are relevant to the potential job opening. Give short, results-oriented statements to support skills. Position your most marketable skills first.

Education: List in reverse chronological order, putting the most salable facts—school or degree—first. Mention honors or achievements, such as a high GPA or Dean's List.

Miscellaneous: Call this section anything applicable: Interests, Activities, Achievements, or Accomplishments.

Give only information that promotes your candidacy for the position for which you are applying.

References: Available upon request. Don't waste space on names and addresses. Have ready on a separate sheet.

Choosing a Resume Format

There are many different but equally acceptable ways to organize your resume. Every resume compiler and career counselor has his or her favorite method and style. The format you use should best present your strongest points and best convey your message to the potential employer. Resume books will use different terms for the various styles, but here are the three most popular types.

1. *The Chronological Resume* is the traditional style, most often used in the workplace and job search. It is also the resume style favored by most employers. That does not mean, however, that it is the most effective. A positive aspect of the chronological resume, aside from it being the traditional approach that employers may expect, is that it emphasizes past jobs that you wish your potential employer to notice. This resume is also very adaptable, with only the reverse chronological order of previous employment an essential ingredient.

2. *The Functional Resume* is most common among those reentering the job market after an absence, career changers, and those wishing to emphasize skills gained through non-work experience. This resume focuses on the many skills gained from employment and the accomplishments one has achieved. It shows a potential employer that you can do and have done a good job. What it doesn't necessarily emphasize is where you have done it and when.

3. *The Combination Resume* merges features of the functional and chronological resumes. This allows job seekers to emphasize accomplishments and skills while still maintaining the traditional format of reverse chronological order of positions held and organizations worked for. This format is perfect if your most current work is not your most impressive.

Sample After-College Chronological Resume

The Chronological Resume format is ideal for someone just graduating with little work experience. Here is a sample:

Michael King
256 Peach Tree Drive
Atlanta, GA 30312
(404) 555-0007

EDUCATION:	**University of Georgia** Athens, GA BA, Political Science, May 1997. Courses include: Business Law, Applied Probability, Statistics, Calculus, Economics, English, Creative Writing, French.
WORK EXPERIENCE:	SALES MANAGEMENT INTERN. Summers 1995–1996. **Nike.** Portland, OR. Managed the sales, distribution, pricing, shelving, and display of all Nike athletic shoes in 30 specialty shoe stores and department stores in the Portland area. Intensive on-the-job and educational training periods in Nike's corporate headquarters. CAMPUS REPRESENTATIVE. School years 1994–1996. **Office of Admissions, University of Georgia.** Organized and implemented an entire recruiting campaign for qualified high school minority students. Received a record number of minority student acceptances and matriculates.
ACTIVITIES AND HONORS:	President, Black Student's Association Recipient, Minority Student Scholarship Freshman Advisor Tutor for high-risk high school students National Collegiate Minority Leadership Award
REFERENCES:	Available upon request.

Sample Career-Changing Functional Resume

The Functional Resume format is ideal for someone changing careers since it emphasizes skills rather than past employment. Here is a sample:

Kathy Lawrence
550 Peach Avenue
Decatur, GA 30032
(503) 555-2436

OBJECTIVE	To obtain a position as an administrative assistant.

AREAS OF EXPERTISE

Administrative
- Independently analyzed a major client's account for an advertising agency.
- Maintained and managed funds in excess of $50,000 for a non-profit organization.
- Managed two rental properties.

Organizational
- Set up procedures for assigned experiments and procured equipment for a research laboratory.
- Planned course syllabi to facilitate learning for students with assessed weaknesses.

Computer
- Managed data input and generated monthly reports.
- Completed courses in Excel spreadsheets and Pagemaker.
- Designed and produced monthly newsletter.

WORK HISTORY	*Computer Operator,* Johnson Corp., Atlanta, GA (1993-present)
	Trouble-shooter in accounting, Cargill, Wilson, and Acree, Decatur, GA (1989-92)
	Instructor, Math Department, Atlanta Graduate Institute (1986-89)
EDUCATION	Atlanta Graduate Institute, MS, Mathematics (1988)
	Marshall University, BA, Mathematics (1985)
	GPA 3.7/4.0
HONORS/ ACTIVITIES	Dean's List, three semesters
	Treasurer for non-profit organization
REFERENCES	Available upon request.

Sample Combination Resume

The Combination Resume allows you to use aspects of both the chronological and functional formats. This type is good for someone whose present work perhaps does not reflect his or her most impressive skills. Here is a sample:

Paul Wheaton
490 Polk St.
College Park, GA 30299
(404) 555-0011

EDUCATION
University of Athens, Marine, GA; GPA 3.7/4.0
MS, Information and Computer Science, December 1992
Blue Mountain State College; GPA 3.4/4.0
AB, Computer Science, May 1986

QUALIFICATIONS
Career-related Projects:
- Designed and implemented multi-tasking operating system for the IBM-PC.
- Implemented compiler for Pascal-like language.
- Designed electronic mail system using PSL/PSA specification.

Languages and Operating Systems:
- Proficient in Ada, Modula-2, Pascal, C+
- Thorough knowledge of IBM-PC hardware.
- Experienced in UNIX, MS-DOS, CP/M operating systems.

Hardware:
- IBM-PC (MS-DOS), Pyramid 90x (UNIX), Cyber 990 (NOS)

WORK EXPERIENCE
Simms Programming Services, Atlanta, GA 3/93-present
UNIX Programmer
Responsible for porting MS-DOS database applications to IBM-PC/AT running Xenix System V. System administration.

IBM Corp., Atlanta, GA 10/90-12/92
Computer Programmer
Performed daily disk backup on Burroughs B-1955 machine. Executed database update programs and checks. User assistance.

Computer companies in Atlanta, GA, area 6/86 - 8/90
Computer Operator
Held full-time positions. Responsible for maintaining computers.

REFERENCES
Available upon request.

Sample Combination Resume for Liberal Arts Major

As mentioned earlier, the Combination Resume allows you to use parts of both the chronological and functional formats. This type is good for liberal arts majors who have several career fields to select among because of their broad educational background. Since Laura (example resume follows) wanted to apply for jobs in broadcasting, magazine publishing, and writing speeches for a Congressman, she used the combination style to avoid writing several different resumes. Here is the sample:

Laura Brown
490 Tech St.
East Point, GA 30000
(404) 555-0011

EDUCATION   Agnes Smith College, Covington, GA; GPA 3.7/4.0
                AB, May 1995
                Major in English literature. Minor in psychology.

                Participated in College-in-Italy Program (Rome).
                Member of Women's Cross Country Running Team.
                Editor *Running Notes.* Reporter for student newspaper.
                Member of Chi Omega sorority. Rush Co-Chairperson and
                Panhellenic Society representative.

EXPERIENCE   **College Sports Information Office,** Dearing, GA
                Reported on all school sports events. Managed post-game
                football press box operations. Published stories about school
                athletes. Wrote press releases.
                Football Statistician, Fall 1993 and fall 1994.
                Compiled statistics. Wrote game summaries and weekly
                reports.

                Brown Computers, Atlanta, GA
                Public Relations Intern, Summers 1993 and 1994.
                Researched information for student advertisements and spe-
                cial publications. Proofread copy and checked facts. Replied to
                reader correspondence. Coordinated Brown Computer's
                School Visitation Program.

Salesperson, Summer 1992.
Completed nightly closings, and maintained various departments in manager's absence. Rotated throughout store as needed. Highest sales for two months.

INTERESTS   Enjoy playing the piano and guitar, oil and watercolor painting. Avid runner. Have traveled in Europe and throughout the western U.S.

REFERENCES   Available upon request.

Resume Checklist

- Brainstorm a list of the skills and talents you want to convey. These may include character traits such as persistence and assertiveness; work skills such as fluency in languages and computer literacy; and transferable skills such as managing, motivating, and leading people, manipulating data, evaluating and analyzing systems.
- Prepare your resume on a computer and printer that give you the same results as a professionally typeset resume.
- Use heavyweight (at least 20 lb.), high-quality paper and a laser printer if at all possible. White, off-white, or light gray papers ($8^1/_2$ x 11 inches) are usually safe, conservative bets. However, if you are in theater, arts, or advertising, you can be a little more daring. If you have the budget, consider buying $9^1/_2$ x $12^1/_2$-inch envelopes so you won't have to fold your resume and cover letter.
- Be concise and brief in your wording.
- Avoid personal pronouns.
- Use active verbs to describe your accomplishments rather than your assigned duties.
- Arrange information in descending order of importance within each section of your resume.
- Be consistent in format and style.
- Tailor your skills and experience as much as possible to each potential job opening.
- Proofread your resume, and then have a few friends proofread it as well.
- Be selective in sending out your resume. Mass mailings usually only result in spending unnecessary time and money.

Using the Computer to Design Your Resume

Welcome to the high-tech world of resume writing. Even if you don't own your own computer, many libraries have them available, and copy stores such as Kinko's rent computer time. So there is no excuse to rule out the computer in designing your resume. There are certain advantages:

- You have the ability to save your resume on a disk, which simplifies editing it for a specific company or position. Revises and updates become simple.
- Computers offer a wide range of type faces, styles (bold, italics, and so on), and sizes. Combined with a laser printout, you can achieve a professional-looking resume at modest expense.

No matter what method you use to prepare your resume, *proofread* it before printing. Misspelled words or typing errors reflect badly on you even if it's not your fault. Recruit a friend to help read your resume, word for word and comma for comma. And don't make last minute changes after everyone has proofed it. Somehow, you *will* end up with an error.

Professional Resume Preparers

It is always better to prepare your own resume, as long as you have reasonable writing skills. However, if you have trouble condensing your writing style and you have no friends who can help, no access to a university career office or books on resumes, then a professional may be able to assist you.

Before choosing a professional resume service, try to get a recommendation from someone whose judgment you trust. Find out the minimum and maximum costs before employing any service. Ask whether the price includes only writing, or typesetting and printing as well. If changes are needed, will it cost extra? Finally, always shop around for the best services available. Don't forget that many career counselors and consultants also provide resume preparation; refer to Chapter 2.

The following are firms that will assist you in preparing your resume. Keep in mind that a listing in this book does not constitute an endorsement.

The laughing stock of the company

Make sure that you don't end up as fodder for employer levity as did the following unfortunates:

One candidate wrote under Job Responsibilities: "Assassinated store manager during busiest retail season." What she meant to write was "assisted."

"Education: College, August 1890–May 1994."

"Here are my qualifications for you to overlook."

"Please call me after 5:30 p.m. because I am self-employed and my employer does not know I am looking for another job."

Reason for leaving last job? The candidate replied: "No special reason." Another replied: "They insisted that all employees get to work by 8:45 every morning. Couldn't work under those conditions."

One applicant submitted a seven-page resume and stated, "This resume is fairly long because I have a lot to offer you."

SELECTED PROFESSIONAL RESUME PREPARERS IN THE ATLANTA AREA

A-Atlanta Discount Business Services
Four locations throughout the Atlanta area
(404) 814-1314
In business since 1976. Offers complete resume writing services, including write-ups. Provides clients with finished disk on resume. Walk-ins accepted but appointments preferred. Major credit cards accepted.

Atlanta Resume Service
5901-C Peachtree Dunwoody Road, Suite 498
Atlanta, GA 30328
(770) 396-9129
In business since 1989. Member of the Professional Association of Resume Writers. Appointments are required for resume writing assistance but will handle walk-ins who only want revisions.

Buckhead Best Resumes
3390 Peachtree Road, Suite 1102
Atlanta, GA 30326
(404) 233-1467
Clients seen by appointment only. Emphasizes its in-depth consultative process that includes a detailed inventory of skills that are "framed" to achieve career goals. Provides services to all levels of professionals. Credit cards not accepted. Member of Georgia Association of Personnel Services.

Buckhead Resume Service
3091 Maple Drive, Suite 204
Atlanta, GA 30305
(404) 237-5115
www.mindspring.com/~resume
Service provided by a writer professional with 12 years of resume-writing expe-

rience. Provides typesetting service in house. Appointments only. Business specializes in management and sales. Major credit cards accepted.

Business World—Professional Resume Writers
3475 Lenox Road N.E., Suite 400
Atlanta, GA 30326
(404) 240-7200
Provides general secretarial services, including resume writing. Several locations throughout the Atlanta metropolitan area. Walk-ins accepted but appointments preferred. Credit cards not accepted.

Career Pro
6075 Roswell Road, Suite 109
Atlanta, GA 30342
(404) 252-8777
Career development service with five affiliated offices in Atlanta. 300 offices nationwide affiliated with Career Pro. In business since 1958. The central location is in Sandy Springs. Service provides in-depth personalized consultation and promises a quick delivery of services, usually same day. Will oversee the writing and formatting of the resume.

Quality Resume Service
2824 Parkridge Drive
Atlanta, GA 30319
(404) 634-4198
In business since 1988. Provides resume consultation services. Handles typesetting, printing, and mailing. Clients seen by appointment only.

Preparing Your Resume for Machine Readers

Today's corporations are taking drastic means to accommodate the overwhelming amount of resumes they receive. Microsoft receives thousands of resumes a week. Could you imagine reading 3,000 resumes in one week? Thus, new techniques such as resume-scanning software have been implemented.

Resumix, Inc., in the Silicon Valley of California, provides software to corporations who have replaced the resume reader with computers capable of scanning resumes and saving corporations valuable time and costs. Therefore, you must not only entice a potential employer with your resume but a computer as well. Your resume is more likely to be scanned by large companies than small, high-tech than non-high-tech.

Here are some hints for preparing the ideal scannable resume:
- Use 8^1/2 x 11-inch paper, light color.
- Avoid dot matrix printouts. Laser prints scan easier.
- If using a computer, use the 12 point font size, and do not condense spacing between letters.
- Avoid using a newspaper-type format, columns, or graphics.

- Be sure to include your name at the top of the second page if your resume is two pages.
- Key words or accomplishments are often scanned; make sure your resume contains words related to the position for which you are applying. Use "hard" vocabulary such as "computer skills," "software packages," etc. Also avoid flowery language.

Resumix provides a brochure, "Preparing the Ideal Scannable Resume." If you are interested, call Resumix at (408) 988-0444.

The Cover Letter Adds a Custom Touch

Never, never send your resume without a cover letter. Whether you are answering a want ad or following up an inquiry call or interview, you should always include a letter with your resume. Use your researching skills to locate the individual doing the hiring. Using the personal touch of addressing your cover letter to a real person will save you the headache of having your resume sent to H.R.'s stack of resumes, or possibly even being tossed out.

A good cover letter should be brief and interesting enough to grab the reader's attention. If you've spoken with the individual, you may want to remind him or her of the conversation. Or, if you and the person to whom you are writing know someone in common, be sure to mention it.

In the next paragraph or two, specify what you could contribute to the company in terms that indicate you've done your homework on the firm and the industry. Use figures and facts to support your accomplishments that are relevant to the job opening.

Finally, in the last paragraph, either request an interview or tell the reader that you will follow-up with a phone call within a week to arrange a mutually convenient meeting.

Sample Cover Letter

Mary Baker
560 Leaf St.
Atlanta, GA 30332

August 12, 1997

Ms. Jacqueline Doe
Wide World Publishing Company
2239 Forest Park Blvd.
Atlanta, GA 31109

Dear Ms. Doe:

As an honors graduate of the University of Athens with two years of copy editing and feature-writing experience with the *Midtown Atlanta Weekly*, I am confident that I would make a successful editorial assistant with Wide World.

Besides my strong editorial background, I offer considerable business experience. I have held summer jobs in an insurance company, a law firm, and a data processing company. My familiarity with word processing should prove particularly useful to Wide World now that you have become fully automated.

I would like to interview with you as soon as possible and would be happy to check in with your office about an appointment. If you prefer, your office can contact me between the hours of 11 a.m. and 3 p.m. at (404) 555-6886.

Sincerely,

Mary Baker

Sample Cover Letter in Reply to Want Ad

Stacy Barnes
34 Sutter St.
Atlanta, GA 30001
(404) 555-2468

May 15, 1997

Mr. Tom White
Anderson Consulting
725 Van St.
Atlanta, GA 30308

Dear Mr. White:

My background seems ideal for your advertisement in the May 13 issue of *The Buckhead Times* for an experienced accountant. My five years of experience in a small accounting firm in Atlanta has prepared me to move on to a more challenging position.

As you can see from my resume, my experience includes not only basic accounting work but also some consulting with a few of our firm's larger clients. This experience combined with an appetite for hard work, an enthusiastic style, and a desire to succeed makes me a strong candidate for your consideration. I assisted the company in expanding its clientele by 30%.

I would appreciate the opportunity to discuss how my background could meet the needs of Anderson Consulting. I will call you within a week to arrange a convenient time to meet.

Sincerely,

Stacy Barnes

Sample Networking Cover Letter

Richard Jackson
560 Bobolink St.
Decatur, GA 30032
(404) 555-6886

December 2, 1997

Mr. James King
3-Q Inc.
452 3rd St.
Dunwoody, GA 30009

Dear James:

Just when everything seemed to be going smoothly at my job, the company gave us a Christmas present that nobody wanted: management announced that half the department will be laid off before the new year. Nobody knows yet just which heads are going to roll. But whether or not my name is on the list, I am definitely back in the job market.

I have already lined up a few interviews. But knowing how uncertain job hunting can be, I can use all the contacts I can get. You know my record—both from when we worked together at 3-Q and since then. But in case you've forgotten the details, I've enclosed my resume. I know that you often hear of job openings as you wend your way about the Atlanta area. I'd certainly appreciate your passing along any leads you think might be worthwhile.

My best to you and Susan for the Holidays.

Cordially,

Rich

Enclosure

Do's and don'ts for cover letters

Do:

- Send a resume with every cover letter.
- Use high-quality, high-rag content paper.
- Target an individual person about the job opening.
- Be brief and interesting enough to capture the reader's attention.
- Tailor your experiences to meet the potential job opening.
- Use acceptable business format; letter should be well spaced on the page.
- Have someone check your letter for grammar, spelling, and formatting mistakes.
- Have an agenda in the letter and follow-up in the amount of time you specified.

Don't:

- Send your first draft of a letter just so you can meet the deadline.
- Send your letter to the president of the company simply because you don't know the name of the hiring authority.
- Include information that can be found on your resume.
- Give only one possible time to meet.
- Call the company four times a day after you have sent the letter.

CYBERTIPS FOR RESUME AND COVER LETTER WRITING

Using the Net to find more sample resumes and cover letters is a good place to start. Many of the job-search services or college career center homepages also have tips on resume and cover letter writing. Some on-line services will also post your resume for employer perusal.

Career Channel—The Job Search
http://riceinfo.rice.edu/projects/careers/Channel/seven.html

Catapult Job Search Guides
http://www.wm.edu/catapult/jsguides.html

Cover Letters by the Rensselaer Polytechnic Institute Writing Center
http://www.rpi.edu/dept/llc/writecenter/web/text/coverltr.html

Interactive Employment Network
http://www.espan.com

Resumes from Yahoo
http://www.yahoo.com/Business/Employment/Resumes/Individual_Resumes

Resumes On-Line
http://199.94.216.72:81/online.html

RECOMMENDED BOOKS ON RESUME WRITING

The following books are full of all the how-to information you'll need to prepare an effective resume and most are available from bookstores or your local library.

Corwin, Leonard. *Your Resume: Key to a Better Job.* New York: Arco, 1988.

Fournier, Myra, and Jeffrey Spin. *Encyclopedia of Job-Winning Resumes.* Ridgefield, CT: Round Lake Publishers, 1991.

Hahn, Harley, and Rick Stout. *The Internet Yellow Pages.* Berkeley, CA: Osborne McGraw-Hill, 1994.

Jackson, Tom. *The Perfect Resume.* New York: Anchor/Doubleday, 1990.

Kennedy, Joyce Lain, and Thomas J. Morrow. *Electronic Resume Revolution.* New York: James Wiley & Sons, 1994.

Krannich, Ronald L., and William J. Banis. *High Impact Resumes and Letters.* Career Management Concepts, 1992.

Lewis, Adele. *How to Write a Better Resume.* Woodbury, NY: Barron's, 1993.

Nadler, Burton Jay. *Liberal Arts Power: How to Sell It on Your Resume.* Princeton, NJ: Peterson's Guides, 1989.

Parker, Yana. *Damn Good Resume Guidelines.* Berkeley, CA: Ten Speed Press, 1989.

Smith, Michael H. *The Resume Writer's Handbook.* New York: Harper and Row, 1994.

Weinstein, Bob. *Resumes Don't Get Jobs: The Realities and Myths of Job Hunting.* New York: McGraw-Hill, 1993.

Yate, Marin. *Resumes That Knock 'em Dead.* Holbrook, MA: Bob Adams, 1992.

seven

The Killer Interview

Your networking paid off and your resume was a success. You are now ready to take the next step in your job search. Unfortunately, though, your resume won't automatically grant you a job, and all the contacts in the world won't do you any good if you don't handle yourself well in an interview. All interviews have the same goal: to convince the interviewer that he or she should hire you or recommend that you be hired. That is what counts. Remember, this interview is all that stands between you and the job, so make it a *killer* interview. This chapter will guide you through the steps and give you an idea of what to expect and what to avoid when interviewing.

Dr. Bob's Six Steps to a Killer Interview

STEP 1: Preparing for the Interview

Good preparation shows ambition and zeal and is a key part of interviewing that is often forgotten. The more you prepare, the more you will be relaxed and comfortable with the interview. Additionally, the more you prepare, the greater your chance of impressing someone with your knowledge of the company and the interview process.

Researching the company before the interview is a must in your preparation. You should be familiar with the following company information before your interview begins:

- The interviewer's name.
- General information about the company, such as the location of the home office, number of plants/stores and their locations, names of parent company, subsidiaries, etc.

- Organizational structure, type of supervision, type of training program.
- Philosophy, goals, and image.
- Financial details, including sales volume, stock price, percent of annual growth in earnings per share, recent profits, etc.
- The competition in the industry and the company's place in it.
- The products or services marketed by the company, including recent media coverage of them.
- Career path in your field.
- Recent news items regarding the company or the industry. It is especially important to check the *Wall Street Journal*'s business section to see if the company you are interviewing with is mentioned on the morning of the interview. Be prepared to speak on many aspects of the company.

Researching Target Companies via the World Wide Web

One of the easiest ways to research a company or organization is to do so over the Net. While not every organization has a WWW address, more and more companies are beginning to see the benefits of a homepage. This should make your Internet surfing for company information much easier. Library Net addresses, mentioned in Chapter 4, are a good place to check; you can also go directly to company Net addresses.

Many public companies have homepages on the Web. They typically provide information about their products and services, and many provide press releases and other news about themselves that is useful to investors. Increasingly, companies are posting employment opportunities on their Web pages.

Commercial Services on the Net—Open Market
http://www.directory.net
A very large index of commercial Web sites. You should be able to find a company Web page here if it exists.

Computer Related Companies
http://www.xnet.com/~blatura/computer.shtml
An excellent list of U.S. computer-related company Web pages.

Corporate Web Registry—Hoover's Company Profiles
http://www.hoovers.com/bizreg.html
Links to over 1,100 corporate Web sites, combined with extensive information about many corporations, including history, current business, personnel, and office locations. A wonderful resource.

Hot 1000 List
http://techweb.cmp.com/techweb/ia/hot1000/hot1.html
This list includes any homepages officially established by or for the company among companies comprising the Fortune 1,000.

Industrial Companies
http://www.xnet.com/~blatura/industry.shtml
A fine list of U.S. industrial company Web pages.

Public Companies
http://networth.galt.com/www/home/insider/publicco.htm
This list includes any homepages officially established by or for the company.
As we go to press, the list contains 688 public companies.

Practicing Before Your Interview
Another key part of preparation and of conducting the most successful of interviews is to practice the interview as much and in as many ways as possible. This can take many forms. However, the best way is to build a list of the questions you feel will be asked and to make sure that you know how to answer them and have answered them out loud to yourself or to someone helping you with a mock interview. Practice your answers and multiple variations of them and you will be much better prepared for the interview.

STEP 2: Dressing Right: Interviewing Fashion Do's and Don'ts

Never underestimate the power of a sharply dressed man or woman during an interview. Proper attire is a key ingredient to a good first impression with your prospective employer. Hygiene is equally important. Shaving should be done the morning before the interview. Perfume and cologne should be low key. Keep the hair trimmed, fingernails clean, and let your credentials and personal charm do the rest.

The Career-Dressed Woman
Within reason, a variety of conservative colors are appropriate for most interview situations. Many tasteful suits are available in black, brown, teal, taupe, olive, forest, maroon, burgundy, and plum. When selecting a suit, especially if you are on a limited budget, focus on classic cuts and styles. The proper fit is just as essential as the suit itself. A good suit should last at least five years. Try to select a high-quality fabric such as wool or wool gabardine. These are the coolest fabrics—making them appropriate not only for the stress of interviewing but also for everyday wear year-round.

If the shoe fits wear it! We see countless well-dressed women with shoes with run-down heels and scraped up toes. Don't brainwash yourself by thinking that they are only shoes and nobody looks at your feet anyway. Shoes are one of those make-or-break elements of your wardrobe. Make sure the local shoe repair has done a good job at keeping yours new-looking.

Keep it feminine: a lot of women still hold the idea that professional means masculine. Not true. Women's professional attire has come into its own since the late '80s and early '90s, when stiffly tailored dark suits paired with floppy bows and ties were all the rage. These have been replaced with soft scarves, unique pins, and more attractive colors and styles. Keep in mind when selecting professional clothing that "feminine" in no way means "sleazy." Tight skirts, too high heels, and low-cut blouses are never appropriate, no matter how conservative their color or casual the office.

The bottom line is that much of business is influenced by image. You may not get that job because you look great, but not looking good may be a reason why you don't get hired.

The Career-Dressed Man

On your big shopping spree for the proper suit, try to be conservative, not flashy. Stick with darker colors like navy blue, dark gray, or black. Single-breasted vs. double-breasted? Whatever you look best in is what you should buy. Usually single-breasted is more conservative and probably best for interviewing.

Shirts and ties are very important in the construction of the perfect suit. Your dress shirts should be comfortable and fit properly around the neck. Tight shirts in the neck area tend to make you resemble Baby Huey or the Pillsbury Doughboy.

The tie can say a lot about the individual, so when choosing your tie be careful and take your time. Try to steer yourself toward the 100% silk ties; they tend to portray a more professional look. Don't allow the tie to overpower your suit with loud colors and crazy patterns. The proper length is also vital in choosing the right tie. Too short a tie makes you look silly. Once knotted, a tie should reach over your belt buckle. Anything higher is not acceptable.

Dress socks are a must. No thick socks and no athletic socks; this is your career, not a gymnasium. Coordinated color socks are essential and they should come over the calf so that when you sit down, you aren't flashing skin between the top of the sock and trouser cuff.

Polished wing-tip shoes are always safe. Make sure that your shoes are as shiny as a new dime. As is the case with women's shoes, your shoes can say a lot about you and should not be in a state of disrepair.

Common Dressing Mistakes Made by Men

Now that you are an expert on career dressing, here are a few mistakes made by men in their quest to dress to impress:

- The belt and suspenders faux pas. You only need one or the other to keep your pants up.
- Make sure that you are not wearing high-water pants. The length of the pant leg should reach the middle of your shoe.
- No knit ties. They went out some years ago with leisure suits.

- Iron your shirt. Wrinkles are not in style.
- No gaudy rings or chains. Save them for bar hopping or the discos. The fact remains that clothes make a difference in our society. One might wish that impressions did not count, but they do!

How to dress

A friend of ours who wanted to break into investment banking finally landed her first big interview with Merrill Lynch. It was fairly easy for her to do her homework on a company of that size. Two days before the interview, however, it suddenly dawned on her that she had no idea how to dress. How did she solve her problem?

"It was pretty easy, actually, and fun, too," says Laura. "All I did was go and hang around outside the office for 15 minutes at lunch time to see what everybody else was wearing."

However, we recommend that even if the office attire is casual, one should still dress professionally. One career counselor recommends that one should "always dress one step above the attire of those in the office where you are interviewing."

STEP 3: The First Impression

The first impression, whether we like it or not, is important in a successful interview. Start off the interview right! Arriving at least ten minutes early helps you relax a little rather than rushing into the meeting all tense and harried. Remember to treat the receptionist, secretary, and anyone else you meet the same way you would treat any potential boss. Be friendly and professional. They often have input into the selection of candidates.

The beginning of the interview is crucial. Many experts feel that the decision to hire you is made during the first four minutes. The rest of the interview is used to justify this earlier decision. Four things are important in creating that first impression. First, a firm handshake, for both men and women, is important. Second, try to make eye contact with the interviewer as much as possible—but don't have a staredown. Third, try to convey a positive attitude with a friendly smile; never underestimate yourself—past jobs and education have equipped you with valuable skills. And finally, say something simple early on to get those first words out of your mouth: "Very nice to meet you" should suffice. It is also important to address your interviewer by last name unless instructed to do otherwise.

STEP 4: Express Yourself

The bulk of the interview is designed for you to answer questions posed by the interviewer. Here are a few tips:

- Be aware of your non-verbal behavior. Wait to sit until you are offered a chair. Look alert, speak in a clear, strong voice, and stay relaxed. Make good eye contact, avoid nervous mannerisms, and try to be a good listener as well as a good talker. Smile.
- Follow the interviewer's lead, but try to get the interviewer to describe the position and duties to you fairly early in the interview so that you can later relate your background and skills in context.
- Be specific, concrete, and detailed in your answers. The more information you volunteer, the better the employer gets to know you and thereby is able to make a wise hiring decision.
- Don't mention salary in a first interview unless the employer does. If asked, give a realistic range and add that the opportunity is the most important factor for you.
- Offer examples of your work and references that will document your best qualities.
- Answer questions as truthfully and as frankly as you can. Never appear to be "glossing over" anything. On the other hand, stick to the point and don't over-answer questions. The interviewer may steer the interview into ticklish political or social questions. If this occurs, answer honestly, trying not to say more than is necessary.
- Never make derogatory remarks about present or former employers or companies.

Questions You May Be Asked During an Interview

Bear in mind that all questions you are asked during an interview serve a specific purpose. Try to put yourself in the interviewer's shoes. Imagine why he or she is asking the questions, and try to provide the answers that, while never dishonest, present you in the most desirable light. Direct your responses toward the particular position for which you are applying. What follows are some questions that employers often ask during interviews. As we mentioned earlier, it is advisable to rehearse answers to these questions prior to your interview so you can appear relaxed and confident.

Ice Breakers

These are designed to put you at ease and to see how well you engage in informal conversation. Be yourself, act natural, and be friendly.

a. Did you have any trouble finding your way here?
b. How was your plane flight?

c. Can you believe this weather?

d. I see you're from Omaha. Why do you want to work in this area?

Work History and Education

These are to assess whether your background and skills are appropriate for the position. Talk about your skills coherently and relate them to the job to be filled. Give specific examples of how you used certain skills in the past. Remember that questions you are asked concerning your past will help the employer determine how you might react and make decisions in the future.

a. *Tell me about yourself.

b. Tell me about the most satisfying job/internship you've ever held.

c. Tell me about the best boss you ever had. The worst.

d. What have you learned from some of the jobs you've held?

e. For what achievements were you recognized by your superiors at your last position?

f. What are you looking for in an employer?

g. What are you seeking in a position?

h. Why did you choose to get a degree in the area that you did?

i. In what activities have you participated outside of work (or class)?

j. How did you finance your education?

k. *What do you like/dislike about your current (or last) job?

Ambitions and Plans

These are questions to evaluate your ambition, how clearly you have thought about your future goals, their feasibility, and how actively you seek to meet them.

a. Are you a joiner or more individually centered? A leader or a group member? A committee member or chairperson? (There isn't necessarily a wrong answer to this type of question. Keep in mind that a ship full of captains will flounder just as badly as a ship with none at all.)

b. What job in our company would you choose if you were free to do so?

c. What does success mean to you? How do you judge it?

d. Assuming you are hired for this job, what do you see as your future?

e. What personal characteristics do you think are necessary for success in this field?

f. How far will you go to get ahead in your career?

g. Are you willing to prove yourself as a staff member of our firm? How do you envision your role?

h. Are you willing to work overtime?

i. *Where do you see yourself five years from now?

j. How much money do you hope to earn in five years? Ten years?

*Note: Questions marked with an asterisk (*) are among the toughest to answer. Further on in this chapter, the "15 Toughest Interview Questions" are treated in some depth so you can "ace" them when the time comes.

Company or Organization

These questions are to determine if you have conscientiously researched the company and if you would be a "match" for them. They also indicate your interest in the company.

a. Do you prefer working for a small or large organization?
b. Do you prefer a private or non-private organization? Why?
c. What do you know about our organization?
d. *Why are you interested in this company?
e. What kind of work are you interested in doing for us?
f. What do you feel our organization has to offer you?
g. *Why do you think you can contribute to our company?

Values and Self-Assessment

These help the interviewer get to know you better and to determine how well you understand yourself. They also help to inform the interviewer of what motivates you.

a. What kinds of personal satisfactions do you hope to gain through work?
b. If you had unlimited funds, what would you do?
c. *If you could live during any time in history, when and where would you live?
d. What motivates you?
e. What are your strengths and weaknesses?
f. How would you describe yourself?
g. What do you do with your free time?
h. What kind of people do you like to work with?
i. How do you adapt to other cultures?
j. *What is your greatest achievement?
k. *How do you manage stress?

How to Handle Objections During the Interview

It is not uncommon to face objections in an interview. It may be that the interviewer believes you lack some skills required. Don't panic! If you keep a level head, you will be able to recover. For example, one woman was applying for an assistant buyer position in the fragrance department of a retail operation although she had never sold perfumes. Her background was in shoes. The interviewer didn't feel she had enough knowledge of perfumes. But by the end of the interview, she had swayed the interviewer with facts of her past achievements as a salesperson, convincing him that skilled people are capable of learning any product line. She even discussed trends in the fragrance industry, which she had researched in a trade magazine—surprising the interviewer, who didn't expect her to know much about the subject.

If an interviewer appears to have an objection to hiring you, ask what it is. With this knowledge, you may be able to change the interviewer's mind or redefine the job description to fit your qualifications.

STEP 5: Questions, You Must Have Questions

A typical interviewer comment toward the close of an interview is to ask if you have any questions. Never just say "no." Keep a list of questions in mind to ask. Sometimes even the worst of interviews can be salvaged by good questions. If you believe that most questions were answered during the interview, try the "not-really-a-question" tactic. This might be a statement such as, "As I mentioned, I believe that my creativity and attention to detail are my strengths. How do you think these would fit into the organization?" Here are a few other questions you might ask.

Questions to Ask Interviewers
- What would a normal working day be like?
- About how many individuals go through your program each year?
- How much contact is there with management?
- During training, are employees transferred among functional fields?
- How soon could I expect to be advanced to the next level in the career path?
- How much travel is normally expected?
- Will I be expected to meet certain deadlines? How frequent are they?
- How often are performance reviews given?
- How much decision-making authority is given after one year?
- Does the company provide any educational benefits?
- How frequently do you relocate professional employees?
- Have any new product lines/services been announced recently?
- What are the essential skills/qualities necessary for an employee to succeed in this position?
- Where are the last two people who held this position (did they leave the company or get promoted)?
- What role would my job play in helping the company achieve its corporate mission and make a profit?
- What are the five most important duties of this job?
- Why did you join the company? What is it about the company that keeps you here?
- What has the company's growth pattern been over the past five years?

At the conclusion of the interview, ask when a hiring decision will be made. This is important not only because it reconfirms your interest in the position but also so you'll know when, realistically, to expect a response. Don't forget, of course, to thank your interviewer for his or her time and to make clear your interest in the position if you feel there may be any doubt about this point.

STEP 6: The Aftermath

As soon as you leave the interview and have a chance, take notes on what you feel you could improve upon for your next interview and on what you feel went particularly well. After all, experience is only valuable to the extent that you're willing to learn from it. It also helps to make a note of something in the interview you might use in your thank-you letter.

The All Important Thank-You Letter

Always follow up each interview with a prompt thank-you letter—written the same day, if possible. The purpose of the letter is to supplement the presentation you made. Thank the interviewer for his or her hospitality. Express continued interest in the position, and mention up to three additional points to sell yourself further. Highlight how your specific experience or knowledge is directly applicable to the company's immediate needs, and if you forgot to mention something important in the interview, say it now. If possible, try to comment on something the interviewer said. Use that comment to show how your interests and skills perfectly match what they're looking for.

The thank-you letter should be sent A.S.A.P.! Your name should remain in front of the interviewer as much as possible. Sending the letter immediately will demonstrate how serious you are about the position. It may well be the final factor in helping you land the job.

Get the most from your references

References should remain confidential and never revealed until a company is close to making you an offer and you want to receive one.

Always brief your references before you supply an interviewer with their names and numbers. Tell the references what company you're interviewing with and what the job is. Give them some background on the company and the responsibilities you'll be asked to handle.

Your references will then be in a position to help sell your abilities. Finally, don't abuse your references. If you give their names too often, they may lose enthusiasm for your cause.

Waiting

Now the waiting begins. Try not to be too impatient, and remember that for the time being no answer is better than a rejection. There could be many reasons why you haven't heard from the company. It could be that the interview process hasn't concluded, or that other commitments have kept the company from making a decision. The most important point to remember during this time is that all your hopes shouldn't be pinned on one or two interviews. The job search is continuous and shouldn't stop until you have accepted a job offer. Keeping all your options open is the best possible plan.

However, if much time has passed and you haven't heard anything from a company in which you are particularly interested, a telephone call or letter asking about the status of your application is appropriate. This inquiry should be stated in a manner that is not pushy but shows your continued interest in the firm. Remember that waiting is an integral part of the job hunt, but a demonstration of your continued interest is appropriate.

Many job seekers experience a kind of euphoria after a good interview. Under the impression that a job offer is imminent, a candidate may discontinue the search. This is a serious mistake. The hiring decision may take weeks or may not be made at all. On average, about six weeks elapse between the time a person makes initial contact with a company and receives a final answer. If you let up on your job search, you will prolong it. Maintain a constant sense of urgency. Get on with the next interview. Your search isn't over until an offer is accepted and you actually begin your new job.

15 Toughest Interview Questions—and How To Answer Them

1. Tell me about yourself. This question, in one form or another, is one of the most likely to be asked. It is also one of the most likely questions to be answered poorly. Answer it without going into your personal life or family background. Stick to your professional and educational background and how it applies to the job you are interested in. Focus on your strengths and—especially with this question—remember to keep your response brief.

2. Teach me how to do something. This question is sometimes used in a consulting or sales company interview. One candidate responded by verbally teaching the interviewer how to play tennis. The subject of the lesson isn't what matters but, rather, the teaching presentation. The interviewer is assessing how well you would do in front of a client. Do you have the skills to impress or persuade a person, and are you articulate and sophisticated in your presentation? Most importantly, can you think on your feet?

3. Should city buses be free? You are probably wondering what free buses have to do with you getting the job. Nothing! Instead, the interviewer wants to see how you think the question through. The interviewer doesn't expect you to have expertise in this area and wants dialogue to occur. Don't be afraid to ask questions to determine whether you are heading in the right direction. Always modify your thinking with whatever information the interviewer may provide to you. Keep in mind that analytical ability is important but so are enthusiasm and creativity.

4. Do you know how to operate a Macintosh computer? On your resume you listed PC knowledge, but you have no experience with the Mac. Then why did the interviewer ask this question? Either the company uses Macs or the interviewer wanted to pull a weakness from your resume. Rather than bluntly saying "no," rephrase your response as: "I have gained a good deal of experience on the PC and with many programs. I feel comfortable with computers, and the transition to the Mac should be fairly easy."

5. Why do you think you can contribute to our company? Most candidates will answer in a typical manner that they are energetic, motivated, and a hard worker. This may or may not be true, but every interviewer has heard this response. What is more effective is to respond with examples or facts from your past experiences that draw the interviewer a picture of how you are a go-getter. This is an excellent question to prepare for, as it gives you an idea of what makes you unique from all other qualified candidates on the market.

6. If you could live during any time in history, when and where would you live? This is an off-the-wall question but it will occur sometimes. The interviewer probably doesn't expect a specific answer. And he may not let you off the hook after you give your answer. Feel free to give yourself time to think before answering; a pensive pause can sometimes even help an interview. Whatever your answer, have a reason for choosing it because almost certainly the interviewer will follow up with, "Why did you choose that?" At work the unexpected happens, and the interviewer wants to see how you deal with it.

7. What is your greatest achievement? This question allows the interviewer to assess both values and skills. What you select as your achievement will express what is important to you. And at the same time your narrative will reveal skills you have acquired. The interviewer will be interested in listening for skills necessary for the job opening.

8. Do you think your grades were a good indication of your academic achievement? If you were an A student, you can respond enthusiastically, "Yes!" However, those of us who had less than fantastic grades will respond differently. There are many reasons you may not have had high grades. For example: you worked full time while attending school or you were involved in many outside organizations. Turn the answer into a positive by explaining the benefits you received from the trade-offs of working and attending school. Emphasize your common sense and creativity rather than your grades. Besides, grades are not everything.

9. Why are you interested in this company? If you've done your homework on the company, you shouldn't sweat over this question. This is your opportunity to show how well your skills and values match that of the company's.

10. What do you like/dislike about your current (or last) job? You need to be alert when answering this question. Criticizing a former employer could send the message that you are a troublemaker or have a negative attitude, which could spell the end to your prospects with this company. Be as positive about your work experience as possible. Emphasize what you contributed and learned from the company. Even a negative experience can be translated into challenges and learning opportunities.

11. Describe how you dealt with a difficult problem. Try to be as positive as you can, and focus on the approach you used rather than any negative outcomes. For example, describe how you examined the problem, developed several alternative solutions, and implemented the solutions. Emphasize any positive outcomes from your solutions.

12. Where do you see yourself five years from now? Be realistic in your answer rather than trying to impress the interviewer. You can reiterate your goals to advance while still being a team player. And you can add that new opportunities are bound to arise within the company, which will also affect what you would like to be doing five years from now. Emphasize how the current job you are interviewing for will prepare you for five-year goals.

13. How do you manage stress? Listen carefully to the question. This isn't asking "can" you manage stress, but rather "how." The basic answer to this question involves giving an example of how you maintained your cool, pulled everyone together, and came up with a positive result, all without becoming overwhelmed.

14. What can you do for our company that someone else cannot? Similar to Question 5, this question usually will come after a description of the job has been provided. You need to reiterate what skills you have that pertain to the position and the company overall. Reemphasize those qualities that you feel are unique and how they might help the organization.

15. Could you explain these gaps in your work history? You may have gaps in your work history for many legitimate reasons. What you want to express is that you enjoy working and that when things aren't going as planned (maybe you were laid off) you are challenged to learn and overcome. Be sure to describe any studying or volunteer work that you may have done while unemployed.

9 Interview Styles to Watch For

The interviewing process can be tricky at times. Most applicants are clueless as to how the interview will go or what it will entail. Many job seekers and career changers will eventually encounter some of these interview types. Knowing a little about each of them is certainly advantageous. Knowing what to expect will boost your confidence and dry out those nervous, sweaty palms.

Behavioral Interviewing. A new technique for interviewing, behavioral interviewing assumes that past behavior predicts future performance. You can easily recognize when an interviewer is using "behavioral interviewing" because you will be asked questions about how you have worked in the past. For example, "Tell me about a time where you successfully learned a new software package"; or, "Tell me about a conflict you had with a co-worker and how you dealt with it." The employer expects you to tell short stories about yourself to give more insight into how you behave at work.

The best strategy to use when answering behavioral interview questions is the STAR technique. STAR stands for situation, task, action, result. First, describe the situation and task you were assigned in order to set the stage. Next, review the action you took. Plan to spend the most time on this part of the answer because your past performance is what the employer is most interested in. Finally, emphasize the results, the outcome of your actions.

Situation: "I was assigned sales manager for a new product my company was introducing."

Task: "I was to develop a marketing plan to determine best sales techniques."

Action: "I created a market survey instrument and conducted a campaign to assess consumer preference. I also conducted blind taste tests at local supermarkets."

Result: "The result was a successful marketing campaign that saw sales of our product skyrocket by 42%."

With STAR, you are able to convince the employer that you are capable of performing the open job by demonstrating your past success.

The Analytical Interview. The analytical interview is designed to let the interviewer see you think on your feet. The interviewer will ask you challenging questions to see how you analyze and perform under pressure. You may hear some off-the-wall questions like the examples below. In some cases you may be given a pen and paper, but don't be surprised if you're not. Most of the time the interviewer is looking for an answer that is simply in the ballpark. If you are totally stumped and caught off guard by the question, think creatively. You also are better off answering humorously than not at all. Remember, the interviewer is interested in your thinking process, not just in how you derived the answer. Here are some questions that may put you on the spot.

- Why are manhole covers round?
- What are the number of square yards of pizza eaten in the U.S. each year?
- How many gas stations would you estimate there are in the United States?

How much does a 747 weigh?

D. N. Meehan, a senior scientist at a large firm, was interviewing a young man. Meehan asked the candidate to estimate the weight of a fully loaded 747 at takeoff. It's pretty obvious that coming up with the correct answer would be very difficult for almost anyone. Since the applicant was not versed in aviation, he felt he would have to come up with something creative and unique in order to leave a lasting impression on the interviewer. The candidate asked if he could use anything in the room and then proceeded to use Meehan's computer. It was a surprise to Meehan when the candidate turned on the "flight simulator" game and came up with the correct answer.

Tennis, anyone?

Theo Kruijssen, a student at Emory University, was asked "How many matches need to be played in a single elimination tennis tournament if there are 256 participants?" Eagerly, Theo began using his math background and developed an equation to solve the problem. Several minutes later, he had his answer. The interviewer, however, was not as impressed as Theo was. The interviewer said that it was quite simple: "There are 255 matches. Each match has one loser and everyone loses once except the winner."

Stress Interviewing. The stress interview is like a horror film. It is more interesting to see than to be in. The intent of the interviewer is to determine how well you can handle pressure or a crisis situation.

Usually, the interviewee doesn't recognize a stress situation. For example, a candidate was taken to lunch by two recruiters. The recruiters informed the candidate that he didn't have the qualifications for the job, and then they began talking among themselves. In reality, they were seeing how he would respond to rejection since the position was in sales, which required dealing with stress and rejection.

Your best strategy for the stress interview is to recognize questions in disguise. Rather than becoming hostile, relax and attempt to present your case to the employer. There are endless cases where the interviewee allows the discussion to get under his skin and make his blood boil. Instead, be humble and try to ignore anything that offends you. Even though questions are designed to insult you, view this as a challenge and answer candidly.

No stress interviewing information would be complete without at least one horror story. A director of a business school placement office told us one that injects new meaning into the word stress. A candidate was interviewing with a Wall Street firm that was known for challenging interviews. He walked into a large boardroom, and at the end of the table, a partner, holding a newspaper in front of his face, said, "Get my attention." Thinking quickly, the candidate took out his lighter and set the newspaper on fire. We're not sure if he got the job, but he did get the partner's attention.

The Manhattan, Kansas, Interview. This type of interview occurs more often than you are aware of since it forms a hidden agenda within the interview itself. We often hear interviewers talk about how they would feel about a candidate if they were stuck with him or her in the airport in Manhattan, Kansas, or anywhere else for that matter, for twenty-four hours. Would you be pals or get on each other's nerves? Many times this assessment is based solely on personality and fit with the interviewer's personality. However, it does serve as a reminder that it is the interviewer who is recommending you for the job, not someone else in the company. You must impress your interviewer while also showing that you're a pretty good person to have around.

Stream of Consciousness Interviewing. This interview goes something like this: "Well let me tell you something about the company, we are located downtown, which is a great place for lunch, as a matter of fact I found a wonderful little restaurant last week that served wonderful pasta, it tasted just like something I had in Italy last year, Italy, now that's a great place to visit, I went there with my sister and we had a blast, Milan, Rome, and Florence, the art is wonderful."

Are you starting to get the picture? Just because you know how to interview doesn't mean your interviewer does. Sometimes you need to learn how to control the interview. For first timers this can be extremely difficult. You also need to be sure that you do not embarrass or insult your interviewer. One way to insert yourself into the stream of consciousness interview is to ask questions about the company and quickly follow up with statements about how your particular strengths would work well in that environment. This type of interview is a real challenge. Make sure that the interviewer leaves with a positive impression of who you are rather than just a feeling of having told a good story.

The Epicurean Interview. If you are in an all-day interview and someone offers to take you to lunch, it may not be as relaxing as it sounds. This is not your moment to put your interviewing skills on the back burner. When going to lunch during the interview process, never let your killer-interview guard down. While conversation may be informal, evaluation is still present. Here are some Epicurean hints for the lunch interview:

- Don't order the most expensive item simply because you are not paying. It is best to order something in the medium price range. Also, don't worry about saving money by ordering the cheapest item; order what you want within reason.
- Stay away from spaghetti, spinach, and shrimp dishes or any other dish that could give you embarrassment. It can be extremely awkward trying to work a piece of food out from between your teeth or slurping up a long pasta noodle.
- If you don't drink alcohol, this is not the time to begin. And if you do drink, we recommend you wait until you have the job. If you must drink, limit yourself to just one. It is best to be as alert as possible during the lunch interview.
- Try to relax. Finding common interests between the interviewer and yourself will help lighten the conversation.

Dear Dr. Bob

How about sharing an interesting Epicurean experience with us.—Sincerely, The Epicurean Club.

Dear Epicurean Club

A student I worked with told me a story about going to a classy restaurant with a potential employer. Having talked a great deal and eaten only a little during the meal, the student decided to order what she thought was a simple dessert. But being a classy restaurant where swank desserts were served, she received a large, flaming dessert. In fact, it was such a large, flaming dessert that the waiter set the plant hanging over the table on fire. Needless to say, the student made a burning impression on the employer. Bon Appetit!

The Athletic Interview. From time to time athleticism, or at least some degree of fitness, can help during an interview. I recall one interview where I was told to meet my potential employer on a popular street corner in New York City. We were to meet and then go someplace to talk. As my luck would have it, by the time the interviewer showed up, he was late for a train at Penn Station. However, he was still interested in talking with me, so in business suits and briefcases we jogged to the station. He made his train and I got a second interview. Always be ready for the unexpected, even if it takes a little more out of you than you expected.

The Grunge Interview. We have talked about proper dress during the interview. There are still those, however, who believe that the best way to interview is to feel comfortable with yourself and your dress. In other words, be yourself and the job is bound to come. Wrong! Take this one opportunity to blend in with those that are interviewing you, and do not make an issue or statement with your clothes. Once you get the job and they see what a great employee you are, they will better understand your dressing desires and requirements. No matter how cool it looks to grunge dress and no matter how comfortable you feel, take our advice and hang up the blue jeans for a few hours.

Dr. Bob's Friendly Interview. As I finished up this section on interviewing, a staff member alerted me to the fact that I had not included my own style of interviewing: the "friendly interview," in which the employer is quite pleasant and lulls you into thinking that he likes everyone. The idea is to catch you off guard with a simple question that might reveal more than you planned about who you are. The way to handle this (and every interview) is to understand that your interview face must be on at all times, always presenting your best side. We all know that everyone has weaknesses; the interview, however, is not the time to let people know about them.

A Few Final Tips on Interviewing

In many ways an interview is like a first date. You can't predict how it will turn out. However, like a date, you can prepare yourself to make the best impression possible. You can also assess whether the company is a good match for you. Just as your first date may not be your best, likewise your first interview may not be your best.

However, you can learn from your mistakes and correct them in future interviews. Most importantly, don't forget to follow-up. If you had the dream date, you wouldn't forget to call again—so you must write the "thank-you letter" to the potential employer.

Rejected? How Can It Happen?

Remember that the world is full of rejections and failures. What would motivate us to improve if we didn't have past failures? Everybody flunks at some point in their life; nobody is perfect. To give you a flavor of how to really fail an interview, here are some major employer turn-offs (provided by the Lindquist-Endicott Report, Northwestern University):

Sloppy appearance. Like it or not, people form lasting impressions of you within the first seconds of the interview. When dressing for an interview, pay close attention to details.

Arrogant attitude. If employers had to sum up the qualities they are looking for in candidates in two words, they would likely be "team player." They want people whose first loyalty is to the company and who are willing to work for the good of the group. Arrogant individualists have no place in this environment.

Limited knowledge about the company or the field. No greater turn-off than to expect the employer to tell you about his or her company. One of Procter and Gamble's favorite interview questions is, "Which of the P&G products is your favorite?" Simple question, but it surprises many.

Asking about the salary or benefits too early. Asking about the salary too early in the interview says nothing about what you can do for the company, only what you want from them. You don't want the employer to think that you are selfish with a one-way mind.

Lack of clarity in long-range goals. Employers want to know why you want a particular job and where you want to go with it. Demonstrate that you have some sort of career plan and that the plan fits in with the company's goals.

Failure to ask for the job. Interviewing is like a sales presentation. After you have spent time marketing yourself, don't forget to close the deal. Ask for the job and let them know you are interested.

How To Bounce Back from Rejection

Do these lines sound familiar? "You're really not the right one." "We liked you, but we've decided not to hire right now." "You really don't have the experience we are looking for." "You are overqualified." These phrases occur more often than we would like. It's important to keep your sanity and courage during the interview process.

Anger, stress, guilt, fear, and anxiety are unfortunate companions to any job search. The strategy, therefore, is to learn to deal with rejection in a healthy and constructive manner and not let it distort your judgment. Develop methods to compensate for the beating your ego may take during the job search. Family and friends can be an excellent source for encouragement and positive support. Don't forget to eat well and exercise to relieve the stress involved in the job search. Be persistent and don't give up! Eddie Rickenbacker once said, "Try like hell to win, but don't cry if you lose." This should be one of your mottoes.

What Do Interviewers Really Want To See?

General Personality. Ambition, poise, sincerity, trustworthiness, initiative, and interest in the firm. (General intelligence is assumed.) Different firms look for different kinds of people, personalities, style, appearance, abilities, and technical skills. Always check the job specifications. Don't waste time talking about a job you can't do or for which you don't have the minimum qualifications.

Personal Appearance. A neat, attractive appearance makes a good impression and demonstrates professionalism.

Work Experience. Again, this varies from job to job, so check job specifications. Be able to articulate the importance of what you did in terms of the job for which you are interviewing and in terms of your own growth or learning. Even if the work experience is unrelated to your new field, employers look upon knowledge of the work environment as an asset.

Verbal Communication Skills. The ability to express yourself articulately is very important. This includes the ability to listen effectively, verbalize thoughts clearly, and express yourself confidently.

Skills. The interviewer will evaluate your skills for the job, such as organization, analysis, and research. It is important to emphasize the skills that you feel the employer is seeking and to give specific examples of how you developed them. This is the main reason why it is important to engage in self-assessment prior to the interview.

Goals/Motivation. Employers will assess your ability to articulate your short-term and long-term goals. You should seem ambitious yet realistic about the training and qualifications needed to advance. Demonstrate your interest in the functional area or industry and a desire to succeed and work hard.

Knowledge of the Interviewer's Company and Industry. At a minimum, you are expected to have done some homework on the company. Don't waste interview time asking questions you could have found answers to in printed material. Know the firm's position and character relative to others in the same industry. General awareness of media coverage of a firm and its industry is usually expected.

CYBERTIPS ON INTERVIEWING

As with most aspects of the job search, the Internet is full of sites with tips on interviewing and the latest in interviewing news. We have listed a few below:

Career Channel
http://riceinfo.rice.edu/projects/careers/Channel/seven/Interview/text/The.interview.html

Career Magazine
http://www.careermag.com/careermag/newsarts/interviewing.html

Catapult
http://www.wm.edu/catapult/catapult.html **or**
http://www.wm.edu/catapult/enelow-i.html

BOOKS ON INTERVIEWING

Biegelein, J.I. *Make Your Job Interview a Success.* New York: Arco, 1994.

Danna, Jo. *Winning the Job Interview Game: Tips for the High-Tech Era.* Briarwood, NY: Palamino Press, 1986.

Fear, Richard A. *The Evaluation Interview.* New York: McGraw-Hill, 1990.

King, Julie Adair. *The Smart Woman's Guide to Interviewing and Salary Negotiation.* Hawthorne, NJ: Career Press, 1993.

Krannich, Caryl R. *Interview for Success.* San Luis Obispo, CA: Impact, 1995.

Marcus, John J. *The Complete Job Interview Handbook.* New York: Harper & Row, 1994.

Medley, H. Anthony. *Sweaty Palms: The Neglected Art of Being Interviewed.* Berkeley, CA: Ten Speed Press, 1992.

Pettus, Theodore. *One On One—Win the Interview, Win the Job.* New York: Random House, 1981.

Smart, Bradford D. *The Smart Interviewer.* New York: John Wiley & Sons, 1990.

Stewart, Charles J., and William B. Cash. *Interviewing Principles and Practices.* Dubuque, IA: William C. Brown Publishers, 1994.

Yate, Martin. *Knock 'em Dead.* Holbrook, MA: Adams Publishing, 1995.

Summer, Temporary, and Part-Time Jobs

For some, getting a job is seen as a summer only or as a temporary proposition. If that is the case, this is the chapter for you. First, summer jobs.

Summer Jobs—Findable and Rewarding

Summer provides the unique opportunity for students to brainstorm about careers that strike their interest. This is an experimental time in which the employer takes only a limited risk. But, how does one go about finding a summer job?

Finding a summer job is very similar to finding a permanent job. Persistence and positive attitude are keys for the high school or college job seeker just as they are for the full-time worker. Here are a few simple hints for prospective summer job seekers.

Set realistic expectations. Don't expect to get rich with summer work and, most importantly, realize that you won't get to the top after a week's work. Some progress can be expected, but summer jobbers should realize that they aren't on the same totem pole as permanent workers.

Have the right attitude. Nothing impresses an employer more than the right attitude. What do they want in an employee? Someone who is loyal, respectful, polite, punctual, enthusiastic, and hardworking. Remember that the number of people who really have all these qualities is small. If you can demonstrate your willingness to be the right person, you may get the job.

Dress right. Dress is a real issue with the summer job seeker. The best way to dress for summer jobs is somewhere between a suit and tie, as parents might encourage, and jeans and T-shirt, as friends might suggest. A collared shirt with slacks or khakis for guys, and slacks or skirt for young women are certainly acceptable. Additionally, wear leather shoes, not sneakers.

Be persistent. As a job seeker you can't be persistent enough. A true key to success in a summer job search is to keep trying, often with the same employer. Many summer success stories come from young people who visit their top five summer job sites of choice once a week until they get a job. One common mistake made by summer job seekers is to stop looking once they think they have a job. Even if an interview goes well or an employer says they like you, you must keep going until you have an actual job offer.

Interview well. Hopefully, after all your searching and preparation, your final challenge will be the interview. But don't be too worried; after all, if you get the interview, you do have a good chance of getting the job, or else the company wouldn't be wasting their time with you. For a successful interview, keep in mind these familiar guidelines: (1) Give specific reasons why you are right for the job; (2) Try to relate every question to your strengths of being loyal, enthusiastic, and other desirable qualities; (3) Inject a little humor into your otherwise serious and hardworking nature—but don't overkill on the comedy; and finally (4) Ask lots of questions to demonstrate your interest in the position.

As you go out into the summer job market, there are a few areas that can present stumbling blocks to your search. These include fear of risk; failing to contact the right person within the company; and taking no for an answer. (In other words, not being persistent enough.) If, on the other hand, you avoid these common traps, you will most likely find yourself on your way to a rewarding summer job experience.

If you are hesitant about working during the summer because you would rather be sitting by the pool, consider the many non-indoor summer opportunities. A summer job doesn't have to be inside an office or fast-food restaurant. There are paid internships offered by non-profit organizations that are not the typical office job environment.

As with any summer job, finding a good one requires starting your search as early as possible. The application process alone takes time, not to mention the research portion.

Dr. Bob's Six-Step Summer Job System

How do you get a job for the summer? Our tried and true system has worked for students and others for years.

1. **Know what you want to do.** Try to make a decision about what you want to do as early as possible. The sooner you decide, the sooner you can begin your search. Don't forget, the Career Center at your school provides resources and counseling to students. (See Chapter 2 for information on choosing a career.)

2. **Develop a resume.** It is important to accomplish this as early as possible since companies and application deadlines are as early as December for some summer jobs. (See Chapter 6 for details on resume and cover letter writing.)

3. **Write a cover letter.** A good cover letter is essential—it directs attention to your resume. Don't forget to have your resume and cover letter critiqued by a friend and career counselor, if possible.

4. **Do research and make contacts.** This step takes the longest, but hard work here can really pay off. Information interviews (see Chapter 5) with people in your field can help develop contacts. Don't forget your Alumni Office to develop a list of prospective employers. Make as many contacts as possible, and as soon as you have your contact list, begin mailing letters and resumes. A helpful tip is to send your letters in batches so you can track them efficiently and follow up each one with a letter.

5. **Follow-up and persistence.** This is the most important step! Make sure that for every letter you send out, for every person you talk to, and for every potential job site you visit, you continue to call back and let them know you are interested. Failure to follow up is disastrous for many a summer job searcher.

6. **Schedule interviews.** As part of your follow-up, try to schedule interviews. Give your letters time to arrive, then follow up with a phone call. This will keep you a step ahead of most college students, who don't start looking for summer jobs until school is out. Finally, make sure you know how to perform the "killer" interview discussed in Chapter 7.

BEST BETS FOR SUMMER EMPLOYMENT IN THE ATLANTA AREA

Atlanta Knights
Omni
100 Techwood Drive
Atlanta, GA 30303
(404) 420-5011
(marketing and public relations)

Atlanta Outward Bound
320 N. McDonough St.
Decatur, GA 30030
(404) 378-0494
(community service/leadership development)

Atlanta Preservation Center
156 7th St., The Desota Suite 3
Atlanta, GA 30308
(404) 876-2041
(preservation organization)

AT&T Global Information Solutions
5 Executive Park Place, N.E.
Atlanta, GA 30329
(404) 321-8826

Boys and Girls Club of America
1230 W. Peachtree St., N.W.
Atlanta, GA 30309
(404) 815-5771
(marketing)

Cable & Wireless
2690 Cumberland Parkway, Suite 490
Atlanta, GA 30309
(770) 434-4161
(telemarketing and computer science)

The Carter Center
1 Copenhill
Atlanta, GA 30307
(404) 420-5101
(development and research)

Chattahoochee Nature Center
9135 Willco Road
Roswell, GA 30075
(770) 992-2053
(outdoor recreation)

Children's Miracle Network Telethon
190 The Exchange, Suite 300
Atlanta, GA 30339
(404) 953-8611
(marketing, development, and public relations)

Circuit City Stores
3755 Atlanta Industrial Parkway
Atlanta, GA 30064
(404) 699-2109
(marketing and business)

Coca-Cola Bottling Company
450 Lee Industrial Blvd.
Austell, GA 30001
(404) 819-2700
(marketing and sales)

C.R. Bard, Inc.
13183 Harland Drive
Covington, GA 30209
(770) 526-4455
(marketing)

Creative Events International
1100 Spring St., Suite 640
Atlanta, GA 30309
(404) 817-0800
(events planning; public relations)

DeKalb County Government
1300 Commerce Drive
Decatur, GA 30030
(404) 371-2885
(public relations and communications)

DeKalb Medical Center
2701 N. Decatur Road
Decatur, GA 30033
(404) 501-5566
(public relations and marketing)

Delta Airlines
Department 961
P.O. Box 20530
Atlanta, GA 30320
(404) 715-2027
(marketing)

Democratic Party of Georgia
1100 Spring St., Suite 710
Atlanta, GA 30309
(404) 874-1996
(politics)

Dittler Brothers
1375 Seaboard Ind. Blvd.
Atlanta, GA 30318
(404) 355-3423
(printing and manufacturing)

DMD Engineering & Testing
2800 Old Alabama Road
Alpharetta, GA 30202
(770) 442-8718
(marketing)

Egleston Children's Hospital
1405 Clifton Road
Atlanta, GA 30322-1101
(404) 315-2009
(marketing, development, and public
relations)

Equitable Real Estate Investment
Management, Inc.
Human Resources, Department SI
1150 Lake Hearn Drive, N.E., Suite 400
Atlanta, GA 30342-1522
(404) 848-8600
(commercial real estate)

Federal Reserve Bank of Atlanta
104 Marietta St., N.W.
Atlanta, GA 30303
(404) 521-8008
(research, business, and finance)

Fernbank Museum of Natural History
767 Clifton Road
Atlanta, GA 30307
(404) 378-0127

Fort Knox Escrow Services
3539-A Church St.
Atlanta, GA 30021
(404) 298-2000
(marketing)

Georgia Public Telecommunications
Commission
1540 Stewart Ave., S.W.
Atlanta, GA 30313
(404) 756-4710
(communications/media)

GTE
245 Perimeter Parkway
Atlanta, GA 30346
(770) 391-8199
(business)

Hands on Atlanta
931 Monroe Drive, Suite 208
Atlanta, GA 30308
(404) 872-2252
(community service)

Jamison Research
50 Perimeter Center East, N.E.,
Suite 450
Atlanta, GA 30346
(770) 399-9401
(commercial real estate)

Judicial Council of Georgia
244 Washington St., S.W., Suite 550
Atlanta, GA 30334
(404) 656-5171
(part of judicial/court system)

Lenox Square
3393 Peachtree Road, N.E.
Atlanta, GA 30326
(404) 233-6767
(marketing)

Marsh & McLennan
3400 Georgia Pacific Center
133 Peachtree St., N.E.
Atlanta, GA 30303
(404) 521-3000
(insurance brokerage)

McCann-Erickson Event Marketing
615 Peachtree St., N.E.
Atlanta, GA 30308
(404) 888-4614
(marketing and advertising)

MCI Telecommunications
MCI Center
3 Ravinia Drive
Atlanta, GA 30346
(770) 668-6670
(industry marketing)

Melita International
5051 Peachtree Corner's Circle
Norcross, GA 30092
(770) 409-4495
(marketing and communications)

Nexus Contemporary Art Center
535 Means St., N.W.
Atlanta, GA 30318
(404) 688-1970
(arts)

Northlake Mall
1000 Northlake Mall
Atlanta, GA 30345
(404) 938-5483
(marketing intern)

Parks and Recreation Department of
Atlanta
675 Ponce de Leon Ave., N.E.
Atlanta, GA
(404) 817-6785
(handles recreational services and
facilities)

Porraro and Associates
1455 Lincoln Parkway, Suite 200
Atlanta, GA 30346
(770) 353-6322
(financial services)

The Princeton Review
455 East Paces Ferry Road
Atlanta, GA 30305
(404) 233-0980
(marketing)

Southern Center for International
Studies
320 West Paces Ferry Road

Atlanta, GA 30305
(404) 656-3804
(research)

Southern Regional Council
134 Peachtree St., Suite 1900
Atlanta, GA 30303-1825
(404) 522-8764
(research)

UCB Chemicals Corporation
2000 Lake Park Drive
Smyrna, GA 30080
(404) 434-6188
(laboratory)

The Weather Channel
2600 Cumberland Parkway
Atlanta, GA 30339
(770) 434-6800
(provides weather information and
public education services)

Woodward Academy
1662 Rugby Ave.
College Park, GA 30337
(404) 765-8220
(pre-school; fund-raising)

Zoo Atlanta
800 Cherokee Ave.
Atlanta, GA 30315
(404) 624-5600
(research and recreation)

Summer Job Hunting on the Net

Be sure and use your computer in your summer job search. Below are a few
sources to get you started.

Career Mosaic
http://www.careermosaic.com/cm/
Information about companies; can post resumes and other job-search assistance; primarily geared toward college students.

Online Career Center
http://www.//occ.com/occ
Information about positions and companies; can submit resume.

Peterson's Education Center
http://www.petersons.com

Provides various services/information e.g. colleges/universities, study abroad programs, summer programs, etc.

CareerNET—Career Resource Center
http://www.careers.org
Be sure to look to CareerNet for links to current jobs, employer sites, newsgroups, and government sites throughout the year.

JobTrak
http://www.jobtrak.com
An excellent place to look for jobs posted at member colleges and universities. You'll need a password however. Check with your college placement or career office.

National Internships
http://campus.net/busemp/nintern/
Student internships and part-time jobs in: Washington, DC; New York City; Northern and Southern CA; Seattle; Texas; and many other places. Job opportunities in the private, non-profit, and government sectors.

Online Career Center
http://occ.com/occ
Try a keyword search on "internship" to get a list of these.

Peace Corps
http://www.clark.net/pub/peace/PeaceCorps.html>
Students can examine frequently asked questions about working for the Peace Corps; timelines for the application process; a list of countries where volunteers are assigned; and a description of the domestic program.

Peterson's Education Center
http://www.petersons.com
Check this new resource for internship opportunities at colleges and universities nationwide. You will also find information on summer job opportunities.

Summer Urban Ministry Opportunities Directory
http://www.fileshop.com/iugm/sumr-dir.html
Lists national and international positions.

RECOMMENDED SOURCES AND GUIDES FOR INTERNSHIPS

The Academy of Television Arts and Sciences
Student Internship Program, 5220 Lankershim Blvd., North Hollywood, CA 91601, (818) 754-2830 (provides internships in the media field).

The American Institute of Architects
Director, Education Programs, 1735 New York Ave., N.W., Washington, DC 20006 (provides information on architectural internships).

Inroads, Inc.
100 South Broadway, P.O. Box 8766, Suite 700, St. Louis, MO 63102 (African-American, Native American, and Hispanic-American students can intern in the areas of business, engineering, and science).

National Audubon Society
Government Affairs Internship Program, 666 Pennsylvania Ave., S.E.,
Washington, DC 20003, (202) 547-9009 (provides internships in resource con-
servation and wildlife management).

National Directory of Internships
National Society for Internships and Experiential Education, 122 St. Mary's St.,
Raleigh, NC 27605 (provides information on internships in a variety of areas).

National Institutes of Health
Summer Internship Program, Office of Education, Bldg. 10, Room 1C129, 9000
Rockville Pike, Bethesda, MD 20892, (301) 402-2176 (provides internships
working alongside influential scientists).

Oldman, Mark, and Samer Hamadeh. *The Princeton Review; America's Top 100
Internships.* New York: Villard Books, 1995.

Temporary/Part-Time Jobs

Locating part-time work in your chosen field is ideal since you can continue to
develop your network of contacts. Many professionals can freelance. An administrative assistant, for example, might be able to find part-time work at a law firm.
An accountant might be able to do taxes on a part-time basis and still gain access
to new referrals.

Another option is independent contracting. For example, if you're a computer programmer and the company you're interviewing with can't justify hiring
someone full time because there isn't enough work, suggest that they hire you on
a temporary basis for specific projects. Or offer to come in one or two days a
week. Or suggest that you work on an as-needed basis. The advantage to the company is that they don't have to pay you benefits (except those you're able to negotiate). The advantage to you is income and experience in your chosen field.

People with technical skills can work themselves into becoming full-time
freelancers in precisely this manner. They might even talk an employer OUT of
hiring them full time and negotiate contract work in order to maintain the freedom of their self-employed status.

Below are some agencies that may assist you in finding a temporary job.

SELECTED AGENCIES FOR PART-TIME AND TEMPORARY WORK

A One Service Personnel
1718 Peachtree St., N.W., Suite 157
Atlanta, GA 30309
(404) 885-9675
Word processing, data entry, and secretarial support.

Accountemps
1816 Independence Square
Dunwoody, GA 30338
(404) 392-0540
Accounting.

Ad Temps
3355 Lenox Road
Atlanta, GA
(404) 938-4290
Advertising, public relations,
radio, TV.

ADIA Disconnected
229 Peachtree St., N.E.
Atlanta, GA
(404) 681-1180
Clerical, technical, communications,
legal, and accounting

**Computer-Aided Engineering
Services**
6095 Barfield Road, Suite 206
Atlanta, GA 30328
(404) 303-8525

Butler Service Group
4960 Peachtree Industrial Blvd.
Norcross, GA 30071
(404) 448-9220
Aerospace, energy, utilities,
electronics, pulp and paper,
pharmaceutical, telecommunications,
and consumer products.

Caldwell Temporary Services
561 Thornton Road, Suite S
Lithia Springs, GA 30057
(404) 739-0796
All fields. Five offices throughout
metro Atlanta.

Corporate Temps
3145 Tucker-Norcross Road, Suite 206
Tucker, GA 30084
(770) 934-1710
Secretarial, administrative, customer
service, and industrial.

DayStar Temporary Services
1201 Peachtree St.
Atlanta, GA 30361
(404) 898-1800

Don Richard Associates of Georgia
3475 Lenox Road, N.E.

Atlanta, GA 30326
(404) 231-3688
Accounting and finance.

DDS Staffing Resources
863 Holcomb Bridge Road, Suite 230
Roswell, GA 30076
(404) 998-7779
Dental and medical temps.

Georgia Temporary Employee
Management Program
133 Peachtree St. N.E., Suite 200
Atlanta, GA 30303
(404) 652-5493
Office automation, executive secretary,
data entry, and technical programmers.

Hire Intellect
1810 Water Place, N.W.
Atlanta, GA 30339
(770) 850-8502
Marketing contractors.

Horizons Resources
1375 Peachtree St., N.E.
Atlanta, GA 30309
(404) 885-9556 603 9330
Specializes in business administration
and banking.

International Insurance Personnel
300 W. Wieuca Road, N.E.
Atlanta, GA 30342
(404) 255-9710
Insurance personnel.

Kelly Services
1201 W. Peachtree St., N.E.
Atlanta, GA 30309
(404) 607-7575
All fields. Eight offices throughout
metro Atlanta.

Lucas Financial Staffing
1827 Powers Ferry Road, S.E.
Marietta, GA 30067
(770) 952-2991

Manpower Temporary Services
260 Peachtree St., Suite 900
Atlanta, GA 30303
(404) 659-3565
All fields. Nine offices throughout
metro Atlanta.

Norrell Staffing Services
1275 Peachtree St., N.E.
Atlanta, GA 30305
(404) 240-3600
All fields. Twelve offices throughout
metro Atlanta.

Olsten Staffing Services
229 Peachtree St., N.E., Suite 901
Atlanta, GA 30303
(404) 659-6111
All fields. Ten offices throughout
metro Atlanta.

Randstad Staffing Services
230 Peachtree St., N.W.
Atlanta, GA 30303

(404) 577-7777
All fields. Nineteen offices throughout metro Atlanta.

**System One Engineering Technical &
MIS Staffing**
5775 Peachtree Dunwoody Road
Atlanta, GA 30326
(404) 252-0099
Engineering, technical, and MIS
staffing.

Temp World Staffing Services
3490 Piedmont Road, Suite 422
Atlanta, GA 30305
(404) 237-9266
Clerical and light industrial.

TRC Staffing Services
1280 W. Peachtree St., N.W.
Atlanta, GA 30309
(404) 874-8899
All fields. Nineteen branches
throughout metro area.

Turning Your Temp Job into Something Permanent

Working as a temporary is a good way to expose yourself to a variety of companies and contacts and to prove your skills to the hiring authority. It can be a foot
in the door at a company you are interested in working for, and, at the same time,
it allows the company to assess your qualifications rather than depending on a 30-
minute interview. So don't take that temporary job too lightly. After all, you never
know when it might turn into something permanent.

RECOMMENDED READING ON TEMPORARY/PART-TIME JOBS

Canape, Charlene. *The Part-Time Solution: The New Strategy for Managing
   Motherhood.* New York: Harper Collins, 1990.
Hawes, Gene R. *College Board Guide to Going to College While Working:
   Strategies for Success.* New York: College Entrance Examination Board (dis-
   tributed by College Board Publications), 1985.
Magid, Renee Y. *When Mothers and Fathers Work: Creative Strategies for
   Balancing Career and Family.* New York: AMACOM, 1987.
Paradis, Adrain A. *Opportunities in Part-Time and Summer Jobs.* Lincolnwood,
   IL: VGM Career Horizons, 1987.
Rothberg and Cook. *Part-Time Professional.* Washington, DC: Acropolis Books, 1985.

How To Handle a New Job and Workplace

A new job, new colleagues, and a new desk — this is what the job search was all about. How do you handle the new job? Well, let the job experts give you some advice.

Walking into your new everyday life, seeing all those new colleagues, and concentrating on fitting into the atmosphere can be overwhelming. But it is important to keep your cool, stay focused, and be yourself. It is natural to be nervous, but how that nervousness manifests itself is important. Showing too much apprehension or bumbling about a bit too much can give others, and cost you, a bad first impression.

How Significant Is the First Day on the Job?

The first day at work can certainly be one of the most important days during your time at a particular company. This is the day that you begin to establish who you are and what you can contribute to the organization. The first day can show your employer a lot. It will give him or her an idea of what you are like as an employee and how you will fit into the workplace.

In order to ease some of the restraint you may be feeling or cure some of those first-day butterflies, here are some tips that will enable you to feel more comfortable. For starters, promptness is essential and says a lot to the employer. This is important for more than just the first day. If you are constantly late, it reveals a sense of irresponsibility and may cause you some grief down the road.

Once you arrive at work on time, determining your duties and what is expected of you is vital. Take a little time to settle in, but try to get on the job soon, and show enthusiasm and contentment with your new job.

You might want to meet with your boss early in the day. This will show motivation and eagerness and will contribute early on to a good first impression. It will also give you an idea of some of the expectations that the company has for you. This and subsequent meetings should help you determine what drives the company and your superiors.

Learn the chain of command and assess the importance of teamwork. Ask about the long-term goals of the company so you can assess your role in it. Keep in mind on your first day that the old saying is true: you never get a second chance to make a first impression.

First Day Do's and Don'ts

It is important to keep in mind some rudimentary but very significant factors in terms of your on-the-job performance. We have formed a Top Ten list that should guide you through a successful first day on the job.

1. **DON'T** expect the red carpet to roll out for you. Employees may not even be expecting you, and special treatment may not be forthcoming.

2. **DON'T** imagine rewarding accomplishments and important responsibilities to await you on your first day. Be prepared for paperwork and orientations.

3. **DON'T** stress. Just take it one step at a time. The company knows you are new and will help you get acclimated; they want you to perform well.

4. **DON'T** be afraid to ask questions, and make sure you realize that no question is a stupid question.

5. **DON'T** be overwhelmed with all the new information. Concentrate on grasping the major points or the most urgent.

6. **DO** enjoy yourself. Think of your job as a challenge and a way to gain new skills for the future.

7. **DO** be prepared. Show everybody that you have your head on straight, can plan ahead, and know what you are doing.

8. **DO** get involved. Interpersonal communication within a company is very important. Be a part of the team, and show other employees that you have some good ideas.

9. **DO** be confident. You were hired because you are qualified. Don't let anything get in your way and make you think otherwise. If the company believes in you, then by all means you should believe in yourself.

10. **DO** stay focused. Try to maintain a working attitude throughout the day. Daydreaming and other distractions will hinder your professional image. Try not to incorporate your personal life with your professional life for the security of your career.

Adjusting Over the Long Run

A new job can be very intimidating and can fill you with mixed emotions about a career. Here are some helpful hints that will enable you to adjust to the company, fit in, and, most importantly, make an impact as a valuable employee.

Develop good communication skills. Has it come to your attention that most top-notch people in a company seem to know one another? Interpersonal communication is a key ingredient in making your job more productive and pleasant. Listen as well to everybody's input, not just those higher up on the career ladder. Keep in mind that you spend a large portion of your life with your workmates, and most of them have something to offer.

Take risks. Don't be afraid to take risks. A leader will have developed enough self-confidence so that taking a few calculated risks is worth the possible payoff. Overcoming skepticism and taking risks can even be the turning point of a career. Just remember to weigh all the options and be prepared for negative as well as positive results.

Work hard. A hard worker always seems to have a brighter future than someone who settles for being just adequate. Let the company know that you are the "go to" person. If you portray that hard-working image, the next step for most supervisors is to trust you with additional duties.

Honesty is the best policy. Try not to make excuses to bail yourself out of hot water. You are better off apologizing and admitting the fact that you made a mistake. Most importantly, never point your finger at other employees. You will only look foolish and cowardly. You want to set a good example, not be the bad example.

Maintaining a Good Relationship with the Boss

Here are some helpful tips to assist you in maintaining a good relationship with your boss.

- Think of your boss as a customer for the product you are trying to sell: yourself. Keep in mind that there is no such thing as impressing your boss too much.

- Value and respect your boss' time. Managers must handle a number of things all at once. If you see that your boss is busy, try to solve the problem yourself or seek assistance from another employee. Freeing your boss from trivial concerns will make everyone's life easier.
- Be open to advice. Don't be offended when your supervisor tries to steer you in the right direction. Make room for criticism, and view it as information that can make you a more effective employee.
- Never make your boss look foolish. Don't challenge his or her judgment in front of other employees. If you feel that you're right, talk to the boss privately. Involving others will just result in dispute and cause havoc.
- Always make your boss look good. Try to keep him/her informed of new issues and ideas. Remember that the better you do, the better the boss looks; and the better the boss looks, the better your career will be.
- Tell your boss about your career objectives or plans for the future. Inform him/her about your ideas and goals of accomplishment. Be optimistic, not skeptical, when discussing career plans with the head person.
- When confrontation with the boss is necessary, try to find an ice-breaking technique to reduce tension. Try to find a common goal or interest in solving the problem. This brings people together and makes them more open to discussion and less defensive.
- Always listen to your boss, but never let him/her walk all over you. Even though you may not have the final say, your judgments deserve to be heard.

A good professional relationship with the boss is vital in terms of job happiness and success. But don't look for the boss to be either perfect or your good buddy. A boss should be a role model and a leader, the person we answer to and respect.

Dear Dr. Bob

Lately, I've noticed my boss taking all the credit for my hard work. He never mentions my name when receiving glowing remarks about a project. What should I do?— Unrecognized Employee

Dear Unrecognized Employee
Your situation is an age-old one. We are supposed to make our bosses look good and hope they will return the favor. Unfortunately, that hasn't happened in your case. I am one that believes "what goes around, comes around" and eventually your efforts will be rewarded. You will have other jobs and other bosses, but your ability will stay with

you. In the meantime, use subtle techniques for claiming what is due. Make sure your name appears on written reports. When people praise your boss, mention how hard the whole department has worked as well. In due time, you will receive your just recognition.

Creativity and Innovation in Your Career

Corporations want individuals that can be assets and contribute to the company. New ideas and different approaches are always encouraged. Be creative. Show the company that you have the zeal and ability to bring new concepts to the company. Try not to be a routine employee who comes to work, takes care of her responsibilities, and leaves work exactly on time everyday.

Don't hesitate when you think you have a new idea that might help the company. The reality is that many companies do not recognize the value of the creative process but only the "bottom line" result. Here are a few tips for breaking your own barriers to creativity.

Postpone judgment. Explore an idea before promoting or nixing it. Even a patently unrealistic idea may lead to a workable solution to a problem.

Look for the second right answer. Avoid the trap of committing too soon to a single solution to a problem. Always look for the second, less obvious answer.

Take risks. How many models for an airplane did Orville and Wilbur Wright fail with before they found one that worked? Think about that the next time you are hesitant in something.

Look for unlikely connections. Computer guru Steve Jobs once said that when he worked for Atari he applied what he learned about movement from a modern dance class in college to the development of video games. Talk about an unlikely connection!

Allow yourself to be foolish. Kids have a leg up on us when it comes to creativity because they are encouraged to be foolish. Creativity flourishes when you allow your mind to romp. Some experts even suggest keeping toys in your office or home to encourage your playful side.

Creativity is within everyone's grasp. It comes out not when you do something that no one has done before but when you do something that *you* have never done before. Recognizing the barriers you yourself have erected to the creative process is the first step to unleashing your potential. Your career and success can only be enhanced once this is done.

Romance in the Office: A Definite Don't

Many dedicated corporate types have found Cupid's arrow piercing their brief-cases and setting their hearts aflutter under their banker pinstripes. What's a person to do when love hits in the workplace? The logical, reasonable answer is, "Don't do it!" But rarely is romance logical or reasonable.

Let's face it. Being in proximity with others for an extended period of time makes the workplace fertile ground for romance to blossom. You share common interests, talk frequently, and may even have similar problems. Next thing you know, you find Mr. or Ms. Right directly under your nose. If you are indeed smitten by a co-worker, we offer a few words of advice about relationships in the workplace.

- Know the company's policy on dating co-workers. Some companies consider it unprofessional or even a conflict of interest. However, it is unlikely that your organization will have a written policy prohibiting such relationships.
- Remember that the workplace is for work. Heated romances should remain outside the workplace.
- Be prepared for people to gossip. Romance is juicy stuff — especially for those who don't have it. There are no easy answers about how to handle gossip. It's best to ignore harmless gossip and to confront people spreading malicious stories (there is harm in a rumor that you or your significant other is pregnant!).
- Think about how to handle the break-up. No one wants to think about the end of a relationship, especially when it is just beginning. However, the number-one workplace hazard is a vindictive ex. Understand that if things don't work out, it is likely that you will still work together. Make sure you are ready for that possibility.
- Finally, never date the boss. Regardless of how professionally you conduct yourself in the office, every action or decision you make will be viewed by others through the lens of your relationship. Additionally, having an ex-significant other for a boss can be terribly awkward.
- If a romance goes sour, there is always the risk of sexual harassment. When one person in a relationship has greater authority over the other, the possibility of sexual harassment exists.

The easiest course is to avoid workplace romances altogether. However, love is capricious, and you may well find that one special person just across the hall. If that's the case, even Cupid understands the importance of separating love and work.

Keeping Your Career on the High Road

Becoming successful and happy is the ultimate dream of those who are trying to get their foot in the door. A true success story involves hard work and a positive professional attitude. Here are some tips that will enable you to take that first step toward a new and fulfilling life.

1. Always maintain a good professional relationship with your co-workers and peers. Knowing a wide array of people is certainly advantageous and can become very helpful when you need a favor or some assistance.
2. Find a mentor, somebody who can develop the best in you and advance your interests in the company.
3. Try to concentrate on small, easy projects at first. Conquering your first assignment will give the company a good initial vision of your work abilities. This will also alleviate the pressures a little and add to your self-esteem and believability.
4. Cater to your clients. Be straightforward and candid with them. Make them see that you are fair and treat them as people not profit figures. Try to value their time by being flexible with your schedule.
5. Never assume that a certain issue is not your job. Try to do whatever you can to make your department and the company work. Even if you are not responsible for certain areas, it won't hinder your career if you attempt to find answers when a problem affects you.
6. Take on as many responsibilities and as much work as you can handle. The operative phrase here, however, is "as much work as you can handle." Willingly accepting additional projects and assignments can ingratiate you with your boss only if you complete them in a timely and professional manner.
7. Accept criticism as a form of information that can make you a better employee. When constructively criticized, determine and take the actions that can correct the problem.
8. Never get stuck in one job. Always look to move forward. If you feel that you don't have a future at a certain company, keep your eyes open for other opportunities. Make sure you gain more and more skills and credibility as you progress.
9. Be a leader. Emphasize your willingness to help others. Gaining leadership status can be challenging, but it will definitely broaden your career in the long run.
10. Stay current on issues in your field. Keeping current enables you to assess the stability of your current job and to predict your next career move.
11. Good people are hard to find. No matter how cliché, it's true. If you excel, you will be in an elite group and in demand by employers.

Keep Your Network Alive

Ideally, this book will help you achieve your dream job. But remember that the average person changes jobs five to eight times in their career. Thus, after you've landed a job, it is important that you notify your network people of your new position and thank them for their assistance. Don't throw away those business cards you worked so hard to accumulate. After all, you never know when you may need to ask them for help again. You've spent months building up a network of professional contacts. Keep your network alive.

Make a "New Year's Resolution" to weigh all aspects of your job annually. Evaluate your current situation and the progress you are making (as measured by increased salary, responsibilities, and skills). Compare the result with what you want from your life's career. Even though you may be completely satisfied in your new job, remember that circumstances can change overnight, and you must always be prepared for the unexpected.

We hope you make good use of the job-search techniques outlined in this book. Perhaps the next time you talk to an unemployed person or someone seeking a new job, you will look at that person with new insight gained from your own job search and career successes. We hope you'll gladly share what you've learned from these pages about how to get a job.

Where Atlanta Works

This chapter contains the names, addresses, and contact numbers of some of Atlanta's top employers of white collar workers. The companies are arranged in categories according to the major products and services they manufacture or provide.

Most entries contain the name of the human resources director or other contact and, where needed, a brief description of the company's business. This listing is intended to help you survey the major potential employers in fields that may interest you. A word of caution: this list is *selective*, not exhaustive. We have not, for example, listed *all* the advertising agencies in the area, as you can find that information in the Yellow Pages. We have simply listed the top twenty-five or so, where the chances of employment are best.

The purpose of this chapter is to get you started, both looking and thinking. This is the kickoff, not the final gun. Browse through the whole chapter, and take some time to check out areas that are unfamiliar to you. Many white collar skills are transferable. People with marketing, management, data processing, accounting, administrative, and other talents are needed in a huge variety of businesses.

Ask yourself in what area your skills could be marketed. Use your imagination, especially if you're in a so-called specialized field. A dietitian, for instance, might look first under Health Care, or maybe Hospitality. But what about museums, banks, or the scores of other places that run their own dining rooms for employees or the public? What about food and consumer magazines? Who invents all those recipes and tests those products?

Much more detailed information on the area's top employers and other, smaller companies can be found in the directories and other resources suggested in Chapter 4. We can't stress strongly enough that you have to do your homework when you're looking for a job, both to unearth places that might need a person with your particular talents and to succeed in the interview once you've lined up a meeting with the hiring authority.

A word about hiring authorities: if you've read Chapter 7, you know that the name of the game is to meet the person with the power to hire you, or get as close to that person as you can. You don't want to go to the chairman or the personnel director if the person who actually makes the decision is the marketing manager or customer service director.

Obviously, we can't list every possible hiring authority in the Atlanta area's "Top 1,500." If we tried, you'd need a wagon to haul this book around. Besides, directories go out of date—even those that are regularly and conscientiously revised. So always *double-check* a contact whose name you get from a book or magazine, including this one. If necessary, call the company's switchboard to confirm who heads a particular department or division.

Here, then, are the Atlanta area's greatest opportunities. The area's top 1,500 employers are arranged in the following categories:

Accounting/Auditing

Advertising Agencies

Aerospace

Apparel/Textiles

Architectural and Design Firms

Automobile/Truck/Transportation Equipment

Banking

Book Publishers

Broadcasting and Television

Chemicals

Computers: Hardware/Software

Computers: Information Management/Consulting

Construction

Cultural Institutions

Drugs and Cosmetics

Educational Institutions

Electronics/Telecommunications

Engineering

Environmental Services

Film, Video, and Related Fields

Food/Beverage Producers and Distributors

Foundations/Philanthropies

Government

Health Care

Hospitality: Hotels and Restaurants
Human Services
Insurance
Law Firms
Management Consultants
Market Research Firms
Media, Print
Museums/Art Galleries
Oil/Gas/Plastics
Paper and Allied Products
Printing
Public Relations
Real Estate
Retailers/Wholesalers
Sports and Recreation
Stock Brokers/Financial Services
Travel/Shipping/Transportation
Utilities

Accounting/Auditing

WEB SITES:

http://www.kentis.com/index.html/
is the accounting professionals resource
center; links to homepages of CPAs.

http://www.unf.edu/students/jmayer/
arl.html
links to resources for accountants and
auditors.

PROFESSIONAL ORGANIZATIONS:

For networking in accounting and related
fields, check out these local professional
organizations listed in Chapter 5. Also see
"Banks" and **"Stock Brokers/Financial
Services."**
**American Institute of CPAs/Georgia
Society of CPAs**

For additional information, you can
contact:

American Institute of CPAs
1211 Ave. of the Americas
New York, NY 10036
(212) 575-6200

American Society of Women Accounts
35 E. Wacker Dr.
Chicago, IL 60601
(312) 726-9030

CPA Associates
201 Route 17 North, 4th Floor
Rutherford, NJ 07070-2574
(201) 804-8686

Institute of Management Accountants
10 Paragon Dr.
Montvale, NJ 07645
(201) 573-9000

**National Association of Black
Accountants**
7249A Hanover Parkway
Greenbelt, MD 20770
(301) 474-6222

National Society of Public Accountants
1010 N. Fairfax St.
Alexandria, VA 22314
(703) 549-6400

PROFESSIONAL PUBLICATIONS:

Accounting Review
Cash Flow
The CPA Journal
D & B Reports
Journal of Accountancy
Management Accounting
National Public Accountant
The Practical Accountant
The Woman CPA

DIRECTORIES:

Accounts Directory (American Directories,
Inc., Omaha, NE)
Accounting Firms and Practitioners
(American Institute of Certified Public
Accountants, New York, NY)
Career Opportunities Handbook (New York
State Public Accounting Firms, New
York, NY)
*Emerson's Directory of Leading U. S.
Accounting Firms* (Emerson's, Seattle, WA)
*National Directory of Certified Public
Accountants* (Peter Norback Publishing
Co., Princeton, NJ)
Who Audits America (Data Financial Press,
Menlo Park, CA)

Employers:

Andersen, Arthur, & Co.
133 Peachtree St., N.E., Suite 2600
Atlanta, GA 30303
(404) 658-1776
Contact: Ms. Smith, Recruiting
Department

Anderson, Hunt & Co.
1950 N. Park Place, Suite 600
Atlanta, GA 30339
(404) 952-6557
Contact: Anita Pittman, Tax Manager

BDO Seidman
285 Peachtree Center Ave., Suite 800
Atlanta, GA 30303
(404) 688-6841
Contact: Garry Weir, Office Manager

Babush, Neiman, Kornman & Johnson
3525 Piedmont Rd., Bldg. 8, Suite 500
Atlanta, GA 30305
(404) 266-1900
Contact: Bill Johnson, Managing Partner

Bennett Thrasher & Co.
115 Perimeter Center Place S., Suite 100
Atlanta, GA 30346
(770) 396-2200

Birnbrey Minsk & Minsk
1801 Peachtree St., Suite 300
Atlanta, GA 30309
(404) 355-3870

Coopers & Lybrand
1155 Peachtree St., N.E.
1100 Campanile Bldg.
Atlanta, GA 30309
(404) 870-1100
Contact: James Klee, Director of
Personnel

DeLoach, Stewart & Co.
780 Johnson Ferry Rd., Suite 325
Atlanta, GA 30342
(770) 256-1606
Contact: Elton Spann

Deloitte & Touche
100 Peachtree St., Suite 1700
Atlanta, GA 30303
(404) 220-1500
Contact for general accounting positions:
Andrea Josey,
Assistant in Human Resources

Ernst & Young
600 Peachtree St., N.E., Suite 2800
Atlanta, GA 30308
(404) 874-8300
Contact: Ms. Terry Curtis

Evans, Porter, Bryan & Co.
235 Peachtree St., N.E.
1800 Gas Light Tower
Atlanta, GA 30303
(404) 586-0133

Frazier & Deeter
1100 Harris Tower
233 Peachtree St., N.E.
Atlanta, GA 30303-1507
(404) 659-2213

Gifford, Hillegass & Ingwersen
233 Peachtree St., Suite 815
Atlanta, GA 30303
(404) 586-0036
Contact: Keven Lucier

Grant Thornton
235 Peachtree St., N.E., Suite 2300
Atlanta, GA 30303-1499
(404) 330-2000
Contact: Ronald C. Baum, Managing
Partner

Gross, Collins & Cress
2625 Cumberland Parkway, Suite 400
Atlanta, GA 30339
(770) 433-1711
Contact: Office Personnel

Habif, Arogeti & Wynne
1073 W. Peachtree St., N.E.
Atlanta, GA 30309
(404) 892-9651
Contact: Marc Kanne, Recruiter

Hyatt, Imler, Ott & Blount
100 Ashford Center North, Suite 200
Atlanta, GA 30338
(770) 394-8800
Contact for general accounting positions:
John Hyatt,
Managing Partner

Jones & Kolb
10 Piedmont Center, Suite 100
Atlanta, GA 30305
(404) 262-7920
Contact: Office Manager

KPMG Peat Marwick
303 Peachtree St., N.E., Suite 200
Atlanta, GA 30308
(404) 222-3000
Contact: Chris Beall, Personnel Director

Mauldin & Jenkins
1640 Powers Ferry Rd., Bldg. 26
Marietta, GA 30067
(770) 955-8600
Send resumes to:
2303 Dawson Rd.
Albany, GA 31707
June Paschal

Metcalf, Rice, Fricke & Davis
950 E. Paces Ferry Rd., Suite 2425
Atlanta, GA 30326
(404) 264-1700
Contact: Office Manager

Price Waterhouse
50 Hurt Plaza, Suite 1700
Atlanta, GA 30303
(404) 658-1800
Contact: Jim Hartsook, Human Resources
Director

Reznick Fedder & Silverman
871 Buford Rd.
Cumming, GA 30131
(770) 844-0644

Smith & Howard
1795 Peachtree St., Suite 300
Atlanta, GA 30309
(404) 874-6244
Contact: James C. Howard, Partner

Smith & Radigan
750 Hammond Dr., Bldg. 2
Atlanta, GA 30328
(404) 255-1300
Contact: Tim Radigan

Tauber & Balser
3340 Peachtree Rd., N.E., Suite 250
Atlanta, GA 30326
(404) 261-7200

Tiller Stewart & Co.
780 Johnson Ferry Rd., Suite 325
Atlanta, GA 30342
(404) 256-1606

Williams Benator & Libby
1040 Crown Pointe Parkway, Suite 400
Atlanta, GA 30338
(770) 512-0500

Windham Brannon
1355 Peachtree St., N.E., Suite 200
Atlanta, GA 30309
(404) 898-2000
Contact: Director of Personnel

Accounting firms big and small

We talked with Richard Craig, a Certified Public Accountant, now a Senior Vice President in finance at a leading data processing firm. We asked how he began his career in accounting and about the advantages and disadvantages associated with the size of the firm you work for.

Said Craig, "I started at Touche Ross (now Deloitte & Touche), one of the big eight (now the big six) accounting firms. Usually, working for a larger firm means learning a specific task. Staffs are larger, so each job is more specialized. You don't usually handle as many components of a job as you would in a smaller firm. You sometimes have more opportunity for hands-on experience in a smaller firm and gain more general management experience," Craig advised.

"But regardless of the size of the firm where you begin your career, if you wish to advance you should remain flexible through the first five years. If your job is not what you expected, be willing to make a change.

"Also, if you want a manager's position, you may have to move around to gain general managerial experience. Sometimes, that will mean a transfer to a department that would not necessarily be your first choice. But if the position rounds out your background, it is usually worth at least a temporary stay."

Advertising Agencies

WEB SITES:

http://www.commercepark.com/AAAA/AAAA.html
is the site of the American Association of Advertising Agencies.

http://www.adage.com/
is the site for *Ad Age Magazine*

PROFESSIONAL ORGANIZATIONS:

For networking in advertising and related fields, check out the following local professional organizations listed in Chapter 5. Also see **"Market Research"** and **"Public Relations."**
Ad2 Atlanta
American Marketing Association
Atlanta Advertising Club
Creative Club of Atlanta
Public Relations Society of America—
  Georgia Chapter
Society for Marketing Professional
  Services

For additional information, you can contact:

American Advertising Federation
1400 K St. N.W., Suite 1000
Washington, DC 20005
(800) 999-2331

American Association of Advertising Agencies
666 Third Ave.
New York, NY 10017
(212) 682-2500

American Marketing Association
250 S. Wacker Dr.
Chicago, Ill 60606
(312) 648-0536

Direct marketing Association
11 W. 42nd St.
New York, NY 10036
(212) 768-7277

Marketing Research Association
2189 Silas Deane Hwy., #5
Rocky Hill, CT 06067
(203) 257-4008

Public Relations Society of America
33 Irving Place, 3rd Floor
New York, NY 10003
(212) 995-2230

Women Executives in Public Relations
P.O. Box 609
Westport, CT 06881
(203) 226-4947

PROFESSIONAL PUBLICATIONS:

Advertising Age
Adweek
Brandweek
Direct Marketing Magazine
Journal of Advertising Research
Madison Ave.
Marketing News
Potentials in Marketing

DIRECTORIES:

Adweek Agency Directory, Southeast
edition (A/S/M Communications, New
York, NY)
*Bradford's Directory of Marketing Research
Agencies* (Bradford Publishing Co.,
Fairfax, VA)
*International Advertising Association
Membership Directory* (IAA, New York,
NY)
*International Membership Directory &
Market Research Guide* (American
Marketing Association, Chicago, IL)
Membership Roster (American Marketing
Association, Chicago, IL)
*O'Dwyer's Directory of Corporate Commu-
nications and O'Dwyer's Directory of
Public Relations Firms* (J.R. O'Dwyer
Company, New York, NY)
Public Relations Journal, Directory issue
(Public Relations Society of America,
New York, NY)
Standard Directory of Advertisers (National
Register Publishing Co., New Provi-
dence, NJ)
Standard Directory of Advertising Agencies
(National Register Publishing Co., New
Providence, NJ)

For those interested in the advertising
field, the industry's *Red Book,* or *Standard
Directory of Advertising Agencies,* is useful
in finding a specific contact in your area
of interest. For example, an artist would
contact the agency's Art Director or
Creative Director. The directory is
available at most libraries.

Employers (if engaged in other
activities as well as advertising, it is so
noted):

Aberdeen Marketing
2030 Powers Ferry Rd., Suite 120
Atlanta, GA 30339
(770) 644-1850

Ad Shop, The
2000 Powers Ferry Rd., Suite2-2
Marietta, GA 30067
(770) 956-7779
Contact: Neal Reynolds, President

Ad Works, The
7000 Central Park Way, N.E.
Atlanta, GA 30328
(770) 399-0844
Contact: Martin Hufham, President

Adair Greene Advertising
200 Atltanta Technology Center
1575 Northside Dr., N.W.
Atlanta, GA 30318
(404) 351-8424
Contact: Warren Greene, President

Adovation
3103 E. Shadowlawn Ave., N.E.
Atlanta, GA 30305
(404) 365-9993

Alexander Communications
2970 Clairmont Rd.
Atlanta, GA 30329
(404) 325-7555
Contact: Sandra Moreland, Vice-President

Anderson Communications
2245 Godby Rd.
Atlanta, GA 30349
(770) 766-8000
Contact: Al Anderson, President

Atlanta Market Research Center
10 Lenox Point, N.E.
Atlanta, GA 30324
(404) 239-0001
Contact: Renea Williams, Market Research

Austin Kelley Public Relations
5901 Peachtree-Dunwoody Rd.,
Suite 200 C
Atlanta, GA 30328
(770) 396-6666
Contact: Maria Beasley, Admin. Director

Aydlotte & Cartwright
6 Concourse Parkway, N.E., Suite 2800
Atlanta, GA 30328
(770) 551-5000
Contact: Account Services: Lynn Gregory;
Creative: Steve Pharr

Bates Associates
161 Spring St., Suite 716
Atlanta, GA 30303
(404) 588-1707
Contact: Elizabeth Bates, President
Public relations

BBDO South
3414 Peachtree Rd., Suite 1600
Atlanta, GA 30326
(404) 231-1700
Contact: Debbie Powell, Director of
Human Resources

Bennett Kuhn Varner
3565 Piedmont Rd., Bldg. 3, Suite 300
Atlanta, GA 30305
(404) 233-0332

Bigelow & Eigel
2880 Dresden Dr.
Atlanta, GA 30341
(770) 216-2160

Bressler & Yauger
3400 Peachtree Rd., Suite 811
Atlanta, GA 30326
(404) 848-9990

Broadus & Associates
3400 Peachtree Rd., N.E., Suite 1100
Atlanta, GA 30326
(404) 237-1503

Brown-Olmstead, A., Associates
127 Peachtree St., Suite 200
The Candler Building
Atlanta, GA 30303

(404) 659-0919
Contact: Katrina Leavelle, Office Manager
Public relations

Campaign Inc.
659 Mimosa Blvd.
Roswell, GA 30075
(770) 640-8806

Carroll/White Advertising
4170 Ashford-Dunwoody Rd., Suite 570
Atlanta, GA 30319
(404) 843-1293

Cascino & Purcell
3333 Peachtree Rd.
1220 East Tower
Atlanta, GA 30326
(404) 237-9945
Contact: John Freebairn, President

Clarion Marketing and Communications
5 Concourse Parkway, Suite 560
Atlanta, GA 30328
(770) 395-3877

Cleveland Clark Inc.
230 Peachtree St., N.W., Suite 1700
Atlanta, GA 30303
(404) 221-0700

Cohn & Wolfe
225 Peachtree St., N.E., Suite 2300
Atlanta, GA 30303
(404) 688-5900
Contact: Pat Cardin, Operating Manager
Public relations

Cole Henderson Drake
400 Colony Square, Suite 500
Atlanta, GA 30361
(404) 892-4500
Contact: Katharynee Beverly, Office
Manager

Cowan & Joseph
400 Perimeter Center Terrace, Suite 160
Atlanta, GA 30346
(770) 395-9255

Creative Services/CSI Advertising
3925 Peachtree Rd., N.E., Suite 200
Atlanta, GA 30319
(404) 262-7424
Contact: Tom Wood, President

Crescent Communications
1200 Ashwood Parkway, Suite 400
Atlanta, GA 30338
(770) 698-8650

Criterion Group, The
12 Piedmont Center, Suite 100
Atlanta, GA 30305
(404) 237-8618
Contact: Cheryl McGregor, Vice-President

Crumbley & Associates
600 W. Peachtree St., N.W., Suite 2300
Atlanta, GA 30308
(404) 892-2300
Contact: Cheryl Lee
Advertising and public relations

Darden Research Corp.
1534 N. Decatur Rd., N.E.
Atlanta, GA 30307
(404) 377-9294
Contact: Claibourne Darden, President
Market research

Davis, Julie, Associates
1 Buckhead Plaza, Suite 520
Atlanta, GA 30305
(404) 231-0660
Contact: Julie Davis
Public relations

Donino & Partners
7000 Central Parkway, Suite 1350
Atlanta, GA 30328
(770) 668-9700

Duffey Communications
11 Piedmont Center, Suite 160
Atlanta, GA 30303
(404) 266-2600
Contact: Jenny Duffey, Principal

Echo Media
2401 Lake Park Dr., Suite 180
Smyrna, GA 30346
(770) 435-4042

Fahlgren Martin
3060 Peachtree Rd., N.W., Suite 730
Atlanta, GA 30305
(404) 364-9999
Contact: Account Services: John Thomas

Fitzgerald & Co.
1 Buckhead Plaza
3060 Peachtree Rd., N.W., Suite 500
Atlanta, GA 30305
(404) 262-8900

Fleishman-Hilliard/Atlanta
233 Peachtree St., Suite 1250
Atlanta, GA 30303
(404) 659-4446
Contact: Randy Siegel, General Manager
and Partner
Public relations

Folio Z Inc.
1201 Peachtree St., N.E., Suite 1550
Atlanta, GA 30361
(404) 881-8765

Freebain & Co.
3343 Peachtree Rd., Suite 1220
Atlanta, GA 30326
(404) 237-9945

Fricks Advertising
6 Concourse Parkway, Suite 3300
Atlanta, GA 30328
(770) 396-6206

Gordon Bailey & Associates
11445 Johns Creek Parkway
Duluth, GA 30155
(770) 232-1711
Contact: Jeri Christopher, V.P. Human
Resources

Gray Matter Marketing
3 Piedmont Center
3405 Piedmont Rd., Suite 550
Atlanta, GA 30305
(404) 266-9258
Contact: Daniel Dodson, Jr.

Headline Group, The
3490 Piedmont Rd., Suite 1504
Atlanta, GA 30305

(404) 262-3000
Contact: Claudia Gaines, President
Public relations

Henderson Agency
3353 Peachtree Rd., Suite 220
Atlanta, GA 30326
(770) 240-4060
Contact: Kerry Graham

Hill & Knowlton
1100 Peachtree St., Suite 2150
Atlanta, GA 30309
(404) 249-8550
Contact: Judy Hamby

Hobson & Associates
5015 Lake Fjord Pass, N.E.
Marietta, GA 30068
(770) 992-9606
Contact: Tony Hobson, President

Hughes Advertising
3333 Peachtree Rd.
Atlanta, GA 30326
(404) 364-2333

Interservice, Erlick & Lavidge
1990 Lakeside Parkway, 3rd Floor
Tucker, GA 30084
(770) 938-3233
Contact: Tom Moseley, Human Resources

Ketchum Public Relations
999 Peachtree St., N.E., Suite 1400
Atlanta, GA 30309
(404) 873-1711
Contact: Jane Shivers, Executive Vice-
President and Director

Kilgannon Group, The
1708 Peachtree St., Suite 303
Atlanta, GA 30309
(404) 876-2800

Kleber & Associates
555 Sun Valley Dr., Suite N-2
Roswell, GA 30076
(770) 518-1000
Contact: Steven L. Kleber

Knapp Inc.
50 Hurt Plaza, Suite 1030
Atlanta, GA 30303
(404) 688-1777
Contact: Kathy Wiggins, Account
Supervisor
Public relations

Madison, T.G.
3340 Peachtree Rd., N.E., Suite 2850
Atlanta, GA 30326
(404) 262-2623

Manning Selvage & Lee/Atlanta
1201 W. Peachtree St., Suite 4800
Atlanta, GA 30309
(404) 875-1444
Contact: Ann Lewin, Managing Director
Public relations

M/A/R/C
5600 Glenridge Dr., N.E., Suite 470
Atlanta, GA 30342
(770) 256-2187
Contact: Nancy Maunder, Office Manager
Consumer research

Marketing Resources
3050 Presidential Dr., Suite 111
Atlanta, GA 30340
(770) 457-6105
Contact: Jan Philman, Account Services

Marketing Specifics
638 Church St., N.E.
Marietta, GA 30060
(770) 426-1107
Contact: Kyle Young, Principal

Marketing Workshop
3725 Da Vinci Court, Suite 200
Norcross, GA 30092
(770) 449-6767
Contact: Dot Lelems, Comptroller

Matlock & Associates
1360 Peachtree St., Suite 220
Atlanta, GA 30309
(404) 872-3200
Contact: George Mattlock, Office
Manager
Public relations

McCann Erickson
615 Peachtree St., N.E.
Atlanta, GA 30365
(404) 873-2321
Contact: Theresa Williams, Human Resources

Mid-American Research
3393 Peachtree Rd., N.E.
Atlanta, GA 30326
(404) 261-8011
4800 Briarcliff Rd. N.E.
Atlanta, GA 30345
(404) 493-1403
Market research

Moore & Symons
3405 Piedmont Rd., N.E., Suite 250
Atlanta, GA 30305
(404) 266-8396
Contact: Mary Anne DeStefano, Office Manager
Market research

Morrison Agency, The
950 E. Paces Ferry Rd.
Atlanta, GA 30326
(404) 233-3405

Ogilvy & Mather
75 14th St., Suite 3000
Atlanta, GA 30309
(404) 888-5100
Contact: Susan Mitchell Sr. V.P., General manager

Parver, Michael, Associates
1800 Peachtree St., Suite 333
Atlanta, GA 30309
(404) 355-5580
Contact: Michael Parver, President

Pollak Levitt Chaiet Advertising
1 Piedmont Center, Suite 505
Atlanta, GA 30305
(404) 261-1566

Pringle Dixon Pringle
303 Peachtree St., N.E., Suite 3150
Atlanta, GA 30308
(404) 688-6720

Contact: Quinn Hudson, Senior Vice-President and Manager
Public relations

Puckett Group, The
2970 Clarimont Rd., Suite 130
Atlanta, GA 30329
(404) 248-1500

Quinn, W.T.
3475 Lenox Rd., Suite 750
Atlanta, GA 30326
(404) 816-0094

Rich/Gardner Advertising
211 Perimeter Center Parkway, Suite 760
Atlanta, GA 30346
(770) 392-0340

Sawyer, Riley, Compton
1100 Abernathy Rd., Suite 800
Atlanta, GA 30328
(770) 393-9849
Contact: Frank Compton, CEO
Advertising, public relations

Smith, Larry, & Associates
3300 Northeast Expressway, Bldg.4, Suite 400
Atlanta, GA 30341
(770) 458-0808

Sullivan Haas Coyle
3350 Peachtree Rd., Suite 950
Atlanta, GA 30326
(404) 231-1661
Contact: Creative: Jerry Sullivan
Contact: Account Services: Bob Coyle
Advertising, public relations

Target Market Team
3350 Peachtree Rd., N.E., Suite 1700
Atlanta, GA 30326
(404) 848-2700
Contact: Ron Bell, President

Tausche Martin Lonsdorf
18 International Blvd.
Atlanta, GA 30303
(404) 221-1188
Contact: Creative: Kurt Tausche, Art Director
Contact: Account Services: Margaret Ann Martin

Thompson, J. Walter, USA/Atlanta
950 E. Paces Ferry Rd.
Atlanta, GA 30326
(404) 365-7300
Contact: Tami Kageorge, Personnel
Director

360
3350 Peachtree Rd., Suite 1550
Atlanta, GA 30326
(404) 261-2360

Tucker Wayne/Luckie & Co.
1100 Peachtree St., N.E., Suite 1800
Atlanta, GA 30343
(404) 347-8700
Contact: Creative: Roy Trimble, Creative
Director
Contact: Account Services: Sid Smith,
President, Advertising

Van Winkle & Associates
1819 Peachtree St., Suite 575
Atlanta, GA 30309
(404) 355-0126

Wemmers Communications
6100 Lake Forrest Dr., Suite 330
Atlanta, GA 30328
(404) 531-0077
Contact: Richard Wemmers, President

WestWayne Inc.
1100 Peachtree St., N.W., Suite 1800
Atlanta, GA 30309
(404) 347-8700

WHM&G Advertising
3340 Peachtree St., N.E., Suite 2250
Atlanta, GA 30326
(404) 814-1410

Wilson, Mike, Public Relations
3400 Peachtree Rd., Suite 1239
Atlanta, GA 30326
(404) 365-9000
Contact: Sheri Mason, President

Aerospace

WEB SITES:

http://www.well.com/user/css/ ALA.HTML
is the homepage of the American Aerospace Industries Association.

http://www.galcit.caltech.edu/~aure/ htmls/aerolinks.html
links to aeronautics resources.

http://brad.net/aero_outlook/
discusses industry trends; links to associations, journals, and government agencies.

PROFESSIONAL ORGANIZATIONS:

For information about aerospace and related fields, you can contact:

Aerospace Education Foundation
1501 Lee Hwy.
Arlington, VA 22209
(703) 247-5839

Aerospace Industries Association of America
1250 I St., N.W.
Washington, DC 20005
(202) 371-8400

Int'l. Association of Machinists & Aerospace Workers
9000 Machinists Place
Upper Marlboro, MD 20772
(301) 967-4500

Society of Senior Aerospace Executives
1100 15th St., N.W., Suite. 300
Washington, DC 20005
(202) 289-0500

Women in Aerospace
922 Pennsylvania Ave., S.E.
Washington, DC 20003
(202) 547-9451

PROFESSIONAL PUBLICATIONS:

Aerospace Daily
Aerospace Engineering
Air Jobs Digest
Aviation Week and Space Technology
Business and Commercial Aviation
Space Commerce Week

DIRECTORIES:

Aviation Week & Space Technology, Marketing Directory issue (McGraw-Hill Publishing Co., New York, NY)
Corporate Technology Directory (Corporate Technology Information Services, Inc., Wellesley, MA)
International ABC Aerospace Directory (Jane's Information Group, Alexandria, VA)
World Aviation Directory & Buyers Guide (McGraw-Hill Publishing Co., New York, NY)

Employers:

Air BP Atlanta
1 Corsair Dr.
Atlanta, GA 30341
(770) 452-0010
Contact: Earl Davis, General Manager
Aircraft broker

Atlanta Propeller Services
4787 Clark Howell Hwy.
College Park, GA 30049
(770) 761-7220
Contact: Sam Parker

Av Fuel Systems Co.
300 Cash Memorial Blvd.
Forest Park, GA 30050
(770) 366-3965
Contact: Ron Semiken General Manager
Aviation fueling equipment

Aviation Atlanta
1950 Airport Rd.
Chamblee, GA 30341
(770) 458-8034
Contact: Ron Sanders, Manager
Training

Colvin Aviation
1080 Ben Epps Dr.
Athens, GA 30605
(706) 458-5100
Contact: Tally Colvin
Charters

Epps Air Service
1 Aviation Way
Atlanta, GA 30341
(770) 458-9851
Contact; Clint Rogers, Flight School
Charters, air ambulance, sales, service,
training, rebuilding

Fokker Aircraft USA
5169 Southridge Parkway
College Park, GA 30349
(770) 991-4600
Contact: Gary Andrews

Global Jet
3 E. Broad St.
Newnan, GA 30263
(770) 254-8326
Contact: John Bone

Graham Airport Engine Service
129 Bethea Rd., Suite 404
Fayetteville, GA 30214
(770) 461-4641
Contact: Randy Graham, Office Manager

Gresham Associates
1 Gresham Landing
Stockbridge, GA 30281
(770) 389-1600
Contact: Michael Meehan, Owner
Charters

Helixpress
2001 Flightway Dr.
Chamblee, GA 30341
(770) 451-7386
Helicopter charter, flight instruction,
tours

Hill Aircraft and Leasing Corp.
3948 Aviation Circle, S.W.
Atlanta, GA 30336
(404) 691-3330
Contact: JoAnn Carter, Finance Manager
Sales, leasing, charters

International Jet Markets
624 Powers Ferry North
Marietta, GA 30067
(770) 971-5401
Contact: Bill Pilker
Aircraft broker

Lockheed Martin Aeronautical Systems
86 S. Cobb Dr., S.E.
Marietta, GA 30063
(770) 494-4411
Contact: Ron Von Matre, Employment
Supervisor
Aircraft manufacturers

McClain International
4785 Roosevelt Hwy.
College Park, GA 30349
(770) 964-3361
Contact: Paul Schwinne, V.P. of
Operations
Manufacturers of aircraft parts and
supplies

Mercury Air Center
DeKalb Peachtree Airport
1951 Airport Rd.
Atlanta, GA 30341
(770) 454-5000
Contact: John Enticknap, General
Manager

Northside Aviation
P.O. Box 490
Kennesaw, GA 30144
(770) 422-4300
Contact: Jennifer Annison, Office
Manager

Peachtree Dekalb Flight Academy
2060 Airport Rd.
Chamblee, GA 30341
(770) 457-8223
Contact: Paula Virshall, Manager

Pope, Mark C., Associates
P.O. Box 1517
Smyrna, GA 30081
(770) 435-2471
Contact: Scott O'Connell, Ground Power
Manager
Ground support and service equipment

Raytheon Aircraft Services
3992 Aviation Circle
Atlanta, GA 30336
(404) 699-9200
Contact: Cy Farmer, Location Manager

Apparel/Textiles

WEB SITES:

http://www.apparelex.com/
has links to over 26,000 apparel and textile
companies.

PROFESSIONAL ORGANIZATIONS:

For networking in the apparel and textile
industries and related fields, check out the
following local professional organizations
listed in Chapter 5:
**American Society of Interior
Designers—Georgia Chapter**
**Georgia Textile Manufacturers
Association**

For additional information, you may
contact:

**American Apparel Manufacturers
Association**
2500 Wilson Blvd., Suite 301
Arlington, VA 22201
(703) 524-1864

Association of Bridal Consultants
200 Chestnutland Rd.
New Milford, CT 06776
(203) 355-0464

Council of Fashion Designers of America
1412 Broadway
New York, NY 10016
(212) 302-1821

**International Association of Clothing
Designers**
475 Park Ave. S.
New York, NY 10016
(212) 685-6602

Sportswear Apparel Association
450 Seventh Ave.
New York, NY 10123
(212) 564-6161

Textile Distributors Association
45 W. 36th St.
New York, NY 10018
(212) 563-0400

Textile Research Institute
P.O. Box 625
Princeton, NJ 08540
(609) 924- 3150

United Textile Workers of America
P.O. Box 749
Voorhees, NJ 08043
(609) 772-9699

PROFESSIONAL PUBLICATIONS:

Apparel Industry Magazine
Fashion Newsletter
Textile Hi-Lights
Textile Research Journal
Textile World
Women's Wear Daily

DIRECTORIES:

Apparel Industry Sourcebook (Denyse &
Co., Inc., North Hollywood, CA)
Apparel Trades Book (Dun & Bradstreet,
Inc., New York, NY)
Davison's Textile Blue Book (Davison
Publishing Co., Ridgewood, NJ)
*Fairchild's Textile & Apparel Financial
Directory* (Fairchild Publications, New
York, NY)

Garment Manufacturer's Index (Klevens Publications, Littlerock, CA)
Membership Directory (American Apparel Manufacturers Association Arlington, VA)

Wholesale/Manufacturers Apparel Directory (American Business Lists, Omaha, NE)

Contracting for a career in fashion

We asked Gary Randazzo, president of a mid-sized contractor of women's apparel, to explain the lines of distribution in the apparel, or garment, industry. "Contractors are the first step in a long and often confusing line of distribution for a garment," says Randazzo. "Contractors put the goods together for manufacturers who do not have their own shops. This is what is known as piece work, assembling garments that have been cut and need only to be sewn together. Some contractors do the actual cutting of the material and construct the garment from the pattern to finished product. The public is generally not aware that contractors even exist, but they are a very important part of the chain.

"Once a garment has been finished, it is usually sent back to the manufacturer for sale to a wholesaler. It is then sold to the retail market. In some instances, large apparel companies can be considered wholesalers and manufacturers. They may also operate retail arms."

We asked if working for a contractor can help round out your experience in the garment industry. "Absolutely. After working for even a small contractor you can move to quality control, product management, and even inventory control for manufacturers or wholesalers. Also, you learn the business from the ground up: working on the shop floor examining dresses, dealing with employees, making contacts with wholesalers and manufacturers. That experience is invaluable in any part of the industry."

Employers:

Action Testing & Consulting Laboratory
1800 Montreal Court
Tucker, GA 30345
(770) 270-9550
Textile consultants

Bridan Industries
6666 Powers Ferry Rd., N.W.
Atlanta, GA 30339
(770) 755-0820
Contact: Personnel
Men's clothing

Dan River
4 Executive Park Dr., Suite 1210
Atlanta, GA 30329
(404) 325-7242
Contact: Lynn Rossman
Textile sales

Guess Jeans
250 Spring St.
Atlanta Apparel Mart
Atlanta, GA 30303
(404) 525-1660
Contact: Lori Pennington, Southeastern
Sales Representative
Women's jeans

Hunt Chemicals
530 Permalume Place, N.W.
Atlanta, GA 30318
(770) 352-1418

J.T.M.
1000 Cobb Place Blvd., N.W.
Kennesaw, GA 30144
(770) 424-1900
Contact: Dave Boyenga
Textile mill supplies

Monsanto Chemical Company
320 Interstate North Parkway, Suite 500
Atlanta, GA 30339
(770) 951-7600
Contact: Louise Harris, Office Manager
Textiles

Oxford Industries
222 Piedmont Ave., N.E.
Atlanta, GA 30308
(404) 659-2424
Contact: Susan Price, Personnel Manager
Men's clothing

Pendleton, Kate
75 Bennett St., N.W.
Atlanta, GA 30309
(404) 350-0737
Textile designer

Playtex Apparel
320 Temple Ave.
Newnan, GA 30264
(404) 253-2121
Underwear

Southeast Sportswear
2910 N. Druide, Suite H
Atlanta, GA 30329
(404) 325-9136
Contact: Dick Padgham

Spring Industries
1301 Hightower Trail, Suite 105
Atlanta, GA 30350
(770) 642-0257
Contact: Rob Rowan, Manager
Springmaid and Wamsutta fabrics

T.C. Marketing
250 Spring St.
Atlanta, GA 30303
(404) 523-0319
Contact: Tom Carroll, Owner
Showroom for men's career apparel

Architectural and Design Firms

WEB SITES:

http://arch.buffalo.edu:8001/internet/ h_firms.html
links to firms and services.

http://archpropplan.auckland.ac.nz/ misc/sources3.html
links to architectural organizations and newsgroups.

http://199.170.0.130/carprof.htm
discusses careers in architecture.

PROFESSIONAL ORGANIZATIONS:

For networking in architecture and related fields, check out the following local professional organizations listed in Chapter 5. Also see **"Construction"** and **"Engineering."**
American Institute of Architects— Atlanta Chapter
American Society of Interior Designers—Georgia Chapter
American Society of Landscape Architects

For additional information, you can contact:

American Institute of Architects
1735 New York Ave. N.W.
Washington, DC 20006
(202) 626-7300

Society of American Registered Architects
1245 S. Highland Ave.
Lombard, IL 60148
(630) 932-4622

PROFESSIONAL PUBLICATIONS:

AIA Journal
Architectural Forum
Architectural Record
Architectural Review
Architecture
Building Design and Construction
Practicing Architect
Progressive Architecture

DIRECTORIES:

AIA Membership Directory (American Institute of Architects, New York, NY)
Architects Directory (American Business Directories, Inc., Omaha, NE)
International Directory of Architects and Architecture (St. James Press, Detroit, MI)
Penguin Directory of Architecture (Viking Penguin, New York, NY)
Society of American Registered Architects National Membership Directory (Society of American Registered Architects, Lombard, IL)

Employers:

Associated Space Design
50 Hurt Plaza, Suite 500
Atlanta, GA 30303
(404) 688-3318
Interior design

Brown, R. L., & Associates
101 W. Ponce de Leon, Suite 670
Decatur, GA 30030
(404) 377-2460
Contact: Barbara Brown

CDH Partners
675 Tower Rd., Suite 200
Marietta, GA 30060
(770) 423-0016

Chapman Coyle Chapman & Associates
1225 Johnson Ferry Rd., Suite 800
Marietta, GA 30068
(770) 973-6644
Contact: Jim Chapman

Cooper Carry & Associates
3520 Piedmont Rd., Suite 200
Atlanta, GA 30305
(404) 237-2000

Culpepper, McAuliffe & Meadows
400 Colony Square, Suite 900
Atlanta, GA 30361
(404) 872-3900

Daly, Leo A., Co.
1201 Peachtree St., N.E., Suite 1730

Atlanta, GA 30361
(404) 874-8333

Diedrich & Associates Architects
3399 Peachtree Rd., N.E., Suite 820
Atlanta, GA 30326
(404) 364-9633
Contact: John Hester, Vice-President

Eason-Earle
4903 Riverdale Rd., Suite 100
Atlanta, GA 30337
(770) 991-3321
Contact: Bill Alexander

Godwin & Associates
7000 Central Parkway, Suite 1020
Atlanta, GA 30328
(770) 804-1280
Contact: Ms. Robin Godwin, Vice-President

Greenberg Farrow Architecture
1755 The Exchange
Atlanta, GA 30339
(770) 303-1033

Heery International
999 Peachtree St., N.E.
Atlanta, GA 30309
(404) 881-9880
Contact: Joyce Hameen, Recruiter
Interior design, management and planning

Hendrick Associates
5 Piedmont Center, Suite 300
Atlanta, GA 30305
(404) 261-9383
Interior design and planning of corporate office and health care facilities

Hirsch/Bedner Associates
909 W. Peachtree St.
Atlanta, GA 30309
(404) 873-4379
Hotel and restaurant interior design

Howell Rusk Dodson Architects
3355 Lenox Rd., N.E., Suite 1190
Atlanta, GA 30326
(404) 266-9631

Jova/Daniels/Busby
1389 Peachtree St., N.E.
Atlanta, GA 30309-3035

Contact: Joseph League, Principal
Interior design and renovation of corporate, financial, and health care facilities

Lord Aeck & Sargent
1201 Peachtree St., Suite 300
Atlanta, GA 30361
(404) 872-0330
Interior design of institutional, university, corporate, and health care facilities

MSTSD Inc.
1401 Peachtree St., N.E., Suite 460
Atlanta, GA 30303
(404) 876-6040

Muldawer Moultrie/Architects & Urban Designers
3904 Randall Rich Rd., N.W., Suite 415
Atlanta, GA 30305
(404) 239-0914
Contact: Paul Muldawer

Nichols Carter Grant Architects
1 Baltimore Place, Suite 401
Atlanta, GA 30308
(404) 892-4510

Niles Bolton & Associates
1 Buckhead Plaza
3060 Peachtree Rd., N.W., Suite 600
Atlanta, GA 30305
(404) 365-7600
Contact: Ray Kimsey, V.P.

Nix Mann & Associates
1382 Peachtree St., N.E.
Atlanta, GA 30309
(404) 873-2300
Contact: Manuel Cedrecha, Partner

O'Neal Inc.
3525 Piedmont Rd., Suite 610
Atlanta, GA 30305
(404) 237-4725

Pieper, O'Brien, Herr, Architects Ltd.
2 Ravinia Dr., Suite 1700
Atlanta, GA 30346
(770) 512-6622
Contact: David Holt, Associate

Portman, John, & Associates
303 Peachtree St., N.E., Suite 4600
Atlanta, GA 30308

(404) 614-5555
Contact: David Holt, Principal

Quantrell Mullins & Associates
999 Peachtree St., Suite 1710
Atlanta, GA 30309
(404) 874-6048
Contact: Henry Mullins, Principal
Interior design of corporate headquarters,
financial, manufacturing, and health care
facilities

Robert & Company
96 Poplar St., N.W.
Atlanta, GA 30335
(404) 577-4000
Contact: Joanne Phippes, Director of
Human Resources

Robertson Loia Roof
5780 Peachtree-Dunwoody Rd., Suite 195
Atlanta, GA 30342
(404) 257-9790

Romm & Pearsall
1375 Peachtree St., N.E., Suite 680
Atlanta, GA 30309
(404) 874-9171
Contact: Stuart Romm, Principal

Rosser International
524 W. Peachtree St., N.W.
Atlanta, GA 30308
(404) 876-3800
Contact: King Evans, Vice-President of
Human Resources

Ruys & Co.
3333 Peachtree Rd., Suite 200
Atlanta, GA 30326
(404) 231-3572
Interior architecture, corporate office
design, tenant development, and space
management services

Sizemore Floyd Architects
1700 Commerce Dr., N.W.
Atlanta, GA 30318
(404) 605-0690

**Smallwood, Reynolds, Stewart, Stewart
& Associates**
1 Piedmont Center
3565 Piedmont Rd., Suite 303

Atlanta, GA 30305
(404) 233-5453
Contact: Keller Smith, Associate
Interior design of corporate office,
hospitality, retail, and educational
facilities

Stang & Newdow
84 Peachtree St., Suite 500
Atlanta, GA 30303
(404) 584-0500

Stevens & Wilkinson Interiors
100 Peachtree St., N.W., Suite 2400
Atlanta, GA 30303
(404) 522-8888
Contact: Thomas O. Ramsey, Senior Vice-
President
Corporate office, health care, government,
and residential design

Stone & Webster Engineering Corp.
1000 Abernathy Rd., Bldg., 400, Suite 165
Atlanta, GA 30328
(770) 481-4100

Thompson Hancock Witte & Associates
4055 Roswell Rd., N.E.
Atlanta, GA 30342
(404) 252-8040

**Thompson, Ventulett, Stainback &
Associates**
1230 Peachtree St., N.E., Suite 2700
Atlanta, GA 30309-3591
(404) 888-6600
Contact: Raymond Stainback, Principal
Interior design of convention center,
corporate office, retail, and performing
arts facilities

**Wakefield Beasley & Associates
Architects**
5275 Triangle Parkway, Suite 200
Norcross, GA 30092
(770) 209-9393

**Warner Summers Ditzel Benefield Ward
& Assoc.**
67 Peachtree Park Dr., Suite 200
Atlanta, GA 30309
(404) 351-6075
Interior design of financial, corporate,
industrial, and institutional facilities

Automobile/Truck/Transportation Equipment

WEB SITES:

http://autocneter.com/cache/indes/
Directory/index.html
is a directory of automobile
manufacturers.

http://www.catalog.com/miata/
carinfo.html
contains links to automotive sites and
companies.

PROFESSIONAL ORGANIZATIONS:

For information on the automotive
industry, you may contact:

**American International Automobile
Dealers Association**
99 Canal Center Plaza, Suite 500
Alexandria, VA 22314
(703) 519-7800

American Trucking Association
2200 Mill Rd.
Alexandria, VA 22314
(703) 838-1700

**ASIA (Automotive Service Industry
Association)**
25 N.W. Point
Elk Grove Village, IL 60007
(847) 228-1310

National Automobile Dealers Association
8400 Westpark Dr.
McLean, VA 22102
(703) 827-7407

Society of Automotive Engineers
400 Commonwealth Dr.
Warrendale, PA 15096
(412) 776-4841

PROFESSIONAL PUBLICATIONS:

Automotive Executive
Automotive Industries Insider
Automotive News
Ward's Automotive Reports

DIRECTORIES:

ASIA Membership Directory (Automotive
Service Industry Assoc., Elk Grove
Village, IL)
Automotive Age, Buyers Guide issue
(Freed-Crown Publishing Co., Van Nuys,
CA)
Automotive News, Market Data Book issue
(Crain Communications, Detroit, MI)
Jobber Topics, Annual Marketing Directory
issue (Irving-Cloud Publishing Co.,
Chicago, IL)
Ward's Automotive Yearbook (Ward's
Communications, Detroit, MI)

Employers:

Ace Atlanta Warehouse
814 Pickens Industrial Dr.
Marietta, GA 30062
(770) 919-0880
Contact: Cheryl Andrews
Automobile electrical equipment

BMW of North America
1280 Hightower Trail
Atlanta, GA 30350
(404) 552-3800
Regional distributorship
Send resume to:
Mary Hayes, Recruiter
300 Chestnut Ridge Rd.
Woodcliff Lake, NJ 07675

Clanton, Billy, Racing
10177 Tara Blvd.
Jonesboro, GA 30236
(770) 471-0233
Contact: Billy Clanton
Distributors for drag racing equipment

Custom Camper Equipment
5151 Highway 54
Lake City, GA 30260
(770) 363-3811
Contact: Wayne Mitchell, President
Truck caps and shells

Davis, J. B., & Son
1059 Grant St., S.E.
Atlanta, GA 30315
(404) 622-6222
Contact: J.B. Davis, Jr., President
Custom-built truck bodies

Dixie Products
2080 Atlanta Rd., S.E.
Smyrna, GA 30080
(770) 432-0626
Contact: Ms. Bobbie Dowdy, Vice-President
Truck washing equipment

Dynatron Bondo Corp.
3700 Atlanta Industrial Parkway, N.W.
Atlanta, GA 30331-1098
(770) 696-2730
Contact: David Lubin, Marketing Director
Manufacturers of body shop supplies

Ford Motor Company
Atlanta Assembly Plant
340 Henry Ford II Ave.
Hapeville, GA 30354
(440) 577-2277
Contact: Tom Cain, Supervisor of Salaried Personnel
Automobile assembly

Fruehauf Truck Equipment
3368 Moreland Ave., S.E.
Conley, GA 30027
(770) 361-3511
Contact: Cherry Eskew, Comptroller

General Motors Doraville Assembly Plant
3900 Motors Industrial Way
Doraville, GA 30360
(770) 455-5101
Contact: Daryl Housewright, Supervisor for Salaried Personnel

Genuine Parts Company
2999 Circle 75 Parkway
Atlanta, GA 30339
(770) 953-1700
Contact: Bill Evans, Director of Human Resources Services
Headquarters

Genuine Parts Company—NAPA
5420 Peachtree Industrial Blvd.
Norcross, GA 30091
(770) 447-5892
Contact: Elaine Bowen, Personnel Manager
Distribution Center

Lift Parts Supply Co.
3955 Moreland Ave.
P.O. Box 835
Conley, GA 30327
(404) 363-2234
Contact; Amita Plumstead
Parts and supplies for industrial trucks

Maaco Auto Painting and Bodyworks
2752 E. Ponce de Leon Ave.
Decatur, GA 30030
(404) 373-1427
Contact: Wes Saunders, Owner
Branches throughout metro area

PPG Finishes
3475 Hamilton Blvd., S.W.
Atlanta, GA 30354
(404) 767-4210
Contact: Les Stanley
Automotive paint supplier

Pep Boys
2726-A Candler Rd.
Decatur, GA 30034
(404) 243-8805
Contact: Alan Sinclair, Southeast Regional Manager
Auto parts. Branches throughout metro area

Banking

WEB SITES:

http://www.wiso.gwdg.de/ifbg/
bank_usa.html
links to homepages of U.S. banks.

http://www.cybercash.com/
directory.html
is a directory of consumer banks.

http://www.bankrate.com/bankrate/
rates/xrefindx.htm
lists names of financial institutions with
Web sites.

PROFESSIONAL ORGANIZATIONS:

For networking in the bank industry and
related fields, check out the following local
professional organizations listed in
Chapter 5. Also see **"Stock Brokers/
Financial Services."**
**Community Bankers Association of
Georgia**
Georgia Bankers Association
Georgia League of Savings Institutions

For additional information, you can
contact:

American Bankers Association
1120 Connecticut Ave., N.W.
Washington, DC 20036
(202) 663-5000

Bank Marketing Association
1120 Connecticut Ave., N.W.
Washington, D.C. 20036
(202) 663-5422

**Mortgage Bankers Association of
America**
1125 15th St., N.W.
Washington, D.C. 20005
(202) 861-6500

National Association of Bank Women
500 N. Michigan Ave.
Chicago, IL 60611
(312) 661-1700

**National Bankers Association (minority
bankers)**
1802 T St., N.W.
Washington, DC 20009
(202) 588-5432

PROFESSIONAL PUBLICATIONS:

ABA Banking Journal
American Banker
Bank Letter
Bank Management
Bankers Magazine
Bankers Monthly
*Barron's National Business and Financial
  Weekly*
D&B Reports

DIRECTORIES:

American Bank Directory (McFadden
  Business Publications, Norcross, GA)
*Directory of American Savings and Loan
  Associations* (T.K. Sanderson Organiza-
  tion, Baltimore, MD)
Financial Yellow Book (Monitor Publish-
  ing, New York, NY)
Money Market Directory (Money Market
  Directories, Charlottesville, VA)
Moody's Bank and Finance Manual
  (Moody's Investors Service, New York,
  NY)
Polk's Bank Directory (R.L. Polk, Nashville,
  TN)
Rand McNally Bankers Directory (Rand
  McNally, Chicago, IL)
Savings and Loan Association Directory
  (American Business Directories, Omaha,
  NE)
Who's Who in International Banking (Reed
  Reference Publishing, New Providence,
  NJ)

Employers:

Bank of Canton
2780 Marietta Hwy.
Canton, GA 30114
(770) 479-1931

Bank of North Georgia
550 Marietta Parkway
Canton, GA 30114
(770) 479-2279

Barnett Bank
3350 Cumberland Circle, 10th Floor
Atlanta, GA 30339
(770) 850-5400
Contact: Sherri Bryant, Employment
Specialist

Brand Banking Co.
106 Crogan St.
Lawrenceville, GA 30245
(770) 963-9224
Contact: Jon Birts, Chairman of the Board

Citizens Trust Bank
712 W. Peachtree St., N.W.
Atlanta, GA 30379
(404) 881-6879
Contact: Marsha Taylor-Holland,
Personnel Director
Main office and five metro branches

Citizens Trust Bank
P.O. Box 4485
Atlanta, GA 30302
(404) 659-5959
Contact: Alberta Martin, Vice-President of
Human Resources

**Clayton County Federal Savings
& Loan Assn.**
101 N. Main St.
Jonesboro, GA 30236
(770) 478-8881
Contact: Heidi Stuebs

Colonial Bank
4800 Ashford-Dunwoody Rd.
Atlanta, GA 30338
(770) 379-8900

Colonial Bank
500 Northridge Rd., Suite 200
Atlanta, GA 30350
(770) 396-3966

Douglas County Bank
5641 Fairburn Rd.
P.O. Box 949
Douglasville, GA 30133
(770) 949-2500
Contact: Frank Boone

Etowah Bank
140 W. Main St.
Canton, GA 30114
(770) 479-8761

Fairburn Banking Co.
65 Washington St.
Fairburn, GA 30213
(770) 964-1551
Contact: Nina Ray, Personnel Director

Federal Reserve Bank
104 Marietta St., N.W.
Atlanta, GA 30303
(404) 521-8500
Contact: Kelley Davis, Employment
Coordinator

Fidelity National Bank
3 Corporate Square
Atlanta, GA 30329
(404) 639-6500
Contact: Tricia Pittman

First Colony Bank
300 S. Main St.
Alpharetta, GA 30201
(770) 751-3100
Contact: Sally Ashworth, Personnel
Director

First Financial Bank
2030 Powers Ferry Rd., N.W., Suite 325
Atlanta, GA 30339
(770) 933-7953

First North American National Bank
1800 Parkway Place, Suite 400
Marietta, GA 30067
(770) 423-7900

First Southern
2727 Panola Rd.
Lithonia, GA 30034
Headquarters and three branches located in Dekalb County.

First State Bank
4806 N. Henry Blvd.
Stockbridge, GA 30281
(770) 474-7293

First Union National Bank
4070 Lavista Rd.
Tucker, GA 30084
(404) 865-3900
Residential mortgage lender

First Union National Bank of Georgia
999 Peachtree St., N.E.
Atlanta, GA 30309
(404) 827-7100
Contact: Human Resources
Headquarters for Georgia's fifth largest bank, with numerous metro branches

Homebanc Mortgage Corp.
5775-E Glenridge Dr.
Atlanta, GA 30328
(404) 303-4000
Residential mortgage lender

HomeSouth Mortage Corp.
1669 Phoenix Parkway, Suite 109
Atlanta, GA 30349
(770) 997-9009
Residential mortgage lender

National Mortgage Investments
1815 North Expressway
Griffin, GA 30223
(770) 227-4734
Residential mortgage lender

NationsBanc Mortgage Corp.
70 Mansell Court, Suite 205
Roswell, GA 30076
(770) 993-0013
Residential mortgage lender

NationsBank
600 Peachtree St., N.E.
Atlanta, GA 30308
(404) 581-2121
Contact: Geri Thomas

Peoples Bank Lithonia
3065 Stone Mountain St.
Lithonia, GA 30058
(770) 482-7200
Contact: Charline Hall, Personnel Director
Main office and one branch

Premier Lending Corp.
2759 Delk Rd., Suite 201
Marietta, GA 30067
(770) 952-0606
Residential mortgage lender

Prudential Bank & Trust Co.
1 Ravinia Dr., Suite 100
Atlanta, GA 30346
(770) 551-6700
Contact: Job Line

Prudential Savings Bank
200 W. Main St.
Cartersville, GA 30120
(770) 382-4171

Regions Bank
6637 Roswell Rd.
Atlanta, GA 30328
(404) 255-8550

South Trust Bank
2000 Riveredge Parkway
Atlanta, GA 30328
(770) 951-4010
Contact: Ellen Hope, Personnel Director
Six Atlanta branches

South Trust Bank
600 Peachtree St.
Atlanta, GA 30308
(770) 951-4000
Contact: Vaughan Cooper, Personnel

Sun America Mortgage Corp.
5775-A Glenridge Dr., Suite 100
Atlanta, GA 30328
(404) 252-0192
Residential mortgage lender

Sunshine Mortgage Corp.
2401 Lake Park Dr., Suite 300
Smyrna, GA 30080
(770) 437-4100
Residential mortgage lender

SunTrust Bank
303 Peachtree St., N.E.
Atlanta, GA 30308
(404) 588-7711
Contact: Karen Summerlin

SunTrust Bank
121 Perimeter Center W.
Atlanta, GA 30346
(770) 551-4100
Residential mortgage lender

Tara State Bank
6375 Highway 85
Riverdale, GA 30274
(770) 996-8272
Contact: Allette Cheaves, Personnel
Director
Two south metro locations

Trust Company Bank
25 Park Place, N.E.
P.O. Box 4418
Atlanta, GA 30302
(404) 588-7711
Contact: Carolyn Cartwright, Personnel
Director

**Tucker Federal Savings & Loan
Association**
2355 Main St.
Tucker, GA 30084
(770) 938-1222

Unity Mortgage Corp.
6600 Peachtree-Dunwoody Rd., Bldg. 600,
Suite 600
Atlanta, GA 30328
(770) 604-4000
Residential mortgage lender

Wachovia Bank
191 Peachtree St., N.E.
Atlanta, GA 30303
(404) 332-5000
Contact: Joe Johnson, Human Resources
Branches throughout metro area

Book Publishers

WEB SITES:

http://www.library.vanderbilt.edu/law/
acqs/pubr.html#links
links to book publishers.

http://www.scescape.com/worldlibrary/
business/companies/publish.html
links to book publishers.

http://www.bocklabs.wisc.edu/ims/
agents.html
is a directory of literary agents.

PROFESSIONAL ORGANIZATIONS:

For networking in book publishing and
related fields, check out the following local
professional organizations listed in
Chapter 5. Also see **"Media, Print."**

Atlanta Writing Resource Center

For additional information, you can
contact:

American Booksellers Association
828 S. Broadway
Tarrytown, NY 10591
(914) 591-2665

Association of American Publishers
71 Fifth Ave.
New York, NY 10010
(212) 255-0200

Book Industry Study Group
160 5th Ave.
New York, NY 10010
(212) 929-1393

**COSMEP, The International Association
of Independent Publishers**
P.O. Box 420703
San Francisco, CA 94142
(415) 922-9490

Publishers Association of the South
P.O. Box 43533
3169 Cahaba Heights Rd.
Birmingham, AL 35243
(205) 967-0580

Southeastern Booksellers Association
R.M. Mills Bookstores
1917 21st Ave.
Nashville, TN 37212

PROFESSIONAL PUBLICATIONS:

American Bookseller
Editor and Publisher
Innovative Publisher
Library Journal
Publishers Weekly
Publishing Trends and Trendsetters
Small Press

DIRECTORIES:

American Book Trade Directory (R.R.
   Bowker, New Providence, NJ)
Literary Agents of North America (Research
   Associates International, New York, NY)
Literary Market Place (R.R. Bowker, New
   Providence, NJ)
*Publishers Directory: A Guide to New and
   Established Private and Special-Interest,
   Avant-Garde and Alternative, Organiza-
   tional Association, Government and
   Institution Presses* (Gale Research,
   Detroit, MI)
Writer's Market (F&W Publications,
   Cincinnati, OH)

Employers:

Consortium Press
1447 Peachtree St., N.E.
Atlanta, GA 30309
(404) 888-9220

Corporate Stories
512 Means St., Suite 200
Atlanta, GA 30318
(404) 681-0909
Contact: Rob Levin

CTB
3260 Peachtree Industrial Blvd., Suite 20
Duluth, GA 30136
(770) 622-4300
Contact: Ben Hicks, Southern Regional
Manager

Fairmont Press
700 Indian Trail-Lilburn Rd.
Lilburn, GA 30247
(770) 925-9388
Contact: Linda Hutchins, Comptroller

Glencoe Division,
McMillan/McGraw Hill
3100 Breckinridge Blvd., Suite 705
Duluth, GA 30136
(770) 717-7007

Harrison Company, The
3110 Crossing Park
Norcross, GA 30071
(770) 447-9150
Contact: Evelyn Knight, Personnel
Director
Law books

Heath, D.C., Co.
2945 Flowers Rd. S., Suite 138
Atlanta, GA 30341
(800) 235-3565
Contact: James Baker, Regional Manager

Houghton Mifflin Co.
7055 Amwiler Industrial Dr.
Atlanta, GA 30360
(770) 449-5881
Contact: Ms. Keith Resseau, Personnel
Manager
Elementary and secondary textbooks

Humanics Publishing Group
1482 Mecaslin St.
Atlanta, GA 30309
(404) 874-2176
Contact: Gary Wilson, Chairman
Children's educational resource books,
children's books,
New Age self-help psychology

Lex Publishing
2161 Monroe Dr., N.E.
Atlanta, GA 30324
(404) 875-5140
Contact: Dala Ford, Vice-President
Electronic publishing

Longstreet Press
2140 New Market Parkway, Suite 122
Marietta, GA 30067
(770) 980-1488
Contact: Chuck Perry, President

MacMillan/McGraw Hill School Division
6510 Jimmy Carter Blvd.
Norcross, GA 30091
(770) 448-7997
Contact: James George, Regional Vice-
President
Elementary textbook publishers

Nexus Contemporary Art Center
535 Means St.
Atlanta, GA 30318
(404) 577-3579
Contact: Michael Goodman or JoAnne
Paschal

Peachtree Publishers, Ltd.
494 Armour Circle, N.E.
Atlanta, GA 30324
(404) 876-8761
Contact: Margret Quinlin, President

Prentice-Hall
66 Luckie St., N.W.
Atlanta, GA 30303
(404) 255-5484
Contact: Charles Coyle, Branch Manager
College division sales office

Pritchett and Hull Associates
3440 Oakcliff Rd., N.E., Suite 110
Atlanta, GA 30340
(404) 451-0602
Contact: M.J. Moody, General Manager
Patient education publications

Scott-Foresman & Co.
1955 Montreal Rd.
Tucker, GA 30084
(770) 939-7210
Contact: Mr. Sandy Brown, Marketing
Manager
Textbooks

Silver, Burdett and Ginn
1925 Century Blvd., N.E.
Atlanta, GA 30345
(770) 321-7455
Contact: Ralph Carlson, Vice-President
and Regional Manager
Elementary textbooks

Turner Publishing Co.
1050 Techwood

Atlanta, GA 30309
(404) 885-4676
Books and videos for children and adults

Wolfe, W. H., Associates
14501 Freemanville Rd.
Alpharetta, GA 30201
(770) 475-6782
Specializes in corporate, family, city, and
county histories

Broadcasting and Television

WEB SITES:

http://www.yahoo.com/text/
Business_and_Economy/Companies/
Media/Television/
links to networks, cable, and local
stations.

http://radio.aiss.uiuc.edu/~rrb/
stations.html
is a guide to radio station sites.

PROFESSIONAL ORGANIZATIONS:

For networking in radio, television, and
related fields, check out the following local
professional organizations listed in
Chapter 5:

Georgia Association of Broadcasters

For additional information, you can
contact:

**American Federation of Television and
Radio Artists**
260 Madison Ave.
New York, NY 10016
(212) 532-0800

American Radio Association
17 Battery Place, Rm. 1443
New York, NY 10004
(212) 809-0600

Association of Independent TV Stations
1200 18th St., N.W.
Washington, DC 20036
(202) 887-1970

Corporation for Public Broadcasting
901 E St., N.W.
Washington, DC 20004
(202) 879-9600

International Radio & Television Society
420 Lexington Ave.
New York, NY 10170
(212) 867-6650

**National Academy of Television Arts and
Sciences**
111 W. 57th St.
New York, NY 10019
(212) 586-8424

**National Association of African-
American Sportswriters and
Broadcasters**
21 Bedford St.
Wyandanch, NY 11798
(516) 491-7774

National Association of Broadcasters
1771 N St., N.W.
Washington, DC 20036
(202) 429-5300

**National Association of Television
Program Executives**
2425 Olympic Blvd., Suite 550E
Santa Monica, CA 90404
(310) 453-4440

National Cable Television Association
1724 Massachusetts Ave., N.W.
Washington, DC 20036
(202) 775-3550

National Radio Broadcasters Association
2033 M St., N.W.
Washington, DC 20036
(202) 429-5420

PROFESSIONAL PUBLICATIONS:

Billboard
Broadcast Communications
Broadcasting and Cable
Broadcasting Magazine
Cable Age
Cable Marketing
Cable World
Communication News
Community TV Review
Radio Only
Radio World
Ross Reports
Television Broadcast
TV Radio Age
Variety

DIRECTORIES:

BPI TV News Contacts (BPI Media
   Services, New York, NY)
Broadcasting /Cablecasting Yearbook
   (Broadcasting Publishing Company,
   Washington, DC)
Broadcasting Cable Sourcebook (Broadcast-
   ing Publishing Company, Washington,
   DC)
*Cable Programming Resource Directory: A
   Guide to Community TV Production
   Facilities and Programming Services and
   Outlets* (Broadcasting Publications,
   Washington, DC)
Cable & Station Coverage Atlas (Warren
   Publishing, Inc., Washington, DC)
*Gale Directory of Publications and
   Broadcast Media* (Gale Research Co.,
   Detroit, MI)
Television & Cable Factbook (Television
   Digest, Washington, DC)
TV/Radio Age Ten-City Directory (TV
   Editorial Corporation, New York, NY)
Who's Who in Television (Packard
   Publishing Co., Hollywood, CA)

Employers:

Atlanta Interfaith Broadcasters
1075 Spring St.
Atlanta, GA 30309
(404) 892-0454
Contact: Ms. O'Lynn Allen, Station
Manager

Christian Television Network
2945 Stone Hogan Rd.
Atlanta, GA 30331
(404) 629-0020
Contact: Nancy Reese, Personnel Director

**CNN Headline News/Cable News
Network**
1 CNN Center
P.O. Box 105366
Atlanta, GA 30348
(404) 827-1500
Contact: Michelle Thomas, Personnel
Director

Cox Enterprises
1400 Lake Hearn Dr., N.E.
Atlanta, GA 30319
(404) 843-5000
Contact: Mary Beth Leamer, Human
Resources

Cripps, Howard/Comcast
3425 Malone Dr.
Chamblee, GA 30341
(770) 451-4785
Contact: Jeanne Muffit, Personnel

Dowden Communications Investors
1100 Abernathy Rd., Suite 1735
Atlanta, GA 30328
(770) 396-1088
Contact: Nancy Wood, Office Manager
Contact: Anne Bulas, Vice-President of
Sales

Georgia Network
1819 Peachtree Rd., Suite 700
Atlanta, GA 30309
(404) 367-9444
Contact: Bob Houghton

JCV-Higgins International
1708 Peachtree St.
Atlanta, GA 30309
(404) 892-8244

Media One
1018 W. Peachtree St., N.W.
Atlanta, GA 30309
(404) 292-8822
Contact: Ernesta Ingram, Personnel
Send resumes to:
P.O. Box 1549
Decatur, GA 30031
Cable system serving city of Atlanta and
DeKalb County

Metromedia International Group
945 E. Paces Ferry Rd., Suite 2210 South
Atlanta, GA 30326
(404) 261-6190
Entertainment and media company

New World Communications Group
3200 Windy Hill Rd., Suite 1100W
Atlanta, GA 30339
(770) 955-0045
Contact: Jim Gorman, Human Resources

People TV/Public Access Channel 12
190 14th St., N.W.
Atlanta, GA 30318
(404) 873-6712
Contact: Chris Leonard, General Manager

Power 99 Radio Station
3405 Piedmont Rd., N.E., Suite 5W

Atlanta, GA 30305
(404) 266-0997
Contact: Mark Renier, General Manager

Raymon Media Group
3333 Peachtree Rd., N.E.
Atlanta, GA 30326
(404) 240-0005
Contact: Paul Ramon, President

Smyrna Cable TV
3773 South Cobb Dr.
Marietta, GA 30080
(770) 433-2338
Contact: Donna Nelson

Spartan Communications
2859 Paces Ferry Rd., Suite 2150
Atlanta, GA 30339
(770) 434-0800

TBS Superstation/TNT
1050 Techwood Dr., N.W.
P.O. Box 105264
Atlanta, GA 30318-5264
(404) 827-1717
Contact: Michelle Thomas, Director of
Corporate Personnel

Turner Broadcasting System
1 CNN Center
P.O. Box 105366
Atlanta, GA 30348-5366
(404) 827-1700
Contact: Director of Human Resources

Breaking into broadcasting

We asked a radio station executive how to get started in broadcasting.

"Persevere," she says. "One of my first interviews was with the personnel director of a television station. 'Do you realize,' he said, 'that the universities in this state graduated hundreds of communications majors last year alone? There aren't that many job openings in the whole state.'

"That was a sobering thought. It discourages a lot of people. But you have to keep in there. Send out resumes, read the trades, see who's switching formats, and all that. Make contacts on the side that might result in a good lead.

"Another important point is to treat your contacts with respect. Broadcasting is a volatile business. You can't afford to burn a lot of bridges or alienate a lot of people. Somebody can be your assistant one day and your boss the next."

WABE-FM 90
740 Bismarck Rd., N.E.
Atlanta, GA 30324
(404) 827-8900
Contact: Milton Clipper, Chief Operation Officer
National Public Radio news, classical music, jazz

WAGA-TV 5
1551 Briarcliff Rd., N.E.
Atlanta, GA 30306
(404) 875-5551
Contact: David Jones, Operations Manager
CBS network affiliate

WALR-FM
209 CNN Center
Atlanta, GA 30303
(404) 688-0068

WAOK Radio Station
1201 Peachtree St., N.E.
Atlanta, GA 30361
(404) 898-8900
Contact: Mike Roberts, Program Director

WATL-Channel 36
1 Monroe Place, N.E.
Atlanta, GA 30324
(404) 881-3600
Contact: Personnel Dept.

WAZX Light 1550 AM/101.9 FM
2460 Atlanta Rd., S.E.
Smyrna, GA 30080
(770) 436-6171
Contact: Humberto Izquierdo

WCNN Radio 68 AM
1601 W. Peachtree St., N.E.
Atlanta, GA 30309
(404) 897-7500
Contact: Sherry Rosenberg, Business Manager
All news

Weather Channel, The
300 Interstate North Parkway
Atlanta, GA 30339
(770) 226-2190
Contact: Doris Shannon, Personnel

WFOX Radio Station
2000 Riveredge Parkway, N.W., Suite 797
Atlanta, GA 30328
(770) 953-9369
Contact: Bill Caghill, Program Director
Sixties, seventies music

WGNX-Channel 46
1810 Briarcliff Rd., N.E.
Atlanta, GA 30329
(404) 325-4646
Contact: Mike Dreaden, News Director

WGST-AM/FM
1819 Peachtree St., Suite 700
Atlanta, GA 30309
(404) 367-0640

WHTA -FM
5526 Old National Hwy., Bldgs. B and C
College Park, GA 30349
(404) 765-9750

WIGO Radio Station
2001 Martin Luther King, Jr., Dr., Suite 520
Atlanta, GA 30310
(404) 752-5460
Contact: Ron Sailor, General Manager

Wireless Cable of Atlanta
3100 Medlock Bridge Rd., Suite 340
Norcross, GA 30071
(770) 409-3570

WJZF-FM
1745 Phoenix Blvd., Suite 100
Atlanta, GA 30349
(770) 996-9341

WKHX KICKS 101.5 FM
210 Interstate North Parkway, 6th Floor
Atlanta, GA 30339
(770) 955-0101
Contact: Neil McGinley, Operations
manager

WKLS Radio Station 96 Rock
1800 Century Blvd., N.E., Suite 1200
Atlanta, GA 30345
(404) 325-0960
Contact: Michael Hughes, Program
Director

WNIV-AM
2970 Peachtree Rd., Suite 970
Atlanta, GA 30305
(404) 365-0970

WNNX-FM
3405 Piedmont Rd., Suite 500
Atlanta, GA 30305
(404) 266-0997

Wometco Cable TV of Clayton County
6435 Tara Blvd., Suite 22
Jonesboro, GA 30236
(770) 478-0010
Contact: Susie Messman, Office Manager

WPBA TV Channel 30
740 Bismarck Rd., N.E.
Atlanta, GA 30324
(404) 827-8900
Contact: Milton Clipper, General Manager
Public Broadcasting TV station

WPCH-FM
1819 Peachtree St., Suite 700
Atlanta, GA 30309
(404) 367-0949

WQXI and 94 Q Radio Stations
3350 Peachtree Rd., N.E.
Atlanta, GA 30326
(404) 261-2970
Contact: Kevin Peterson, Program
Director

WRFG-FM Radio Station
1083 Austin Ave., N.E.
Atlanta, GA 30307
(404) 523-3471

Contact: Tom Davis, Program Director
Community access radio. Mostly
volunteer staff

WSB Radio and Television
1601 W. Peachtree St., N.E.
Atlanta, GA 30309
(404) 897-7000
Contact: Al Blink, News Office
Television station is ABC-TV network
affiliate. AM and FM
radio stations

WSSA Radio Station 1570 AM
2424 Old Rex Morrow Rd.
Morrow, GA 30260
(770) 361-8843
Contact: Vic Stevens, Program Director
Easy-listening Christian music

WSTR-FM
3350 Peachtree Rd., Penthouse Suite
Atlanta, GA 30326
(404) 261-2970

WTJH Inspirational Radio
2146 Dodson Dr.
East Point, GA 30344
(770) 344-2233
Contact: Silas Buchanan, General
Manager

WUPA TV 69
2700 Northeast Expressway Access Rd.,
N.E.
Atlanta, GA 30345
(404) 325-6929
Contact: Linda Danna, General Manager

WVEE-FM
1201 Peachtree St., N.E.
Atlanta, GA 30361
(404) 989-8900

WXIA TV-11 Alive
1611 W. Peachtree St., N.E.
Atlanta, GA 30309
(404) 892-1611
Contact: Nancy Putney, Vice-President for
Production
NBC network affiliate

WYAY 106 FM & 104 FM
210 Interstate North Parkway, 6th Floor
Marietta, GA 30339
(770) 955-0106
Contact: Sue Flinchun, Office Manager

WZGC Z-93 Radio Station
1100 Johnson Ferry Rd., N.E., Suite 593
Atlanta, GA 30342
(770) 851-9393
Contact: Gary Lewis, General Manager
Album rock

Chemicals

WEB SITES:

**http://www.yahoo.com/
Business_and_Economy/Companies/
Chemicals/**
lists chemical companies and sites.

**http://nearnet.gnn.com/wic/
chem.06.html**
is the homepage of the American
Chemical Society.

To learn more about the chemical
industry, you can contact:

PROFESSIONAL ORGANIZATIONS:

American Chemical Society
1155 16th St., N.W.
Washington, DC 20036
(202) 872-4600

Chemical Manufacturers Association
2501 M St., N.W.
Washington, DC 20037
(202) 887-1100

**Chemical Specialties Manufacturers
Association**
1913 I St., N.W.
Washington, DC 20006
(202) 872-8110

PROFESSIONAL PUBLICATIONS:

Chemical Business
Chemical Engineering News
Chemical Industry Update
Chemical Week

DIRECTORIES:

Chem-Sources U.S.A. (Chemical Sources
International, Clemson, SC)
Chemclopedia (American Chemical
Society, Washington, DC)
Chemical and Engineering News, Career
Opportunities issue (American
Chemical Society, Washington, DC)
Chemical Week, Buyer's Guide issue
(McGraw-Hill, New York, NY)
*Chemical Week: Financial Survey of the 300
Largest Companies* (McGraw-Hill, New
York, NY)

Employers:

Air Products & Chemicals
990 Hammond Dr., Suite 890
Atlanta, GA 30328
(770) 671-1891
Contact: Charles Bennett, Regional
Manager
Manufacturing materials for paints,
adhesives, and paper coatings

Alchem Chemical Company
5360 Tulane Dr., S.W.
Atlanta, GA 30336
(404) 696-9202
Contact: Bart Whitaker, President
Chemicals for the compounding and
coating industries

Alchemy-South, Ltd.
1345 Owenby Dr.
Marietta, GA 30066
(770) 427-1234
Contact: Tom Welch, President

Alpha Metals
200 Technology Dr.
Alpharetta, GA 30302
(770) 475-6100
Contact: Sue Odem, Personnel Supervisor
Soldering chemicals

American Industrial Chemical Corp.
1819 S. Cobb Industrial Blvd., S.W.
Smyrna, GA 30082
(770) 434-8300
Contact: Bill Lipton, President
Chemicals for the textile and compounding trades

Amrep Inc.
900 Industrial Park Dr., N.E.
Marietta, GA 30062
(770) 422-2071
Contact: Diane Caldwell, Human
Resources
Aerosols, specialty lubricants, organic and
biodegradable

Aqua Engineer Industrial Cleaning Equipment
6955 Oak Ridge Parkway, S.W., Suite D
Austell, GA 30001
(770) 944-6677
Contact: Sandy Gray
Steam cleaning and pressure washing
equipment and chemicals

Ashland Chemical Company Division of Ashland Oil
4550 Northeast Expressway Access Rd.
Doraville, GA 30340
(770) 448-7010
Contact: Dan Brown, Plant Manager

Burris Chemicals
2225 Lawrence Ave.
East Point, GA 30344
(770) 761-5942
Contact: Randall Pegram, Division
President

Chemtech Industries—SSC Division
1550 E. Taylor Ave.
East Point, GA 30344
(770) 394-4141
Contact: Julie Heard, Personnel

Dow Chemical USA
115 Perimeter Center Place, Suite 590
Atlanta, GA 30346
(770) 394-4141
Contact: Sandy Wotring, Office Manager

Ecolab
2221 New Market Parkway, S.E., Suite 142
Marietta, GA 30067
(770) 953-2583
Contact: Wayne Francis, Regional
Manager
Ware washing specialists

General Chemical Corp.
1427 Central Ave.
P.O. Box 90220
East Point, GA 30344
(770) 761-1181
Contact: Mr. Gaddy, Plant Supervisor
Aluminum sulfate manufacturers

General Polymers
2060 Defoor Hills Rd., N.W.
Atlanta, GA 30318
(404) 352-2315
Contact: Stephen Fusi, District Manager
Industrial chemicals and solvents division

Georgia Gulf Corp.
400 Perimeter Center Terrace, Suite 595
Atlanta, GA 30346
(770) 395-4500
Contact: John Hager, Director of Human
Resources

Hunt Chemicals
530 Permalume Place, N.W.
Atlanta, GA 30318
(404) 352-1418
Contact: Sam Medhear, President

J.B. Distributing of Madison
95 Milton Ave., S.E.
Atlanta. GA 30315
Contact: John Burnette, President
Blending, compounding, analysis of
solvents, and industrial and
specialty chemicals

Kerr-McGee Chemical Corporation
2200 Northlake Parkway, Suite 277
Tucker, GA 30084
(770) 934-9781
Contact: Carlton Staples, Regional Sales
Manager

LaRoche Industries
1100 Johnson Ferry Rd., N.E.
Atlanta, GA 30342
(404) 851-0300
Contact: Joe Martucci, Executive Director
of Human Resources

M&J Solvents Co.
1577 Marietta Rd., N.W.
P.O. Box 19703, Station N
Atlanta, GA 30325
(404) 355-8240
Contact: Michael McQuen, General
Manager
Solvent recovery

Monsanto Chemical Company
320 Interstate North Parkway, N.W.,
Suite 500
Atlanta, GA 30339
(770) 951-7600
Direct resumes to:
Monsanto Chemical Company
800 N. Lindberg Blvd.
St. Louis, MO 63167
Attn: Anne H. Roberts, Manager of
Professional Employment

Purex Industrial Division
3300 Montreal Industrial Way
Tucker, GA 30084
(770) 939-8820
Contact: Gil Sisson, Regional Manager
Cleaning chemicals for industrial use

Computers: Hardware/Software

WEB SITES:

http://www.zdnet.com/~zdi/tblazer/
compani.html
lists sites of hardware manufacturers and
software developers.

http://www.stars.com/Jobs.html
lists computer opportunities related to
Web development.

PROFESSIONAL ORGANIZATIONS:

For networking in the computer industry,
check out the following local professional
organization listed in Chapter 5. See also
"Computers/Information Management"
and "Electronics/Telecommunications."

Society for Technical Communication

For more information, you can contact:

American Society of Computer Dealers
P.O. Box 100
Hohokus, NJ 07423
(201) 444-5006

Association of Computer Professionals
9 Forest Dr.
Plainview, NY 11803
(516) 938-8223

Association for Women in Computing
6421 N. 24th St.
Arlington, VA 22207
(703) 536-2088

**Computer and Communications
Industry Association**
666 11th St., N.W.
Washington, DC 20001
(202) 783-0070

**Data Processing Management
Association**
505 Busse Hwy.
Park Ridge, IL 60068
(847) 825-8124

Information Industry Association
555 New Jersey Ave., N.W., Suite 800
Washington, DC 20001
(202) 639-8262

**Information Technology Association of
America**
1616 N. Ft. Myer Dr.
Arlington, VA 22209
(703) 522-5055

**Institute of Electrical & Electronics
Engineers (IEEE)**
345 E. 47th St.
New York, NY 10017
(212) 705-7900

**National Computer Graphics
Association**
2722 Merrilee Dr.
Fairfax, VA 22031
(703) 698-9600

**Semiconductor Equipment and
Materials International**
805 E. Middlefield Rd.
Mountain View, CA 94043
(415) 964-5111

Software Publishers Association
1730 M St., N.W., Suite 700
Washington, DC 20036
(202) 452-1600

PROFESSIONAL PUBLICATIONS:

BYTE
Computer Industry Report
Computer World
Datamation
Electronic Business
Electronic News
Info World
Journal of Software Maintenance
Microtimes
MIS News
PC Magazine
PC Week
PC World

DIRECTORIES:

Data Communications Buyers Guide
(McGraw-Hill, New York, NY)

Data Sources: Hardware-Data Communications Directory (Ziff-Davis, New York, NY)

Data Sources: Software Directory (Ziff-Davis, New York, NY)

Datapro Directory of Microcomputer Software (Datapro Information Services Group, Delran, NJ)

Engineering, Science and Computer Jobs
(Peterson's Guides, Princeton, NJ)

Guide to High Technology Companies
(Corp. Technology Information Services, Woburn, MA)

ICP Software Directory (International Computer Programs, Indianapolis, IN)

Membership Directory (Information Technology Assoc. of America, Arlington, VA)

Software Publishers' Catalog Annual
(Meckler Corp., Westport, CT)

Booting up big $$$ in computer sales

Philip Daniels competes in the fast lane as a computer sales engineer. His clients are Fortune 500 companies, and his products are communications boards, controllers, and disk and tape subsystems manufactured by a relatively new specialty company. "It's an emotionally and physically stressful environment where I constantly have to prove myself," says Philip.

We asked how he got there and what keeps him successful. "I use every skill and all the experience I've ever had," said the former teacher and editorial assistant for a steel company's community relations department. "When I decided to go back to school for an associate's degree in computers, I needed a job as well. So I sold cars, and that provided invaluable marketing and people experience, plus communications skills that are absolutely essential in my present business.

"Once I got into computer courses, I realized I couldn't settle for a $25,000 programming job and began laying more plans. And, incidentally, you must prepare yourself for the entry position in this field. My first job—strictly commission—was with a small systems house, and within a year I was director of marketing with a sales staff of six. I got a total overview of the business so that I could talk from that perspective on my next round of interviews.

"I used an employment agent who specializes in computer sales to get this position and was very specific with him about my requirements."

Asked to explain his current success, Philip responds: "I'd have to say the number one factor is technical expertise—with sales ability second. I read, listen, and pick brains to stay on top of the products and a changing market place so that my company provides a service to the client by sending me. By the way, with little more education than a $25,000 programmer, I'll make at least three times that this year. And the perks are great, too."

Employers:

A.D.A.M. Software
1600 River Edge Parkway, Suite 800
Atlanta, GA 30328
(770) 980-0888

ADVANCED Control Systems
2755 Northwoods Parkway
Norcross, GA 30072
(770) 451-4586
Contact: Elaine Meggs, Personnel

Alltel Healthcare Information Services
200 Ashford Center N.
Atlanta, GA 30338
(404) 847-5000

American Megatrends
6145-F Northbelt Parkway
Norcross, GA 30071
(770) 263-8181
Contact: Personnel

American Software
470 E. Paces Ferry Rd.
Atlanta, GA 30305
(770) 261-4381
Contact: Kevin Burdette, Corporate Recruiter

American Technical Services Group
5680 Oakbrook Parkway, Suite 165
Norcross, GA 30093
(770) 447-9444
Contact: Marie Robinson, Director of Human Resources

Brock Control Systems
2859 Paces Ferry Rd., Suite 1000
Atlanta, GA 30339
(770) 431-1200
Contact: Ms. Marty Conn, Human Resouces

Bull Information Systems
6 West Druid Hills Dr.
Atlanta, GA 30329
(404) 982-2027
Contact: Richard Copeland, Human Resources

Byers Engineering Co.
6285 Barfield Rd.
Atlanta, GA 30328
(404) 843-1000
Contact: Cindy Lawrence, Controller
Manufactures computer graphics and provides engineering services for utilities

Cap Gemini America
400 Perimeter Center, Suite 400
Atlanta, GA 30346
(770) 677-3520
Contact: Max Machacek

Checkfree Corp.
4411 E. Jones Bridge Rd.
Norcross, GA 30092
(770) 441-3387
Contact: Pete Knight

Chromatics
2558 Mountain Industrial Blvd.
Tucker, GA 30084
(770) 493-7000
Contact: Joclyn Johnson

CLR
2400 Lake Park Dr.
Smyrna, GA 30080
(770) 432-1996
Contact: Human Resources

COIN Financial Systems
3300 Breckinridge Blvd.
Duluth, GA 30136
(770) 717-1700
Contact: Karen McGhee

Dickens Data Systems
1175 Northmeadow Parkway, Suite 150
Roswell, GA 30076
(770) 475-8860

Digital Communications Associates
1000 Alderman Dr.
Alpharetta, GA 30202
(770) 442-4000

Dun & Bradstreet Software
66 Perimeter Center East
Atlanta, GA 30346
(404) 239-2000

EDS
200 Galleria Parkway, Suite 870
Atlanta, GA 30339
(770) 297-3700
Information technology, computer
systems, consulting facilities management

Electromagnetic Sciences
660 Engineering Dr.
Norcross, GA 30092
(770) 263-9200
Contact: Mike Robertson, Personnel
Manager

Encore Systems
900 Circle 75 Parkway, Suite 1700
Atlanta, GA 30339
(770) 612-3900

Energy Management Associates
100 Northcreek, Suite 800
Atlanta, GA 30327
(770) 261-5256
Contact: Barbara Bell-Dees

First Data Corp.
6567 The Corners Parkway
Norcross, GA 30092
(770) 441-7793
Contact: Human Resources, Charlotte,
NC (704) 549-7000

**First Financial Management
Corporation**
3 Corporate Square, Suite 700
Atlanta, GA 30329
(770) 321-0120

Fisher Business Systems
1950 Spectrum Circle, Suite 400
Marietta, GA 30067
(770) 578-1771

FormMaker Software
2300 Windy Ridge Parkway, Suite 400 N.
Atlanta, GA 30339
(770) 859-9900

GE Computer Corp.
6875 Jimmy Carter Blvd., Suite 3200
Norcross, GA 30071
(770) 246-6300

GEAC Computer Corp.
66 Perimeter Center East
Atlanta, GA 30346
(770) 239-2000
Contact: Human Resources

Harbinger Corp.
1055 Lenox Park Blvd.
Atlanta, GA 30319
(404) 841-4334
Contact: Lisa Phillips

Hayes Microcomputer Products
5835 Peachtree Corners East
Norcross, GA 30092
(770) 840-9200
Contact: Human Resources

HBO & Co.
301 Perimeter Center North
Atlanta, GA 30346
(770) 393-6000
Contact: Christine Rumsey, Human
Resources

Hewlett-Packard Company
20 Perimeter Summit Blvd.
Atlanta, GA 30319
(404) 648-0000
Contact: Staffing Representative

IBM Corp.
1201 W. Peachtree St., Suite 500
Atlanta, GA 30367-1200
(800) 964-4473

Imnet Systems
8601 Dunwoody Place, Suite 420
Atlanta, GA 30350
(404) 998-2200

INFAX
2485 Lithonia Industrial Blvd.
Lithonia, GA 30058
(770) 482-2755
Contact: Human Resources

Information America
600 W. Peachtree St., Suite 1200
Atlanta, GA 30308
(404) 892-1800
Contact: Ed Porter, Human Resources

Information Systems of America
500 Northridge Rd.
Atlanta, GA 30350
(770) 587-6800
Contact: Human Resources

Intecolor Corp.
2150 Boggs Rd.
Duluth, GA 30136
(770) 623-9145
Contact: Susan Eadie, Personnel

IQ Software Corp.
3295 River Exchange Dr., Suite 550
Norcross, GA 30092
(770) 446-8880
Contact: Barbara Jones, Human Resources

KnowledgeWare
3340 Peachtree Rd. N.E.
Atlanta, GA 30326
(770) 231-8575

Lanier Worldwide
2300 Parklake Dr., N.E.
Atlanta, GA 30345
(770) 496-9500
Contact: Louise Flint, Human Resources

Lotus Development Corp.
1000 Abernathy Rd., N.E.
Atlanta, GA 30328
(770) 391-0011
Contact: Lori Scarborough, Personnel
Director

Microbilt
6190 Powers Ferry Rd., Suite 400
Atlanta, GA 30339
(770) 955-0313

MindSpring Enterprises
1430 W. Peachtree St., Suite 400
Atlanta, GA 30309
(404) 815-0770

NCR Corp.
5335 Triangle Parkway, Suite 200
Norcross, GA 30092
(770) 840-2740
Contact: Bob Bender, Director of
Personnel

Network Connection, The
1324 Union Hill Rd.
Alpharetta, GA 30201
(770) 751-0889
Contact: Barbara Riner, Vice-President

Peachtree Software
1505 Pavilion Place
Norcross, GA 30093
(770) 724-4000
Contact: Bonnie Steward Human
Resources Manager

Proto Systems of Atlanta
625 Sims Industrial Blvd.
Alpharetta, GA 30201
(770) 475-1330
Contact: Beverly Butner, Human
Resources

Sales Technologies
3399 Peachtree Rd., Suite 700
Atlanta, GA 30326
Contact: Anna Lynn Witherington

Scientific Games
1500 Bluegrass Lakes Parkway
Alpharetta, GA 30201
(770) 664-3700

Servantis Systems
4411 E. Jones Bridge Rd.
Norcross, GA 30092
(770) 441-3387

System Works, The
1640 Powers Ferry Rd., Bldg. 11
Marietta, GA 30067
(770) 952-8444
Contact: Alice Welden, Director of
Human Resources

TSW International
3301 Windy Ridge Parkway
Atlanta, GA 30339
(770) 989-4132

UniComp
1800 Sandy Plains Parkway, Suite 305
Marietta, GA 30066
(770) 424-3684

Universal Data Consultants
6630 Bay Circle
Norcross, GA 30071
(770) 446-6733

U.S. Dateq
5555 Triangle Parkway, Suite 400
Norcross, GA 30092
(770) 446-8282
Contact: Brian Sims, Personnel

XcelleNet
5 Concourse Parkway, Suite 850
Atlanta, GA 30328
(770) 804-8100
Contact: Joel Miller, Vice-President of
Personnel

Computers: Information Management/Consulting

WEB SITES:

http://www.acm.ndsu.nodak.edu/ ~acmco/
discusses careers in computer consulting.

http://204.252.76.40/0002c2a.html
is a news update on the information services industry.

http://www.wdn.com/aop/
is the homepage for the Assocation of Online Professionals.

PROFESSIONAL ORGANIZATIONS:

For local networking groups, see the preceding section. For additional information, contact the following organizations:

American Society for Information Science
8720 Georgia Ave., Suite. 501
Silver Spring, MD 20910
(301) 495-0900

Association of Independent Information Professionals
245 5th Ave., Suite 2103
New York, NY 10016
(212) 779-1855

IEEE Computer Society
1730 Massachusetts Ave., N.W.
Washington, DC 20036
(202) 371-0101

Information Industry Association
1625 Massachusetts Ave. N.W., Suite 700
Washington, DC 20036
(202) 986-0280

ITI Information Technology Industry Council
1250 I St., N.W., Suite 200
Washington, DC 20005
(202) 737-8888

Society for Information Management
401 N. Michigan Ave.
Chicago, IL 60611
(312) 644-6610
Special Interest Group on Data Communication

Association for Computing Machinery
1515 Broadway
New York, NY 10036
(212) 869-7440

Women in Information Processing
P.O. Box 39173
Washington, DC 20016
(202) 328-6161

PROFESSIONAL PUBLICATIONS:

CIO: The Magazine for Information Executives
Computer Communications Review
Computerworld: Newsweekly for Information Systems Management
Data Communications
EDI News
Information Processing and Management
InformationWEEK
Internet Business Report
Link-Up
Network World
Networking Management
Online

DIRECTORIES:

Computers and Computing Information Resources Directory (Gale Research, Detroit, MI)
Data Sources (Ziff-Davis Publishing, New York, NY)
Directory of Top Computer Executives (Applied Computer Research, Phoenix, AZ)
Information Industry Directory (Gale Research, Detroit, MI)
Information Sources (Information Industry Association, Washington, DC)

Networking in new media

For get-togethers in cyberspace try these sites:

Worldwide Web Artists Consortium
(212) 358-8220
http://wwwac.org
Contact: Kim Dawson, Director, Human Resources

Webgirls: networking for cyberfemales
(212) 642-8012
asherman@interport.net

ECHO (East Coast Hangout)
(212) 292-0900
info@echonyc.com

Employers:

Billing and Professional Services
4500 Hugh Howell Rd.
Tucker, GA 30084
(770) 270-4150
Contact: James Hansard, Personnel
Manager
Serves medical professionals

Compuserve Information Services
2 Concourse Parkway
Corporate Center W., Suite 500
Atlanta, GA 30328
(770) 393-3004

Computer Business Systems
5 Dunwoody Park, N.E., Suite 127
Atlanta, GA 30338
(770) 393-0868
Contact: Wayne Akins, President
Information management consulting,
accounts receivable, list
maintenance, etc.

Computer Generation
5775 Peachtree-Dunwoody Rd.
Bldg. G, 4th Floor
Atlanta, GA 30342
(770) 705-2800

Consultec
9040 Roswell Rd., Suite 700
Atlanta, GA 30350
(770) 594-7799

Datafax
2260 Northwest Parkway, Suite C
Marietta, GA 30067
(770) 988-9628
Contact: Linda Hursh, Manager
Data entry, conversion, direct mail
advertising

Datamatx Incorporated
3146 Northeast Expressway Access Rd.
Chamblee, GA 30341
(770) 936-5600
Contact: Robert Grant
Laser printing, mailing services

GE Information Services
9000 Central Parkway, N.E., Suite 500
Atlanta, GA 30328
(770) 698-4400
Resume to:
7000 Central Parkway, Suite 1300
Atlanta, GA 30028
Contact: Kim Vanderzee
Data processing, value-added networking,
point-of-sale systems,
electronic interchange of business,
medical and international trade data

Honeywell Inc.
5375 Oakbrook Parkway
Norcross, GA 30093
(770) 381-4844

IBM Corp.
4111 Northside Parkway
Atlanta, GA 30327
(404) 238-6165

Input Services
1090 Northcase Parkway, Suite 3
Marietta, GA 30067
(770) 952-8094
Contact: Nina Lauter, Data Processing
Manager

ISI
380 Northwoods Circle
Norcross, GA 30092
(770) 246-3000
Contact: Peggy Daniel, Human Resources
Manager
Systems development, consulting, hands-
on training, programming,
software engineering, network specialists

Management Control Methods
2258 Northlake Parkway
Tucker, GA 30084
(770) 934-0480
Contact: Richard D. Mosrie, President
Peak loads, mailings, inventories, word
processing

National Business Systems
8215 Roswell Rd., Bldg. 500
Atlanta, GA 30350
(404) 390-0477
Contact: Darrell Billings, Operations
Manager
Secured data storage

National Data Corp.
2 National Data Plaza
Atlanta, GA 30329
(404) 728-2000

NCR Corporation
130 Technology Park
Norcross, GA 30092
(770) 441-8400
Contact: Bonnie Lytle, Administrative
Supervisor

Programming Alternatives
3105 Medlock Bridge Rd.
Norcross, GA 30071
(770) 447-0609
Contact: Valeri Haralson, Recruiting
Manager
Contract programming, contract
engineering, consulting

Quantum Consulting Network
6 Concourse Parkway, Suite 2990
Atlanta, GA 30328
(770) 393-7420
Contact: Daniel Carpenter, President

Romac and Associates
3 Ravinia Dr., N.E., Suite 1460
Atlanta, GA 30346
(770) 604-3880
Consulting, programming, analysis
design, training

Sales Technologies
3399 Peachtree Rd., Suite 700
Atlanta, GA 30326
(404) 841-4000

SCS/Computer
5680 Oakbrook Parkway, Suite 149
Norcross, GA 30093
(770) 368-1040
Contact: Ms. Frankie Reed

**Societe Internationale de Telecommuni-
cations Aeronautics**
2380 Godby Rd.
College Park, GA 30349
(770) 761-5461
Send resume to:
Societe Internationale de Telecommunications Aeronautics
3100 Cumberland Circle, Suite 200
Atlanta, GA 30339
(404) 850-4500

Construction

WEB SITES:

http://www.copywriter.com/ab/
constr.html
lists bulletin boards and discussion groups
for the industry; offers links to other
industry sites including Construction
Online.

http://scescape.com/worldlibrary/
business/companies/construct/html
links to construction companies

PROFESSIONAL ORGANIZATIONS:

For networking in the construction
industry and related fields, check out the
following local professional organizations
listed in Chapter 5. Also see
"Engineering."
**American Society of Heating,
  Refrigeration & Air**
**American Society of Landscape
  Architects**
**Association of Builders & Contractors of
  Georgia**
**Association of Mechanical Contractors
  of Atlanta**
**Homebuilders Association of Metro
  Atlanta**
Homebuilders Association of Georgia
**Society for Marketing Professional
  Services**

For additional information, you may
contact:

Associated Builders & Contractors
729 15th St., N.W.
Washington, DC 20005
(202) 637-8800

**Associated General Contractors of
America**
1957 E St., N.W.
Washington, DC 20006
(202) 393-2040

**Construction Management Association
of America**
12355 Sunrise Valley Dr., Suite 640
Reston, VA 22091
(703) 391-1200

Construction Specifications Institute
601 Madison St.
Alexandria, VA 22314

**National Association of Home Builders
of the U.S.**
1201 15th St., N.W.
Washington, DC 20005
(202) 822-0200

**National Association of Minority
Contractors**
1333 F St., N.W.
Washington, DC 20004
(202) 347-8259

**National Association of Women in
Construction**
327 S. Adams St.
Fort Worth, TX 76014
(817) 877-5551

PROFESSIONAL PUBLICATIONS:

Associated Construction Publications
Builder
Building & Contractor
Building Design & Construction
Construction Review
Construction Weekly
Constructor
ENR: Engineering News Record

DIRECTORIES:

*Associated Builders & Contractors
  Membership Directory* (Associated
  Builders & Contractors, Washington,
  DC)
Blue Book of Major Homebuilders (LSI
  Systems, Crofton, MD)
*Construction Equipment, Construction
  Giants* (Cahners Publishing, Des Plaines,
  IL)

Constructor, Directory issue (Associated General Contractors of America, Washington, DC)
Who's Who in Engineering (Engineers Joint Council, New York, NY)

Employers:

Alumax Inc.
5655 Peachtree Parkway
Norcross, GA 30092
(770) 246-6600
Aluminum products

Aviation Constructors
2690 Cumberland Parkway
Atlanta, GA 30339
(770) 431-0800

Baston-Cook of Atlanta
700 Galleria Parkway, N.W., Suite 550
Atlanta, GA 30339
(770) 955-1951
Contact: Randy Thompason, Asst. Vice-President

Beers Inc.
70 Ellis St., N.E.
Atlanta, GA 30303
(404) 659-1970
Contact: Elmon Henry, Executive Vice-President

Black, Marvin M. Co.
5437 Spalding Dr.
Norcross, GA 30092
(770) 448-7179
Contact: Mike Black, President

Brasfield & Gorrie
4151 Ashford-Dunwoody Rd., Suite 525
Atlanta, GA 30319
(770) 988-0996
Contact: Rob Taylor, Director of Business Development

Brownlow & Sons Co.
1654 Roswell Rd.
Marietta, GA 30062
(770) 977-8404

Choate Construction Co.
1640 Powers Ferry Rd., Bldg. 11, Suite 300

Marietta, GA 30067
(770) 644-2170

Citadel Corp.
6075 The Corners Parkway
Norcross, GA 30092
(770) 242-0604

Cleveland Group
2690 Cumberland Parkway, Suite 200
Atlanta, GA 30339
(770) 436-0879

Conlan Co., The
1800 Parkway Place, Suite 1010
Marietta, GA 30067
(770) 423-8000

Ellis-Don Construction
3100 Medlock Bridge Rd., Suite 335
Norcross, GA 30071
(770) 409-9985

Flagler Co.
2126 DeFoors Ferry Rd., N.W.
Atlanta, GA 30318
(404) 351-0007
Contact: Thorne Flagler, President

Glenn Sims Remodeling Co.
1924 Tucker Industrial Rd.
Tucker, GA 30084
(770) 934-9576

Griffin, R.J., & Co.
800 Mt. Vernon Hwy., Suite 200
Atlanta, GA 30328
(770) 551-8883
Contact: David Paris, Executive Vice-President

Hails Construction
10886 Crabapple Rd.
Roswell, GA 30075
(770) 993-8290
Contact: Roger Watson, Vice-President

Hardin Construction
1380 W. Paces Ferry Rd., N.W.
Atlanta, GA 30327
(404) 264-0404
Contact: JoAnn Weinberg, Personnel Director

HCB Contractors
3495 Piedmont Rd., N.E., Bldg. 10,
Suite 510
Atlanta, GA 30305
(404) 261-2200
Contact: Frank Spears, Vice-President and
District Manager

Holder Corporation
3333 Cumberland Circle, N.W., Suite 400
Atlanta, GA 30339
(770) 988-3000
Contact: Ms. Lee Johnston, Human
Resources

Home Rebuilders, The
1629 Monroe Dr.
Atlanta, GA 30324
(404) 876-3000

Kajima Construction Services
2859 Paces Ferry Rd., Suite 1500
Atlanta, GA 30339
(770) 431-6300

Keene Construction Co.
6500 McDonough Dr., Suite D-5
Norcross, GA 30093
(770) 448-8010

Lennon Co., The
5920 Roswell Rd., Suite B106-107
Atlanta, GA 30328
(404) 252-9848

Leslie Contracting
213 Jeff Davis Place, Suite 101
Fayetteville, GA 30214
(770) 460-7400

McDevitt Street Bovis
7000 Central Parkway, Suite 1400
Atlanta, GA 30328
(770) 481-9380

Metric Constructors
1395 S. Marietta Parkway, Suite 910
Marietta, GA 30067
(770) 428-4999
Contact: Jim Taylor, Regional Manager

National Service Industries
1420 Peachtree St., N.E.
Atlanta, GA 30309
(404) 853-1000
Lighting equipment

New South Construction Co.
1800 Phoenix Blvd., Suite 206
Atlanta, GA 30349
(770) 996-5600

Patton, M.G., Construction Co.
6645 Peachtree-Dunwoody Rd., N.E.
Atlanta, GA 30328
(770) 522-0005

Piedmont Residential
3023 Maple Dr.
Atlanta, GA 30305
(404) 841-9301

Pinkerton & Laws
1810 Water Place, Suite 220
Atlanta, GA 30339
(770) 956-9000

Raco General Contractors
1401 Dalon Rd.
Atlanta, GA 30306
(404) 873-3567

Rawn Construction Co.
3723 Clairmont Rd.
Atlanta, GA 30341
(404) 452-1295

Russell, H.J., Construction Co.
504 Fair St., S.W.
Atlanta, GA 30313
(404) 330-1000

SawHorse Inc.
5600 Roswell Rd., N.W., Suite N-368
Atlanta, GA 30042
(404) 256-2567

**Southeastern Construction
& Management**
3198 Cains Hill Place
Atlanta, GA 30305
(404) 365-7757

Southern Energy/Four Seasons
1955 Cliff Valley Way, Suite 235
Atlanta, GA 30329
(404) 315-0445

Southern Traditional Builders
635 Holmes St.
Atlanta, GA 30318
(404) 355-1332

Turner Construction Co.
7000 Central Parkway, Suite 650
Atlanta, GA 30328
(770) 551-2100

Van Winkle Consolidated Co.
652 Bellemeade Ave., N.W.

Atlanta, GA 30318
(770) 351-2132
Contact: Bryant McDaniel, Marketing
Director

Winter Construction Co., The
530 Means St., N.W., Suite 200
Atlanta, GA 30318
(404) 588-3300
Contact: Erin White, Marketing Coordinator

Weeks Construction Services
4497 Park Dr.
Norcross, GA 30093
(770) 923-4076

Cultural Institutions

WEB SITES:

**http://www.sirius.com/~robinson/
musprof.html**
is a resource for curators, researchers, and
museum staff.

**http://www.imagesite.com/muse/
museylpgs.html**
contains the museums and galleries Yellow
Pages.

**http://www.concourse.com/wwar/
galleries.html**
contains contact information for galleries.

PROFESSIONAL ORGANIZATIONS:

For networking among cultural institutions, museums, and the arts, check out
the following professional organizations
listed in Chapter 5. See also **"Museums/
Art Galleries."**

**Atlanta Writing Resource Center
Southern Arts Federation**

For more information, you can contact:

American Association of Museums
1225 I St., N.W.
Washington, DC 20005
(202) 289-1818

American Federation of Arts
41 E. 65th St.
New York, NY 10021
(212) 988-7700

**Amusement and Music Operators
Association**
401 N. Michigan Ave.
Chicago, IL 60611
(312) 644-6610

Arts and Business Council
25 W. 45th St.
New York, NY 10036
(212) 819-9287

**National Assembly of Local Arts
Agencies**
1420 K St., N.W.
Washington, DC 20005
(202) 371-2830

National Assembly of State Arts Agencies
1010 Vermont Ave., N.W.
Washington, DC 20005
(202) 347-6352

PROFESSIONAL PUBLICATIONS:

Art Business News
ArtCom
Artweek
BAM
Mix
Museum News
Music Journal
Performance
Show Business
Variety

DIRECTORIES:

Art Business News: Guide to Galleries, Museums, and Artists (Brant Art Publications, New York, NY)
Directory for the Arts (Center for Arts Information, New York, NY)
NASAA Directory (National Assembly of State Arts Agencies, Washington, DC)
Official Museum Directory (American Association of Museums, Washington, DC)
Who's Who in American Art (R.R. Bowker, New Providence, NJ)

Employers:

Alliance Theatre Company and Alliance Theatre School
1280 Peachtree St., N.E.
Atlanta, GA 30309
(404) 898-1132
Contact: Sallie Lawrence, Personnel Director

APEX Museum
135 Auburn Ave., N.E.
Atlanta, GA 30303
(404) 521-2739
Contact: Daniel Moore, President

Atlanta African Film Society
111 James P. Brawley Dr., S.W.

Atlanta, GA 30314
(404) 525-1136

Atlanta Bach Choir
1026 Ponce de Leon Ave., N.E.
Atlanta, GA 30306
(404) 872-2224

Atlanta Ballet Company
477 Peachtree St., N.E.
Atlanta, GA 30308
(404) 892-3303
Contact: Chuck Johnston, Executive Director

Atlanta Botanical Gardens
1345 Piedmont Ave., N.E.
Atlanta, GA 30309
(404) 876-5859
Contact: Calvin Cloud, Business Manager

Atlanta Boys Choir
1215 S. Ponce de Leon Ave., N.E.
P.O. Box 8583, Station F
Atlanta, GA 30306
(404) 378-0064
Contact: Fletcher Wolfe, Director

Atlanta Historical Society
3101 Andrews Dr., N.W.
Atlanta, GA 30305
(404) 814-4000
Contact: Rick Beard, Director

Atlanta Museum
537 Peachtree St., N.E.
Atlanta, GA 30308
(404) 872-8233
Contact: J.H. Elliott, Director

Atlanta Opera
1800 Peachtree St., N.W., Suite 620
Atlanta, GA 30309
(404) 355-3311
Contact: William Fred Scott, Artistic Director

Atlanta Shakespeare Company
499 Peachtree St.
Atlanta, GA 30308
(404) 874-5299
Contact: Tony Wright, Assoc. Director

Atlanta Symphony Orchestra
1293 Peachtree St., N.E.
Atlanta, GA 30309
(404) 898-1182
Contact: Linda Moxley, Director of
Marketing

Big Shanty Museum
2829 Cherokee St., N.W.
Kennesaw, GA 30144
(404) 427-2117
Contact: Katherine Fletcher, Director
Houses Civil War locomotive "The
General" of *The Great Locomotive
Chase* saga

Buckhead Roxy
3110 Roswell Rd., N.E.
Atlanta, GA 30324
(404) 233-7699
Contact: Dave Scruggs, Director

Bulloch Hall
180 Bulloch Ave.
Roswell, GA 30075
(404) 992-1731
Contact: Pam Humphries, Director

Center for Puppetry Arts
1404 Spring St., N.W.
Atlanta, GA 30309
(404) 873-3391
Contact: Lisa Rhodes, Administrative
Director

Center Stage Theatre
1374 W. Peachtree St., N.E.
Atlanta, GA 30309
(404) 874-1511
Contact: Ted Mankin, General Manager

Chattahoochee Nature Center
9135 Willeo Rd.
Roswell, GA 30075
(404) 992-2055
Contact: Greg Greer, Administrative
Executive
Trails, exhibits, and store

Dunwoody Stage Door Players
5339 Chamblee-Dunwoody Rd.
Dunwoody, GA 30338
(404) 396-1726
Contact: Peggy Brown, Administrative
Director

Fernbank Museum of Natural History
767 Clifton Rd., N.E.
Atlanta, GA 30307
(404) 378-0127

Fernbank Science Center
156 Heaton Park Dr., N.E.
Atlanta, GA 30307
(404) 378-4311
Contact: Mary Hiers, Director
Natural sciences museum, planetarium,
and forest with trails

Fox Theatre
660 Peachtree St., N.E.
Atlanta, GA 30365
(404) 881-2100
Contact: Roxanne Smith, Marketing
Director

Georgia Shakespeare Festival
501 Means St., N.W.
Atlanta, GA 30318
(404) 233-1717
Contact: Richard Garner, Producing
Director

Herndon Home
587 University Place, N.W.
Atlanta, GA 30314
(404) 581-9813
Contact: Carole Merritt, Director

High Museum of Art
1280 Peachtree St., N.E.
Atlanta, GA 30309
(404) 892-3600
Contact: Ned Rifkin, Director

**High Museum of Art Folk Art &
Photography Galleries**
30 John Wesley Dobbs Ave.
Atlanta, GA 30303
(404) 577-6940
Contact: Ellen Sleurov, Curator

Horizon Theatre Company
1083 Austin Ave., N.E.
Atlanta, GA 30307
(404) 584-7450
Mailing address:
P.O. Box 5376, Station E
Atlanta, GA 30307
Contact: Lisa and Jeff Adler, Co-Artistic
Directors

Image Film and Video Center
75 Bennett St., N.W.
Atlanta, GA 30309
(404) 352-4225
Contact: Nancy Kiracofe, Operations
Manager

Jomandi Productions
1444 Mayson St., N.E.
Atlanta, GA 30324
(404) 876-6346
Contact: Marsha Jackson, Managing
Director

Mitchell, Ruth, Dance Company
3509 Northside Parkway, N.W.
Atlanta, GA 30327
(404) 237-8829

Neighborhood Playhouse
430 W. Trinity Place
Decatur, GA 30030
(404) 373-3904
Contact: Sondra Nelson, Artistic/
Executive Director

Nexus Contemporary Arts Center
535 Means St., N.W.
Atlanta, GA 30318
(404) 688-2500
Contact: Louise Shaw, Executive Director

Onstage Atlanta
235 E. Ponce de Leon Ave.
Decatur, GA 30030
(404) 373-3039
Contact: Marc Gowan, Executive Artistic
Director

**Science and Technology Museum of
Atlanta (SCITEK)**
395 Piedmont Ave., N.E.
Atlanta, GA 30308
(404) 522-5500
Contact: Victoria Rogers, Vice-President
of External Affairs

Seven Stages
1105 Euclid Ave., N.E.
Atlanta, GA 30307
(404) 522-0911
Contact: Del Hamilton, Artistic Director

Southeastern Savoyards
2160 Adams Dr., N.W.
Atlanta, GA 30318
(404) 396-0620
Contact: Mr. Lynn Thompson, Artistic
Director

Theatre Gael
173 14th St.
Atlanta, GA 30309
(404) 876-1138

Theatre of the Stars
4469 Stella Dr., N.E.
Atlanta, GA 30355
(404) 252-8960
Mail to:
P.O. Box 11748
Atlanta, GA 30355
Contact: Louise Hudson, Executive
Producer

Theatrical Outfit, The
1012 Peachtree St., N.E.
Atlanta, GA 30309
(404) 872-0665
Mail to:
P.O. Box 7098
Atlanta, GA 30357
Contact: Phillip DePoy, Artistic Director

Woodruff Arts Center
1280 Peachtree St., N.E.
Atlanta, GA 30309
(404) 892-3600
Arts complex that is home to the Atlanta
Symphony Orchestra,
Alliance Theater Company, Atlanta
College of Art

Drugs and Cosmetics

WEB SITES:

http://pharminfo.com/pharmmall/
pm_hp.html
is the pharmaceutical information
network.

PROFESSIONAL ORGANIZATIONS:

For networking in the drug industry and
related fields, you may
want to check out this professional
organization listed in Chapter 5. Also see
"Chemicals."

International Food Additives Council

For more information, you can contact:

American Pharmaceutical Association
2215 Constitution Ave., N.W.
Washington, DC 20037
(202) 628-4410

**Cosmetic, Toiletry, and Fragrance
Association**
1101 17th St., N.W.
Washington, DC 20036
(202) 331-1770

**Health Industry Distributors
Association**
225 Reinekers Lane, #650
Alexandria, VA 22314
(703) 549-4432

**Health Industry Manufacturers
Association**
1200 G St., N.W., #400
Washington, DC 20005
(202) 452-8240

**National Association of Medical
Suppliers**
625 Slaters Lane, #200
Alexandria, VA 22314
(703) 836-6263

**National Association of Pharmaceutical
Manufacturers**
320 Old Country Rd.
Garden City, NY 11530
(516) 741-3699

**Pharmaceutical Manufacturers
Association**
1100 15th St., N.W.
Washington, DC 20005
(202) 835-3400

PROFESSIONAL PUBLICATIONS:

American Druggist
CFTA Newsletter
Cosmetics and Toiletries
Cosmetic World News
Drug Topics
*Journal of Pharmaceutical Marketing and
   Management*
NAPM News Bulletin
PMA Newsletter
Soap/Cosmetics/Chemical Specialties

DIRECTORIES:

Drug Topics Red Book (Litton Publica-
   tions, Oradell, NJ)
Fragrance Foundation Reference Guide
   (Fragrance Foundation, New York, NY)
NACDS Membership Directory (National
   Association of Chain Drugstores,
   Arlington, VA)
NWDA Membership Directory (National
   Wholesale Druggists Association,
   Scarsdale, NY)
Pharmaceutical Manufacturers of the U.S.
   (Noyes Data Corp., Park Ridge, NJ)
*Who's Who: The CFTA Membership
   Directory* (Cosmetic, Toiletry and
   Fragrance Association, Washington, DC)

Employers:

Action Testing & Consulting Laboratory
1800 Montreal Court
Tucker, GA 30084
(770) 270-9550
Contact: Jim Muenster, Assistant Director

Bronner Brothers Cosmetics
2141 Powers Ferry Rd.
Marietta, GA 30067
(404) 988-0015
Makers of ethnic hair care products for
over 40 years

Cheatham Chemical Company
1550 Roadhaven Dr.
Stone Mountain, GA 30083
(770) 414-7283
Contact: Michael Barker, Vice-President of
Sales

**Dante, Stephen, Cosmetics/Total
Accessories**
Atlanta Apparel Mart
250 Spring St., Suite 7 South 114
Atlanta, GA 30303
(404) 688-7807
Contact: Ms. Ellie Wolf, Owner

Hawaiian Tropic
616 Valley Brook Rd.
Decatur, GA 30033
(404) 296-5080
Contact: Ken Herring, Owner

International Murex Technologies Corp.
3075 Northwoods Circle
Norcross, GA 30071
(770) 662-0660
Medical products

**Jennings, Frankie, International
Cosmetics**
1625 John Calvin Ave.
College Park, GA 30337
(404) 758-1910
Contact: Ms. Frankie Jennings, President
Private label manufacturing, packaging.
Sales

K.H.E. Kulture House
650 Evans St., S.W.
Atlanta, GA 30310
(404) 753-3403
Contact: Khalilah Hasan, Owner
Essential oils, wholesale and retail

**Merck Sharp & Dohme Division of
Merck & Co.**
2825 Northwoods Parkway
Norcross, GA 30071
(770) 662-7200
Contact: Bob Vincent, Regional Director
Biological products

Mikart Inc.
2090 Marietta Blvd., N.W.
Atlanta, GA 30318
(404) 351-4510
Contact: Cerie McDonald, Vice-President
Drug manufacturer

Perryman Sales
5099 Southridge Parkway, Suite 108
Atlanta, GA 30349
(770) 991-9114
Contact: Gail Seabron

**Wyeth-Ayerst Laboratories Division of
American Home Products**
1000 Union Court
Kennesaw, GA 30144
(770) 421-0039
Contact: Jim French, Sales Division
Manager
Drug manufacturer

Educational Institutions

WEB SITES:

http://www.petersons.com:8080/
links to public and private schools,
colleges, and universities, arranged by
geography.

http://chronicle.ment.edu/
is the homepage of *ACADEME This Week;*
lists job opportunities.

PROFESSIONAL ORGANIZATIONS:

For networking in education and related
fields, check out the following profes-
sional organizations listed in Chapter 5:
**American Association of University
    Women—Atlanta Chapter
Atlanta Association of Educators
Fulton County Association of Educators
Georgia Association of Educators
Georgia Vocational Association
Professional Association of Georgia
    Educators
Southeastern Library Association**

For additional information, you can
contact:

**American Association of School
Administrators**
1801 N. Moore St.
Arlington, VA 22209
(703) 528-0700

**American Association of University
Women**
1111 16th St., N.W.
Washington, DC 20036
(202) 785-7700

Association of School Business Officials
11401 N. Shore Dr.
Reston, VA 22090
(703) 478-0405

**Council for Educational Development
and Research**
200 L St., N.W.
Washington, DC 20036
(202) 223-1593

National Education Association
1201 16th St., N.W.
Washington, DC 20036
(202) 833-4000

PROFESSIONAL PUBLICATIONS:

*The Chronicle of Higher Education
Education Week
Georgia Teacher
Instructor Magazine
School Administrator
Teaching Exceptional Children
Teaching Pre-K - 8
Technology and Learning
Today's Catholic Teacher*

DIRECTORIES:

College Blue Book (Macmillan, New York,
    NY)
Four Year Colleges (Peterson's Guides,
    Princeton, NJ)
Georgia Post-Secondary School Directory
    (Georgia Student Finance Authority,
    Tucker, GA)
*Georgia Public Education: State and Local
    Schools and Staff* (Georgia Department
    of Education, Atlanta, GA)
*Guide to Secondary Schools, Georgia/South
    Carolina Edition* (College Board, New
    York, NY)
Private Schools of the U.S. (Market Data
    Retrieval, Shelton, CT)
Public Schools USA (Williamson Publica-
    tions, Charlotte, NC)
QED's School Guide, Georgia edition
    (Quality Education Data, Denver, CO)
Yearbook of Higher Education (Marquis
    Publishing Co., Chicago, IL)

Employers, Elementary and High School:

Atlanta Board of Education
210 Pryor St., S.W.
Atlanta, GA 30335
(404) 827-8000
Contact: Barbara Howery, Human Resources

Children's School, The
345 10th St., N.E.
Atlanta, GA 30309
(404) 873-6985
Contact: Marcia Spiller, Principal

Children's World Learning Centers
1835 Savoy Dr., Suite 210
Atlanta, GA 30341
(770) 458-4646

Christ the King
46 Peachtree Way, N.E.
Atlanta, GA 30305
(404) 233-0383
Contact: Peggy Warner, Principal

Clayton County Board of Education
120 Smith St.
Jonesboro, GA 30236
(770) 473-2712
Contact: William Chavis, Director of Certified Personnel; Marty Whiteman, Classified Personnel

Cobb County Board of Education
514 Glover St., S.E.
Marietta, GA 30060
(770) 426-3300
Contact: James Wilson, Personnel Director
For teaching positions contact: George Hall, elementary; Liz Cole, middle; Dianne William, high

Decatur Board of Education
320 N. McDonough St.
Decatur, GA 30030
(404) 370-4400
Contact: Joann Podharez, Personnel

DeKalb County Board of Education
3770 N. Decatur Rd.
Decatur, GA 30032
(404) 297-1200
Contact: Bobbie Stephens

Douglas County Board of Education
9030 Highway 5
P.O. Box 1077
Douglasville, GA 30133
(770) 920-4000
Contact: Marysue Murray, Personnel Administrator

Epstein School of Atlanta, The
335 Colewood Way, N.W.
Atlanta, GA 30328
(404) 843-0111
Contact: Roz Cohen, Asst. Head of School

Fayette County Board of Education
210 W. Stonewall Ave.
Fayetteville, GA 30214
(770) 460-3535
Contact: Barry James, Personnel Director

Fulton County Board of Education
786 Cleveland Ave., S.W.
Atlanta, GA 30315
(404) 768-3600
Contact: Michael Gray, Director of Elementary Education; Norman Barchi, Director of Middle and High School Education

Galloway School
215 W. Weiuca Rd., N.W.
Atlanta, GA 30342
(404) 252-8389
Contact: Gordan Mathis, Upper Learning Principal; Jamie Tender, Middle Learning; Linda Camp, Early Learning

Georgia Department of Education
James "Sloppy" Floyd Veterans Building
1862 Twin Towers East
Atlanta, GA 30334
(404) 656-2510
Contact: Gene Abshier, Personnel Director

Greater Atlanta Christian School
1575 Indian Trail Rd.
Norcross, GA 30093
(770) 243-2000
Contact: David Fincher, Academic Vice-President

Gwinnett County Public Schools
52 Gwinnett Dr.
Lawrenceville, GA 30245
(770) 513-6656
Contact: Glenn Pethel, Personnel Director, elementary; Wendel L. Jackson, middle and high school

Hebrew Academy of Atlanta
5200 Northland Dr., N.E.
Atlanta, GA 30342
(404) 843-9900
Contact: Richard Wagner

Heiskell School, The
3260 Northside Dr., N.W.
Atlanta, GA 30305
(404) 262-2233
Contact: Mrs. James M. Heiskell

Henry County Schools
396 Tomlinson St.
P.O. Box 479
McDonough, GA 30253
(770) 957-6601
Contact: Richard Binkney, Personnel Director

Holy Innocents' Episcopal School
805 Mt. Vernon Hwy., N.W.
Atlanta, GA 30327
(404) 255-4026
Contact: Susan Groesbeck, Headmaster

Katherine & Jacob Greenfield Hebrew Academy of Atlanta
5200 Northland Dr., N.E.
Atlanta, GA 30342
(404) 843-9900

Killian Hill Christian School
151 Arcado Rd.
Lilburn, GA 30226
(770) 921-3224
Contact: Paul Williams, Administrator of the School

Landmark Christian School
50 E. Broad St.
Fairburn, GA 30213
(770) 306-0647

Lovett School, The
4075 Paces Ferry Rd., N.W.
Atlanta, GA 30327
(404) 262-3032
Contact: Jim Hendrix, Assistant to Headmaster

Marist School
3790 Ashford-Dunwoody Rd., N.E.
Atlanta, GA 30319
(770) 457-7201
Contact: Michael Maher, Headmaster

Masters Christian Academy
1985 LaVista Rd., N.E.
Atlanta, GA 30329
(404) 325-8540
Contact: Paul Humphrey, Principal

Montessori Institute of America
2355 Virginia Place, N.E.
Atlanta, GA 30305
(404) 233-1961
Contact: Lillian Bryan

Mount Paran Christian School
1700 Allgood Rd., N.E.
Marietta, GA 30062
(770) 578-0182
Contact: Susan King, Head Master

Mount Vernon Presbyterian
471 Mt. Vernon Hwy., N.E.
Atlanta, GA 30328
(404) 255-8557

Mount Zion Christian Academy
7102 Mt. Zion Blvd.
Jonesboro, GA 30236
(770) 478-9903

Our Lady of Assumption
1320 Hearst Dr., N.E.
Atlanta, GA 30319
(404) 364-1902
Contact: Joan Tiernan, Principal

Pace Academy
966 W. Paces Ferry Rd., N.W.

Atlanta, GA 30318
(404) 262-1345

Paideia School, The
1509 Ponce de Leon Ave.
Atlanta, GA 30307
(404) 377-3491
Contact: Paul Bianchi, Headmaster

Paulding County Schools
522 Hardee St.
Dallas, GA 30132
(770) 443-8000
Contact: Trudy Sowar, Personnel Director

Primrose School Franchising Co.
199 S. Erwin St.
Cartersville, GA 30120
(770) 606-9600

Providence Christian Academy
4575 Lawrenceville Hwy.
Lilburn, GA 30247
(770) 279-7200

Rockdale County School System
954 Main St.
Conyers, GA 30207
(770) 483-4713
Contact: Valerie Sue Smith, Director of
Human Resources

St. Pius X Catholic High School
2674 Johnson Rd., N.E.
Atlanta, GA 30345
(404) 636-3023
Contact: Mr. Sasso, Principal

St. Thomas More
630 W. Ponce de Leon Ave.
Decatur, GA 30030
(404) 373-8456
Contact: Thomas Collins, Principal

Sheltering Arms Child Development
350 Techwood Dr.
Atlanta, GA 30313
(404) 527-7475

Stone Mountain Christian School
P.O. Box 509
Stone Mountain, GA 30086
(770) 469-3431
Contact: John Tomlinson, Principal

Walker School, The
700 Cobb Parkway
Marietta, GA 30062
(770) 427-4666
Contact: Donald Robertson, Headmaster

Wesleyan School
86 Mt. Vernon
Sandy Springs, GA 30328
(404) 255-8557

Westminster Schools, The
1424 W. Paces Ferry Rd., N.W.
Atlanta, GA 30327
(404) 355-8673
Contact: William Clarkson, President

Wood Acres Country Day School
1772 Johnson Ferry Rd.
Marietta, GA 30062
(770) 971-1880
Contact: Kay & Dave Clark, owners

Woodward Academy
1662 Rugby Ave.
College Park, GA 30337
(404) 765-8200
Contact: Tom Jackson, President

Employers, Higher Education:

Agnes Scott College
141 E. College Ave.
Decatur, GA 30030
(404) 371-6285
Contact: Janet Gould, Director of
Personnel Services

American College for the Applied Arts
3330 Peachtree Rd., N.E.
Atlanta, GA 30326
(404) 231-9000
Contact: James Todd, Director

Atlanta Area Technical School
1560 Stewart Ave., S.W.
Atlanta, GA 30310
(404) 756-3700
Contact: Brenda Jones, President

Atlanta Christian College
2605 Ben Hill Rd.
East Point, GA 30344

(404) 761-8861
Contact: Edwin Groover, President
Four-year bible college

Atlanta College of Art
1280 Peachtree St., N.E.
Atlanta, GA 30309
(404) 898-1164
Contact: Diane Floyd, Business Manager

Atlanta Metropolitan College
1630 Stewart Ave., S.W.
Atlanta, GA 30310
(404) 756-4000

Atlanta School of Biblical Studies
4468 Covington Hwy.
P.O. Box 361786
Decatur, GA 30036
(404) 284-0037
Contact: Donald J. Musin, President

Carroll Technical Institute
997 S. Highway 16
Carrollton, GA 30117
(770) 836-6800

Chattahoochee Technical Institute
980 S. Cobb Dr.
Marietta, GA 30060
(770) 528-4500
Contact: Jean Hollis

Clark Atlanta University
223 James P. Brawley Dr., S.W.
Atlanta, GA 30314
(404) 880-8000
Contact: Gwendolyn Lytle, Human
Resource Director

Clayton State College
5900 N. Lee St.
Morrow, GA 30260
(770) 961-3526
Contact: Annette Butler, Personnel
Director

Columbia Theological Seminary
701 Columbia Dr.
P.O. Box 520
Decatur, GA 30031
(404) 378-8821

Contact: James Hudnut-Beumler,
Academic Dean's Office

Creative Circus
1935 Cliff Valley Way, N.E., Suite 210
Atlanta, GA 30329
(404) 633-1990
Contact: Rochelle Moore, Director of
Education

DeKalb College
3251 Panthersville Rd.
Decatur, GA 30034
(404) 244-2376
Contact: Barbara Disney, Director of
Human Resources

DeKalb Technical Institute
495 N. Indian Creek Dr.
Clarkston, GA 30021
(404) 297-9522
Contact: James Gray, Personnel

DeVry Institute of Technology
250 N. Arcadia Ave.
Decatur, GA 30030
(404) 292-7900
Contact: Steven Massie, Human Resource
Manager

Emory University
1762 Clifton Rd.
Atlanta, GA 30322
(404) 727-7611
Contact: Alice Miller, Associate Vice-
President, Human Resources

Georgia Institute of Technology
225 North Ave., N.W.
Atlanta, GA 30332
(404) 894-2000
Contact: Barry Chuck Dunbar, Associate
Vice-President

Georgia State University
University Plaza
Atlanta, GA 30303
(404) 651-2000
Contact: Connie Rifkind, Director of
Personnel

Griffin Technical Institute
501 Varsity Rd.
Griffin, GA 30223
(770) 228-7348

Gwinnett Technical School
5150 Sugarloaf Parkway
Lawrenceville, GA 30243
(770) 962-7580
Contact: Personnel for part-time
positions.
For full-time positions
Contact: Glenn Pethel, Personnel Director

**Interdenominational Theological
Seminary**
671 Beckwith St., S.W.
Atlanta, GA 30314
(404) 527-7700
Contact: Dr. Moore, Administrative Office

Kennesaw State University
3455 Frey Lake Rd.
Marietta, GA 30061
(770) 423-6000
Contact: Ed Rugg, Vice-President of
Academic Affairs

Life Chiropractic College
1269 Barclay Circle, S.E.
Marietta, GA 30060
(770) 424-0554
Contact: Dr. Rowberry, Academic Dean

Marshall, John, Law School
805 Peachtree St., N.E., Suite 400
Atlanta, GA 30308
(404) 872-3593
Contact: Robert J. Dagostino, President

Mercer University Atlanta
3001 Mercer University Dr.
Atlanta, GA 30341
(770) 986-3000
Contact: Sandy Givens, Director of
Personnel

Morehouse College
830 Westview Dr., S.W.
Atlanta, GA 30314
(404) 681-2800
Contact: Craig Triplett, Personnel

Morehouse School of Medicine
720 Westview Dr., S.W.
Atlanta, GA 30310-1495
(404) 752-1500
Contact: James Allen, Asst. Director

Morris Brown College
643 Martin Luther King, Jr., Dr., N.W.
Atlanta, GA 30314
(404) 220-0270
Contact: Julia King, Director of Human
Resources

North Metro Technical Institute
5198 Ross Rd.
Acworth, GA 30319
(770) 975-4010

Oglethorpe University
4484 Peachtree Rd., N.E.
Atlanta, GA 30319
(404) 261-1441
Contact: Linda Bucki, Vice-President for
Administration

**Portfolio Center for Art, Design and
Photography**
125 Bennett St., N.W.
Atlanta, GA 30309
(404) 351-5055
Contact: John Hunsinger, Director of
Admissions

Southern Polytechnic State University
1100 S. Marietta Parkway
Marietta, GA 30060-2896
(404) 528-7267
Contact: Don Green, Personnel Director

Spelman College
350 Spelman Lane, S.W.
Atlanta, GA 30314
(404) 681-3643
Contact: Forrest Tennant, Human
Resources

State University of Georgia
1600 Maple St.
Carrollton, GA 30118
(770) 836-6500

Electronics/Telecommunications

WEB SITES:

http://arioch.gsfc.nasa.gov/wwwvl/
ee.html
is the Web's virtual electrical engineering
library.

http://www.wiltel.com/library/
library.html
is a telecommunications library.

http://www.utsi.com/telecomm.html
links to telecom companies.

http://www.spp.umich.edu/telecom/
online-pubs.html
links to telecom companies and on-line
publications.

PROFESSIONAL ORGANIZATIONS:

For networking in the electronics industry
and related fields, check out these
organizations listed in Chapter 5. Also see
"**Computers**" sections.

**National Contract Management
Association**

For additional information, you can
contact:

American Electronics Association
5201 Great American Parkway
Santa Clara, CA 95054
(408) 987-4200

Electronics Industries Association
2500 Wilson Blvd.
Arlington, VA 22201
(703) 907-7500

**Institute of Electrical & Electronics
Engineers (IEEE)**
1730 Massachusetts Ave., N.W.
Washington, DC 20036
(202) 371-0101

Telecommunications Association
74 New Montgomery St., Suite 230
San Francisco, CA 94105
(415) 777-4647

PROFESSIONAL PUBLICATIONS:

Communications Daily
Electronic Business
Electronic News
Electronics
Technology News of America
Telecommunications Week
Telephony

DIRECTORIES:

American Electronics Association Directory
(American Electronics Association, Santa
Clara, CA)
Corporate Technology Directory (Corporate
Technology Information Services, Inc.,
Woburn, MA)
Directory and Buyers Guide (Telephony,
Chicago, IL)
EIA Trade Directory and Membership List
(Electronics Industries Association,
Washington, DC)
Telecommunications Directory (Gale
Research, Detroit, MI)
U.S. Electronics Industry Directory (Harris
Publications, Twinsburg, OH)
Who's Who in Electronics (Harris Publica-
tions, Twinsburg, OH)

Employers:

AirTouch
4151 Ashford-Dunwoody Rd.
Atlanta, GA 30319
P.O. Box 105477
Atlanta, GA 30348-9504
(404) 257-5000
Contact: Dianne Monk, Human Resources
Department
Cellular phone service operator

American Indetel Communications
3000 Northwood Parkway
Norcross, GA 30071
(770) 446-3031
Contact: Pam Burke, Office Manager
Business telephone systems

Attachmate
1000 Alderman Dr.
Alpharetta, GA 30202
(770) 442-4000
Contact: Michael Barnes, Recruiter
Atlanta's third largest high-tech company.
Provides data communications equipment
and systems

AT&T
1200 Peachtree St., N.E.
Atlanta, GA 30309
(404) 810-7001
Contact: Management Employment
Office
Long distance network services, telecommunications equipment, telephone
switching equipment, communications
cable, computers, telephones. Atlanta's
largest telecommunications company

BellSouth Corp.
1155 Peachtree St., N.E.
Atlanta, GA 30309
(404) 249-2000
Contact: Buddy Henry, Executive Vice-
President Corporate Relations
Telecommunications holding company,
local and long distance telephone service,
telecommunications products and services

BT North America
2 Paces Ferry W.
2727 Paces Ferry Rd., Suite 1500
Atlanta, GA 30339
(770) 333-4600
Outsourcing of international data, image
and voice telecommunication network
solutions

**Burnup & Simms Communications
Services**
5555 Oakbrook Dr., Suite 620
Norcross, GA 30093
(770) 662-8310
Design, installation, and maintenance of
communication cabling systems and
networks

Butler Telecommunications Group
4960 Peachtree Industrial Blvd., Suite 210
Norcross, GA 30071
(770) 448-9220
Contact: Joe Meador, Recruiter
Engineering and construction services to
the telecommunications industry

Byers Engineering
6285 Barfield Rd.
Atlanta, GA 30328
(404) 843-1000
Contact: Cindy Lawrence, Controller
Manufactures computer graphics and
provides engineering services for utilities

Cable Consultants
3850 Peachtree Industrial Blvd.
Duluth, GA 30136
(770) 441-0854
Contact: Ms. Martyh Bostwick, Office
Manager
Engineering, design, and installation of
voice and data networks

Communications Technology Corp.
6049 Boatrock Blvd.
Atlanta, GA 30336
(404) 346-3967
Contact: Pamela Johnson, Personnel
Manager
Manufacturers of outside plant telecom-
munications equipment

Computer Communications Specialists
6529 Jimmy Carter Blvd.
Norcross, GA 30071
(770) 441-3114
Contact: Lois Swartwood, Human
Resources
Manufactures and sells voice and data
processing systems

Convergent Media Systems
3490 Piedmont Rd., Suite 800
Atlanta, GA 30305
(404) 262-1555
Contact: Sam Sanders, Director of Human
Resources
Satellite video conferencing

Cox Communications
1400 Lake Hearn Dr., N.E.
Atlanta, GA 30319
(404) 843-5000
Contact: Mary Leamer, Human Resources
Development and operation of cable
systems for Cox Enterprises Inc.

Electromagnetic Sciences
660 Engineering Dr.
Norcross, GA 30092
(770) 263-9200
Designs and manufactures microwave
equipment and radio-linked data
communications equipment

Electronic Technical Applications of America
1395 S. Marietta Parkway, S.E., Bldg. 200,
Suite 206
Marietta, GA 30067
(770) 428-1901
Contact: Roger Malsbury, Owner
Electronic instrument repair and
calibration

Electronic Tele-Communications
3620 Clearview Parkway
Atlanta, GA 30340
(770) 457-5600
Design, marketing, and service of voice
and call processing systems

ERDAS
2801 Buford Hwy., Suite 300
Atlanta, GA 30329
(404) 248-9000
Contact: Bill Pennington, Manager of
Human Resources
Produces image processing and geo-
graphic mapping systems

Ernest Telecom
6475 Jimmy Carter Blvd., Suite 300
Norcross, GA 30071
(770) 448-7788
Contact: Pam Ernest, Vice-President
Manufactures a computer card for pay
telephones

Fulton Communications Telephone Co.
3146 Reps Miller Rd.
Norcross, GA 30071
(770) 446-3100
Contact: Ken DeMarcus, President
Business communications systems

GTE Mobile Communications
245 Perimeter Center Parkway, N.E.
Atlanta, GA 30346
(770) 391-8000
Contact: Ronald J. Meadows, Manager of
Corporate Selling
Telephone service, communications
engineering, network services, government systems

GTE Supply
2580 Cumberland Parkway, N.W.
Atlanta, GA 30339
(770) 433-1838
Contact: Bob Patterson, National Sales
Manager
Electronic mail service

Hitachi American Ltd., Telecommunications Division
3617 Parkway Lane, Suite 100
Norcross, GA 30092
(770) 446-8820
Contact: Monica Lay, Human Resources
Digital PBX systems and facsimile
machines, research, manufacturing, sales,
service

Information Dynamics
1600 Oakbrook Dr., Suite 580
Norcross, GA 30091
(770) 449-5083
Contact: Rick Purnell, Sales Manager

MCI Center
3 Ravinia Dr.
Atlanta, GA 30346-2102
(770) 280-6535
Contact: Bob Green, Director of Personnel
Long distance telephone company

Melita International
5051 Peachtree Circle
Norcross, GA 30092
(770) 446-7800
Contact: Elaine Raglannd, Human
Resources
Researches and develops, manufactures,
and markets automated telephone call
processing systems

Mitsubishi Electric Sales America
6100 Atlantic Blvd.
Norcross, GA 30071
(770) 448-1263
Contact: JoAnne Mocny, Administrator,
Human Resources

National Data Corporation
1 National Data Plaza
Atlanta, GA 30329
(404) 728-2000
Contact: Don Howard, Vice-President of
Human Resources
Provides data communications equipment
and systems

Northern Telecom
5555 Windward Parkway, Suite B
Alpharetta, GA 30201
(770) 661-5000
Manufacturing, marketing, and sales of
telecommunications switching products

Northern Wire and Cable
5555 Oakbrook Parkway, Bldg. 400, Suite
400
Norcross, GA 30093
(770) 955-6800
Contact: Kristen Walsh

Nova Information Systems
5 Concourse Parkway, Suite 700
Atlanta, GA 30328
(770) 396-1456
Bank-card processing and transaction
networking services

Protech Systems
679 Arnold Mill Rd.
Woodstock, GA 30188
(770) 926-0342
Contact: Sue Marchman, Office Manager
Printed and etched circuits

Seams Business Communications
1600 Riveredge Parkway, Suite 900
Atlanta, GA 30328
(770) 956-2000
Sales, installation, and service of business
telephone systems

Scientific-Atlanta Inc.
1 Technology Parkway South
Norcross, GA 30092
(770) 903-5000
Contact: Brian Koenig, Vice-President of
Human Resources
Atlanta's largest high-tech company.
Manufactures communication products,
defense systems, and test instruments

**Southern Bell Telephone and Telegraph
Co.**
Send resumes to:
100 Perimeter Center Place, Rm. 193
Atlanta, GA 30346
(800) 407-0281
Local telephone company for metro
Atlanta area

Sprint
3065 Cumberland Circle
Atlanta, GA 30339
(404) 649-8000
Contact: Mr. Orbin Harris, Human
Resources Department

Superior Tele Tec
150 Interstate North Parkway
Atlanta, GA 30339
(770) 953-8338
Manufactures telecommunications cable
and voice/data transmission systems

Utility Consultants
1800 Water Place, N.W., Suite 200
Atlanta, GA 30339
(770) 955-9922
Contact: Ken Taylor, Manager
Engineering, construction, installation,
maintenance, and other services to
telecommunications, power, and CATV
industries

Video Display Corp.
1868 Tucker Industrial Dr.
Tucker, GA 30084
(770) 938-2080
Contact: Vicky McCall, Personnel Manager
Produces cathode ray tubes and optic components

Walters Communications
2690-C Summers St.
Kennesaw, GA 30144
(770) 422-1430
Contact: Pete Walters, Owner
Fiber optic splicing and installation

Wegener Corporation
11350 Technology Circle
Duluth, GA 30155
(770) 623-0096
Contact: Elaine Miller, Personnel Manager
Produces satellite communications electronics

Engineering

WEB SITES:

http://www.webcreations.com/bolton/ is a job-search page for engineers.

http://www.techweb.comp.com/current is a job listing and career information site for technical careers.

http://www.ieee.org/jobs.html lists engineering jobs.

PROFESSIONAL ORGANIZATIONS:

For networking in engineering and related fields, check out the following professional organizations listed in Chapter 5. You may also want to look at the sections on "Architecture," "Construction," and "Environmental Services."
American Society of Heating, Refrigeration and Air
American Society of Mechanical Engineers
Association of Energy Engineers
Georgia Society of Professional Engineers
Society for Marketing Professional Services

For additional information, you can contact:

American Society of Civil Engineers
345 E. 47th St.
New York, NY 10017
(212) 705-7496

American Society of Mechanical Engineers
345 E. 47th St.
New York, NY 10017
(212) 705-7722

Institute of Electrical & Electronics Engineers (IEEE)
345 E. 47th St.
New York, NY 10017
(212) 705-7900

National Society of Professional Engineers
1420 King St.
Alexandria, VA 22314
(703) 684-2800

National Society of Women Engineers
120 Wall St., 11th Floor
New York, NY 10005
(212) 509-9577

PROFESSIONAL PUBLICATIONS:

Building Design & Construction
Chemical Engineering
Civil Engineering News
Electronic Engineering Times
ENR: Engineering News Record

DIRECTORIES:

*American Consulting Engineers Council
Directory* (American Consulting
Engineers Council, Washington, DC)
Directory of Contract Service Firms (C.E.
Publications, Kenmore, WA)
Engineering, Science and Computer Jobs
(Peterson's Guides, Princeton, NJ)
IEEE Directory (Institute of Electrical and
Electronics Engineers, New York, NY)
Official Register (American Society of Civil
Engineers, New York, NY)
Professional Engineering Directory
(National Society of Professional
Engineers, Alexandria, VA)
Who's Who in Engineering (American
Association of Engineering Societies,
Washington, DC)

Employers:
A & C Consultants
1797 N.E. Expressway
Atlanta, GA 30329
(404) 633-9099
Contact: Dean Alford, President

Applied Engineering and Science
2261 Perimeter Park Dr., Suite One
Atlanta, GA 30341
(770) 454-1818
Contact: Ms. Chris Stamile

Armour Cape & Pond
2635 Century Parkway, Suite 800
Atlanta, GA 30345
(404) 633-8998

ATC/ATEC Associates
1300 Williams Dr., N.E., Suite A
Marietta, GA 30066
(770) 427-9456
Contact: Kay Abramson, Human
Resources Manager

Atlanta Testing & Engineering
11420 Johns Creek Parkway
Duluth, GA 30136
(770) 476-3555
Contact: Clinton Hammond, Comptroller

Bennett & Pless
1900 Century Place
Atlanta, GA 30345
(404) 325-2000
Contact: Nancy Pless, Personnel Director

Byers Engineering Co.
6285 Barfield Rd.
Atlanta, GA 30328
(404) 843-1000
Contact: Kenneth G. Byers, Jr., President

Camp Dresser & McKee
2100 Riveredge Parkway, Suite 500
Atlanta, GA 30328
(770) 971-5407

Caraustar Industries
3100 Washington St.
Austell, GA 30001
(770) 948-3101
Contact: Richard France, Director of
Human Resources

Childress Hunt & Associates
3107 Medlock Bridge Rd.
Norcross, GA 30071
(770) 446-3779
Contact: Bill Childress

Civil Engineering Consultants
1225 Johnson Ferry Rd., N.E., Suite 855
Marietta, GA 30068
(770) 977-5747
Contact: Susan Upchurch, Office Manager

Crown Anderson
306 Dividend Dr.
Peachtree City, GA 30269
(770) 486-2000
Air pollution control systems; design,
supply, and installation of hazardous
chemical and medical waste incineration
systems; storage

Dames & Moore
235 Peachtree Rd., N.E.
North Tower, Suite 2000
Atlanta, GA 30303
(404) 577-2122

Dynamic Metals
584 Edgewood Ave.
Atlanta, GA 30312
(404) 577-2398
Contact: Gene Labus, Controller
Metals recycling

Emcon
1560 Oakbrook Dr., Suite 100
Norcross, GA 30093
(770) 447-4665

Engineering Associates
2625 Cumberland Parkway, Suite 100
Atlanta, GA 30339
(770) 432-8833
Contact: Jan Barber, Personnel Director

Facility Group, The
2233 Lake Park Dr.
Smyrna, GA 30080
(770) 437-2700

Franco, A.M., Engineers
409 Blanton Rd., N.W.
Atlanta, GA 30342
(404) 255-8313
Contact: Aaron Franco, Owner

Golder Associates Inc.
3730 Chamblee-Tucker Rd.
Atlanta, GA 30341
(770) 496-1893
Contact: Kim Scott, Coordinator

Harrington Engineers
2981 Church St.
East Point, GA 30344
(404) 761-0767
Contact: B.W. Harrington, Owner

Harrington George & Dunn
1401 Peachtree St., N.E., Suite 120
Atlanta, GA 30309
(404) 885-1555
Contact: Anthony George, Director of
Human Resources

Hibble Peters & Dawson
3000 Clearview Ave.
Doraville, GA 30340
(770) 455-7707
Contact: Ron Tate, Business Manager

Jordon, Jones & Goulding
2000 Clearview Ave., N.E.
Atlanta, GA 30340
(770) 455-8555
Contact: Carol Clary, Human Resources
Recruiter

Law Companies Group
3 Ravinia Dr., Suite 1830
Atlanta, GA 30346
(770) 396-8000
Contact: Amy Cantin, Corporate
Personnel Director

**Law Engineering & Environmental
Services**
114 Town Park Dr.
Kennesaw, GA 30144
(770) 421-3400

Lockwood Greene Engineers
250 Williams St., N.W.
Atlanta, GA 30303
(404) 525-0500
Contact: Donald R. Luger or W.M. Leslie,
Managing Principals

Lynch, Jack, & Associates
2142 Vista Dale Court
Tucker, GA 30084
P.O. Box 420127
Atlanta, GA 30342
(770) 939-2616
Contact: Jack Lynch, President

Mayes Sudderth & Etheredge
2217 Roswell Rd., Suite G100
Marietta, GA 30062
(770) 971-5407

Metcalf & Eddy
1201 Peachtree St., N.E., Suite 1101
Atlanta, GA 30361
(404) 881-8010
Contact: J.C. Goldman, Senior Vice-
President

Neilsen Structural Engineers
3475 Lenox Rd., N.E., Suite 200
Atlanta, GA 30326
(404) 231-8693
Contact: Harold Neilsen, President

Newcomb & Boyd Consulting Engineers
1 Northside 75
Atlanta, GA 30318
(404) 352-3930
Contact: Warren Shiver, Senior Partner

O'Neal Inc.
3525 Piedmont Rd., Suite 610
Atlanta, GA 30305
(404) 237-4725

Palmer Engineering Co.
3690 N. Peachtree Rd.
Chamblee, GA 30341
(770) 452-8255
Contact: W.F. Palmer, Jr., President

Pharr Engineering
1770 Century Circle, N.E., Suite 22
Atlanta, GA 30345
(404) 325-3441
Contact: Michael Williamson, Vice-President

Piedmont, Olsen, Hensley
3200 Professional Parkway, Suite 200
Atlanta, GA 30339
(770) 952-8861
Contact: Susan Strickland, Office Manager

Post, Buckley, Schuh & Jernigan
1575 Northside Dr., Suite 350
Atlanta, GA 30318
(404) 351-5608

Robert & Co.
96 Poplar St., N.W.
Atlanta, GA 30335
(404) 577-4000
Contact: L.W. Robert, Managing Partner

Sandwell Inc.
2690 Cumberland Parkway
Atlanta, GA 30339
(770) 433-9336

Simons Engineering
1 W. Court Square
Decatur, GA 30030
(404) 370-3200
Contact: Mary Arnold, Human Resources

Southern Engineering Company
1800 Peachtree St.
Atlanta, GA 30367-8301
(404) 352-9200
Contact: R. Drayton, Vice-President of Personnel

Starzer & Ritchie
2323 Perimeter Park Dr., Suite 100
Atlanta, GA 30341
(770) 455-3404
Contact: Hubert Starzer, President

Thompson, W.L., Consulting Engineers
3475 Lenox Rd., N.E., Suite 300
Atlanta, GA 30326
(404) 266-1400
Contact: W.L. Thompson, Chief Executive Officer

Tolson-Simpson & Associates, Consulting Engineers
6025 The Corners Parkway, Suite 207
Norcross, GA 30092
(770) 263-1034
Contact: Jim Freedman

United Consulting Group
625 Holcomb Bridge Rd.
Norcross, GA 30071
(770) 209-0029

Weems-Doer Engineers
1655 Tully Circle, N.E.
Atlanta, GA 30329
(404) 321-7544
Contact: Mr. Weems, President

Williams, Russell and Johnson
771 Spring St., N.W.
Atlanta, GA 30308
(404) 853-6800
Contact: Beverly Mosby, Personnel

Yeung and Viness
2080 Peachtree Industrial Court, Suite 112
Chamblee, GA 30341
(770) 457-3688
Contact: Mr. Viness, Owner

Environmental Services

WEB SITES:

http://envirolink.org/envirowebs.html
links to publications, organizations, government, and industry sites.

http://www.econet.apc.org/econet/
links to industry news and organizations.

PROFESSIONAL ORGANIZATIONS:

You may also want to check out the section on **"Engineering."** For information about environmental services and related fields, you may contact:

Alliance for Environmental Education
10751 Ambassador Dr., Suite 201
Manassas, VA 22110
(703) 335-1025

The Conservation Foundation
1250 24th St., N.W.
Washington, DC 20037
(202) 293-4800

Earthwatch
P.O. Box 403N
Watertown, MA 02272
(617) 926-8200

Environmental Careers Organization
286 Congress St., 3rd Floor
Boston, MA 02210-1009
(617) 426-4783

Greenpeace USA
1436 U St., N.W.
Washington, DC 20009
(202) 462-1177

National Assoc. for Environmental Professionals
5165 MacArthur Blvd., N.W.
Washington, DC 20016
(202) 966-1500

National Wildlife Federation
1400 16th St., N.W.
Washington, DC 20036-2266
(202) 797-6800

Sierra Club
730 Polk St.
San Francisco, CA 94109
(415) 776-2211

Water Environment Federation
601 Wythe St.
Alexandria, VA 22314
(703) 684-2400

PROFESSIONAL PUBLICATIONS:

E, The Environmental Magazine
Ecology USA
Environmental Business Journal
Environmental Report
EPA Journal
Pollution Engineering
Water Engineering and Management
Water and Wastes Digest

DIRECTORIES:

The Complete Guide to Environmental Careers (The CEIP Fund, Island Press, Washington, DC)
Conservation Directory (National Wildlife Federation, Washington, DC)
Directory of National Environmental Organizations (U.S. Environmental Directories, St. Paul, MN)
EI Environmental Services (Environmental Information, Bloomington, MN)
The Environmental Career Guide (John Wiley & Sons, New York, NY)
Green at Work: Finding a Business Career that Works for the Environment (Island Press, Washington, DC)

A "growth" industry

An environmental consultant friend of ours says the enforcement of federal regulations and emphasis on compliance with hazardous waste removal and clean air and water acts has put increased demands on her office. Opportunities for lawyers, engineers, and environmentalists are growing in large corporations and non-profit organizations. As she says, "It's a growth industry."

Employers:

ATC/ATEC Associates
1300 Williams Dr.
Marietta, GA 30066
(770) 427-9456
Contact: Kay Abramson, Human Resources Coordinator
Environmental engineering and consulting, remediation services, geotechnical engineering

Applied Engineering and Science
2261 Perimeter Park Dr., Suite 1
Atlanta, GA 30341
(770) 454-1818
Contact: Barbara Boyle, Administrative Assistant
Hazardous waste treatment and management, industrial wastewater studies and treatment

Associated Environmental
1325 N. Meadow Park, Suite 114
Roswell, GA 30076
(770) 569-1712
Contact: Human Resources
Underground storage tank management, environmental property assessment, hazardous waste management

Atlanta Testing and Engineering
11420 Johns Creek Parkway
Duluth, GA 30155
(770) 476-3555
Contact: Greg Fischer, Environmental Manager
Geotechnical engineering, construction materials testing, environmental service

Brown & Caldwell
53 Perimeter Center E., Suite 500
Atlanta, GA 30346
(770) 394-2997
Water, wastewater, storm water, energy, air, and hazardous waste engineering

Browning-Ferris Industries of Georgia
8607 Roberts Dr., Suite 100
Atlanta, GA 30350
(770) 640-2300
Contact: Ms. Pat Abel
Residential and commercial recycling, waste collection, transportation and disposal; design, construction, and operation of sanitary landfills

Camp Dresser & McKee
2100 Riveredge Parkway, Suite 500
Atlanta, GA 30328
(770) 971-5407
Industrial and municipal hazardous waste, engineering, design, and construction

Caraustar Industries
3100 Washington St.
Austell, GA 30001
(770) 948-3101
Contact: Richard France, Director of Human Resources

Central Metals Co.
1765 The Exchange, Suite 500
Atlanta, GA 30339
(770) 951-6700
Contact: Martin Kogon, Vice-President
Recycling—glass, aluminum, other metals

CH2M Hill
115 Perimeter Center Place N.E., Suite 700
Atlanta, GA 30345
(770) 604-9095
Environmental consulting and strategy
development, process technology, design,
and construction

Chemical Waste Management
2600 Delk Rd., Suite 100
Marietta, GA 30067
(770) 951-6700
Waste reduction, treatment, disposal,
transportation, storage, recycling

Clayton Environmental Consultants
400 Chastain Center Blvd., N.W.,
Suite 490
Kennesaw, GA 30144
(770) 499-7500
Occupational health and safety, environmental engineering and remediation,
litigation support, and analytical
laboratory

Crown Anderson
306 Dividend Dr.
Peachtree City, GA 30269
(770) 631-0453
Contact: Joseph Accort
Air pollution control systems; design,
supply, and installation of hazardous
chemical and medical waste incineration
systems; storage

Dames & Moore
235 Peachtree Rd., N.E.
North Tower, Suite 2000
Atlanta, GA 30303
(404) 577-2122
Remedial design and construction services

DPC General Contractors
250 Arizona Ave., Bldg. A
Atlanta, GA 30307
(404) 373-0561
Asbestos and lead abatement, demolition/
hauling, underground tank removal and
installation, and soil remediation

Dynamic Metals
584 Edgewood Ave.
Atlanta, GA 30312
(404) 577-2398
Contact: Gene Labus, Controller
Metals recycling

Earth Tech
2264 Northwest Parkway, Suite E
Marietta, GA 30067
(770) 850-0777
Contact: Jan Dorsch
Site remediation investigations and risk
assessment; UST services; PCB decontamination; sampling and analyses

Emcon
1560 Oakbrook Dr., Suite 100
Norcross, GA 30093
(770) 447-4665
Solid and hazardous waste management
and design, regulatory/compliance audits,
industrial hygiene and safety

Engineering Science
57 Executive Park, Suite 590
Atlanta, GA 30329
(404) 325-0770
Contact: Rose Deslauries, Personnel
Director
Hazardous waste management, industrial
and municipal waste treatment, laboratory analyses

Federal Environmental Services
1100 Northmeadow Parkway, Suite 108
Roswell, GA 30076
(770) 740-1000
Contact: Speer Mabry
Engineering, consulting, lab analysis,
remediation, recycling, transportation,
disposal

Foster Wheeler Environmental Corp.
302 Research Dr.
Norcross, GA 30092
(770) 825-7200
Engineering, consulting, and remediation

GeoSyntec Consultants
1100 Lake Hearn Dr., N.E., Suite 200
Atlanta, GA 30342
(404) 705-9500
Geoenvironmental engineering, hazardous and solid waste engineering, and management

Golder Associates
3730 Chamblee-Tucker Rd.
Atlanta, GA 30341
(770) 496-1893
Contact: Kimberly Scott
Consulting, hydrogeology; geotechnical engineering; solid, hazardous, and nuclear waste disposal management; mining engineering; water resources management

Jordan, Jones & Goulding
2000 Clearview Ave., N.E.
Atlanta, GA 30340
(770) 455-8555
Municipal and industrial wastewater treatment; hazardous and solid waste management; regulatory compliance programs; air and odor studies

Kemron Environmental Service
2987 Clairmont Rd., Suite 150
Atlanta, GA 30329
(404) 636-0928
Contact: Wendy Sexton
Environmental assessments; wetlands ecology delineation; hazardous waste management; soil and groundwater remediation; endangered species surveys

Lake Engineering
35 Glenlake Parkway, Suite 500
Atlanta, GA 30328
(770) 395-0464
Air, solid, and hazardous waste, process design, and water

Law Companies Group
3 Ravinia Dr., Suite 1830
Atlanta, GA 30346
(770) 396-8000
Contact: George Furguson, Director of Human Resources

Environmental engineering and earth science consulting; air quality, site assessment; solid waste management

Lockwood Greene Engineers
250 Williams St., Suite 4000
Atlanta, GA 30303
(404) 525-0500
Contact: Kathy Pleggi, Recruiting Specialist
Environmental testing, waste treatment design, water supply management, air emissions control, hazardous waste, solvents control

Metro Alloys
717 Highland Ave.
Atlanta, GA 30312
(404) 688-6063
Contact: Bruce Berman, Vice-President
Metals recycling

Mindis Recycling
1990 DeFoor Ave.
Atlanta, GA 30318
(404) 262-0400
Contact: Laury Bagen, Director of Human Resources
Recycling: newspapers, glass, aluminum, other metals, plastics, corrugated materials

Newell Recycling Co.
1359 Central Ave.
Atlanta, GA 30344
(404) 766-1621
Contact: Joan Blalock, Office Manager
Metals recycling

OHM Remediation Services Corp.
5335 Triangle Parkway, Suite 450
Norcross, GA 30092
(770) 729-3900
Site remediation and closure; emergency response; hydrogeological site assessment; facility decommissioning; groundwater treatment; remedial design and construction

Parsons Engineering Science
57 Executive Park South
Atlanta, GA 30329
(404) 235-2300
Hazardous waste reduction, wastewater
treatment plant design, risk assessment,
and plant operations

Permafix Environmental Services
6075 Roswell Rd., Suite 602
Atlanta, GA 30328
(404) 847-9990
Hazardous waste treatment, wastewater
treatment, and reclamation

Purafil Inc.
2654 Weaver Way
Doraville, GA 30340
(770) 662- 8545
Contact: Beth Gular, Engineering
Air purification systems, monitoring,
instrumentation, environmental testing
services

Radian International
1979 Lakeside Parkway, Suite 800
Tucker, GA 30084
(770) 414-4522
Environmental engineering, remediation,
and information

Recycall Corp.
922 Memorial Dr.
Atlanta, GA 30316
(404) 688-6824
Recycles aluminum, paper, office paper

Recycle America of Atlanta
255 Ottley Dr., N.E.
Atlanta, GA 30371
(404) 892-8480
Contact: Sylvia Dean, Personnel
Recycles newspaper, glass, plastics,
aluminum, corrugated materials

Rust Environmental and Infrastructure
1650 Oakbrook Dr., Suite 445
Norcross, GA 30093
(770) 417-1680
Hydrogeology investigations; remedial

engineering; underground storage tank
closures; environmental site assessments;
storm water control

Southeast Recycling Corp.
200 Powers Ferry Rd., Suite 600
Marietta, GA 30067
(770) 955-6300
Contact: Ron Secrest, Human Resources
Manager
Recycles newspapers, aluminum, plastic,
glass, corrugated material, all grades of
paper

Spatco Environmental Services
3300 Holcolm Bridge Rd., Suite 222
Norcross, GA 30092
(770) 409-7820
Contact: Mac Bowes, Manager
Soil, groundwater, and hazardous waste
management and remediation;
bioremediation; site assessments; drilling;
decontamination and construction

Waste Abatement Technology
1235 F Kennestone Circle
Marietta, GA 30066
(770) 427-1947
Contact: Margaret Cain, Office Manager
Hazardous and solid waste site cleanup;
groundwater remediation; soil treatment;
lagoon closure; drum characterization and
removal

Waste Management of North America
1765 The Exchange, Suite 500
Atlanta, GA 30339
Contact: Jennifer Williams, Human
Resources
Waste reduction, recycling, solid waste
collection and disposal

Westinghouse Remediation Services
675 Park North Blvd., Suite 100
Clarkston, GA 30083
(404) 299-4713
Soil and groundwater containment,
decontamination and dismantling, and
groundwater recovery and treatment

Weston, Roy F.
1880-H Beaver Ridge Circle
Norcross, GA 30071
(770) 263-5400
Turnkey remedial design and construction; site investigation; hydrogeology; solid waste planning; landfill design and construction

Winter Environmental Services
530 Means St., Suite 100
Atlanta, GA 30318
(404) 588-0288
Site remediation, asbestos abatement, plant services, and brownfield developments

Film, Video, and Related Fields

WEB SITES:

**http://www.fleethouse.com/fhcanada/
western/bc/van/entertan/hqe/vrhq-
lnk.htm**
is a comprehensive guide to theater, film, television, and music industries.

http://www.ern.com/ern.htm
has links to companies and individuals in the entertainment industry.

PROFESSIONAL ORGANIZATIONS:

For networking in film, videotape, and related fields, check out these professional organizations listed in Chapter 5. You may also want to look at the section on **"Broadcasting and Television."**

**Atlanta Producers Association, The
(TAPA)
Atlanta Songwriters Association**

For additional information, you can contact:

**Academy of Motion Picture Arts and
Sciences**
8949 Wilshire Blvd.
Beverly Hills, CA 90211
(310) 247-3000

American Film Institute
Kennedy Center for Performing Arts
Washington, DC 20566
(202) 828-4000

Film Arts Foundation
346 9th St.
San Francisco, CA 94103
(415) 552-8760

PROFESSIONAL PUBLICATIONS:

American Film
Back Stage
Billboard
Box Office
Film Comment
Film Journal
Variety
Videography

DIRECTORIES:

Audio-Visual Communications: Who's Who
(Media Horizons, New York, NY)
Audio-Visual Marketplace (R.R. Bowker,
New York, NY)
*Back Stage Film/Tape/Syndication
Directory* (Back Stage Publications, New
York, NY)
Film Producers, Studios, and Agents Guide
(Lone Eagle Publishing, Beverly Hills,
CA)
Who's Who in the Motion Picture Industry
and *Who's Who in Television* (Packard
Publishing Co., Beverly Hills, CA)

Employers:

Atlanta Audio-Visuals
66 12th St., N.E.
Atlanta, GA 30309
(404) 876-7841

Atlanta Slide Art Productions
1459 Montreal Rd., Suite 206
Tucker, GA 30084
(404) 491-3608
Contact: Ms. Pat Sharp, Manager
Full-service slide production studio

Atlanta Video
1708 Peachtree St., Suite 107
Atlanta, GA 30309
(404) 873-2571
Contact: William A. Brown, Owner
Corporate videos

Atlanta Video Production Center
800 Forest St., N.W.
Atlanta, GA 30318
(404) 355-3398
Contact: Joe Gora, President
Complete videotape production and post-
production services

Chambliss-Wolff
2135 DeFoor Hills Rd., N.W.
Atlanta, GA 30318
(404) 355-1077
Contact: David Wolff, Director and
Owner
Commercials, industrial films

Cinefilm Laboratory
2156 Faulkner Rd., N.E.
Atlanta, GA 30324
(404) 633-1448
Contact: Bill Thornton, Owner
Film laboratory, editing

Cinema Concepts Theatre Service Co.
2030 Powers Ferry Rd., N.W., Suite 214
Atlanta, GA 30339
(404) 956-7460
Contact: Richard Neville, Production
Supervisor
35mm animations

Corporate Audio Visual Services
580 Dutch Valley Rd.
Atlanta, GA 30324
(404) 881-8234
Large-screen production systems

Corporate Video Marketing
122 Fowler St., N.W.
Atlanta, GA 30310
Contact: Rick Richey, Production
Manager
Multi-camera remote productions,
computer graphics

Doppler Recording Studios
1922 Piedmont Circle, N.E.
Atlanta, GA 30324
(404) 873-6941
Contact: Bill Quinn, Studio Manager
Atlanta's largest recording studio complex

First Light Films
1245 Fowler St., N.W.
Atlanta, GA 30318
(404) 876-7373
Contact: Vivian Jones, General Manager

Fowler Communications
5600 Roswell Rd., N.W.
Prado East Suite 100
Atlanta, GA
(404) 255-7177
Sales, design, rental, service

Gannett Production Services
1611 W. Peachtree St., N.E.
Atlanta, GA 30309
(404) 873-9182
Contact: Jerry Michel, Production
Manager

Image America
771 Miami Circle, N.E.
Atlanta, GA 30324
(404) 266-3340
Contact: David Harrell, President/Owner
Production, rental, staging, slides,
duplication

Morton, Jack, Productions
17 Executive Park Dr., N.E., Suite 200

Atlanta, GA 30329
(404) 329-8500
Contact: Nan O'Connor, General
Manager and Vice-President
Audio-visuals, film, videotape, multi-media productions

National Sound and Video
6500 McDonough Dr.
Norcross, GA 30091
(404) 447-0101
Recording, sound systems, projection, post-production

Productions Services—Atlanta
2000 Lakewood Way, S.W.
Atlanta, GA 30315
(404) 622-1311
Contact: Bill Orr, Accounting & Personnel
Manager
Equipment rental, special effects

Production Shop, The
3 Piedmont Center, N.E.
Atlanta, GA 30305
(404) 261-3443
Contact: Maggie Anderson, President

Professional Photographic Resources
667 11th St., N.W.

Atlanta, GA 30318
(404) 885-1885
Contact: David Chapman, Manager

Siebke Inc.
7160 Riverside Dr., N.W.
Sandy Springs, GA 30328
(404) 396-1595
Contact: Judy Siebke, Owner

Southern Tracks Recording Studio
3051 Clairmont Rd., N.E.
Atlanta, GA 30329
(404) 329-0147
Contact: Mike Clark, Owner

Technical Industries of Georgia
6000 Peachtree Rd., N.E.
Atlanta, GA 30350
(404) 455-7610
Sound and video, sales and rentals, multimedia, engineering and design

Vanderkloot Film & Television
750 Ralph McGill Blvd., N.E.
Atlanta, GA 30312
(404) 221-0236
Contact: Mark Wagner, Production
Manager
Production, editing

Breaking into film production

Tracey Barnett was working in public relations when she decided to break into film production. Although she didn't know anyone in the industry when she began, today she is a successful freelance production manager. We asked her how she did it.

"Most important was my desire to do it," says Tracey, "and I didn't get discouraged. I began by making a few contacts in the industry through people I knew in related fields. Then I set up interviews with these contacts. At the end of each interview, I asked for the names of three to five other contacts. This strategy opened a lot of doors for me. I followed up each interview with a phone call. I also kept in touch with my contacts on a monthly basis."

We asked Tracey what jobs are available for beginners in the film business and what qualifications are needed for those jobs.

"Entry-level positions include production assistant, stylist, assistant wardrobe manager, and grip," says Tracey. "There are no special requirements for these jobs. You don't need a degree in film to work in the business. In fact, people with film degrees begin at the same level as everybody else. What does count is intelligence and the ability to get things done quickly and efficiently. You need to think on your feet and be able to anticipate what needs to be done."

According to Tracey, freelance production assistants begin at about $150-$200 per day. More experienced production assistants can make as much as $300 per day. "But keep in mind that as a freelancer, you don't have the security of a regular paycheck," says Tracey. "You may not work every day." She advises those who need a more reliable income to look for a staff position in the industry.

Tracey advises those who want to break into the film business to keep at it: "Don't count your inexperience as a negative. Tenacity and enthusiasm will get you the first job. Approach your contacts and keep approaching them—over and over and over again."

Food/Beverage Producers and Distributors

WEB SITES:

http://www.pvo.com/~pvo-plus/
provides a directory of food and beverage
businesses, industry professionals, events,
and an interactive bulletin board.

http://www.fmi.org
Food Marketing Institute

http://wwwfpi.org/fpi
Food Service and Packaging Institute

http://www.snax.com
Snack Food Association

http://www.Tmrinc.com/ifpd
International Food Products Directory

PROFESSIONAL ORGANIZATIONS:

You may also want to look at the section
on "**Hospitality.**"

For additional information, you can
contact:

Association of Food Industries
5 Ravinia Dr.
Matawan, NJ 07747
(908) 583-8188

Distilled Spirits Council
1250 I St., N.W.
Washington, DC 20006
(202) 452-8444

Food Marketing Institute
800 Connecticut Ave., N.W.
Washington, DC 20006
(202) 452-8444

**National Association of Beverage
Retailers**
5101 River Rd.
Bethesda, MD 20816
(310) 656-1494

National Food Brokers Association
1010 Massachusetts Ave., N.W.
Washington, DC 20001
(202) 789-2844

National Frozen Foods Association
4755 Linglestown Rd.
Harrisburg, PA 17112
(717) 657-8601

National Soft Drink Association
1101 16th St., N.W.
Washington, DC 20036
(202) 463-6732

United Dairy Industry Association
10255 W. Higgins Rd., Suite 900
Rosemont, IL 60018
(847) 803-2000

Wine & Spirits Wholesalers of America
1023 15th St., N.W.
Washington, DC 20005
(202) 371-9792

PROFESSIONAL PUBLICATIONS:

Beverage World
Fancy Food
Food and Beverage Marketing
Food Industry News
Food Management
Foodservice Product News
Georgia Grocer
Grocery Marketing
Progressive Grocer
Wines and Vines

DIRECTORIES:

*Hereld's 5000: The Directory of Leading
    U.S. Food and Beverage Manufacturers*
    (SIC Publishing, Hamden, CT)
*Impact Yearbook: A Directory of the Wine
    and Spirits Industry* (M. Shanken
    Communications, New York, NY)
Modern Brewery Age Blue Book (Business
    Journals, Norwalk, CT)

*National Association of Specialty Food &
Confection Brokers Directory of Members*
(NASFCB, Van Nuys, CA)
National Beverage Marketing Directory
(Beverage Marketing Corp., New York,
NY)
NFBA Directory (National Food Brokers
Association, Washington, DC)
*Wines & Vines Buyers Guide: Directory of
the Wine Industry in North America*
(The Hiaring Co., San Rafael, CA)

Employers:

Atlanta Beverage Company
5000 Fulton Industrial Blvd., S.W.
Atlanta, GA 30336
(404) 699-6700
Contact: Elaine Slocombe, Human
Resources
Authorized distributors of Anheuser
Busch

Cagle's
2000 Hills Ave., N.W.
Atlanta, GA 30318
(404) 355-2820
Poultry products

Coca-Cola Co.
1 Coca-Cola Plaza, N.W.
Atlanta, GA 30339
(404) 676-2121
Contact: Human Resources Director
Company headquarters for the U.S.

Belca Foodservice
4795 Fulton Industrial Blvd., S.W.
Atlanta, GA 30336
(404) 699-1211
Contact: Ed Zimmerman, General
Manager

Better Brands
755 Jefferson St., N.W.
Atlanta, GA 30377
(404) 872-4731
Contact: Betty Jordan, Personnel
Distributors for Miller, Lowenbrau, other
beers

Cannon Meats
1985 Powers Ferry Rd., S.E.
Marietta, GA 30067
(770) 952-7191
Contact: Bob Cannon, Owner

City Beverage Co.
566 Wells St., S.W.
Atlanta, GA 30312
(404) 522-4200
Contact: Brenda Robinson, Director of
Personnel
Beer wholesaler

Coca-Cola Company, The
1 Coca-Cola Plaza
Atlanta, GA 30313
(404) 676-2665
Contact: Staffing Department
International headquarters

DeKalb Farmers Market
3000 E. Ponce de Leon Ave.
Decatur, GA 30030
(404) 377-6401
Contact: Personnel
Wholesale and retail meat, seafood,
produce

General Mills
1080 Holcomb Bridge Rd.
Roswell, GA 30076
(770) 587-3333
Contact: B.J. Johnson, Regional Operations Manager

General Wholesale Beer Co.
1271 Tacoma Dr., N.W.
Atlanta, GA 30318
(404) 351-3626
Contact: Hal Shaw, Sales Supervisor

Georgia Marketing Services
P.O. Box 2186
Norcross, GA 30071
(770) 246-9400
Contact: Jim Robbins, President
Food broker

Georgia Spice Company
3600 Atlanta Industrial Parkway, N.W.
Atlanta, GA 30331
(404) 696-6200
Contact: Bob Shapiro, Vice-President
Formulating, packaging, and blending
spices for the food industry

Habersham Vineyards & Winery
200 Northcreek, Suite 405
Atlanta, GA 30327
(404) 239-9463
Contact: Tom Slick, President
Representative for winery located in
nearby Baldwin, GA

Harry's Farmers Market
1180 Upper Hembree Rd.
Roswell, GA 30076
(770) 664-6300
Contact: Kathi Howard, Personnel
Manager
Wholesale and retail meat, seafood,
produce, gourmet foods

Inland Seafood
1222 Menlo Dr., N.W.
Atlanta, GA 30318
(404) 350-5850
Contact: Eric Sussman, Comptroller
Seafood wholesaler

Los Amigos Tortilla Mfg.
251 Armour Dr., N.E.
Atlanta, GA 30324
(404) 876-8153
Contact: Ruben Rodriguez, Sales Manager

National Distributing Co.
1 National Dr., N.W.
Atlanta, GA 30336
(404) 696-9440
Contact: Fred Bleiberg, Operations
Manager
Liquor wholesaler

Pepsi-Cola Bottling Company of Atlanta
1480 Chattahoochee Ave., N.W.
Atlanta, GA 355-1480
Contact: Tim Goodley, Personnel

Pya/Monarch
5501 Fulton Industrial Blvd.
Atlanta, GA 30336
(404) 346-1400
Contact: Don Foster, Vice-President of
Sales
Wholesaler for meat, seafood, produce,
eggs, canned goods, dry goods, paper and
plastic table-top items

Royal Oak Enterprises
900 Ashwood Parkway, Suite 800
Atlanta, GA 30338
(404) 393-1430

Ruth's Salads
135 Lake Mirror Rd.
Forest Park, GA 30050
(404) 361-1410
Contact: Bill Rudisil, Regional Sales
Manager

Salad Factory
1576 Atlanta Rd., S.E.
Marietta, GA 30060
(770) 427-8791
Contact: Carol Helton, Owner
Salad bar vegetables, prepared salads

Stroup's Brokerage Co.
600 Houze Way, Suite C3
P.O. Box 121
Roswell, GA 30076
(770) 587-4300
Contact: Robert Stroup, Owner
Food broker, specializing in food
ingredients

United Distributors
2627 Collins Springs Dr., S.E.
Smyrna, GA 30080
(404) 799-0333
Contact: John Fleming , On-Premises
Division Manager
Beer distributor

Foundations/Philanthropies

WEB SITES:

http://www.duke.edu/~ptavern/
Pete.Philanthropic.html
provides links to philanthropies,
nonprofits, foundations, charities, and
organizations.

http://www.mtn.org/nonprofit.html
lists nonprofit sites.

PROFESSIONAL ORGANIZATIONS:

For information on foundations and
related fields you can contact the following
local organizations listed in Chapter 5:
**Association of Fund Raisers & Direct
Sellers**
Georgia Society of Association Executives

For additional information on foundations
and related fields you can contact:

Council on Foundations
1828 L St., N.W., Suite 300
Washington, DC. 20036
(202) 466-6512

The Foundation Center
79 5th Ave.
New York, NY 10003
(212) 620-4230

National Charities Information Bureau
19 Union Square W., 6th Floor
New York, NY 10003
(212) 929-6300

PROFESSIONAL PUBLICATIONS:

Charities USA
Chronicle of Philanthropy
Foundation News
The Humanist

DIRECTORIES:

*America's New Foundations: The
   Sourceboook on Recently Created
   Philanthropies* (Gale Research, Detroit,
   MI)

*Corporate 500: The Directory of Corporate
   Philanthropy* (Gale Research, Detroit,
   MI)
*Foundation Directory and Corporate
   Foundation Profiles* (Foundation Center,
   New York, NY)

Employers:

American Jewish Committee
7 Piedmont Center, Suite 315
Atlanta, GA 30305
(404) 233-5501
Contact: Shery Frank, Southeastern Area
Director

American Red Cross
1955 Monroe Dr., N.E.
Atlanta, GA 30324
(404) 881-9800
Contact: Lamar Scotti, Personnel Director
Metropolitan Atlanta chapter, provides
disaster aid

Arthritis Foundation
1330 W. Peachtree St.
Atlanta, GA 30309
(404) 872-7100
Contact: Don Riggin, President
National headquarters; awards grants in
arthritis

Campbell, John Bulow, Foundation
25 Park Place, N.E.
1530 Trust Company Tower
Atlanta, GA 30303
(404) 658-9066
Contact: John W. Stephenson, Executive
Director

CF Foundation
600 Peachtree St., N.E.
Atlanta, GA 30308
(404) 892-4464
Contact: Greg Giornelli, Executive
Director
Primarily focuses on community service

Coca-Cola Foundation, The
P.O. Drawer 1734
Atlanta, GA 30301
(404) 676-2121
Contact: Donald Green, President
Primary focus is educational projects

Day, Cecil B., Foundation
4725 Peachtree Corners Circle, Suite 300
Norcross, GA 30092
(404) 446-1500
Contact: Edward L. White, Jr., President
Philanthropic organization; no particular
focus

Foundation Center
50 Hurt Plaza, S.E.
Atlanta, GA 30303
(404) 880-0095
Contact: Director Pattie Johnson
Research library on foundations

Gwinnett Foundation
1770 Indian Trail-Lilburn Rd., N.W.
Norcross, GA 30093
(770) 564-3451
Contact: Joe Estafen
Community foundation that supports
nonprofits in Gwinnett County

**King, Martin Luther, Jr., Center for
Nonviolent Social Change**
449 Auburn Ave., N.E.
Atlanta, GA 30312
(404) 524-1956
Contact: Johnny Mack, Executive Director
Sponsors programs related to nonviolence

**Metropolitan Atlanta Community
Foundation**
50 Hurt Plaza, S.E.
Atlanta, GA 30303
(404) 688-5525
Contact: Alicia Philipp, Executive Director
Awards grants to nonprofit organizations,
primarily for children and youth

National Kidney Foundation of Georgia
1655 Tullie Circle, N.E.
Atlanta, GA 30329
(404) 248-1315
Contact: Susie Oringel
Provides support for projects with
patients, doctors, and community work
pertaining to kidney disease

Sickle Cell Foundation of Georgia
2391 Benjamin E. Mays Dr., S.W.
Atlanta, GA 30311
(404) 755-1641
Contact: Jean Brannan, Executive Director
Sponsors program to identify and assist
sickle cell patients; some scholarships

United Way of Atlanta
100 Edgewood Ave., N.E.
Atlanta, GA 30303
(404) 527-7200
Contact: Mark O'Connell, President
Well known private funding source for
nonprofit agencies in the Atlanta area

Watkins Christian Foundation
1958 Monroe Dr., N.E.
Atlanta, GA 30324-4887
(404) 872-3841
Contact: Bill Watkins, Chairman of the
Board

Woodruff, Robert W., Foundation
50 Hurt Plaza, Suite 1200
Atlanta, GA 30303
(404) 522-6755
Contact: Charles H. McTier, President
Primarily provides assistance to Atlanta
area community organizations

Government

WEB SITES:

http://lcweb.loc.gov/global/executive/
general_resources.html
links to federal government sites.

http://www.law.vill.edu/Fed-Agency/
fedwebloc.html
lists over 200 federal government Web
servers.

http://www.wpi.edu/Academics/IMS/
Library/jobguide/gov.html
lists government job openings.

http://www.Atlanta.org/phone/
citydir.htm
City of Atlanta directory page.

http://www.atlanta.org
City of Atlanta homepage.

http://www.state.ga.us/homeng.htm/
State of Georgia homepage.

PROFESSIONAL ORGANIZATIONS:

For networking in government and related
fields, contact the following local professional organization listed in Chapter 5:

Georgia Municipal Association

For additional information about jobs in
government and related fields, you can
contact the following organizations:

**American Federation of Government
Employees**
80 F St., N.W.
Washington, DC 20001
(202) 737-8700

**American Federation of State, County
and Municipal Employees**
1625 L St., N.W.
Washington, D.C. 20036
(202) 452-4800

**National Association of Government
Employees**
2011 Crystal Dr., Suite 206
Arlington, VA 22202
(703) 979-0290

PROFESSIONAL PUBLICATIONS:

AFSCME Leader
City and State
Federal Employee News Digest
Federal Jobs Digest
Federal Staffing Digest
Federal Times
Government Executive
The Government Manager
The Public Employee Magazine
Public Employee Press

DIRECTORIES:

*Braddock's Federal-State-Local Government
   Directory* (Braddock Communications,
   Alexandria, VA)
Directory of Georgia Municipal Officials
   (Georgia Municipal Association, Atlanta,
   GA)
Federal Yellow Book (Monitor Publishing
   Co., New York, NY)
*Georgia Official Directory of United States
   Congressmen, State and County Officers*
   (Georgia Secretary of State, Atlanta, GA)
Georgia Official and Statistical Register
   (Georgia Secretary of State, Atlanta, GA)
*Members of the General Assembly of
   Georgia* (House of Representatives, State
   Capitol, Atlanta, GA)

Employers, Fulton County:

To apply for a position with Fulton
County, you must visit the Fulton County
Government Center, Suite 3030 at 141
Pryor St. which is located in downtown
Atlanta. The hours are 8:30 a.m.-5:00
p.m., Monday-Friday. Current vacancy
announcements are posted on a bulletin

board. Applicants must complete an application. Resumes are not accepted in lieu of applications.

Community Services and Job Training
141 Pryor St., N.W.
Atlanta, GA 30303
(404) 730-7921

Extension Service
141 Pryor St., N.W.
Atlanta, GA 30303
(404) 730-7000

Family and Children Services
230 Peachtree St., N.W.
Atlanta, GA 30303
(404) 756-4900

Finance Department
141 Pryor St., N.W.
Atlanta, GA 30303
(404) 730-7600

Health Department
99 Butler St., S.E.
Atlanta, GA 30303
(404) 730-1211

Inspections and Zoning Enforcement
141 Pryor St., N.W.
Atlanta, GA 30303
(404) 730-5858

Parks and Recreation
1575 Northside Dr.
Atlanta, GA 30318
(404) 730-6200

Personnel Department
141 Pryor St., N.W., Suite 3030
Atlanta, GA 30303
(404) 730-6700

Planning and Economic Development
141 Pryor St., N.W.
Atlanta, GA 30303
(404) 730-8000

Public Library
1 Margaret Mitchell Square
Atlanta, GA 30303
(404) 730-1700

Public Works
141 Pryor St., N.W.
Atlanta, GA 30303
(404) 730-6833

Purchasing Department
130 Peachtree St., N.E.
Atlanta, GA 30303
(404) 730-5800

Tax Commissioner
141 Pryor St., N.W.
Atlanta, GA 30303
(404) 730-6400

Employers, City of Atlanta:

To apply for a position with the City of Atlanta, go to the Personnel Department at 68 Mitchell St., N.W., which is located in downtown Atlanta. The hours are 8:30 a.m-4:30 p.m., Monday-Friday. You can also call the job information hotline at (404) 330-6456 for the latest listing of job vacancies.

Atlanta Department of Corrections
236 Peachtree St., S.W.
Atlanta, GA 30303
(404) 865-8080

Aviation Department
Hartsfield International Airport
Atlanta, GA 30354
(404) 530-6620

Finance Department
68 Mitchell St., S.W.
Atlanta, GA 30303
(404) 330-6442

Housing and Community Development Department
68 Mitchell St., S.W.
Atlanta, GA 30303
(404) 330-6390

Parks and Recreation Bureau
675 Ponce de Leon Ave., N.E.
Atlanta, GA 30308
(404) 817-6752

Personnel and Human Resources Department
68 Mitchell St., S.W.
Atlanta, GA 30303
(404) 330-6360

Public Works
68 Mitchell St., S.W.
Atlanta, GA 30303
(404) 330-6254

Employers, State of Georgia:

For detailed information about the State of Georgia employment process, call (404) 656-2724. The State Merit System processes applications for employment. It is located in the West Tower of the Twin Towers building which is located at the corner of Piedmont Ave. and Martin Luther King, Jr., Dr. in Suite 418. The hours are 8:00 a.m.-4:30 p.m., Monday-Friday. Each day at 9:30 a.m., an information presentation is conducted to provide employment information about the Merit System.

Administrative Services
200 Piedmont Ave., N.E.
Atlanta, GA 30334
(404) 656-5764

Agriculture, Georgia State Department of
19 Martin Luther King, Jr., Dr.
Atlanta, GA 30334
(404) 656-3615

Community Affairs, Georgia State Department of
100 Peachtree St., N.E., 1200 Equitable Bldg.
Atlanta, GA 30303
(404) 656-6390

Education, Georgia Department of
James "Sloppy" Floyd Veterans Building
1654 Twin Towers East
Atlanta, GA 30334
(404) 656-2510

Human Resources, Georgia Department of
47 Trinity Ave., S.W., Rm. 212H
Atlanta, GA 30334
(404) 656-6750

Industry and Trade, Georgia Department of
285 Peachtree Center Ave., Suite 1000
Atlanta, GA 30303
(404) 656-3710

Insurance Commissioner's Office, Georgia
2 Martin Luther King, Jr., Dr.
Atlanta, GA 30334
(404) 656-2082

Investigation, Georgia Bureau of
3121 Panthersville Rd.
Decatur, GA 30034
(404) 244-2508

Labor, Georgia Department of
148 International Blvd., N.E.
Atlanta, GA 30303
(404) 656-3182

Mental Health Institute, Georgia
1256 Briarcliff Rd., N.E.
Atlanta, GA 30306
(404) 894-5659

Merit System of Personnel, Georgia
200 Piedmont Ave., S.E.
Suite 418 West Towers
Atlanta, GA 30334
(404) 656-2705
Hotline: (404) 656-2724

Natural Resources, Georgia Department of
205 Butler St., S.E.
Atlanta, Georgia 30334
(404) 656-2695
Hotline: (404) 656-7567

Pardons and Parole, Georgia Department of
2 Martin Luther King, Jr., Dr.
Atlanta, GA 30334
(404) 656-5716

Public Safety, Georgia Department of
959 E. Confederate Ave., S.E.
Atlanta, GA 30316
(404) 624-7550

Public Telecommunications—Georgia Public Television Broadcasting
1540 Stewart Ave., S.W.
Atlanta, GA 30310
(404) 756-2400

Regional Hospital at Atlanta, Georgia
3073 Panthersville Rd.
Decatur, GA 30034
(404) 243-2470

Revenue, Georgia Department of
270 Washington St., Rm. 411
Atlanta, GA 30334
(404) 656-4010

Secretary of State, Georgia
2 Martin Luther King, Jr., Dr.
820 West Tower
Atlanta, GA 30334
(404) 656-5551

Technical and Adult Education, Georgia Department of
1800 Century Place, N.E.
Atlanta, GA 30345-4304
(404) 679-1763

Transportation, Georgia Department of
2 Capitol Square
Atlanta, GA 30334
(404) 656-5260

Employers, United States:

One official source for information on federal positions in Atlanta is called *Career Connections in Atlanta*. It is a telephone service that can be accessed by calling (404) 331-4315. The recording has several menu options, including the option of having applications mailed to your home. Information on federal jobs and the application process is available at the Office of Personnel Management listed below.

Agriculture, U.S. Department of
Southeastern Regional Office
1718 Peachtree St., N.W.
Atlanta, GA 30309
(404) 347-3926

Army Corps of Engineers, U.S.
77 Forsyth St., S.W.
Atlanta, GA 30335-6801
(404) 331-6683

Centers for Disease Control and Prevention, U.S.
1600 Clifton Rd., N.E.
Atlanta, GA 30329
(404) 639-3615
Hotline: (404) 332-4577

Environmental Protection Agency, Region IV, U.S.
345 Courtland St., N.E.
Atlanta, GA 30365
(404) 347-3486
Hotline: (800) 833-8130

Federal Aviation Administration
1701 Columbia Ave.
College Park, GA
(404) 305-5330

Health and Human Services, U.S. Department of
Atlanta Regional Office
101 Marietta Tower
Atlanta, GA 30323
(404) 331-2205

Labor, U.S. Department of
1371 Peachtree St., N.E.
Atlanta, GA 30367
(404) 347-7692

National Park Service
Southeast Regional Office
75 Spring St., S.W.
Atlanta, GA 30303
(404) 331-5714

Nuclear Regulatory Commission, U.S.
101 Marietta St., N.W.
Atlanta, GA 30323
(404) 331-5609

Personnel Management, U.S. Office of
75 Spring St., S.W.
Atlanta, GA 30303
(404) 331-4531

Small Business Administration, U.S.
1375 Peachtree St., N.E.
Atlanta, GA 30367
(404) 347-4943

Treasury, Internal Revenue Service, U.S.
Department of the
4800 Buford Hwy.
Chamblee, GA 30362
(770) 455-2448
Hotline: (770) 455-2455

Health Care

WEB SITES:

http://debra.dgbt.doc.ca/~mike/
healthnet/key.html
links to health care resources.

http://demOnmac.mgh.harvard.edu/
hospitalweb.html
a comprehensive list of hospitals on the
Web.

http://www.nscnet.com/jobheath.htm
lists health care employment
opportunities.

http:www.usadata.com/usdata/market/
atl95hca.htm
listing of Atlanta health care providers.

PROFESSIONAL ORGANIZATIONS:

For networking in health care and related
fields, check out the following local
professional organizations listed in
Chapter 5:
American Academy of Psychotherapists
American Association of Occupational
   Health Nurses
American Association of Osteopathic
   Specialists
American Hospital Association
Association of Black Cardiologists
Georgia Association of Home Health
   Agencies
Georgia Chiropractors Association
Georgia Dental Association

Georgia Nurses Association
Georgia Pharmaceutical Association
Georgia Psychological Association
Medical Association of Georgia

For additional information, you can
contact:

American Dental Association
211 E. Chicago Ave.
Chicago, IL 60611
(312) 440-2500

American Health Care Association
1201 L St., N.W.
Washington, DC 20005
(202) 842-4444

American Medical Association
515 N. State St.
Chicago, IL 60610
(312) 464-5000

American Public Health Association
1015 15th St., N.W.
Washington, DC 20005
(202) 789-5600

Group Health Association of America
1129 20th St., N.W., Suite 600
Washington, DC 20036
(202) 778-3200

National Association for Home Care
519 C St., N.E., Stanton Park
Washington, DC 20002
(202) 547-7424

National Association of Social Workers
750 1st St., N.E.
Washington, DC 20002
(202) 408-8600

National Council of Community Mental Health Centers
12300 Twinbrook Parkway, Suite 320
Rockville, MD 20852
(301) 984-6200

PROFESSIONAL PUBLICATIONS:

American Journal of Nursing
American Journal of Public Health
Business and Health
The Dental Assistant
Health News Daily
Healthcare Executive
Healthcare Marketing Report
HMO Magazine
Home Care News
Home Health Line
Hospital Practice
Hospitals
JAMA (Journal of the American Medical Association)
Managed Care Outlook
Modern Healthcare

DIRECTORIES:

AHA Guide to the Health Care Field (American Hospital Association, Chicago, IL)
Atlanta Business Chronicle Annual Book of Lists, Atlanta's Largest Hospitals, Georgia's Largest HMOs (Atlanta Business Chronicle, Atlanta, GA)
Atlanta Medical Facilities (Atlanta Chamber of Commerce, Atlanta, GA)
Blue Book Digest of HMOs (National Association of Employers on Health Care Action, Boca Raton, FL)
Directory of Health Care Coalitions in the U.S. (American Hospital Association, Chicago, IL)
Directory of Hospitals (SMG Marketing Group, Chicago, IL)

Encyclopedia of Medical Organizations and Agencies (Gale Research, Detroit, MI)
HMO/PPO Directory (Medical Economics Data, Montrale, NJ)
Home Health Agency Report and Directory and Home Health Agency Chain Directory (SMG Marketing Group, Chicago, IL)
KBL Healthcare Handbook (KBL Healthcare, New York, NY)
Managed Health Care Directory (American Managed Care and Review Association, Washington, DC)

Employers:

Aetna Health Plan
3500 Piedmont Rd., Suite 300
Atlanta, GA 30305-1565
(404) 814-4322
Contact: Joe Wild, General Manager

Beech Street—PPO
500 Northridge Rd., Suite 800
Atlanta, GA 30350
(770) 518-5300

BlueChoice PPO
3350 Peachtree Rd.
Atlanta, GA 30326
(404) 842-8000

Blue Cross and Blue Shield of Georgia
3350 Peachtree Rd.
Atlanta, GA 30326
(404) 842-8445

Central Home Health Care
6666 Powers Ferry Rd., Suite 220
Atlanta, GA 30339
(770) 953-8570
Contact: Patricia Waller

Cigna Co.
100 Peachtree St., Suite 700
Atlanta, GA 30303
(404) 681-7000
Contact: Alexis Perry, Human Resources

Cobb Hospital
3950 Austell Rd.
Austell, GA 30001
(770) 732-4010

Columbia East Side Medical Center
1700 Medical Way
Snellville, GA 30278
(404) 979-0200
Contact: Sissy Stone, Human Resources

Columbia West Paces Medical Center
3200 Howell Mill Rd., N.W.
Atlanta, GA 30327
(404) 351-0351
Contact: Clay Boyles, Director of Staff
Services

CompDent
8800 Roswell Rd., Suite 244
Atlanta, GA 30350
(770) 998-8936
Managed dental care

Crawford Long Hospital of Emory University
550 Peachtree St., N.E.
Atlanta, GA 30365
(404) 686-2536
Contact: Tom Cushman

Decatur Hospital
450 N. Candler St.
Decatur, GA 30030
(404) 377-0221
Hiring done through DeKalb Medical Center

DeKalb Medical Center
2701 N. Decatur Rd.
Decatur, GA 30033
(404) 297-2700
Contact: Tom Crawford, Director of Personnel

Dunwoody Medical Center
4575 N. Shallowford Rd.
Atlanta, GA 30338
(770) 454-2000

Eastside Medical Center
1700 Medical Way
Snellville, GA 30278
(770) 979-0200

Egleston Children's Hospital at Emory University
1405 Clifton Rd., N.E.
Atlanta, GA 30322
(404) 325-6000

Emory Adventist Hospital
3949 South Cobb Dr.
Smyrna, GA 30080
(404) 434-0710
Contact: Peggy Seckler, Director of Human Resources

Emory Clinic
1365 Clifton Rd.
Atlanta, GA 30322
(404) 321-0111

Emory University Hospital
1364 Clifton Rd., N.E.
Atlanta, GA 30322
(404) 712-5750
Contact: Margaret Bloomquist

Extended Community Home Health of Atlanta
4151 Memorial Dr., Suite 223-A
Decatur, GA 30032
(404) 292-3007
Contact: Human Resources

Georgia Baptist Home Care Services
100 10th St., N.W., Suite 800
Atlanta, GA 30309
(404) 265-1144
Contact: Joanne Onken

Georgia Baptist Health Care System/ Georgia Baptist Medical Center
303 Parkway Dr., N.E.
Atlanta, GA 30312
(404) 265-4227
Contact: Patti Askew, Director of Human Resources

Grady Memorial Hospital
80 Butler St., S.E.
Atlanta, GA 30335
(404) 616-4307
Contact: Derck Carissimi, Vice-President of Human Resources

GranCare
1 Ravinia Dr., Suite 1500
Atlanta, GA 30346
(770) 393-0199
Health-care provider

Gwinnett Medical Center
1000 Medical Center Blvd.
Lawrenceville, GA 30245
(770) 995-4321
Contact: Steve Madeau, Vice-President of
Human Resources

Healthdyne Technologies
1255 Kennestone Circle
Marietta, GA 30066
(770) 499-1212
Designs, manufactures, and markets
medical devices, primarily for home use

HealthStar Managed Care Corp.
4 Concourse Parkway, Suite 215
Atlanta, GA 30328
(770) 396-1009

Henrietta Egleston Hospital for Children
1405 Clifton Rd., N.E.
Atlanta, GA 30322
(404) 325-6000
Contact: Angela Fletcher, Human
Resources

Henry Medical Center
1133 Eagle's Landing Parkway
Stockbridge, GA 30281-5099
(770) 389-2200

Housecall Medical Resources
1000 Abernathy Rd., Bldg. 400, Suite 1825
Atlanta, GA 30328
(770) 379-9000
Home health care

Isolyser Co.
4320 International Blvd.
Norcross, GA 30093
(770) 381-7566
Disinfects and disposes of medical waste

**Kaiser Foundation Health Plan of
Georgia/Maxicare Southeast Health
Plans**
3495 Piedmont Rd., N.E.
Atlanta, GA 30305
(404) 233-0555
Contact: Tammy Jones, Human Resources
Manager

Kennestone Hospital
677 Church St.
Marietta, GA 30060
(770) 793-7070
Contact: Chris Jackson, Personnel
Manager

Kennestone Hospital at Windy Hill
2540 Windy Hill Rd.
Marietta, GA 30067
(770) 644-1000
Contact: Ed Newman, Personnel Manager

Matria Health Care
1850 Parkway Place
Marietta, GA 30067
(770) 423-4500
Contact: Marty LeMasurier, Vice-
President Employee Relations
Provides maternity management health-
care services

Medaphis Corp.
2700 Cumberland Parkway, Suite 300
Atlanta, GA 30339
(770) 319-3300
Health-care management services

Metlife Health Care Network of Georgia
1130 Northchase Parkway, S.E.
Marietta, GA 30067
(770) 955-7975

Metro Home Health Services
2045 Peachtree Rd., N.E., Suite 100
Atlanta, GA 30309
(404) 350-0484
Contact: Debra Schiller

Morehouse Medical Associates
75 Piedmont Ave., Suite 700
Atlanta, GA 30303
(404) 756-1400

North Fulton Regional Hospital
3000 Hospital Blvd.
Roswell, GA 30076
(770) 751-2500
Contact: Lynn Haynes, Director of
Human Resources

Northlake Regional Medical Center
1455 Montreal Rd.
Atlanta, GA 30085
(770) 270-3000
Contact: Cindy Ackerman, Director of
Personnel

Northside Hospital
1000 Johnson Ferry Rd.
Atlanta, GA 30342
(404) 851-8000
Contact: Heather Fritzler, Human
Resources

**Northside Hospital Home Health
Services**
5825 Glenridge Dr., Bldg. 4
Atlanta, GA 30328
(404) 851-6293
Contact: Barbara Moore

Parkway Medical Center
1000 Thornton Rd.
Lithia Springs, GA 3057
(770) 732-7777

Piedmont Hospital
1968 Peachtree Rd., N.W.
Atlanta, GA 30309
(404) 605-5000
Contact: Derek Carissimi

Piedmont Physicians Group
1968 Peachtree Rd., N.W.
Atlanta, GA 30309
(404) 350-3847

Preferred Plan of Georgia
3150 Holcomb Bridge Rd., Suite 210
Norcross, GA 30071
(770) 849-9849

Private Healthcare Systems
1000 Abernathy Rd., Suite 940
Atlanta, GA 30328
(770) 394-1084

Promina Northwest Health System
3950 Austell Rd.
Austell, GA 30001
(770) 732-4040
Contact: Human Resources

Prudential Health Care Plan
2859 Paces Ferry Rd., Suite 401
Atlanta, GA 30339
(404) 801-7500

Quantam Radiology
100 Galleria Parkway, Suite 1450
Atlanta, GA 30339
(770) 952-8899

Rockdale Hospital
1412 Milstead Ave.
Conyers, GA 30207
(770) 918-3000

Saint Joseph's Hospital of Atlanta
5665 Peachtree-Dunwoody Rd., N.E.
Atlanta, GA 30342
(404) 851-7001

Scottish Rite Children's Hospital
1001 Johnson Ferry Rd.
Atlanta, GA 30342
(404) 256-5252
Contact: Tina Bendock, Human Resources

Shallowford Community Hospital
4575 N. Shallowford Rd.
Atlanta, GA 30338
(404) 454-2000
Contact: Sissy Stone, Director of Human
Resources

South Fulton Medical Center
1170 Cleveland Ave.
East Point, GA 30344
(404) 305-3500
Contact: Lew Castle, Human Resources
Director

Southcare/Principal PPO
400 Northcreek
3715 Northside Parkway, Suite 300
Atlanta, GA 30327
(404) 231-9911

Southeast Permanente Medical Group
3495 Piedmont Rd., N.E.
Atlanta, GA 30305
(404) 364-7000

Southern Regional Medical Center
11 Upper Riverdale Rd., S.W.
Riverdale, GA 30274
(404) 991-8000
Contact: Larry Hodges, Director of
Human Resources

Southwest Hospital and Medical Center
501 Fairburn Rd., S.W.
Atlanta, GA 30331
(404) 699-1111
Contact: Samuel Bowens, Director of
Human Resources

Spalding Regional Hospital
601 S. 8th St.
Griffin, GA 30223
(770) 228-2721

Staff Builders Home Health
1835 Savoy Dr., Suite 205
Atlanta, GA 30341
(770) 457-1245
Contact: Pam Coltrane

Tanner Medical Center/Carrollton
705 Dixie St.
Carrollton, GA 30117
(770) 836-9580

TheraTx
1105 Sanctuary Parkway, Suite 100
Alpharetta, GA 30201
(770) 752-8888
Health-care services

United Healthcare of Georgia
2970 Clairmont Ave., Suite 300
Atlanta, GA 30329-1634
(404) 982-8840
Contact: Alana Rivard, Human Resources
Coordinator

VA Medical Center Atlanta
1670 Clairmont Rd.
Decatur, GA 30033
(404) 321-6111
Contact: David Fitkin

Visiting Nurse Health System
133 Luckie St., N.W.
Atlanta, GA 30303
(404) 527-0660
Contact: John Good, Vice-President of
Human Resources

Wesley Woods Geriatric Hospital
1817 Clifton Rd.
Atlanta, GA 30329
(404) 728-6200
Contact: Deborah Mills, Director of
Personnel

West Georgia Medical Center
1514 Vernon Rd.
LaGrange, GA 30240
(770) 882-1411

West Paces Medical Center
3200 Howell Mill Rd., N.W.
Atlanta, GA 30327
(404) 351-0351

Hospitality: Hotels and Restaurants

WEB SITES:

http://www.hospitalitynet.nl/
is a central source for the hospitality
industry; includes a "virtual job exchange."

http://www.vnr.com/vnr/arch_ch.html
is the culinary and hospitality on-line
newsletter.

**http://clever.net/medium/html/
hotels.html**
is the Atlanta Hotel Guide.

htttp://www.evmedia.com/Atlanta.html
is an Atlanta hotel listing, including prices.

PROFESSIONAL ORGANIZATIONS:

For networking in the hospitality industry
and related fields, check out the following
local professional organizations listed in
Chapter 5:
**Asian American Hotel Owners
    Association**
**Association for Convention Operations
    Management**
Georgia Hospitality & Travel Association

For more information, you can contact:

American Hotel & Motel Association
1201 New York Ave., N.W.
Washington, DC 20005
(202) 789-3100

Chefs de Cuisine Association of America
155 E. 55th St., Suite 302B
New York, NY 10022
(212) 832-4949

Hotel Sales and Marketing Association
1300 L St., N.W., Suite 800
Washington, DC 20005
(202) 789-0089

**International Association of Convention
and Visitors Bureaus**
P.O. Box 758
Champaign, IL 61824
(217) 359-8881

National Restaurant Association
1200 17th St., N.W.
Washington, DC 20036
(202) 331-5900

PROFESSIONAL PUBLICATIONS:

Club Management
Food Management
Food and Wine
Hotel and Motel Management
Hotel and Resort Industry
Meetings and Conventions
Nation's Restaurant News
Restaurant Business
Restaurant Hospitality
Restaurant and Institutions

DIRECTORIES:

Directory of Hotel and Motel Companies
    (American Hotel Association Directory
    Corp. New York, NY)
Hotel and Motel Redbook (American Hotel
    and Motel Association, Washington,
    DC)
Meetings and Conventions Magazine,
    Directory issue (Murdoch Magazines,
    New York, NY)
National Restaurant Association Directory
    (National Restaurant Association,
    Washington, DC)
Restaurant Hospitality, Hospitality 500
    issue (Penton/IPC, Inc., Columbus, OH)

Hotel management: more than "Puttin' on the Ritz"

With a little more than two years' experience in the hotel business, Nancy Gordon landed a job as sales manager for the Ritz-Carlton Hotel. We asked her for an overview of the hospitality industry.

"If you want to move up quickly," says Nancy, "this industry is the place to be. It's anything but a dead-end business. Some people stay with the same organization for most of their careers. But I'd say the average is probably around five years with any given company. People are constantly calling and making job offers.

"I studied hotel management and general business. Nevertheless, you can't just walk out of college and into a middle management position. I started as a receptionist at the Ritz-Carlton. Then I became a secretary. I don't know anyone who hasn't paid dues for a year or two. If you're interested in food or beverages, you might move up to dining room assistant. Essentially, you'd be doing the same thing as a secretary—typing up contracts or menus, that sort of thing. You really have to learn the business from the bottom up.

"In sales you move from secretarial work to a full-fledged sales position. I was a sales representative, then was promoted to sales manager. The next step might logically be director of sales or marketing, where I'd be responsible for advertising and marketing strategies, developing budgets and so on. An equivalent position would be director of food and beverages, the person who's responsible for all the food and drink served in the hotel, room service, all the dining rooms, special banquets, everything. After director of sales or of food and beverages, you go on to general manager.

"I'd say the competition is about average—not nearly as fierce as the advertising industry, for example. Earning potential is pretty good, too, depending, of course, on the size of the hotel, the city you're in, and what kind of company you're working for. You start pretty low, maybe around $23,000 a year. But each time you move up, you get a hefty raise, or ought to."

Hotel Employers:

Atlanta Airport Hilton & Towers
1031 Virginia Ave.
Atlanta, GA 30354
(404) 767-9000
Contact: Darech Turan

Atlanta Airport Marriott
4711 Best Rd.
College Park, GA 30337
(404) 766-7900
Contact: Bob Stewart

Atlanta Hilton & Towers
255 Courtland St., N.E.
Atlanta, GA 30303
(404) 659-2000
Contact: Bentley Kriewald

Atlanta Marriott Marquis
265 Peachtree Center Ave.
Atlanta, GA 30303
(404) 521-0000
Contact: Ann McCarthy

Atlanta Marriott Northwest
200 Interstate North Parkway
Atlanta, GA 30339
(7704) 952-7900
Contact: Gary Hughes

Atlanta Marriott Perimeter Center
246 Perimeter Center Parkway
Atlanta, GA 30346
(770) 394-6500
Contact: Mary Rich

Atlanta Renaissance Hotel—Airport
4736 Best Rd.
College Park, GA 30337
(404) 762-7676
Contact: Elizabeth Adocchio

Atlanta Renaissance Hotel—Downtown
590 W. Peachtree St., N.W.
Atlanta, GA 30308
(404) 881-6000
Contact: Sharon Clakum

Courtyard by Marriott
175 Piedmont Ave., N.E.
Atlanta, GA 30303
(404) 659-2727

Crowne Plaza-Ravinia
4355 Ashford-Dunwoody Rd.
Atlanta, GA 30346
(770) 395-7700
Contact: Debbie Grant

Doubletree Hotel at Concourse
7 Concourse Parkway
Atlanta, GA 30328
(770) 395-3900
Contact: Brad Conner

Downtown Court Hotel
175 Piedmont Ave.
Atlanta, GA 30303
(404) 659-2727
Contact: Teresa Dobson

Grand Hotel
75 14th St.
Atlanta, GA 30309
(404) 881-9898
Contact: Lauri Craig

Holiday Inn—Airport North
1380 Virginia Ave.
East Point, GA 30344
(404) 762-8411

Holiday Inn & Conference Center
418 Armour Dr.
Atlanta, GA 30324
(404) 873-4661
Contact: Ted Clark

Holiday Inn Worldwide
3 Ravinia Dr., Suite 2900
Atlanta, GA 30346
(770) 604-2000
17 Atlanta locations

Hotel Nikko Atlanta
3300 Peachtree Rd., N.E.
Atlanta, GA 30305
(404) 365-8100
Contact: Julie Cook

Hyatt Regency Atlanta
265 Peachtree St.
Atlanta, GA 30303
(404) 577-1234
Contact: Joe Demille

Johnson, W.B., Properties
3414 Peachtree Rd., Suite 300
Atlanta, GA 30326
(404) 365-9800

Marriott, J.W., at Lenox
3300 Lenox Rd., N.E.
Atlanta, GA 30326
(404) 262-3344
Contact: Bob Schuler

Marriott Perimeter Center
246 Perimeter Center Parkway
Atlanta, GA 30346
(770) 394-6500

Omni Hotel at CNN Center
100 CNN Center
Atlanta, GA 30335
(404) 659-0000
Contact: Beth Sarles

Radisson Hotel Atlanta
165 Courtland & International Blvd.
Atlanta, GA 30303
(404) 659-6500
Contact: Mindy Laffler

Ramada Hotel Dunwoody
Interstate 285 at Chamblee-Dunwoody
Rd.
Atlanta, GA 30338
(770) 394-5000
Contact: Janet Rogers

Renaissance Waverly Hotel
2450 Galleria Parkway
Atlanta, GA 30339
(770) 953-4500
Contact: Perry Grice

Ritz-Carlton Atlanta
181 Peachtree St., N.E.
Atlanta, GA 30303
(404) 659-0400
Contact: Scott Russell

Ritz-Carlton, Buckhead
3434 Peachtree Rd., N.E.
Atlanta, GA 30326
(404) 237-2700
Contact: Emme Lou Jenkins

Sheraton Atlanta Airport
1325 Virginia Ave.
Atlanta, GA 30344
(404) 768-6660
Contact: Patricia Williams

Sheraton Colony Square Hotel
188 14th St., N.E.
Atlanta, GA 30361
(404) 892-6000
Contact: Natalie Shaw

Sheraton Gateway
1900 Sullivan Rd.
College Park, GA 30337
(404) 997-2770
Contact: Jean Spaulding

Stouffer Renaissance Hotel
1 Hartsfield Centre Parkway
Atlanta, GA 30354
(404) 209-9999
Contact: Jim Day

Swissotel Atlanta
3391 Peachtree Rd., N.E.
Atlanta, GA 30326
(404) 365-0065
Contact: Rick Cunningham

Westin Peachtree Plaza
210 Peachtree St., N.W.
Atlanta, GA 30303
(404) 659-1400
Contact: Erik Smith

Wyndham Garden Hotel—Midtown
125 10th St.
Atlanta, GA 30308
(404) 873-4800
Contact: Lou Mayne

Restaurant Employers:

There are hundreds of restaurants in the Atlanta metropolitan area. The following listing includes selected restaurant chains and some of the most famous of Atlanta's eateries.

Abbey Restaurant, The
163 Ponce de Leon Ave., N.E.
Atlanta, GA 30308
(404) 876-8532
Contact: Laura Lorazsky
Downtown formal dining restaurant

America's Favorite Chicken Co.
6 Concourse Parkway, Suite 1700
Atlanta, GA 30328
(770) 391-9500
Fast-food chicken

Atlanta Fish Market
265 Pharr Rd.
Atlanta, GA 30305
(404) 262-3165
Contact: David Abes
Fresh seafood

Benihana of Tokyo
2143 Peachtree Rd., N.E.
Atlanta, GA 30309
(404) 355-8565
Contact: Michael Barver
Flagship of three Atlanta restaurants in this national chain

Blimpie International
1775 The Exchange, Suite 600
Atlanta, GA 30339
(770) 984-2707
168 Atlanta locations; subs and salads

Blue Ridge Grill
1261 W. Paces Ferry Rd.
Atlanta, GA 30327
(404) 233-5030
American, contemporary Southern cuisine

Bone's Restaurant
3130 Piedmont Rd.
Atlanta, GA 30305
(404) 237-2663
Contact: Emile Blau
American cuisine

Buckhead Diner
3073 Piedmont Rd.
Atlanta, GA 30305
(404) 262-3336
Contact: David Reiley
Modern American cuisine

Cheesecake Factory, The
3024 Peachtree Rd., N.W.
Atlanta, GA 30305
(404) 816-2555
Contact: Randy Cook
American cuisine

Chequers Seafood Grill
236 Perimeter Center Parkway
Atlanta, GA 30346
(770) 391-9383
Fresh seafood, steaks, pastas

Chick-Fil-A
5200 Buffington Rd.
Atlanta, GA 30349
(404) 765-8000
Flagship restaurant of this Atlanta-based chain

Chops
70 W. Paces Ferry Rd.
Atlanta, GA 30305
(404) 262-2675
Contact: Daniel Zilleweger
Popular steakhouse

Church's Chicken
6 Concourse Parkway, Suite 1700
Atlanta, GA 30328
(770) 391-9500
48 Atlanta locations; quick-service chicken

Coach & Six Restaurant and Lounge
1776 Peachtree St., N.W
Atlanta, GA 30309
(404) 872-6666
Contact: Sue Hauvlin, Owner
Long-established, white-tablecloth restaurant

Dailey's Restaurant and Bar
17 International Blvd.
Atlanta, GA 30303
(404) 681-3303
Contact: Sally Sexton, Manager
Fine dining

Dante's Down the Hatch
60 Upper Alabama St., S.W., Suite 001
Atlanta, GA 30303
(404) 577-1801
Contact: Ann Tyus
Jazz and fondue in Underground Atlanta
and Buckhead

**Gorin's Homemade Ice Cream &
Sandwiches**
357 Executive Park, Suite 440
Atlanta, GA 30329
(404) 248-9900
Contact: Patia Connell
Main office for this chain with 21
locations

Hooters of America
1815 The Exchange
Atlanta, GA 30339
(770) 951-2040
Restaurant chain

Houlihan's at Park Place
4505 Ashford-Dunwoody Rd.
Atlanta, GA 30346
(770) 394-8921
American cuisine

Houston's—Lenox
3321 Lenox Rd.
Atlanta, GA 30326
(404) 237-7534
Contact: Lori Canvkenberge
Restaurant chain; American cuisine

Houston's—Peachtree
2166 Peachtree Rd.
Atlanta, GA 30309
(404) 351-2442
Restaurant chain; American cuisine

Houston's—West Paces
3539 Northside Parkway

Atlanta, GA 30327
(404) 262-7130
Restaurant chain; American cuisine

JFS International
2532 Panola Rd.
Lithonia, GA 30058
(770) 987-4509
Contact: Milton Saner, Owner
Kentucky Fried Chicken franchise

Kudzu Cafe
3215 Peachtree Rd.
Atlanta, GA 30305
(404) 262-0661
Contact: Mike Vajac
Contemporary Southern food

La-Van Hawkins Inner City Foods
2254 Ravenwood Trail
Marietta, GA 30066
(770) 924-0738
Fast-food hamburger restaurants

Liberty House Restaurant Corp.
3423 Piedmont Rd., N.E., Suite 318
Atlanta, GA 30305
(404) 262-3130
Contact: Richard Lewis
Manages several upscale restaurants in
Buckhead

Longhorn Steaks
8215 Roswell Rd., Bldg. 200
Atlanta, GA 30350
(770) 399-9595
Over 15 Atlanta area locations

Mansion, The
179 Ponce de Leon Ave., N.E.
Atlanta, GA 30308
(404) 876-0727
Contact: Nazid Ahsan

McDonald's Restaurants
5901 Peachtree-Dunwoody Rd., N.E.,
Suite C-500
Atlanta, GA 30328
(770) 698-7498
Contact: Darrlyn Miller
Handles hiring for all of Georgia and part
of Alabama

Melears Barbecue
P.O. Box 327
Fayetteville, GA 30214
(770) 461-7180
Contact: Kenneth Melear
Barbecue restaurant and catering

Mick's
Corporate Office
489 Peachtree St.
Atlanta, GA 30308
(404) 872-1400
Contact: Teresa Sariani
Contemporary casual dining; 10 restaurants in the Atlanta area

Murray's Fixture Company
3917 Oakcliff Industrial Court
Doraville, GA 30340
(404) 242-7649
Restaurant equipment

National Service Industries
NSI Center
1420 Peachtree St., N.E.
Atlanta, GA 30309
(404) 853-1000
Contact: James S. Balloun
Linen services

OK Café & Take Away
1284 W. Paces Ferry Rd.
Atlanta, GA 30327
(404) 233-2888
American cuisine

103 West
103 W. Paces Ferry Rd.
Atlanta, GA 30327
(404) 233-5993
Fine dining

Paschal's Center
830 Martin Luther King, Jr., Dr., S.W.
Atlanta, GA 30314
(404) 577-3150
Contact: Constance Jenkins, Manager
Long-established soul food restaurant and caterer; managed by Clark Atlanta University

Peasant Restaurants
489 Peachtree St., N.E.
Atlanta, GA 30308
(404) 872-1400
Contact: Teresa Sirriani
Headquarters for an Atlanta chain of fine dining restaurants

Pizza Hut (Corporate Office)
400 Northridge Rd., Suite 600
Atlanta, GA 30350
(404) 998-7272
Contact: Rodney Whitmore, Human Resources Director
Office for this chain with more than 60 metro outlets

Po Folks Caterin' Center
6131 Peachtree Parkway
Norcross, GA 30092
(404) 874-5555
Contact: Scott Ray
Catering center for metro Atlanta Po Folks restaurants

Popeye's Chicken & Biscuits
6 Concourse Parkway, Suite 1700
Atlanta, GA 30328
(770) 391-9500
24 Atlanta locations; quick-service chicken

Ray's on the River
6700 Powers Ferry Rd.
Atlanta, GA 30339
(770) 955-1187
Contact: Bryan Housely
Fresh seafood

Rio Bravo Cantina
3172 Roswell Rd.
Atlanta, GA 30305
(404)   262-7431
Mexican/Tex-Mex cuisine

RTM Restaurant Group
5995 Barfield Rd.
Atlanta, GA 30328
(404) 256-4900
Fast food

Ruth's Chris Steak House
5788 Roswell Rd.
Atlanta, GA 30328
(404) 255-0035
Contact: John Haros
Steakhouse

Taco Mac
1006 N. Highland Ave., N.E.
Atlanta, GA 30306
(404) 873-6529
Contact: Lisa Durham
Flagship for this local three-restaurant
chain

Tavern at Phipps
3500 Peachtree Rd.
Atlanta, GA 30326
(404) 814-9640
American bistro

T.G.I. Friday's
5600 Roswell Rd., N.W.
Atlanta, GA 30342
(404) 256-2482

Home Office
P.O. Box 809062
Dallas, TX 75380
Atlanta flagship of this national chain

Three Dollar Café—Windy Hill
2580 Windy Hill Rd.
Marietta, GA 30067
(770) 850-0868
American cuisine

Varsity, The
61 North Ave., N.W.
Atlanta, GA 30308
(404) 881-1707
American/fast food. An Atlanta landmark.

Waffle House
5986 Financial Dr.
Norcross, GA 30071
(770) 729-5700
Contact: Chris Jacobson
Corporate headquarters for this chain,
with approximately 50 Atlanta locations

Human Services

WEB SITES:

http://lib4.fisher.su.oz.au/Social_Work/
socwkls.html
links to journals, newsgroups, and
listserves.

http://caster.ssw.upenn.edu/cont-ed/
index.html
offers social work courses via the Internet.

http://http.bsd.uchicago.edu/~r-tell/
socwork.html
provides comprehensive links to social
work sites.

PROFESSIONAL ASSOCIATIONS:

For networking in human services and
related fields, check out the following local
professional organizations listed in
Chapter 5. Also see **"Foundations"** and
"Health Care."
**Association of Fund Raisers & Direct
Sellers**
**National Association of Social Workers—
Georgia Chapter**

For more information, you can contact:

Center for Human Services
7200 Wisconsin Ave., Suite 600
Chevy Chase, MD 20814
(301) 654-8338

National Association of Social Workers
750 1st St., N.E.
Washington, DC 20002
(202) 408-8600

Nonprofit Resource Center
50 Hurt Plaza, S.E.
Atlanta, GA 30303
(404) 688-4845

United Way of Metropolitan Atlanta
100 Edgewood Ave., N.E.
Atlanta, GA 30303
(404) 527-7200

PROFESSIONAL PUBLICATIONS:

Children and Youth Services Review
Community Jobs
Journal of Social Welfare
The Nonprofit Times

DIRECTORIES:

Directory of Agencies (National Association
of Social Workers, Washington, DC)
*National Directory of Children and Youth
Services* (Marion Peterson, Longmont,
CO)
*National Directory of Private Social
Agencies* (Croner Publications, Queens
Village, NY)
Public Welfare Directory (American Public
Welfare Association, Washington, DC)

Employers:

AID Atlanta
1438 W. Peachtree St.
Atlanta, GA 30309
(404) 872-0600
Contact: Tony Braswell, Director

Alzheimer's Association
2130 Raymond Dr.
Atlanta, GA 30329
(404) 451-1300

**American Cancer Society/Atlanta Unit
Division**
2200 Lake Blvd., N.E., Suite C
Atlanta, GA 30319
(404) 841-0700
Contact: Feliciano Mendez

**American Civil Liberties Union of
Georgia**
142 Mitchell St., S.W.
Atlanta, GA 30303
(404) 523-5398

American Diabetes Association
1 Corporate Square, N.E., Suite 127
Atlanta, GA 30329
(404) 320-7100
Contact: Nancy Allen, Director

American Red Cross—Metropolitan Atlanta Chapter
1925 Monroe Dr., N.E.
Atlanta, GA 30324
(404) 881-9800
http://www.redcross.org/atlanta/
Contact: Roger Svoboda, President

Amnesty International
131 Ponce de Leon, Suite 220
Atlanta, GA 30308
(404) 876-5661
Contact: Ajamu Baraka

Arthritis Foundation, Georgia Chapter
550 Pharr Rd., Suite 550
Atlanta, GA 30305
(404) 237-8771
Contact: Jim Peniston

Association for Retarded Citizens of Georgia
2860 East Point St.
East Point, GA
(404) 761-3150
Contact: Tom Query, Executive Director

Atlanta Children's Shelter
607 Peachtree St., N.E.
Atlanta, GA 30308
(404) 892-3713
Contact: Jacqueline Brown

Atlanta Jewish Community Center
1745 Peachtree Rd., N.E.
Atlanta, GA 30309
(404) 875-7881
Contact: Harry Stern

Atlanta Legal Aid Society
151 Spring St., N.W.
Atlanta, GA 30303
(404) 524-5811
Contact: Steven Gottlieb

Atlanta Urban League
100 Edgewood Ave., Suite 600
Atlanta, GA 30303
(404) 659-1150
Contact: Lyndon Wade

Big Brothers/Big Sisters of Metropolitan Atlanta
Boys Clubs of Metropolitan Atlanta
100 Edgewood Ave., N.E., Suite 710
Atlanta, GA 30303
(404) 527-7610
Contact: Janice McKenzie-Crayton, President

Boys Clubs of America
1230 W. Peachtree St., N.W.
Atlanta, GA 30309
(404) 892-3317
Contact: David Roark

Boy Scouts of America—Atlanta Area Council
100 Edgewood Ave., N.E., 4th Floor
Atlanta, GA 30303
(404) 577-4810
Contact: Archie Crain

CARE
151 Ellis St., N.E.
Atlanta, GA 30303
(404) 681-2552
Contact: Peter Bell

City of Hope/Cancer & Major Diseases Center
600 W Peachtree St., Suite 1450
Atlanta, GA 30308
(404) 873-6030
Contact: Lisa Grissom

Clayton County Community Services Authority
1000 Main St.
Forest Park, GA 30050
(404) 363-0575
Contact: Charles Grant

Families First
P.O. Box 7948, Station C
Atlanta, GA 30357
(404) 853-2800
Contact: Robert Weaver

Georgia Society to Prevent Blindness
455 E. Paces Ferry Rd., Suite 222
Atlanta, GA 30305
(404) 266-0071
Contact: Jenny Pomeroy

Goodwill Industries
2201 Glenwood Ave., S.E.
Atlanta, GA 30316
(404) 377-0441
Contact: Raymond Bishop

King, Martin Luther, Jr., Center for Social Change
449 Auburn Ave., N.E.
Atlanta, GA 30312
(404) 524-1956
Contact: Tony Gomez

Leukemia Society of America—Georgia Chapter
6201 Powers Ferry Rd., Suite 380
Atlanta, GA 30339
(7704) 859-0899
Contact: Laurie Papelian

Lupus Foundation of America
285 Interstate North Parkway, Suite 150
Atlanta, GA 30339-2203
(770) 952-3891
Contact: Phyllis Keeler

March of Dimes Regional Office
1775 The Exchange, Suite 630
Atlanta, GA 30339
(770) 612-9177
Contact: Joe Campbell

Multiple Sclerosis Society-Georgia Chapter
1100 Circle 75 Parkway, Suite 630
Atlanta, GA 30339
(770) 984-9080
Contact: Terri Pendergast

Muscular Dystrophy Association
2187 Northlake Parkway, Bldg. 9, Suite 116
Tucker, GA 30084
(770) 621-9800
Contact: Sylvia Brown

NAACP, Regional Office
970 Martin Luther King, Jr., Dr., S.W.
Atlanta, GA 30314
(404) 688-8868
Contact: Nelson B. Rivers

National Conference of Christians and Jews
3300 Buckeye Rd.
Chamblee, GA 30341
(770) 451-2434
Contact: Jimmy Harper, Executive Director

National Kidney Foundation of Georgia
1655 Tullie Circle, Suite 111
Atlanta, GA 30329
(404) 248-1315
Contact: Christopher Starr

North Fulton Human Service Center
89 Grove Way
Roswell, GA 30075-4532
(770) 992-4339
Contact: Bill Stokes

Northwest Georgia Girl Scout Council
100 Edgewood Ave., N.E., Suite 1100
Atlanta, GA 30335
(404) 527-7500
Contact: Pat Tunno

Salvation Army, The
675 Seminole Ave., N.E.
Atlanta, GA 30306
(404) 873-3101
Contact: John Smiles

Save the Children
1447 Peachtree St., Suite 700
Atlanta, GA 30309
(404) 885-1578
Contact: Donna Overcast, Director

Senior Citizen Services of Metropolitan Atlanta
1705 Commerce Dr., N.E.
Atlanta, GA 30318
(404) 351-3889
Contact: Vivian Minor, Executive Director

Southern Christian Leadership Conference—National Office
334 Auburn Ave., N.E.
Atlanta, GA 30312
(404) 522-1420
Contact: Rev. E. Randel Osburn

United Way of Metropolitan Atlanta
100 Edgewood Ave., N.E.
Atlanta, GA 30303
(404) 527-7200
Contact: Mark O'Connell

Visiting Nurses Association of Metropolitan Atlanta
133 Luckie St., N.W.
Atlanta, GA 30303
(404) 527-0660
Contact: John Good, Vice-President of Human Resources

Young Men's Christian Association of Metropolitan Atlanta
100 Edgewood Ave., N.E., Suite 902
Atlanta, GA 30303
(404) 588-9622
Contact: Katie Carstens, Human Resources

Young Women's Christian Association of Metropolitan Atlanta
100 Edgewood Ave., N.E., Suite 806
Atlanta, GA 30303
(404) 527-7575
Contact: Debra Hart Fisher, Executive Director

Turning volunteer work into a job

After spending many years working as a volunteer for various organizations, Marion Simon's daughters advised her to "stop giving it away." She decided to look for paid employment. But because she had never had a paid job, Simon was not sure how to begin her job search.

"As a woman in my middle years, I wondered where in the world I would go," says Marion. "I had a good education and a great deal of volunteer experience. I had planned and orchestrated large benefits and had done an inordinate amount of fund-raising over the years. I also had done community work in the inner city.

"I talked to some career counselors at a local college and they helped me put together a resume. Then I began to talk to people I knew. They offered me various jobs, none of which thrilled me.

"Then I happened to mention my job search to the president of a hospital where I had done a great deal of volunteer work," says Marion. "He asked me not to take a job until I had talked to him. Later, he hired me as his special assistant, with the charge to 'humanize the hospital.' Over a period of time, I developed a patient representative department.

"When I began the job 11 years ago, I was a one-person operation. As time went on, I added staff. I currently supervise a staff of 9, plus about 25 volunteers. The job of patient representative is now a full-fledged profession. Many women in the field began as volunteers. They knew a lot about the hospital where they were volunteering and thus made the transition into a paid position more easily."

We asked Simon what advice she has for volunteers who want to move into the paid workforce. "Go to the career counseling departments of some small colleges. If they suggest that you need additional training, get it. Nevertheless, before you go back to school, investigate the kinds of jobs available in your chosen field. Think about how you can use your volunteer experience in a paid position. Take what you've done and build from it."

Insurance

WEB SITES:

http://insurancenet.com/index.html
links to a directory of insurance resources on the Net.

http://www.onramp.net/ICC/
provides employment, educational, and informational services for the insurance industry.

http://www.rampages.onramp.net/~jlnixon
is the insurance career connection.

http:www.cba.uga.edu/insurance/inews.htm
site of the University of Georgia Terry College of Business "Risk Management and Insurance" newsletter.

http:www.com/acbd/busi_ins.html
is the site of a listing of insurance brokers.

PROFESSIONAL ORGANIZATIONS:

For networking in insurance and related fields, check out the following professional organization listed in Chapter 5:
Atlanta Association of Life Underwriters

For more information, you can contact:

American Insurance Association
1130 Connecticut Ave., N.W.
Washington, DC 20036
(202) 828-7100

National Association of Independent Insurers
2600 River Rd.
Des Plaines, IL 60018
(847) 297-7800

Society of Certified Insurance Counselors
P.O. Box 27027
Austin, TX 78755
(512) 345-7932

PROFESSIONAL PUBLICATIONS:

Best's Review
Independent Agent
Insurance Advocate
Insurance Journal
Insurance Week
National Underwriter

DIRECTORIES:

Best's Insurance Reports (A.M. Best Co., Oldwick, NJ)

Financial Times World Insurance (Gale Research, Detroit, MI)

Hine's Directory of Insurance Adjusters (Hines Legal Directory, Glen Ellyn, IL)

Insurance Almanac (Underwriter Publishing Co., Englewood, NJ)

S&P's Insurance Book (Standard and Pool's Rating Group, New York, NY)

Employers:

Alexander & Alexander Consulting Group
3565 Piedmont Rd., Bldg. 1, Suite 600
Atlanta, GA 30363
(404) 264-3141
Benefit consultants

Alexander, Steve, Insurance Agency
P.O. Box 7886
Atlanta, GA 30357
(404) 892-2985
Contact: Joy Porter, Office Manager

American Family Life Assurance Company of Columbus
7076 Peachtree Industrial Blvd.
Norcross, GA 30071
(770) 449-5215
Contact: Doris Bracket, District Sales Coordinator

American National Insurance Company Sales Office
1000 Circle 75 Parkway, Suite 701
Atlanta, GA 30339-3026
(404) 952-5333
Contact: Larry Lamunyon, District Manager

Anderson, Arthur
133 Peachtree St., N.E.
Atlanta, GA 30303
(404) 658-1776
Benefit consultant

Associated Doctors Health & Life Insurance Co.
1475 Buford Dr., Suite 403-125
Lawrenceville, Georgia 30243
(770) 433-2737
Contact: Mark Lloyd

Atlanta Life Insurance Co.
100 Auburn Ave., N.E.
Atlanta, GA 30303
(404) 659-2100
Contact: Leanne Gordon
One of the nation's largest minority-owned insurance companies

Bankers Fidelity Life Insurance Co.
4370 Peachtree Rd., N.E.
Atlanta, GA 30319
(404) 266-5500
Contact: Barbara Sides, Human Resources

Blue Cross and Blue Shield of Georgia
3350 Peachtree Rd., N.E.
Atlanta, GA 30326
(404) 842-8445

Buck Consultants
200 Galleria Parkway, N.W., Suite 1200
Atlanta, GA 30339
(770) 955-2488
Benefit consultants

Chastain Davis & Pearre Insurance
53 Perimeter Center East, Suite 400
Atlanta, GA 30346
(404) 551-3270
Contact: Harold Davis, Owner

Confederation Life Insurance and Annuity Co.
260 Interstate North Circle
Atlanta, GA 30339
(770) 953-5100
Contact: Steve Sprague

Coopers & Lybrand—Human Resource Advisory Group
1155 Peachtree St.
Atlanta, GA 30309
(404) 870-1309
Benefit consultants

Corporate Insurance Agency
Two Ravinia Dr., Suite 1430
Atlanta, GA 30346
(770) 390-1880

Cotton States Insurance
244 Perimeter Center Parkway, N.E.
Atlanta, GA 30346
(770) 391-8600
Contact: Joyce McWhorter, Human
Resources

Dean & Tanner Insurance Agency
3833 Roswell Rd., Suite 107B
Atlanta, GA 30342
(404) 261-1180
Contact: Jim Dean, Owner

Delta Life Insurance Co.
4370 Peachtree Rd., N.E.
Atlanta, GA 30319
(404) 231-2111
Contact: Jim Falkler

Draper Owens Co.
6000 Lake Forest Dr., Suite 325
Atlanta, GA 30328
(404) 256-6600
Contact: Clyde Mynatt

Eve-O'Neal
2970 Peachtree Rd., N.W., Suite 650
Atlanta, GA 30305
(404) 262-3616

**Financial Life Insurance Company of
Georgia**
191 Peachtree St., N.E.
Atlanta, GA 30303
(404) 332-6270
Contact: Hugh O'Neal, President

Fuqua Enterprises
1201 W. Peachtree St., N.W.
Atlanta, GA 30309
(404) 815-2000

Greater Georgia Life Insurance Company
3350 Peachtree Rd., N.E.
Atlanta, GA 30326
(404) 842-8001
Contact: Belinda Bennett, Human
Resources Specialist

Haas & Dodd
7000 Peachtree-Dunwoody Rd., N.E.
P.O. Box 720436
Atlanta, GA 30358-2436
(404) 698-7400
Contact: Kim Langley, Office Manager

Hay Group
5901-A Peachtree-Dunwoody Rd.,
Suite 450
Atlanta, GA 30328
(770) 394-5500
Benefit consultants

Hazlehurst & Associates
400 Perimeter Center Terrace, Suite 850
Atlanta, GA 30346
(770) 395-9880
Benefit consultants

Hewitt Associates
2100 River Edge Parkway, Suite 900
Atlanta, GA 30328
(770) 956-7777
Benefit consultants

ING Insurance
5780 Powers Ferry Rd., N.W.
Atlanta, GA 30327-4390
(770) 980-5100
Contact: Charles Lewis, Vice-President of
Human Resources

ITT Hartford
4170 Ashford-Dunwoody Rd., N.E.
Atlanta, GA 30319
(404) 256-1155
Contact: Debbie Bauguss, Personnel

Johnson & Higgins of Georgia
191 Peachtree St., N.E., Suite 3400
Atlanta, GA 30303
(404) 586-0000
Contact: Carol Collier, Vice-President of
Human Resources

Jones-Logan Co.
8060 Roswell Rd., Suite 200
Atlanta, GA 30350
(770) 394-7814
Contact: Pat Hayes, Office Manager

Kemper Insurance
2877 Brandywine Rd.
Atlanta, GA 30341
(770) 986-0303
Contact: Dan Moleni, Manager of Human Resources

Lanigan Insurance Agency
3610 Piedmont Rd., N.E.
Atlanta, GA 30305
(404) 261-8942
Contact: John Lanigan, President

Liberty National Life Insurance Company
5300 Frontage Rd., Suite H
Forest Park, GA 30050
(404) 608-0033
Contact: Ed Wiggs, District Manager

Life Insurance Company of Georgia
5780 Powers Ferry Rd., N.W.
Atlanta, GA 30327
(770) 980-5100

Martin & Associates Berkshire Life Insurance
1050 Crown Pointe Parkway, Suite 920
Atlanta, GA 30338
(770) 551-6300
Contact: John E. Martin, Jr., General Agent

Maryland Casualty Company
1100 Ashwood Parkway
P.O. Box 105009
Atlanta, GA 30348
(770) 399-5555
Contact: Vicky Burger, Assistant Manager of Human Resources

McEver & Co.
3715 Northside Parkway, N.W., Suite 125
Atlanta, GA 30327
(404) 262-7200
Contact: Robert McEver

Mercer, William M., Inc.
133 Peachtree St., N.E., Suite 3700
Atlanta, GA 30303
(404) 521-2200
Benefit consultants

Merritt & McKenzie Insurance Agency
3715 Northside Parkway, N.W.
Suite 400 North Creek
Atlanta, GA 30327
(404) 266-7160
Contact: Gary Ralston

Metropolitan Life Insurance Co.
3200 Highland Parkway, S.E., Suite 400
Smyrna, GA 30082
(770) 432-7738
Contact: Linda McCoy, Office Manager

New York Life Insurance Co.
400 Embassy Row, Suite 100
Atlanta, GA 30328
(404) 395-2500
Contact: John Allen, Jr., General Manager

Northwestern Mutual Life Insurance Co.
1360 Peachtree St.
Atlanta, GA 30309
(404) 885-6500
Contact: Nancy Inman, Human Resources

Primerica Life Insurance Co.
3120 Breckinridge Blvd.
Duluth, GA 30199
(770) 381-1000
Contact: Peggy Hilton, Recruiting

Prudential Insurance Company of America, The
3495 Piedmont Rd.
12 Piedmont Center, Suite 300
Atlanta, GA 30305
(404) 262-2600
Contact: Ron Smith, Human Resources

Sutter & McLellan
3861 Holcomb Bridge Rd.
Norcross, GA 30092
(770) 246-8300
Contact: Karen Koskonas

Towers Perrin
950 E. Paces Ferry Rd., Suite 1100
Atlanta, GA 30326
(404) 365-1600
Benefit consultants

Travelers Insurance
Commercial Insurance Division
3500 Piedmont Rd., Security Center, Suite 400
Atlanta, GA 30305
(404) 814-4700
Contact: Regina Presybysz

United Family Life Insurance Co.
230 John Wesley Dobbs Ave.
Atlanta, GA 30303
(404) 659-3300
Contact: Michelle Iverson, Human Resources

Vickery Insurance Agency
P.O. Box 1202
McDonough, GA 30253
(770) 957-7093
Contact: Charles Vickery, Owner

Watson Wyatt Worldwide
4170 Ashford-Dunwoody Rd., N.E.
Atlanta, GA 30319
(404) 252-4030
Benefit consultants

Law Firms

WEB SITES:

http://www.law.indiana.edu/law/lawindex.html
is a virtual law library; also connects to all law firms on the Net.

http://www.abanet.org/
is the homepage of the American Bar Association.

http://holmes.law.cwru.edu/cwrulaw/career/career.html
links to career opportunities in the field.

http://hg.org/firms-georgia.html
list of major law firms in Atlanta; can search by attorney and firm specialties; link to Georgia law schools and area bar associations.

http:lawforum.net/states/ga/lawfirms.htm
is the State Directory of Georgia Law Firms; has an employment link.

PROFESSIONAL ORGANIZATIONS:

For networking in law and related fields, check out the following local professional organizations listed in Chapter 5:
Atlanta Bar Association
Gate City Bar Association
Georgia Association of Criminal Defense Lawyers
Georgia Association of Legal Assistants
Lawyers Club of Atlanta

For more information, you can contact:

American Bar Association
750 N. Lake Shore Dr.
Chicago, IL 60611
(312) 988-5000

National Association of Legal Assistants
1601 S. Main St.
Tulsa, OK 74119
(918) 587-6828

National Bar Association (Minority Lawyers)
1225 11th St., N.W.
Washington, DC 20001
(202) 842-3900

National Federation of Paralegal Associations
P.O. Box 33108
Kansas City, MO 64114
(816) 941-4000

National Paralegal Association
P.O. Box 406
Solebury, PA 18963
(215) 297-8333

PROFESSIONAL PUBLICATIONS:

ABA Journal
American Lawyer
Fulton County Daily Report
Lawyer's Weekly
The National Law Journal
The Paralegal
The Practical Lawyer

DIRECTORIES:

ABA Directory (American Bar Association,
Chicago, IL)
*Atlanta Business Chronicle Annual Book of
Lists—Largest Law Firms* (Atlanta
Business Chronicle, Atlanta, GA)
Directory of Local Paralegal Clubs
(National Paralegal Association,
Solebury, PA)
Georgia Legal Directory (Legal Directories
Publishing Company, Dallas, TX)
Law Firms Yellow Book (Monitor Publish-
ing Co., New York, NY)
Martindale-Hubbell Law Directory (Reed
Reference Publishing, New Providence,
NJ)
*NLDA Directory of Legal Aid and Defender
Offices* (National Legal Aid and Defender
Association, Washington, DC)
Of Counsel 500 (Prentice Hall Law and
Business, Englewood Cliffs, NJ)

Employers:

Alston & Bird
1 Atlantic Center
1201 W. Peachtree St.
Atlanta, GA 30309-3424
(404) 881-7000
Contact: Cathy Benson, Director of
Personnel
Atlanta's second largest law firm;
litigation, banking, and corporate finance

Arnall Golden & Gregory
1 Atlantic Center
1201 W. Peachtree St.
Atlanta, GA 30309
(404) 873-8500

Constangy, Brooks & Smith
230 Peachtree St., N.E.
Atlanta, GA 30303
(404) 525-8622
Contact: Cathy Hood, Office Manager
Labor and employment law, environmental law, ERISA

Drew, Eckl & Farnham
880 W. Peachtree St.
Atlanta, GA 30309
(404) 885-1400
Contact: Joanna Lan, Recruiting Coordi-
nator
Mail to:
P.O. Box 7600
Atlanta, GA 30357
General civil practice

Fisher & Phillips
1500 Resurgens Plaza
945 E. Paces Ferry Rd., N.E.
Atlanta, GA 30326
(404) 231-1400
Contact: Janice Kilgore
Labor and employment law

Ford & Harrison
1275 Peachtree St., N.E.
Atlanta, GA 30309
(404) 888-3800
Contact: Jessica Royston, Recruiting
Coordinator
Labor and employment

Glass, McCullough, Sherrill & Harrold
1409 Peachtree St., N.E.
Atlanta, GA 30309
(404) 885-1500
Contact: Kathy Cavanaugh, Human
Resource Director
Commercial and residential real estate,
litigation, corporate

Greene, Buckley, Jones & McQueen
285 Peachtree Center Ave., N.E.
Marquis Tower, Suite 1400
Atlanta, GA 30303
(404) 522-3541
Contact: Al Copija, Assistant
Administrator
General civil, corporate, litigation,
insurance defense

Hawkins & Darnell
303 Peachtree St.
Atlanta, GA 30308
(404) 614-7400
Product and general liability and
environmental and business litigation

Holland & Knight
1201 W. Peachtree St., N.E., Suite 2000
Atlanta, GA 30309-3400
(404) 817-8500
Contact: Molly Harvey, Recruiting
Coordinator
Corporate and litigation

Hunton & Williams
600 Peachtree St., N.E., Suite 4100
Atlanta, GA 30308
(404) 888-4000
Corporate, litigation, environmental, and
labor

Jones & Askew
191 Peachtree St., N.E., 37th Floor
Atlanta, GA 30303-1769
(404) 818-3700
Contact: Thomas Hodge, Hiring Partner
Patent, trademark and copyright law,
litigation

Jones Day Atlanta
One Peachtree Center
303 Peachtree St., N.E., Suite 3500
Atlanta, GA 30308
(404) 521-3939
Contact: Virginia Wells, Personnel
Administrator
Corporate banking, real estate, environ-
ment, and intellectual property

Kilpatrick Stockton
1100 Peachtree St., Suite 2800
Atlanta, GA 30309
(404) 815-6500
Contact: William Brewster, Hiring Partner

King and Spalding
191 Peachtree St., N.E.
Atlanta, GA 30303-1763
(404) 572-4600
Contact: Gearlinne Eley, Personnel
Director
Largest law firm in Atlanta

Kutak Rock & Campbell
225 Peachtree St., N.E., Suite 2100
4400 Georgia-Pacific Center
Atlanta, GA 30303
(404) 222-4600
Contact: Becky Horner, Administrative
Assistant
Public and corporate finance, corporate
litigation, real estate

Long, Aldridge and Norman
One Peachtree Center
303 Peachtree St., Suite 5300
Atlanta, GA 30308
(404) 527-4000
Contact: Terry Moore, Human Resources
Corporate, securities, tax, litigation, real
estate

Long, Weinberg, Ansley & Wheeler
999 Peachtree St., N.E., Suite 2700
Atlanta, GA 30309
(404) 876-2700
Contact: Greg Rimes, Office Manager
Insurance litigation, aviation, professional
negligence, products liability, environmental, health care

Morris, Manning & Martin
Atlanta Financial Center
3343 Peachtree Rd., N.E., Suite 1600
Atlanta, GA 30326
(404) 233-7000
Contact: Jackie Williams, Director of
Personnel
General corporate, computer law, real
estate, litigation, tax, estate planning

Nelson, Mullins, Riley & Scarborough
1201 Peachtree St., Bldg. 400, Suite 2200
Atlanta, GA 30361
(404) 817-6000
Contact: Sylvia Kochler, Hiring Partner
Aviation, products liability, corporate and
securities, and technology

Paul, Hastings, Janofsky & Walker
600 Peachtree St., N.E., Suite 2400
Atlanta, GA 30308
(404) 815-2400
Corporate, tax, litigation, employment
law, and real estate

Peterson, Dillard, Young, Asselin, Powell
230 Peachtree St., N.W., Suite 1100
Atlanta, GA 30303
(404) 523-3300
Contact: Kathy McCollister, Office
Manager
Construction law, litigation, business law,
real estate

Powell, Goldstein, Frazer & Murphy
191 Peachtree St., N.E., 16th Floor
Atlanta, GA 30303
(404) 572-6600
Contact: Carol Faubert, Director of
Personnel
Banking and corporate finance; litigation

Rogers & Hardin
International Tower, Suite 2700
229 Peachtree St., N.E.
Atlanta, GA 30303
(404) 522-4700
Contact: Jane Berlin, Administrator
Securities litigation, mergers & acquisitions, corporate, employment, commercial litigation

Smith, Currie & Hancock
233 Peachtree St., N.E.
Atlanta, GA 30303-1530
(404) 521-3800
Contact: Debra Henderson, Recruiting
Coordinator
Construction law, labor, employment law

Smith, Gambrell & Russell
1230 Peachtree St., N.E., Suite 3100
Atlanta, GA 30309-3592
(404) 815-3500
Contact: Sherri Knight, Recruiting
Coordinator

Sutherland, Asbill & Brennan
999 Peachtree St., N.E.
Atlanta, GA 30309-3996
(404) 853-8000
Contact: Linda Newman, Personnel
Administrator

Swift, Currie, McGhee & Hiers
1355 Peachtree St., N.E., Suite 300
Atlanta, GA 30309
(404) 874-8800
Contact: Katherine Shirley
Business litigation, corporate, securities,
business defense

Troutman, Sanders, LLP
600 Peachtree St., N.E., Suite 5200
Atlanta, GA 30308
(404) 885-3000
Contact: Sue Ellen Maneely, Director of
Personnel
General civil law practice

Webb, Carlock, Copeland, Semler & Stair
285 Peachtree Center Ave., Suite 2600
Atlanta, GA 30303
(404) 522-8220
Insurance defense litigation

Womble, Carlyle, Sandridge & Rice
1275 Peachtree St., N.E., Suite 700
Atlanta, GA 30309
(404) 872-7000
Corporate, real estate, litigation, financial
institutions, health care

Management Consultants

WEB SITES:

http://www.scescape.com/worldlibrary/
business/companies/consult.html
Links to consulting companies.

PROFESSIONAL ORGANIZATIONS:

For networking in management consulting and related fields, check out the following local professional organizations listed in Chapter 5:

Administrative Management Society
American Management Association
Consulting Engineers Council of Georgia
Georgia Association of Personnel Services

For more information, you can contact:

Association of Management Consulting Firms (ACME)
230 Park Ave.
New York, NY 10169
(212) 949-6571

Institute of Management Consultants
521 Fifth Ave.
New York, NY 10175
(212) 697-8262

National Management Association
2210 Arbor Blvd.
Dayton, OH 45439
(513) 294-0421

PROFESSIONAL PUBLICATIONS:

Academy of Management Journal
Academy of Management Review
ACME Newsletter
Administrative Management
Business Quarterly
Consultants News
Executive
Harvard Business Review
Management Review

DIRECTORIES:

ACME Directory (Association of Management Consultants, New York, NY)
Bradford's Directory of Management Consultants (Bradford Publications, Fairfax, VA)
Consultants and Consulting Organizations (Gale Research, Detroit, MI)
Directory of Management Consultants (Kennedy Publications, Fitzwilliam, NH)
Dun's Consultants Directory (Dun and Bradstreet Corp., Parsippany, NJ)
IMC Directory (Institute of Management Consultants, New York, NY)

Employers:

Andersen Consulting
133 Peachtree St., N.E., Suite 2600
Atlanta, GA 30303
(404) 880-9100
Contact: Kitty Stumler, Director of Human Resources

Atlanta Consulting Group
1600 Parkwood Circle, Suite 200
Atlanta, GA 30339
(770) 952-8000
Contact: Marylea Lightner, Director of Professional Services

Bekaert Associates
2440 Sandy Plains Rd., N.E.
Marietta, GA 30060
(770) 565-9430

Booz-Allen & Hamilton
229 Peachtree St., N.E., Suite 1520
Atlanta, GA 30303
(404) 659-3600
Send resumes to:
Human Resources
8283 Greensboro Dr., Dept. STIT
McLean, VA 22102

Boston Consulting Group
600 Peachtree St., N.E.
Atlanta, GA
(404) 877-5200
Contact: Jennifer Schonheiter, Recruiting
Assistant

Coopers & Lybrand
1100 Campanile Bldg.
1155 Peachtree St., N.E.
Atlanta, GA 30309
(404) 870-1100
Northridge Office: (770) 643-0175

Crawford & Co.
5620 Glenridge Dr., N.E.
Atlanta, GA 30342
(404) 256-0830

Deloitte Touche Consulting Group
285 Peachtree Center Ave., Suite 2000
Atlanta, GA 30303
(404) 220-1500
Contact: Human Resources

Executive Adventure
400 Colony Square
Atlanta, GA 30303
(404) 870-9071
Contact: Bob Carr, Chief Executive Officer

Executive Expeditions
131 Village Parkway, N.E., Suite 4
Marietta, GA 30067
(770) 951-2173
Contact: John D. Schmidt, President

Fagin Advisory Services
990 Hammond Dr., N.E.
Atlanta, GA 30328
(770) 390-9005
Contact: Barbara Schaffer

Garr Consulting Group, The
1240 Powers Ferry Rd., S.E.
Atlanta, GA 30067
(770) 955-6142
Contact: Pam McClure, Human Resources

Grissom, John, and Associates
2189 Cascade Rd., S.W.
Atlanta, GA 30311
(404) 755-4542
Contact: John Grissom, owner

Hamilton/KSA
1355 Peachtree St., N.E., Suite 900
Atlanta, GA 30309
(404) 892-3436
Contact: Fran Preston, Recruiter

Hay Group
5901-A Peachtree-Dunwoody Rd., N.E.
Bldg. A, Suite 450
Atlanta, GA 30328
(770) 394-5500
Contact: Corina Hill, Office Manager

Hewitt Associates
2100 River Edge Parkway, N.W.
Marietta, GA 30328
(770) 956-7777
Contact: Valerie Cushing

ICCA Pro-Med
11660 Alpharetta Hwy., Suite 650
Roswell, GA 30076
(770) 752-5570
Contact: Tanya Gessger

Kearney, A.T.
1100 Abernathy Rd., Suite 900
Atlanta, GA 30328
(770) 393-9900
Contact: Barbara Macceo, Office Manager

Kurt Salmon Associates
1355 Peachtree St., N.E.
Atlanta, GA 30309
(404) 892-0321
Contact: Donna Simmons, Recruiting
Coordinator

Manning Selvage & Lee
1201 W. Peachtree St.
Atlanta, GA 30309
(404) 875-1444
Contact: Jan Lewin, Managing Director

McFarlane & Company
1 Park Place, N.W.
Atlanta, GA 30318
(404) 352-2290
Contact: Ian McFarlane, President

McGarvy-Ross Consulting
289 Washington Ave., N.E.
Marietta, GA 30060
(770) 428-8899
Contact: James McGarvy, President

Miller Howard Consulting Group
750 Hammond Dr.
Bldg. 12, Suite 200
Atlanta, GA 30328
(404) 255-6523
Contact: Michelle Tisdale, Marketing
Director

MSI Division of MSI International
1050 Crown Point Parkway, Suite 100
Atlanta, GA 30338
(770) 394-2494
Contact: Jim Watson, Vice-President

ODR Inc.
2900 Chamblee-Tucker Rd.
Atlanta, GA 30341
(770)455-7145
Contact: Michaelene Conner, Vice-
President, Core Services

Omega Hospitality Group
2033 Monroe Dr., N.E.
Atlanta, GA 30324
(404) 873-2000
Contact: David Zakin, Principal

Park Square
142 S. Park Square, N.E.
Marietta, GA 30060
(770) 428-2900
Contact: Angie Wissing, Director of
Human Resources

Southern Electric International
900 Ashwood Parkway
Dunwoody, GA 30338
(770) 379-7000
Contact: Lee Martin, Human Resources

Spencer Stuart
1201 W. Peachtree St., Suite 3230
Atlanta, GA 30309
(404) 892-2800
Contact: Karen Connors, Director of
Research

Sperduto & Associates
235 Peachtree St., N.E., Suite 300
Atlanta, GA 30303
(404) 577-1178
Contact: Debbie D'Anna, Office Manager

Tilinghast-A Towers Perrin Company
950 E. Paces Ferry Rd., N.E., Suite 1100
Atlanta, GA 30326
(404) 261-5420
Contact: Gretchen Thompson, Personnel
Manager

Turknett Associates Leadership Group
2310 Parklake Dr., N.E., Suite 1100
Atlanta, GA 30345
(770) 270-1723
Contact: Glendale Jones, Office Manager

Market Research Firms

WEB SITES:

http://www.ama.org/
is the homepage of the American
Marketing Association.

http://www.sme.com/dmweb/
is the Direct Marketing Web.

http://www.com/acvb/busi_adv.htm/
listing of advertising agencies, public
relations, and marketing firms in the
Atlanta area.

PROFESSIONAL ORGANIZATIONS:

For networking in market research and
related fields, check out the following local
professional organizations listed in
Chapter 5. Also see **"Advertising
Agencies"** and **"Public Relations."**

Ad2 Atlanta
American Marketing Association
**Public Relations Society of America—
Georgia Chapter**

For more information, you can contact:

American Marketing Association
250 S. Wacker Dr.
Chicago, IL 60606
(312) 648-0536

**Council of American Survey Research
Organizations**
3 Upper Devon, Belle Terre
Port Jefferson, NY 11777
(516) 928-6954

Marketing Research Association
2189 Silas Deane Hwy., Suite 5
Rocky Hill, CT 06067
(203) 257-4008

**National Association of Market
Developers**
1422 W. Peachtree St., N.W., Suite 500
Atlanta, GA 30309
(404) 892-0444

**Sales and Marketing Executives
International**
Statler Office Tower, No. 458
Cleveland, OH 44115
(216) 771-6650

PROFESSIONAL PUBLICATIONS:

Direct Marketing Magazine
Industrial Marketing
Journal of Marketing Research
Marketing and Media Decisions
Marketing Times

DIRECTORIES:

*Bradford's Directory of Marketing Research
Agencies* (Bradford Publishing Co.,
Fairfax, VA)
*Handbook of Independent Advertising and
Marketing Services* (Executive Commu-
nications, Inc., New York, NY)
*International Membership Directory and
Marketing Services Guide* (American
Marketing Association, Chicago, IL)
Membership Roster (American Marketing
Association, Chicago, IL)
*Multinational Marketing and Employment
Directory* (World Trade Academy Press,
Inc., New York, NY)

Employers:

Atlanta Marketing Research Center
P.O. Box 13463
Atlanta, GA 30324
(404) 239-0001
Contact: John Lockyear

Booth Research Services
1120 Hope Rd.
Dunwoody, GA 30350
(770) 992-2200
Contact: Andrea Gordon, Human
Resources

Carpax Associates
5755 Dupree Dr., N.W.
Atlanta, GA 30327
(770) 859-9075
Contact: Lydia Simpson, Office Manager

Compass Marketing Research
3725 Da Vinci Court, N.W.
Norcross, GA 30092
(770) 448-0754
Contact: Wendy Meyers, Human Resources

Darden Research Corporation
1534 N. Decatur Rd., N.E.
Atlanta, GA 30307
(404) 377-9294

Eagle Research Atlanta
1 Dunwoody Park
Dunwoody, GA 30338
(770) 395-6090
Contact: Schavonne Maxwell, Personnel Director

Gallup Organization
3333 Peachtree Rd., N.E.
Atlanta, GA 30326
(404) 816-4115
Contact: Njeri Collier, Office Manager

Guideline Research/Atlanta
3675 Crestwood Parkway, N.W.
Duluth, GA 30136
(770) 717-7844
Contact: Rick Tate, President

Key Marketing & Research
4002 Summerwood Lane
Roswell, GA 30202
(770) 772-6060
Contact: Jennifer Schaeffer, Operations Scheduler

Marketing Spectrum
990 Hammond Dr., N.E.
Atlanta, GA 30328
(770) 395-7244
Contact: Joyce McNeil, Office Manager

PVR
11445 Johns Creek Parkway
Duluth, GA 30155
(770) 232-0322

Plexus Marketing Group
1140 Hammond Dr., N.E.
Atlanta, GA 30328
(770) 390-9692
Contact: Lisa Hamett, Operations Manager

Polaris Marketing Research
359 E. Paces Ferry Rd., Suite 300
Atlanta, GA 30305
(404) 816-0353
Contact: Lucy Klausner, Vice-President

Questnet Communications
6201 Powers Ferry Rd., N.W.
Atlanta, GA 30339
(404) 303-8881
Contact: Bonnie Wade, Human Resources

Research Design Associates
721 E. Ponce de Leon Ave.
Decatur, GA 30030
(404) 373-4637

Research Inc.
7000 Peachtree-Dunwoody Rd., N.E.
Atlanta, GA 30328
(770) 481-0292
Contact: Debbie McNamara, Research Director

Tourmaline Marketing
3715 Northside Parkway, N.W.
Atlanta, GA 30328
(404) 240-7300
Contact: Milt Donaldson, Comptroller

Winfield Group, The
1280 W. Peachtree St.
Atlanta, GA 30309
(404) 888-0530
Contact: Pamela Griffin, Senior Program Manager

Media, Print

WEB SITES:

http://www.enews.com/
is the homepage of the Web's electronic
newsstand.

http://www.mediainfo.com/edpub/e-
papers.home.page.html
links to newspapers on the Net.

http://ic.corpnet.com/~aking/webinfo/
webzines.html
links to Web magazines.

Virtually all large companies, as well as
major newspapers, magazines, and
reference publishers, have an electronic
publishing division. Check out the
homepage of the publication or business
of interest to learn about their electronic
division.

PROFESSIONAL ORGANIZATIONS:

For networking in the magazine and
newspaper publishing business, check out
the following local professional organizations listed in Chapter 5. Also see **"Book
Publishers."**

**Atlanta Press Club, The
Georgia Press Association**

For additional information, you can
contact:

**American Newspaper Publishers
Association**
11600 Sunrise Valley Dr.
Reston, VA 22091
(703) 648-1000

Electronic Publishers Association
611 Lighthouse Ave.
Santa Cruz, CA 95060
(408) 423-8580

**National Association of Desktop
Publishers**
462 Old Boston St.
Boston, MA 01983
(800) 874-4113

National Newspaper Association
1525 Wilson Blvd.
Arlington, VA 22209
(703) 907-7900

Newsletter Publishers Association
1401 Wilson Blvd., Suite 207
Arlington, VA 22209
(703) 527-2333

Newspaper Features Council
37 Arch St.
Greenwich, CT 06830
(203) 661-3386

Suburban Newspapers of America
401 N. Michigan Ave.
Chicago, IL 60611
(312) 644-6610

Writers Guild of America, East
555 W. 57th St.
New York, NY 10019
(212) 767-7800

PROFESSIONAL PUBLICATIONS:

American Journalism Review
*Business Publishing: The Magazine for
   Desktop Publishers*
The Columbia Journalism Review
Desktop Printing and Publishing
Editor and Publisher
Electronic Publishing
Folio
Suburban Voice
The Writer
Writer's Digest

DIRECTORIES:

*Editor and Publisher International
   Yearbook* (Editor and Publisher, New
   York, NY)
*Electronic News Financial Fact Book and
   Directory* (Fairchild Publications, New
   York, NY)

Hispanic Media and Markets Directory (Standard Rate and Data Service, Wilmette, IL)

Literary Market Place (R.R. Bowker, New Providence, NJ)

Magazine Industry Market Place (R.R. Bowker, Inc., New Providence, NJ)

National Directory of Magazines (Oxbridge Communications, Inc., New York, NY)

SNA Membership Directory (Suburban Newspapers of America, Chicago, IL)

Employers:

Also see listings of area newspapers in Chapter 1 and trade journals in Chapter 4.

Atlanta Homes and Lifestyle
1100 Johnson Ferry Rd., Suite 595
Atlanta, GA 30345
(404) 252-6670
Contact: Barbara Tapp, Editor

Atlanta Magazine
1360 Peachtree St., N.E.
Atlanta, GA 30309
(404) 872-3100
Contact: Lee Walburn, Editor

Atlanta Sports & Fitness
359 E. Paces Ferry Rd., N.E.
Atlanta, GA 30305
(404) 842-0359
Contact: Laura Weldon, Editor

Business Week/Atlanta Bureau
229 Peachtree St., N.E.
Atlanta, GA 30303
(404) 521-3288
Contact: David Greising

DBR Publishing Company
2965 Flowers Rd., S.
Chamblee, GA 30341
(770) 458-2609
Contact: Stephanie Rikard, Manager

Dale Gordon Publishing
1801 Piedmont Ave., N.E.
Atlanta, GA 30324
(404) 875-4434
Contact: Dale Gordon, Owner

Fairchild Publications
57 Executive Park South, N.E.
Atlanta, GA 30329
(404) 633-9253
Contact: Georgia Lee, Editor

Georgia Journal
329 Durand Falls Dr.
Decatur, GA 30031
(404) 377-4275
Contact: David Olier, Editor

Georgia Trend Magazine
1770 Indian Trail-Lilburn Rd., N.W., Suite 350
Norcross, GA 30093
(770) 931-9410
Contact: Tom Berry, Editor

Golf World Magazine
2915 Piedmont Rd., N.E.
Atlanta, GA 30305
(404) 266-8811
Contact: Terry Galvin, Editor

Grier's Almanac Publishing Co.
5123 Charmant Place
Doraville, GA 30360
(770) 395-6381
Contact: Brian Bachler, Editor

Guide to Georgia
1655 Peachtree St., N.E.
Atlanta, GA 30309
(404) 892-0961
Contact: Pat Samford, Editor

Health News Magazine
1275 Ellsworth Industrial Dr., N.W.
Atlanta, GA 30302
(404) 755-9600
Contact: Lumumba Faiz, Editor

IDG Communications
990 Hammond Dr., N.E.
Atlanta, GA 30328
(770) 394-0758
Job hotline: (800) 343-4935

INC Magazine
3060 Peachtree St., N.W.
Atlanta, GA 30305
(404) 264-8989
Contact: Greg Bowerman, Regional
Manager

Industrial Engineering Magazine
25 Technology Park
Norcross, GA 30092
(770) 449-0461
Contact: Gary Ferguson, Editor

Intertech Publishing Company
6151 Powers Ferry Rd., N.W., Suite 200
Atlanta, GA 30339
(770) 955-2500
Contact: John Skeels, Vice-President

Know Atlanta—Newcomer Guide
7840 Roswell Rd.
Dunwoody, GA 30350
(770) 512-0016
Contact: Sheryl Fenton, Editor

Media 3 Publications
4721 Chamblee-Dunwoody Rd.,
Suite 100B
Atlanta, GA 30338
(770) 394-2811
Contact: Pat Adams, Manager

Newsweek Magazine
285 Peachtree Center Ave., Suite 2402
Atlanta, GA 30303
(404) 581-0000
Contact: Dan Peterson, Editor

Papermaker Magazine
57 Executive Park South, N.E., Suite 310
Atlanta, GA 30329
(404) 325-9153
Contact: Jerry Koncel, Editor

Shore Varrone
6255 Barfield Rd., N.E.
Atlanta, GA 30321
(404) 252-8831
Contact: Doug Shore, Owner

Southern Progress Magazine
1760 Peachtree St., N.W.
Atlanta, GA 30309
(404) 874-4462
Contact: Steve Cummings, Advertising
Manager

Standard & Poor's Corporation
4170 Ashford-Dunwoody Rd., Suite 520
Atlanta, GA 30319
(404) 843-4774
Contact: Jim Craig, Manager

Style Magazine
1575 Northside Dr., N.W.
Atlanta, GA 30318
(404) 352-2400
Contact: Neil Rubin, Editor

TAPPI Journal
15 Technology Parkway South
Norcross, GA 30092
(770) 446-1400
Contact: Don Meadows, Editor

TV Guide Magazine
2200 Century Parkway, N.E.
Atlanta, GA 30345
(404) 325-2490
Contact: Sybil Freeman, Sales
Representative

Upscale Communications
600 Bronner Brothers Way, S.W.
Atlanta, GA 30310
(404) 758-7467
Contact: Sheila Bronner, Editor

U.S. News and World Report
233 Peachtree St., N.W.
Atlanta, GA 30303
(404) 688-1331
Contact: Jill Jordan Cedar

Museums/Art Galleries

WEB SITES:

http://www.comlab.ox.ac.uk/archive/
other/museums.html
searches for museums on the Web.

http://www.mcp.com/hayden/museum-
book/sites.html
links to gallery sites.

http://www.clever.net/high/html/arts/
museum.htm/
listing of cultural institutions in Atlanta.

PROFESSSIONAL ORGANIZATIONS:

Also see **"Cultural Institutions."** For
information about the museum and
gallery professions, you can contact:

American Association of Museums
1225 I St., N.W., Suite 200
Washington, D.C. 20005
(202) 289-1818

American Federation of Arts
41 E. 65th St.
New York, NY 10021
(212) 988-7700

Arts and Business Council
25 W. 45th St.
New York, NY 10036
(212) 819-9287

Association of Art Museum Directors
41 E. 65th St.
New York, NY 10021
(212) 249-4423

**International Foundation for Art
Research**
46 E. 70th St.
New York, NY 10021
(212) 879-1780

**National Antique and Art Dealers
Association of America**
15 E. 57th St.
New York, NY 10022
(212) 826-9707

Women's Caucus for Art
P.O. Box 2646
New York, NY 10022
(718) 727-8125

PROFESSIONAL PUBLICATIONS:

Art Business News
Art Marketing Letter
The ART Newsletter
Art World
Museum World

DIRECTORIES:

American Art Directory (R.R. Bowker, New
 Providence, NJ)
*Art Business News: Guide to Galleries,
 Museums and Artists* (Brant Art Publica-
 tions, New York, NY)
Art Marketing Sourcebook (ArtNetwork,
 Renaissance, CA)
Art Now Gallery Guides (Art Now, Clinton,
 NJ)
Official Museum Directory (American
 Association of Museums, Washington,
 DC)
Who's Who in American Art (R.R. Bowker,
 New Providence, NJ)

Working in the nonprofit world

We asked Tom Sanberg, once Director of Development for a prominent museum, what it takes to make it in the non-profit world.

"Most of the people who enjoy nonprofit work and are successful at it tend to be other-directed. They get satisfaction out of working for a so-called worthy cause. There are very few high-paying jobs in not-for-profit institutions. An executive-level job at a museum, for example, probably pays about half what a job with similar responsibilities would pay in a profit-making company of the same size.

"One of the fastest-growing specialties within the nonprofit world is fundraising management, probably because nonprofit institutions rely so heavily on grants and contributions," Tom adds. He notes that universities now offer courses in fundraising.

Museum Employers:

APEX Museum
135 Auburn Ave.
Atlanta, GA 30303
(404) 521-2654
Contact: Dan Moore, Director

Atlanta Heritage Row
55 Upper Alabama St., S.W.
Atlanta, GA 30303
(404) 584-7879
Contact: Lynn Rollins, Director

Atlanta History Center
130 W. Paces Ferry Rd., N.W.
Atlanta, GA 30305
(404) 814-4000
Contact: Rick Beard, Director

Atlanta International Museum of Art and Design
285 Peachtree Center Ave., N.E.
Atlanta, GA 30303
(404) 688-2467
Contact: Angelyn S. Chandler, Director

Carlos, Michael C., Museum at Emory University
571 Kilgore St.
Atlanta, GA 30312

(404) 727-4282
Contact: Tony Hirschell, Director

Fernbank Museum of Natural History
767 Clifton Rd., N.E.
Atlanta, GA 30307
(404) 378-0127
Contact: Kay Davis, Director

Fernbank Science Center
156 Heaton Park Dr., N.E.
Atlanta, GA 30307
(404) 378-4311
Contact: Mary Hiers, Director

Herndon Home
587 University Place, N.W.
Atlanta, GA 30314
(404) 581-9813
Contact: Carole Merritt, Director

Jimmy Carter Library & Museum
441 Freedom Parkway
Atlanta, GA 30307
(404) 331-0296
Contact: Don Schewe, Director

Kennesaw Civil War Museum , The
2829 Cherokee St.
Kennesaw, GA 30144
(770) 427-2117
Contact: Dawn Collins, Director, Museum and Preservation Services

SCITREK Science and Technology Museum
395 Piedmont Ave., N.E.
Atlanta, GA 30308
(404) 522-5500
Contact: Mary Kay Roarabaugh, Director

Wren's Nest—The Joel Chandler Harris Association
1050 Ralph D. Abernathy Blvd., S.W.
Atlanta, GA 30310-1812
(404) 753-8535
Contact: Carole Mumford, Director

Art Gallery Employers:

Alpha/Omega Galleries
11060 Alpharetta Hwy.
Roswell, GA 30076
(770) 640-1954
Contact: Kurt Shiveman

Avery Gallery
390 Roswell St., S.E.
Marietta, GA 30060
(770) 427-2459
Contact: Shae Avery

Bennett St. Gallery
22 Bennett St., N.W.
Atlanta, GA 30309
(404) 352-8775
Contact: Suzie Pryor

Burnnoff Gallery
1529 Piedmont Ave., N.E.
Atlanta, GA 30324
(404) 875-3475
Contact: Dennis Burnham

Gallery of Spalding Corners
7722 Spalding Dr.
Norcross, GA 30092
(770) 447-4814
Contact: Valerie Brown

Global Art Galleries
2115 Hills Ave., N.W.
Atlanta, GA 30080
(404) 351-5111
Contact: Dave Kaufer

Gold, Fay, Gallery
247 Buckhead Ave., N.E.
Atlanta, GA 30305
(404) 233-3843

High Museum of Art
1280 Peachtree St., N.E.
Atlanta, GA 30309
(404) 733-4400
Contact: Ned Rifkin

High Museum of Art: Folk Art and Photography Galleries
30 John Wesley Dobbs Ave., N.E.
Atlanta, GA 30303
(404) 577-6940
Contact: Ned Rifkin

Hope Gallery, The
595 Piedmont Ave., N.E.
Atlanta, GA 30308
(404) 892-0534
Contact: Hope Davis

Jackson Fine Art Gallery
3115 E. Shadowlawn Ave.
Atlanta, GA 30305
(404) 233-3739
Contact: Jane Jackson

Lowe Gallery, The
75 Bennett St., N.W.
Atlanta, GA 30309
(404) 352-8114
Contact: Laura Nix

Tolliver, William, Art Gallery
2300 Peachtree Rd., N.W.
Atlanta, GA 30309
(404) 350-0811
Contact: Debra Collier

Wentworth Galleries Ltd
4400 Ashford-Dunwoody Rd., N.E.
Atlanta, GA 30346
(770) 913-0641
Contact: Cindy Brian

Oil/Gas/Plastics

WEB SITES:

http://www.oilnetwork.com/
services.html
is a network of oil companies on the
Internet; also maintains a job center.

http://www.pennwell.com/ogj.html
is the homepage of *Oil and Gas Journal.*

http://www.utsi.com/oil_gas.html
links to oil and gas industry sites.

http://www.echi.com/live.visit/visit.html
is the Plastics Network; connects to
companies and directories.

PROFESSIONAL ORGANIZATIONS:

For networking in oil, gas, plastics, and
related fields, check out the following local
professional organizations listed in
Chapter 5. Also see **"Chemicals"** and
"Engineering."

American Society of Heating,
  Refrigerating & Air
Association of Energy Engineers
Association of Mechanical Contractors
  of Atlanta

For more information, you can contact:

American Gas Association
1515 Wilson Blvd.
Arlington, VA 22209
(703) 841-8400

American Petroleum Institute
1220 L St., N.W.
Washington, D.C. 20005
(202) 682-8000

**Petroleum Industry Research
Foundation**
122 E. 42nd St.
New York, NY 10168
(212) 867-0052

Society of Plastics Engineers
14 Fairfield Dr.
Brookfield, CT 06804
(203) 775-0471

Society of the Plastics Industry
1275 K St., N.W.
Washington, DC 20005
(202) 371-5200

PROFESSIONAL PUBLICATIONS:

Drilling Contractor
Gas Industries Magazine
Lundberg Letter
Modern Plastics
National Petroleum News
Oil Daily
Oil and Gas Journal
Plastics World
World Oil

DIRECTORIES:

Energy Job Finder (Mainstream Access,
  New York, NY)
Gas Industry Training Directory (American
  Gas Association, Arlington, VA)
International Petroleum Encyclopedia
  (PennWell Publishing Co., Tulsa, OK)
Modern Plastics, Encyclopedia issue
  (McGraw-Hill, New York, NY)
National Petroleum News-Market Facts
  (Hunter Publishing Co., Des Plaines, IL)
Oil and Gas Directory (Geophysical
  Directory, Inc., Houston, TX)
Plastics World, Directory issue (Cahners,
  Newton, MA)
US Oil Industry Directory (PenWell
  Publishing, Tulsa, OK)

Employers:

Adco International Plastics Corp.
1256 Sandtown Rd.
Marietta, GA 30060
(770) 425-1234
Contact: Shirley Couch
Injection molding

AGL Resources Service Co./Atlanta Gas Light Co.
1219 Caroline St., N.E.
Atlanta, GA 30307
(404) 584-4705
Contact: Human Resources
Gas company—primary supplier for Atlanta metro area

Allied Plastics—A Division of Atlanta Belting
4840 N. Royal Atlanta Dr.
Tucker, GA 30084
(770) 939-8030
Contact: Bob Purcell, General Manager
Vacuum forming, thermoforming, and acrylic fabrication

American Petroleum Products
1200 Oakleigh Dr.
East Point, GA 30344
(404) 768-1900
Contact: William Click, Comptroller
Sells oil lubricants

AmeriGas
P.O. Drawer 87516
Atlanta, GA 30337
(404) 763-8235
Contact: William Evans, Human Resources Manager
Propane company

Atlanta Chemical Corp./Plastics Division
3400 Atlanta Industrial Parkway, N.W.
Atlanta, GA 30331
(404) 696-1000
Contact: Gail Sammons, Office Manager
Plastics manufacturer

Atlanta Plastics
5360 Snapfinger Woods Dr.
Decatur, GA 30035
(770) 987-9090
Contact: Paul Bunning, President
Fabricator and designer

Austell Gas System
2838 Washington St.
P.O. Box 685
Atlanta, GA 30001

(770) 948-1841
Contact: Human Resources Department
Supplier of natural gas

Barber Oil Co.
930 Front St.
Mabelton, GA 30059
(770) 948-5271
Contact: Edwin Barber, President
Petroleum supplier

Custom Plastics
250 Laredo Dr.
Decatur, GA 30030
(404) 373-1691
Contact: Scarlett Luke, Executive Vice-President
Plastics fabricator

Eastern Manufacturing
3178 Oakcliff Industrial St.
Doraville, GA 30340
(770) 457-6426
Contact: Office Manager

Garnett Oil & Gas
3525 Piedmont Rd., N.E.
Atlanta, GA 30305
(404) 261-7280
Contact: Bill Garnett, President
Oil and gas exploration and development

J.C. Oil
4199 Club Dr., N.E.
P.O. Box 191301
Atlanta, GA 30319
(404) 237-1280
Contact: John H. Clifton
Oil field service, oil land leases

Kentex Industries
5304 Panola Industrial Blvd.
Decatur, GA 30035
(770) 981-2550
Contact: Jake Kennington III
Job shop manufacturing company

McLure Oil Co.
2394 Mount Vernon Commons, Suite 220
Dunwoody, GA 30338
(770) 396-6655

Petroleum Source & Systems Group
2957 Clairmont Rd.
Atlanta, GA 30329
(404) 321-5711
Contact: Roger Murray, Chief Operating
Officer
Natural gas; fuel management

Pharr Machinery & Steel Co.
6365 McDonough Dr.
Norcross, GA 30093
(770) 448-4451
Contact: Human Resources
Mining equipment and supplies

Phillips Petroleum Co.
5399 Peachtree Industrial Blvd.
Chamblee, GA 30341
(770) 454-7021
Contact: Bob Brown, Manager
Crude oil purchasing

Plastech Corporation
2080 General Truman St., N.W.
Atlanta, GA 30346
(404) 355-9682
Contact: Larry Lee, Owner
Expandable products, custom-formulated
polyurethane

Plastic Suppliers
1174 Hayes Industrial Dr., N.E.
Marietta, GA 30062
(770) 424-0702
Contact: Dennis Cerny, Branch Manager
Distributors and converters of plastic film
and sheet

Plastics Engineering Laboratories
1800 MacLeod Dr.
Lawrenceville, GA 30243
(770) 962-4261
Plastics research and consulting

Taylor Gas
84 Jonesboro Rd.
Fairburn, GA 30213
(770) 964-3357
Contact: John Taylor, President
Gas company

Wilson, Ralph, Plastics Company
2323 Park Central Blvd.
Decatur, GA 30031
(770) 593-2424
Mail to:
P.O. Box 549
Decatur, GA 30031-5049
Contact: Debbie Brown, Office Manager
Decorative laminates

Paper and Allied Products

WEB SITES:

http://www.tappi.org/
is the homepage of the Technical
Association of the Paper and Pulp
Industry.

**http://www.curbet.com/print/
merch.html**
links to paper merchants.

PROFESSIONAL ORGANIZATIONS:

For networking in paper and allied
products and related fields, check out the
following local professional organization
listed in Chapter 5:
**Technical Association of the Pulp and
Paper Industry**

For more information about the paper
industry, you can contact:

American Forest and Paper Association
260 Madison Ave.
New York, NY 10016
(212) 340-0600

American Paper Institute
260 Madison Ave.
New York, NY 10016
(212) 340-0600

National Paper Trade Association
c/o John J. Buckley
111 Great Neck Rd.
Great Neck, NY 11021
(516) 829-3070

Paper Industry Management Association
1699 Wall St., Suite 212
Mount Prospect, IL 60056
(847) 956-0250

Sales Association of the Paper Industry
P.O. Box 21926
Columbus, OH 43221
(614) 326-3911

**Technical Association of the Paper and
Pulp Industry**
Technology Park, Box 105113
Atlanta, GA 30348
(404) 446-1400

PROFESSIONAL PUBLICATIONS:

Good Packaging Magazine
Packaging
Paper Age
Paper Sales
Pulp and Paper
Pulp and Paper Week
TAPPI Journal

DIRECTORIES:

American Papermaker, Mill and Personnel
   issue (ASM Communications, Inc.,
   Atlanta, GA)
*Lockwood-Post's Directory of the Paper and
   Allied Trades* (Miller Freeman, New
   York, NY)
Paper Yearbook (Harcourt Brace
   Jovanovich, New York, NY)
Pulp and Paper, Buyer's Guide issue
   (Miller Freeman, San Francisco, CA)
TAPPI Membership Directory (Technical
   Association of the Paper and Pulp
   Industry, Atlanta, GA)
*Walden's ABC Guide and Paper Production
   Yearbook* (Walden-Mott Corp., Ramsey,
   NJ)

Employers:

American Business Products
2100 River Edge Parkway, Suite 1200
Atlanta, GA 30328
(770) 953-8300
Business suppliers

APD Automatic Packaging Machinery
1500 Hillcrest Rd.
Norcross, GA 30093
(770) 921-6300
Contact: Kelly Pounds, Office Manager
Packaging machinery

Associated Paper
1202 Royal Dr.
Conyers, GA 30207
(770) 929-1987
Contact: Dave Benton, Vice-President of
Operations
Paper distributors

Atlanta Broom Company
4750 Bakers Ferry Rd., S.W.
Atlanta, GA 30336
(404) 696-4600
Contact: David Spain, Office Manager
Bags, boxes, film and foil, tissues, plates,
cups, trays

Avon Corrugated
1013 Lees Mill Rd.
College Park, GA 30349
(770) 997-9620
Tape boxes, mailing containers

Fulton Paper Company
6255 Boat Rock Blvd., S.W.
Atlanta, GA 30336
(404) 629-1044
Contact: Richard Smith, General Manager

Gaylord Container Corporation
4351 Pleasantdale Rd.
Doraville, GA 30340
(404) 448-9110
Contact: Jeff Mauk, Production Manager

Georgia-Pacific Corporation
133 Peachtree St., N.E.
Atlanta, GA 30303
(404) 652-4000
Contact: Corporate Staffing
Paper and forest products

Industrial Paper Corp.
300 Villanova Dr.
Atlanta, GA 30336
(404) 346-5800
Contact: Mark Lichtenstein, President
Complete line of packaging machines,
films, service

Kliklok Corporation
5224 Snapfinger Woods Dr.

Decatur, GA 30035
(770) 981-5200
Contact: Susie Dodson, Personnel
Manager
Packaging machinery

LaBoiteaux Company
8525 Dunwoody Place
Atlanta, GA 30350
(770) 998-8000
Contact: Joe Harper, Eastern Division
Manager
Brokers for packaging materials

Packaging Corp. of America
3200 Lakewood Ave.
East Point, GA 30344
(404) 753-9784 X227
Contact: Beverly Gwynn, Personnel
Manager
Package development

Payne, Lee, Associates
2925 Ridgewood Circle, N.W.
Atlanta, GA 30327
(404) 350-6976
Contact: Lee Payne, President
Package design

Piedmont National Corporation
1561 Southland Circle, N.W.
Atlanta, GA 30318
(404) 351-6130
Contact: Kim Walton, Vice-President of
Administration
Bags, wrappings, tape, boxes, twine

Sabin Robbins Paper Co.
4601 Welcome All Rd.
College Park, GA 30349
(404) 767-9418
Contact: Rick Whitescarver, Division
Manager

Unisource
3587 Oakcliff Rd.
Doraville, GA 30340
(770) 447-9418
Contact: Ron Allred, Branch Manager
Papers for printing, copying, and
duplicating

Printing

WEB SITE:

http://www.curbet.com/print/plink.html links to commercial printers, paper merchants, and printing associations.

PROFESSIONAL ASSOCIATIONS:

For more information about the printing industry, you can contact:

National Association of Printers and Lithographers
780 Palisade Ave.
Teaneck, NJ 07666
(201) 342-0700

Printing Industries of America
100 Dangerfield Rd.
Alexandria, VA 22314
(703) 519-8100

Technical Association of the Graphic Arts
68 Lomb Memorial Dr.
Rochester, NY 14623
(716) 475-7470

PROFESSIONAL PUBLICATIONS:

American Printer
Graphic Arts Monthly
Printing Impressions
Printing News
Who's Printing What

DIRECTORIES:

Directory of Typographic Services (National Composition Association, Arlington, VA)
Graphic Arts Blue Book (A.F. Lewis & Co., New York, NY)
Graphic Arts Monthly—Printing Industry Sourcebook (Cahners Magazines, New York, NY)

Employers:

American Signature
3101 McCall Dr.
Atlanta, GA 30340
(404) 451-4511
Contact: Lisa Bunce, Personnel Manager

Austin Printing
2123 Liddell Dr., N.E.
Atlanta, GA 30324
(404) 875-9653

Bennett Graphics
125 Royal Woods Court, Suite 100
Tucker, GA 30084
(770) 723-1192

Braceland
5800 Tulane Dr., S.W.
Atlanta, GA 30336
(404) 696-7900
Contact: Kathy Rogers, Personnel

Cadmus Marketing Services
2300 DeFoor Hills Rd.
Atlanta, GA 30318
(404) 355-7220
Contact: Sylvia Keller, Human Resources

Color Graphics
4540 Frederick Dr., S.W.
Atlanta, GA 30336
(404) 696-1515
Contact: Buddy Towery, President

Corporate Printers
2195 Pendley Rd.
Cumming, GA 30130
(770) 688-6652

Darby Printing Co.
6215 Purdue Dr., S.W.
Atlanta, GA 30336
(404) 344-2665
Contact: Morris Hack, Human Resources

Dittler Brothers
1375 Seaboard Industrial Blvd.
Atlanta, GA 30318
(404) 355-3423
Contact: Stephanie Bayer, Corporate Recruiter

Executive Printing
830 Kennesaw Ave.
Marietta, GA 30060
(770) 428-1554
Contact: Denise Badera, Office Manager

Gannett Offset Atlanta
120 James Aldredge Blvd.
Atlanta, GA 30336
(404) 699-6200

Geographics
3450 Browns Mill Rd.
Atlanta, GA 30354
(404) 768-5805
Contact: Norvin Hagan, President

Graphic Communications Corp.
394 N. Clayton St.
Lawrenceville, GA 30245
(770) 963-1871
Contact: Hoyt Tuggle, President

Graphic Industries
2155 Monroe Dr., N.E.
Atlanta, GA 30324
(404) 874-3327
Contact: Mark Polk III, President

Harris Specialty Lithographers
1519 Stoneridge Dr.
Stone Mountain, GA 30083
(770) 938-7650
Contact: Larry Shamblin, Vice-President

IPD Printing & Distributing
5800 Peachtree Rd.
Chamblee, GA 30341
(770) 458-6351
Contact: Chuck Hartman, Director of Administration

Label America
5430 E. Ponce de Leon Ave.
Stone Mountain, GA 30083
(770) 934-8040

Master Promotions and Graphics
1540 Westfork Dr.
Lithia Springs, GA 30057
(770) 944-9040
Contact: Tom White, President

Moore Copies
3343 Peachtree Rd., N.E.
Atlanta, GA 30326
(404) 231-1380
Contact: Betty Moore, Owner

National Graphics
725 Dekalb Industrial Way
Decatur, GA 30033
(404) 292-6933

Network Publications
2 Pamplin Dr.
Lawrenceville, GA 302443
(770) 962-7220

Phoenix Communications
5664 New Peachtree Rd.
Atlanta, GA 30341
(404) 457-1301
Contact: Richard Roberts, Vice-President

Scientific Games Holdings Corp.
1500 Bluegrass Lakes Parkway
Alpharetta, GA 30201
(770) 664-3700
Contact: Lucy Neely, Human Resources Manager

Seiz Printing
4525 Acworth Industrial Dr.
Acworth, GA 30101
(770) 917-7000
Contact: Earl Sutherland, General Manager

Southern Signatures
201 Armour Dr.
Atlanta, GA 30324
(404) 872-4411
Contact: Leeann Phillips, Human Resources Manager

Stein Printing Co.
2161 Monroe Dr., N.E.
Atlanta, GA 30324
(404) 875-0421
Contact: Glynis Henderson, Production
Manager

Stevens Graphics
713 R.D. Abernathy Blvd., S.W.
Atlanta, GA 30310
(404) 753-1121
Contact: Ricki Bryant, Human Resources
Director

**Treasure Chest Advertising, Atlanta
Division**
3271 Hamilton Blvd., S.E.
Atlanta, GA 30354
(404) 761-2100
Contact: Xiamara Gonzales, Human
Resources Director

Tucker Castleberry
3500 McCall Place
Atlanta, GA 30340
(707) 454-1580
Contact: Pete Livezey, Vice-President

Voxcom Inc.
100 Clover Green
Peachtree City, GA 30269
(770) 487-7575
Contact: Annie Haynes, Human Resources
Manager

Walton Press
402 Mayfield Dr.
Monroe, GA 30655
(770) 267-2596

Webco Printing
350 Great Southwest Parkway
Atlanta, GA 30336
(404) 696-4590
Contact: Allen Bodenhagen, Human
Resources Director

Williams Printing Company
1240 Spring St., N.W.
Atlanta, GA 30309
(404) 875-6611
Contact: Gloria Schmidt, Office Manager

Public Relations

WEB SITES:

http://www.prsa.org/
is the homepage of the Public Relations Society of America.

http://www.com/acvb/busi_adv.htm
listing of advertising agencies, public relations, and marketing firms in the Atlanta area.

PROFESSIONAL ORGANIZATIONS:

For networking in public relations and related fields, check out the following local professional organization listed in Chapter 5. Also see **"Advertising Agencies"** and **"Market Research Firms."**

**Public Relations Society of America—
   Georgia Chapter**

PROFESSIONAL PUBLICATIONS:

Communication World
O'Dwyer's Newsletter
PR News
PR Reporter
Public Relations Journal
Publicist

DIRECTORIES:

Bacon's Publicity Checker (Bacon's
   Publishing Company, Chicago, IL)
*National Directory of Corporate Public
   Affairs* (Columbia Books, Washington,
   DC)
*O'Dwyer's Directory of Corporate Commu-
   nications* and *O'Dwyer's Directory of
   Public Relations Firms* (J.R. O'Dwyer
   Co., New York, NY)
Public Relations Journal, Register issue
   (Public Relations Society of America,
   New York, NY)
Who's Who in P.R. (P.R. Publishing Co.,
   Exeter, NH)

Employers:

A. Brown Olmstead Associates
127 Peachtree St., N.E.
Atlanta, GA 30303
(404) 659-0919
Contact: Kristy Angevine

Alexander Communications
400 Colony Square, Suite 980
Atlanta, GA 30361
(404) 897-2300
Contact: Cynthia Costa

Anderson Communications
2245 Godby Rd.
College Park, GA 30349
(404) 766-8000
Contact: John Turner

Baron, McDonald & Wells
6292 Lawrenceville Hwy., Suite C
Tucker, GA 30084
(770) 492-0373

Bockel & Company
3379 Peachtree Rd., N.E.
Atlanta, GA 30326
(404) 814-0500
Contact: David Bockel, President

Cohn & Wolfe
225 Peachtree St., Suite 2300
Atlanta, GA 30303
(404) 688-5900
Contact: Bob Cohn

Communications Masters
3627 W. Lawrenceville St.
Duluth, GA 30136
(770) 495-8330

Communications 21
560 Pharr Rd., Suite 21
Atlanta, GA 30305
(404) 814-1330

Cookerly & Co.
5 Piedmont Center, Suite 400
Atlanta, GA 30305
(404) 816-2037

Copithorne & Bellows
1050 Crowne Pointe Parkway, Suite 340
Atlanta, GA 30338
(770) 392-8611
Contact: Michelle Marriott

Cornerstone Communications Group
1360 Peachtree St., N.E., Suite 950
Atlanta, GA 30309
(404) 249-8833

Crumbley & Associates
600 W. Peachtree St., N.W., Suite 2300
Atlanta, GA 30308
(404) 892-2300
Contact: Cheryl Lee
Advertising and public relations

Custer Gamwell Communications
47 Perimeter Center E., Suite 460
Atlanta, GA 30346
(770) 396-3996

Davis, Julie, Associates
1 Buckhead Plaza, Suite 520
Atlanta, GA 30305
(404) 231-0660
Contact: Julie Davis, President

DeMoss Group, The
3473 Satellite Blvd., Suite 211
Duluth, GA 30136
(770) 813-0000

Dowling, Langley & Associates
1360 Peachtree St., N.E., Suite 360
Atlanta, GA 30309
(404) 892-0100

Ducharme Communications
400 N. Ridge Rd., Suite 510
Atlanta, GA 30350
(770) 594-0110
Contact: Mark Ducharme

Duffey Communications
11 Piedmont Center, Suite 600
Atlanta, GA 30305
(404) 266-2600
Contact: Jenny Duffey

Edelman Public Relations Worldwide
3525 Piedmont Rd., Bldg. 8, Suite 610
Atlanta, GA 30305
(404) 237-1952

ELG Creative Services
1100 Circle 75 Parkway, Suite 800
Atlanta, GA 30339
(770) 984-2293

First Class
1272 Oakcrest Dr., S.W.
Atlanta, GA 30311
(404) 696-9999

Fleishman-Hillard International Communications
233 Peachtree St., N.E., Suite 1250
Atlanta, GA 30303
(404) 659-4446
Contact: Cathy Scott

Freebairn & Co.
3343 Peachtree Rd., Suite 1220
Atlanta, GA 30326
(404) 237-9945

GCI Atlanta
1355 Peachtree St., N.E., Suite 590
Atlanta, GA 30030
(404) 873-5330

Golin/Harris Communications
50 Hurt Plaza, S.E., Suite 1220
Atlanta, GA 30303
(404) 681-3808
Contact: Margaret Murphy, General Manager

Hayslett Sorrel & Lane
5784 Lake Forrest Dr., Suite 265
Atlanta, GA 30328
(404) 303-1755

Headline Group, The
3490 Piedmont Rd., Suite 1504
Atlanta, GA 30305
(404) 262-3000
Contact: Lee Yarbrough

Hill and Knowlton
1100 Peachtree St., Suite 2150
Atlanta, GA 30328
(404) 249-8550

Hollingsworth, Colborne & Associates
57 Forsyth St., Suite 1050
Atlanta, GA 30303
(404) 577-3856

**Horton Lind Communications and
Public Relations**
3281 W. Shadowlawn Ave., N.E.
Atlanta, GA 30305
(404) 364-9401

Images USA
1718 Peachtree Rd., Suite 650S
Atlanta, GA 30309
(404) 892-2931

Jackson Spalding Ledlie
1201 Peachtree St. N.E., Suite 1905
Atlanta, GA 30361
(404) 874-8389

Keene, Pamala A., Public Relations
2401 Lake Park Dr., Suite 262
Smyrna, GA 30080
(770) 333-0123

Ketchum Public Relations Worldwide
999 Peachtree St., Suite 1850
Atlanta, GA 30309
(404) 877-1800
Contact: Jane Shivers

Knapp Inc.
50 Hurt Plaza, Suite 1030
Atlanta, GA 30303
(404) 688-1777
Contact: John Knapp, President

Landmark Communications
3814 Satellite Blvd., Suite 200
Duluth, GA 30136
(770) 813-1000

Leathurbury Group, The
452-B E. Paces Ferry Rd.
Atlanta, GA 30305
(404) 364-0035

Manning Selvage & Lee
1201 W. Peachtree St., Suite 4800
Atlanta, GA 30309
(404) 875-1444
Contact: Jan Lewin, Managing Director

Mathon & Associates
1885 Moores Mill Rd.
Atlanta, GA 30318
(404) 352-8015

Matlock & Associates
1360 Peachtree St., N.E., Suite 220
Atlanta, GA 30305
(404) 872-3200
Contact: Nichole Taylor, Client Services
Mgr.

Mazie Hale Public Relations
2964 Peachtree Rd., N.W., Suite 530
Atlanta, GA 30305
(404) 261-7080
Contact: Mazie Hale

Mills, William, Agency
3091 E. Shadowlawn Ave.
Atlanta, GA 30305
(404) 261-4900
Contact: Scott Mills

Ogilvy & Mather Public Relations
75 14th St., N.W., Suite 3000
Atlanta, GA 30309
(404) 888-5100
Contact: Susan Mitchell

Parver, Michael, Associates
1800 Peachtree St., N.E., Suite 333
Atlanta, GA 30309
(404) 355-5580
Contact: Julie Southwell

Primedia
600 W. Peachtree St., Suite 1600
Atlanta, GA 30308
(404) 892-2287

Pringle Dixon Pringle
303 Peachtree St., N.E., Suite 3150
Atlanta, GA 30308
(404) 688-6720
Contact: Kim McNeill

Randolph Partnership, The
1201 Peachtree St., N.E.
Atlanta, GA 30361
(404) 892-4505

Roundtree Group
8325 Dunwoody Place, Bldg. 2
Atlanta, GA 30350
(770) 645-4545
Contact: Pam Cash

Roy Communications
1987 Wellbourne Dr.
Atlanta, GA 30324
(404) 874-7119

RP Communications
220 Drummen Court, N.E.
Atlanta, GA 30328
(770) 392-0007

Sawyer Riley Compton
1100 Abernathy Rd., N.E., Suite 800
Atlanta, GA 30328
(770) 393-9849
Contact: Connie Reeves

Tortorici & Co
4406 Peachtree Rd., N.E.
Atlanta, GA 30319
(404) 365-9393

Treco-Jones Public Relations
1800 Century Blvd., Suite 1225
Atlanta, GA 30345
(404) 320-7269

Wilson, Mike, Public Relations
3400 Peachtree Rd., Suite 1239
Atlanta, GA 30326
(404) 365-9000

Real Estate

WEB SITE:

http://addcom.com/darlings/links.htm
links to real estate sites including
RealtyLinks and the Internet Real Estate
Directory.

PROFESSIONAL ORGANIZATIONS:

To learn more about the real estate
industry, you can contact the following
local professional organizations listed in
Chapter 5:
**Association of Builders and Contractors
of Georgia
Atlanta Board of Realtors
Atlanta Builders Exchange
Construction Suppliers Association
Georgia Association of Realtors
Gwinnett County Board of Realtors
Homebuilders Association of Georgia
Homebuilders Association of Metro
Atlanta**

For more information, you can contact:

**American Society of Real Estate
Counselors**
430 N. Michigan Ave.
Chicago, IL 60611
(312) 329-6000

International Real Estate Institute
8383 E. Evans Rd.
Scottsdale, AZ 85260
(602) 998-8267

National Association of Realtors
430 N. Michigan Ave.
Chicago, IL 60611
(312) 329-8200

PROFESSIONAL PUBLICATIONS:

Journal of Property Management
National Real Estate Investor
Real Estate Issues
Real Estate News
Real Estate Review
Realty and Building

DIRECTORIES:

American Real Estate Guide (LL&IL
Publishing, Marhasset, NY)
*American Society of Real Estate Counselors
Directory* (ASREC, Chicago, IL)
Directory of Certified Residential Brokers
(Retail National Marketing Institute,
Chicago, IL)
National Real Estate Investor Directory
(Real Estate Publications, Tampa, FL)
National Roster of Realtors (Stamats
Communications, Cedar Rapids, IA)

Employers:

Ackerman & Co.
1040 Crown Pointe Parkway, Suite 200
Atlanta, GA 30338
(770) 392-0440
Contact: Steve Silverstein
Commercial and residential real estate
development and sales

AFCO Realty Associates
4200 Northside Parkway, Bldg. 12
Atlanta, GA 30327
(404) 233-1700
Contact: Chandler Braden, Vice-President
Office and industrial sales and leasing

Apartment Group, The
3340 Peachtree Rd., N.E., Suite 2180
Atlanta, GA 30326
(404) 812-8100

Apartment Realty Advisors
4000 Cumberland Parkway, Suite 1950
Atlanta, GA 30339
(770) 438-6710
Contact: J.T. Clark
Asset management for multifamily units

Bowers, Richard, & Co.
3475 Lenox Rd., Suite 800
Atlanta, GA 30326
(404) 816-1600
Property management, relocation
services, and development

Brannen/Goodard Co.
3390 Peachtree Rd., N.E., Suite 1200
Atlanta, GA 30326
(404) 812-4000
Contact: Gail Anderson
Commercial brokerage and advisory
services

Brown Realty Advisors
419 E. Crossville Rd., Suite 103
Roswell, GA 30075
(770) 594-1915
Contact: Liz Ganor
Commercial real estate broker

Bryant & Associates
3350 Peachtree Rd., Suite 1250
Atlanta, GA 30326
(404) 262-2828
Contact: Kathy Godwin
Commercial brokerage and asset
management

Buckhead Brokers Realty
5395 Roswell Rd., N.E.
Atlanta, GA 30342
(404) 252-7030
Contact: Bob Sheehan
Full-service brokerage and management

Bullock, Terrell & Mannelly
400 Perimeter Center Terrace, Suite 145
Atlanta, GA 30346
(770) 391-1900
Contact: Joe Terrell, Partner
Full-service real estate brokerage

Carter, Ben, Associates
950 E. Paces Ferry Rd., Suite 975
Atlanta, GA 30326
(404) 364-3222
Asset management, development, and
acquisitions

Carter & Associates
1275 Peachtree St., N.E.
Atlanta, GA 30367
(404) 888-3000
Contact: Pam Trocino, Personnel Director
Property management and corporate
development, research, and services

CB Commercial Real Estate
100 Galleria Parkway, Suite 500
Atlanta, GA 30339
(770) 951-7800
Contact: Karen Munnay
Diverse services, including appraisal,
advisory services, and financial services

Coldwell Banker—Atlanta
400 Northridge Rd., Suite 100
Atlanta, GA 30350
(770) 642-3600

Coldwell Banker North Metro Realty
4690 S. Lee St.
Buford, GA 30518
(770) 945-6736
Contact: Jonell Chester, Broker
Several offices in the Atlanta area;
commercial and residential real estate
brokerage

Colliers Cauble & Co.
1355 Peachtree St., Suite 500
Atlanta, GA 30309
(404) 888-9000
Management and development

Compass Management and Leasing
100 Peachtree St., Suite 2200
Atlanta, GA 30303
(404) 659-2777
Commercial property management and
development

Cousins Properties
2500 Windy Ridge Parkway, Suite 1600
Atlanta, GA 30339
(770) 955-2200
Commercial property management and
development

Cushman & Wakefield of Georgia
1201 W. Peachtree St., N.W., Suite 3300
Atlanta, GA 30309
(404) 875-1000
Contact: Lisa Bobbitt, Office
Administrator
Atlanta's largest commercial real estate
brokerage

Faison
5 Concourse Parkway, Suite 2000
Atlanta, GA 30328
(770) 698-2200
Contact: Sandra Brooks, Human
Resources Director
Full-service real estate, commercial
property management

Gables Residential Trust
2859 Paces Ferry Rd.
Atlanta, GA 30339
(770) 436-4600
Apartment property management

Galbreath Co., The
4200 Northside Parkway, Bldg. 12
Atlanta, GA 30327
(404) 233-1700

Grubb & Ellis
400 Northridge Rd., Suite 1200
Atlanta, GA 30350
(404) 522-5477
Contact: Robert J. Boyd, Senior Vice-
President
Full-service real estate company

Hodges, M.D., Enterprises
300 Great Southwest Parkway
Atlanta, GA 30336
(404) 691-4007

Hodges Ward Elliott Inc.
3399 Peachtree Rd., N.E., Suite 1200
Atlanta, GA 30326
(404) 233-6000
Hotel investment and brokerage

Industrial Developments International
3343 Peachtree Rd., N.E., Suite 1050
Atlanta, GA 30326
(404) 233-6080

Insignia Commercal Group
5665 New Northside Dr., Suite 350
Atlanta, GA 30328
(770) 916-9090
Commercial and apartment property
management

JDN Realty Corp.
3340 Peachtree Rd., N.E., Suite 1530
Atlanta, GA 30326
(404) 262-3252
Developer

Koll Management Services
3399 Peachtree Rd., Suite 1900
Atlanta, GA 30326
(404) 842-1200
Contact: Ed Milton, Senior Vice-President
Real estate sales, leasing, consulting

Lane Co.
1050 Crown Point Parkway, Suite 500
Atlanta, GA 30338
(770) 668-0070
Apartment property management

LaVista Associates
3201 Peachtree Corners Circle
Norcross, GA 30092
(770) 448-6400
Contact: Don Perry, Jr., President
Commercial real estate brokerage

LeCraw, Julian, & Co.
1575 Northside Dr., Bldg. 100, Suite 200
Atlanta, GA 30318
(404) 352-2800
Asset and property management

Ledic Management Group
2727 Paces Ferry Rd., N.W., Suite 225
Atlanta, GA 30339
(770) 435-9200
Apartment property management

McDonald Development Co.
3715 Northside Parkway, Suite 650
Atlanta, GA 30327
(404) 239-0885

Metro Brokers
750 Hammond Dr., Bldg. 1
Atlanta, GA 30328
(404) 843-2500
Contact: John Hartram, Owner
Residential and commercial real estate
brokers

MK Management Co.
1011 Collier Rd., N.W.
Atlanta, GA 30318
(404) 355-6000
Commercial property management

Morris & Raper Realtors
990 Hammond Dr., Suite 710
Atlanta, GA 30328
(770) 671-0088

Myrick Co., The
6025 The Corners Parkway, Suite 100
Norcross, GA 30092
(770) 449-5622
Contact: Jack Myrick, Jr.
Property and asset management

Norman, Harry, Realtors
5229 Roswell Rd., N.E.
Atlanta, GA 30342
(404) 252-4034
Contact: George Conley

Northside Realty
6065 Roswell Rd., Suite 600
Atlanta, GA 30328
(404) 252-3393
Contact: Debbie McKay

Pinnacle Management Co.
5600 Roswell Rd., Suite 201 N.
Atlanta, GA 30342
(404) 252-8900
Apartment property management

Portman Co., The
303 Peachtree St., N.E., Suite 4600
Atlanta, GA 30308
(404) 614-5252
Developer

Portman-Barry Commercial Real Estate Brokerage Co.
1000 Abernathy Rd., Suite 220
Atlanta, GA 30328
(770) 668-2200

Post Properties
3350 Cumberland Circle
Atlanta, GA 30339
(770) 350-4400
Apartment property management

Prudential Atlanta Realty
1000 Abernathy Rd., Suite 600
Atlanta, GA 30328
(770) 399-3000

Prudential Atlanta Realty—Roswell
863 Holcomb Bridge Rd.
Roswell, GA 30376
(770) 992-4100
Contact: Edward Erbesfield

Pruitt, Jenny, & Associates
990 Hammond Dr., Suite 1035
Atlanta, GA 30328
(770) 394-5400
5 offices in Atlanta

Ram Partners
3350 Cumberland Circle, Suite 2050
Atlanta, GA 30339
(770) 850-0830
Apartment property management

RE/MAX of Georgia
1100 Abernathy Rd., Bldg. 500, Suite 705
Atlanta, GA 30328
(770) 393-1137
Contact: Joyce Cheshire, Office Manager
Residential real estate brokers with sales
offices throughout the metro area

Ridgewood Properties
2859 Paces Ferry Rd., Suite 700
Atlanta, GA 30339
(770) 434-3670

Royal LePage Commercial Real Estate Services of Atlanta
3060 Peachtree Rd., Suite 1500
Atlanta, GA 30305
(404) 262-1300
Contact: Gail Burton, Administrative
Manager

Security Capital Atlantic
6 Piedmont Center, Suite 600
Atlanta, GA 30305
(404) 237-9292

Seefried Properties
4200 Northside Parkway, Suite 225
Atlanta, GA 30327
(404) 233-0204
Developer

Selig Enterprises
1100 Spring St., Suite 550
Atlanta, GA 30309
(404) 876-5511
Commercial property management

Sentinel Real Estate
6540 Powers Ferry Rd., Suite 325
Atlanta, GA 30339
(770) 988-9770
Apartment property management

Sharp Boylston Companies
3490 Piedmont Rd., Suite 650
Atlanta, GA 30305
(404) 261-1881
Contact: Davis Branch, Chairman & CEO
Commercial real estate brokerage

Shopping Center Group, The
6520 Powers Ferry Rd., Suite 250
Atlanta, GA 30339
(770) 955-2434
Shopping center leasing, tenant representation

Simpson/Antonio Group, The
100 Galleria Parkway, Suite 1070
Atlanta, GA 30339
(770) 951-1919
Contact: Jim Simpson, Chairman
Commercial real estate brokers

Staubach Company Southwest, The
1230 Peachtree St., N.E., Suite 2900
Atlanta, GA 30309
(404) 347-8050
Strategic planning, site selection,
development management and design

Technology Park—Atlanta
11555 Medlock Bridge Rd., Suite 150
Duluth, GA 30155
(770) 497-1400
Developer

Thomas Enterprises
300 Village Green Circle, Suite 200
Smyrna, GA 30080
(770) 801-8222
Developer

Trammell Crow Co.
3101 Tower Creek Parkway
Atlanta, GA 30339
(770) 644-2200
Property and facility management and
development

United Retail
8215 Roswell Rd., B1500
Atlanta, GA 30350
(770) 512-8200
Contact: Robert D. Zurcher, Personnel
Manager

Weeks Corp.
4497 Park Dr.
Norcross, GA 30093
(770) 923-4076
Commercial property management and
developer

Weiland, John Homes
1950 Sullivan Rd.
Atlanta, GA 30328
(770) 996-1400
Contact: Terry Russell
Residential real estate development and
building; 3 Atlanta offices

Westminster Group, The
3715 Northside Parkway
400 Northcreek, Suite 550
Atlanta, GA 30327
(404) 261-6500
Contact: Jim Sibley, President
Consulting and research

Wilson and Nolan
11 Piedmont Center, Suite 905
Atlanta, GA 30305
(404) 231-2272
Contact: Mary Yarber, Office Manager

Location, location, location

Bob Kramer is a partner in a firm that leases downtown office space. We talked with him recently about getting started in commercial real estate. "Leasing commercial real estate is a very tough business," says Kramer. "You don't make any money during your first year or two in the business. There's a very high attrition rate.

"But if you stick with it, you can make more money than your peers in other fields ever dreamed of. Six-figure incomes are not uncommon among people who have been in the business only five years.

"At our firm, we don't hire people right out of school; we look for people with some experience in the business world and in real estate. But many of the larger firms will hire recent grads and train them. In fact, some large firms have formal training programs.

"If you're a young person just starting out, I'd suggest getting a job with a bigger firm. Then be like a blotter—soak up everything they can teach you. After a few years, reevaluate your position with the company. The problem with the bigger firms is that they sometimes tend to ignore you once they've trained you. In a smaller firm, the senior people see more of a relationship between your success and the overall success of the company. Also, there's a lot of competition within a large firm. It's easy to get lost in the shuffle."

We asked Kramer what qualifications are needed to succeed in commercial real estate. "You have to be tough because you'll face a certain amount of rejection. You have to be hungry because this is an extremely competitive business. A college degree is helpful, but it isn't required. This business is basically sales—getting out and seeing people, convincing them that your skills and knowledge are up to snuff. When you're just starting out, it's also very important to have a mentor in the company—someone to help you and look out for you."

Retailers/Wholesalers

WEB SITES:

http://www.pncl.co.uk/subs/james/vl/
vretail.html
is the WWW virtual library homepage for
retailing.

http://www.retail-experts.com/
provides education and resources to
retailers.

http://www.inetbiz.com/market/
is a worldwide marketplace of wholesalers.

PROFESSIONAL ORGANIZATIONS:

For networking in retailing and wholesaling, check out the following local professional organizations listed in Chapter 5:
**American Society of Interior Designers—
Georgia Chapter
Georgia Retail Association**

For more information, you can contact:

**National Association of Convenience
Stores**
1605 King St.
Alexandria, VA 22314
(703) 684-3600

**National Association of Wholesale
Distributors**
1725 K St., N.W., 3rd Floor
Washington, DC 20006
(202) 872-0885

National Retail Federation
325 7th St., N.W., Suite 1000
Washington, DC 20004
(202) 783-7971

National Retail Merchants Federation
325 7th St., N.W., Suite 1000
Washington, DC 20004
(202) 783-7971

PROFESSIONAL PUBLICATIONS:

Chain Store Age
Inside Retailing
Journal of Retailing
Merchandising
New York Apparel News
Store Planning
Stores
Women's Wear Daily

DIRECTORIES:

American Manufacturers Directory
(American Business Information,
Omaha, NE)
*American Wholesalers and Distributors
Directory* (Gale Research, Inc., Detroit,
MI)
Convenience Stores Membership Directory
(National Association of Convenience
Stores, Alexandria, VA)
Fairchild's Financial Manual of Retail Stores
(Fairchild Books, New York, NY)
*Sheldon's Retail Directory of the U.S. and
Canada* (PS & H, Inc., New York, NY)

Employers:

Allen, Ivan, Co.
221 Peachtree Center Ave., N.E.
Atlanta, GA 30303
(404) 332-3000
Contact: Nancy Pavery, Director of Human
Resources
Office furnishing and supplies

A & P Food Stores
1200 White St., S.W.
Atlanta, GA 30310
(404) 758-4544
Contact: James Crews, Director of
Personnel
Supermarkets

Atlanta Market Center
240 Peachtree St., N.W.
Atlanta, GA 30303
(404) 220-2000

Big B Drugs
2563 N. Decatur Rd.
Decatur, GA 30033
(404) 377-1757
Drugstores

Borders Book Shop
3655 Roswell Rd., N.E.
Atlanta, GA 30342
(404) 237-0707
Contact: Nancy Teele, Manager

Bruno's
5511 Chamblee-Dunwoody Rd.
Dunwoody, GA 30338
(770) 394-3630
Contact: Manager
Grocery stores; some superstores

Coles, The Book People
Town Center At Cobb
400 Earnest Barrett Parkway
Kennesaw, GA 30144
(770) 423-1579
Contact: Maria Garcia, Manager

Cumberland Mall
1000 Cumberland Mall, N.W.
Atlanta, GA 30339
(770) 435-2206

Dalton, B., Bookseller
154-A Lenox Square
3393 Peachtree Rd., N.E.
Atlanta, GA 30326
(404) 231-8516
Must contact individual stores and obtain
application

Eckerd Drugs
36 Herring Rd.
Newnan, GA 30265
(404) 688-8770
Drugstores

Gwinnett Place Mall
2100 Pleasant Hill Rd.
Duluth, GA 30136
(770) 476-5160

Harris Teeter
3954 Peachtree Rd., N.E.
Atlanta, GA 30319

(404) 814-5990
Contact: Manager of individual stores
Gourmet grocery stores

Home Depot, The
send resume to:
The Home Depot
2455 Paces Ferry Rd.
Atlanta, GA 30339-4024
(770) 433-8211
Contact: Human Resources
Building materials

K-Mart Corp.
5265 Old Dixie Rd.
Forest Park, GA 30050
(404) 363-6830
Discount department stores

Kroger Co.
2175 Parklake Dr., N.E.
Atlanta, GA 30345
(770) 496-7467
Contact: Glenn Jenkins, Human Resources Director
Supermarkets

Lenox Square
3393 Peachtree Rd.
Atlanta, GA 30326
(4040 233-6767

Macy, R.H., & Co.
180 Peachtree St., N.W.
Atlanta, GA 30303
(800) 603-6229
Department stores

National Vision Associates
296 Grayson Hwy.
Lawrenceville, GA 30245
(770) 822-3600
Vision centers

Neiman-Marcus Co.
3393 Peachtree Rd., N.E.
Atlanta, GA 30326
(404) 266-8200
Contact: Scott Murphy, Human Resources
Director
Department stores

North Point Mall
1000 North Point Circle
Alpharetta, GA 30202
(770) 740-9273

Northlake Mall
1000 Northlake Parkway
Atlanta, GA 30345
(770) 938-3564

Oxford Books
360 Pharr Rd., N.E.
Atlanta, GA 30305
(404) 262-3333
Contact: Ruper LeCraw, Owner

Paradise Shops, The
5950 Fulton Industrial Blvd., S.W.
Atlanta, GA 30336
(404) 344-7905
Newsstands

Penney, J.C., Co. (District Office)
4500-A Ashford-Dunwoody Rd.
Atlanta, GA 30346
(404) 897-5600
Contact: Eugene Gilmore, Human
Resources Director
Department stores

Perimeter Mall
4400 Ashford-Dunwoody Rd., N.E.
Atlanta, GA 30346
(770) 394-4270

Phipps Plaza
3500 Peachtree Rd.
Atlanta, GA 30326
(404) 262-0992

Publix (Atlanta Division Office)
2849 Paces Ferry Rd., N.W.
Atlanta, GA 30339
(770) 435-0990 X4
Contact: Russ Paul, Human Resources

Rich's Inc.
223 Perimeter Center Parkway
Atlanta, GA 30346
(770) 913-5176
Contact: Stephanie Neff, Executive
Recruiting
Department stores

Sears, Roebuck & Co.
3585 Northside Parkway, N.W.
Atlanta, GA 30327
(404) 264-1341
Department stores

Southlake Mall
1000 Southlake Mall
Morrow, GA 30260
(770) 961-1050

Town Center at Cobb
400 Ernest Barrett Parkway
Kennesaw, GA 30144
(770) 424-9486

Toys 'R Us
Management Positions write:
3710 Atlanta Industrial Parkway
Atlanta, GA 30331-1026

Waldenbooks
L-91 Lenox Square
3393 Peachtree Rd., N.E.
Atlanta, GA 30326
(404) 261-2781
Bookstores

Winn-Dixie Stores
P.O. Box 4809
Atlanta, GA 30302
(404) 346-2400
Contact: J.R. Stuckey, Human Resources
Supermarkets

Wolf Camera
1706 Chantilly Dr., N.E.
Atlanta, GA 30324
(404) 633-9000
Contact: Missy Strickland, Personnel
Camera and video stores

Sports and Recreation

WEB SITES:

http://www.sportsite.com/mac/allshop/
sgma/html/sgma_hp.html
is the SportsLink page, listing companies,
publications, industry news, and jobs.

http://www.onlinesports.com/pages/
CareerCenter.html
is the on-line Sports Career Center, with
career opportunities and a resume bank.

http://www.fitnessworld.com/
is the homepage of *Fitness World.*

PROFESSIONAL ORGANIZATIONS:

For networking in the sports and
recreation fields, check out the following
local professional organizations listed in
Chapter 5:
Atlanta Songwriters Association

For more information, you can contact:

**Aerobic and Fitness Association of
America**
1520 Ventura Blvd.
Sherman Oaks, CA 91403
(818) 905-0040

**American Association for Leisure and
Recreation**
1900 Association Dr.
Reston, VA 22091
(703) 476-3472

American Fitness Association
6285 E. Spring St., No. 404
Long Beach, CA 90808
(310) 402-3952

Association for Fitness in Business
60 Revere Dr., Suite 500
Northbrook, IL 60062
(847) 636-6621

Association of Physical Fitness Centers
600 Jefferson St., Suite 202
Rockville, MD 20852
(301) 424-7744

**IDEA: The International Association of
Fitness Professionals**
6190 Cornerstone Court E., Suite 204
San Diego, CA 92121
(800) 999-4332

National Recreation & Parks Association
2775 S. Quincy St., Suite 300
Arlington, VA 22206
(703) 820-4940

National Sporting Goods Association
1699 Wall St.
Mount Prospect, IL 60056
(847) 439-4000

Society of Recreation Executives
P.O. Drawer 17148
Pensacola, FL 35222
(904) 477-2123

PROFESSIONAL PUBLICATIONS:

American Fitness
Athletic Business
Athletic Management
Fitness Management
Parks and Recreation
Sports Industry News

DIRECTORIES:

American Fitness Association Directory
(American Fitness Association, Long
Beach, CA)
Athletic Business, Professional Directory
Section (Athletic Business Publications,
Madison, WI)
Fitness Management Source Book (Leisure
Publications, Los Angeles, CA)
Health Clubs Directory (American
Business Directories, Omaha, NE)
Information Sources in Sports and Leisure
(K.G. Saur, New Providence, NJ)
*New American Guide to Athletics, Sports,
and Recreation* (New American Library,
New York, NY)

Recreation Centers Directory (American Business Directories, Omaha, NE)
Sports Administration Guide and Directory (National Sports Marketing Bureau, New York, NY)
Sports Market Place (Sports Guide, Phoenix, AZ)
Who's Who in Recreation (Society of Recreation Executives, Pensacola, FL)
Who's Who in Sports and Fitness (American Fitness Association, Long Beach, CA)

Employers, Sports:

Athletic Club NE
1515 Sheridan Rd., N.E.
Atlanta, GA 30324
(404) 325-2700
Contact: Craig Black, Athletic Director

Atlanta Braves Baseball Club
521 Capitol Ave., S.E.
Atlanta, GA 30312
(404) 522-7630
National League baseball franchise

Atlanta Falcons Football Club
1 Falcon Place
Suwanee, GA 30174
Call employment line: (770) 945-1111
National Football League franchise

Atlanta Hawks Basketball Club
1 CNN Center, South Tower, Suite 405
Atlanta, GA 30303
(404) 827-3800
Contact: Lisa Stricklin
National Basketball Association franchise

Atlanta Ruckus
(soccer)
539 W. Paces Ferry Rd., N.W.
Atlanta, GA 30305
(770) 645-6655

Australian Body Works
3495 Piedmont Rd., Bldg. 12
Atlanta, GA 30305
(404) 848-0222
Fitness center

Bally Total Fitness
6780 Roswell Rd., N.W.
Atlanta, GA 30328
(770) 392-1861
Contact: Gina Bonds

Buckhead Towne Club
2900 S. Pharr Court, N.W.
Atlanta, GA 30305
(404) 262-3455
Fitness center

City Athletic Club
1 CNN Center, Suite 211
Atlanta, GA 30303
(404) 659-4097
Fitness center

City of Atlanta Department of Parks, Recreation and Cultural Affairs
City Hall East
675 Ponce de Leon Ave., N.E., 8th Floor
Atlanta, GA 30308
(404) 817-6793
Personnel Department for City of Atlanta:
68 Mitchell St., S.W., Rm. 2107
Atlanta, GA 30335-0306
(404) 330-6377
Must get application to send with resume

Concourse Athletic Club
8 Concourse Parkway
Atlanta, GA 30328
(770) 698-2000
Fitness center

Corporate Sports Executive Design/ Managed Health Clubs
6400 Highlands Parkway
Smyrna, GA 30082
(770) 432-0100
Fitness center; indoor golf

Court Sport
5338 Goose Creek Cove
Norcross, GA 30092
(770) 263-7680
Contact: Gary Smith, Owner
Court equipment, lighting, resurfacing, stringing supplies

Day, Cecil B., Wellness Center
1445 Mount Vernon Rd.
Atlanta, GA 30338
(770) 393-9355
Fitness center

Douglasville Health & Athletic Club
8741 Hospital Dr.
Douglasville, GA 30134
(770) 949-7507

Eagle Watch Country Club
3055 Eagle Watch Dr.
Woodstock, GA 30188
(770) 591-1000
Contact: Mark Williams, Club Manager
Public golf course

Fitness Factory
500-N Amsterdam Ave.
Atlanta, GA 30303
(404) 815-7900

Fitness International
2410 Wisteria Dr., Suite B
Snellville, GA 30278
(770) 736-8001
Fitness center, spa

Fox Creek Executive & Golf Range
1501 Windy Hill Rd.
Smyrna, GA 30080
(770) 435-1000
Contact: Hank Caulkins, General
Manager

Georgia's Stone Mountain Park Golf Course
Stone Mountain, GA 30086
(770) 498-5717
Contact: Dwayne Laricey, Manager
Public golf course

Gold's Aerobic-Athletic Club
720 N. Glynn St.
Fayetteville, GA 30214
(770) 461-9962
5 locations in metro Atlanta

Golf Training Systems
3400 Corporate Way, Suite G
Duluth, GA 30136
(770) 623-6400

Highland Athletic Club at Georgia Baptist Medical Center
303 Parkway Dr., Box 62
Atlanta, GA 30312
(404) 265-4759
Fitness center

Holiday Fitness and Racquet Club
6780 Roswell Rd., N.W.
Atlanta, GA 30328
(404) 392-1861
Contact: Tim Hilton or Mike Tuzzo,
Operations
Health club

Main Event Fitness
5294 Buford Hwy.
Atlanta, GA 30340
(770) 452-1133

Metro Atlanta YMCA
100 Edgewood Ave., N.E., Suite 902
Atlanta, GA 30303
(404) 588-9622
Fitness center, youth programs

Metropolitan Golf & Tennis Club
3000 Fairington Parkway
Lithonia, GA 30038
(770) 981-7686
Contact: Sue Osborne, Director of Human
Resources
Semi-private club

Peachtree Center Athletic Club
227 Courtland St.
Atlanta, GA 30303
(404) 523-3833
Fitness center, swimming classes, day spa

Piedmont Hospital Health & Fitness Club
2001 Peachtree Rd., N.E., Suite 100
Atlanta, GA 30309
(404) 605-1965

Promina Health Place: Center for Wellness
65 S. Medical Dr.
Marietta, GA 30060
(770) 793-7300
Fitness center, seniors exercise program

Southern Athletic Club
754 Beaver Ruin Rd.
Lilburn, GA 30247
(770) 923-5400

Sporting Club, The
1515 Sheridan Rd., N.E.
Atlanta, GA 30324
(404) 325-2700
Contact: Ron Ruth, Athletic Director
Health club

Sporting Club, The, at Windy Hill
135 Interstate North Parkway, N.W.
Atlanta, GA 30039
(770) 953-1100
Health club

Sportslife
1775 Water Place, N.W.
Atlanta, GA 30339
(770) 952-3200
Contact: Steve Wilson
Fitness center, indoor/outdoor tennis

SportsLife
P.O. Box 6909
Marietta, GA 30065
(770) 984-0031
Contact: Vickie White, Human Resources
Corporate office for metro health clubs

Vinings Club, The
2859 Paces Ferry Rd.
Atlanta, GA 30339
(770) 433-1155
Fitness center

Workout America
691 Highway 138
Riverdale, GA 30274
(770) 991-3314
Fitness center

World Gym Aerobics & Fitness
4771 Britt Rd., Suite F-1
Norcross, GA 30093
(770) 414-1121

YWCA of Greater Atlanta
100 Edgewood Ave., Suite 800
Atlanta, GA 30303
(404) 527-7575
Fitness center, tai chi, karate

Employers, Recreation:

Atlanta Botanical Garden
1345 Piedmont Ave.
Atlanta, GA 30309
(404) 876-5859
http:/www.ajc.com/atl/botanica.htm

Atlanta Cyclorama
800-C Cherokee Ave., S.E.
Atlanta, GA 30315
(404) 658-7625

Chattahoochee Outdoor Center
1990 Island Ford Parkway
Dunwoody, GA 30050
(770) 395-6851

Georgia's Stone Mountain
P.O. Box 778
Stone Mountain, GA 30086
(770) 498-5670
Contact: Jackie Kelley, Director of
Personnel
Historic/amusement park

Lake Lanier Islands Hotel and Golf Club
7000 Holiday Rd.
Lake Lanier Islands, GA 30518
(770) 945-8787
Contact: Joyce Ruiz, Director of Human
Resources
Metro area lake resort

Six Flags Over Georgia
P.O. Box 43187
Atlanta, GA 30378
(770) 739-3410
Contact: Kathryn Dunn, Human
Resources
Amusement park

White Water American Adventures
250 N. Cobb Parkway, N.E.
Marietta, GA 30062
(770) 424-9283
Contact: Jo Chandler, Personnel
Water park

Zoo Atlanta
800 Cherokee Ave., S.E.
Atlanta, GA 30315
(404) 624-5600
Contact: Margeria Waterman, Senior
Vice-President of Human Resources

Stock Brokers/Financial Services

WEB SITES:

http://bank.net/home.rich.html
links to investment industry sites and
directories.

http://www.io.org/~invest/places.htm
links to finance-related groups, newsletters, and corporate information.

**http://www.nextnet.com/iwctr/
iwctr.html**
is the homepage of *Securities Industry
Daily;* links to employment opportunities.

PROFESSIONAL ORGANIZATIONS:

For networking in finance and related
fields, check out the following local
professional organizations listed in
Chapter 5. Also see **"Banking."**

**Georgia Securities Association
International Association for Financial
Planning—Atlanta Chapter**

For more information, you can contact:

**Association for Investment Management
and Research**
5 Boar's Head Lane
Charlottesville, VA 22903
(804) 977-6600

Financial Executives Institute
10 Madison Ave.
Morristown, NJ 07960
(201) 898-4600

**National Association of Personal
Financial Advisors**
1130 Lake Cook Rd., Suite 105
Buffalo Grove, IL 60089
(847) 537-7722

**National Association of Securities
Dealers**
1735 K St., N.W.
Washington, D.C. 20006
(202) 728-8000

National Venture Capital Association
1655 N. Fort Meyer Dr.
Arlington, VA 22209
(703) 351-5269

Securities Industry Association
635 Slaters Lane, Suite 110
Alexandria, VA 22314
(703) 683-2075

PROFESSIONAL PUBLICATIONS:

*Barron's National Business and Financial
  Weekly*
CFO
D & B Reports
Commodity Journal
Corporate Finance Letter
Corporate Financing Week
Credit and Financial Management
Dun's Business Month
Financial Executive
Financial World
Institutional Investor
Investment Dealer's Digest
Journal of Finance
Securities Week
Stock Market Magazine
Traders Magazine
Wall St. Letter

DIRECTORIES:

Corporate Finance Sourcebook (National
  Register Publishing, New Providence,
  N.J.)
CUSIP Master Directory (Standard &
  Poor's New York, NY)
Directory of Registered Investment Advisors
  (Money Market Directories,
  Charlottesville, VA)
Financial Yellow Book (Monitor Publishing
  Co., New York, NY)
*Handbook of Financial Markets and
  Institutions* (John Wiley and Sons, New
  York, NY)

Investment & Securities Directory
(American Business Directories, Omaha,
NE)
Money Market Directory (Money Market
Directories, Charlottesville, VA)
Nelson's Directory of Investment Research
(W.R. Nelson, Port Chester, NY)
Securities Industry Yearbook (Securities
Industry Association, New York, NY)
Security Dealers of North America
(Standard and Poor's, New York, NY)
STA Traders Annual (Securities Traders
Association, New York, NY)
Who's Who in Finance and Industry (Reed
Reference Publishing, New Providence,
NJ)

Employers:

American Wealth Management
3525 Peidmont Rd., Bldg. 7, Suite 520
Atlanta, GA 30305
(404) 262-2719

Argent Securities
3340 Peachtree Rd., Suite 450
Atlanta, GA 30326
(404) 237-1100

Baird, Robert W., & Co.
400 Interstate North Parkway, Suite 1700
Atlanta, GA 30339
(770) 955-6611
Contact: Tamara Haber, Office
Administrator

Bear Stearns & Co.
950 E. Paces Ferry Rd., N.E., Suite 2300
Atlanta, GA 30326
(404) 842-4000
Contact: Damion Carufe, Senior Managing Director

Bradford, J.C., & Co.
5 Concourse Parkway, Suite 2750
Atlanta, GA 30328
(770) 394-4500
Contact: Mike Moore

Brown, Alex & Sons
3565 Piedmont Rd., Bldg. 1, Suite 400
Atlanta, GA 30305
(404) 261-1000
Contact: Julia West, Branch Coordinator

Buckhead Financial Corp.
3475 Lenox Rd., Suite 600
Atlanta, GA 30326
(404) 233-2792
Contact: Cathy Sweeney, Vice-President of
Operations

Carnegie Wealth Management
3500 Piedmont Rd., N.E., Suite 220
Atlanta, GA 30305
(404) 231-9230
Contact: Donna Howell, Senior Vice-
President

Charles, J.W., Financial Services
11 Piedmont Center, Suite 800
Atlanta, GA 30305
(404) 240-1000

Cigna Financial Advisors
1800 Parkway Place, S.E., Suite 900
Marietta, GA 30067-8295
(770) 426-4600
Contact: Frauncee Ladd, Office Administrator

Dean Witter
3414 Peachtree Rd., Suite 628
Atlanta, GA 30326
(404) 266-4822
Contact: Bruce Alanzo, Regional Director

**Donaldson, Lufkin & Jenrette Securities
Corp.**
1201 W. Peachtree St., Suite 3650
Atlanta, GA 30309
(404) 897-3300

Dreyfus Service Corporation
3384 Peachtree Rd., Suite 100
Atlanta, GA 30326
(404) 262-1061
Contact: Rhonda Heard, Office Manager

Edwards, A.G.
3399 Peachtree Rd., N.E., Suite 1150
Atlanta, GA 30326
(404) 237-2210
Contact: Terri Anderson, Personnel
Manager

Equifax Inc.
P.O. Box 4081
Atlanta, GA 30309
(404) 885-8000
Credit reporting services

Fidelity National Capital Investors
3490 Piedmont Center, Suite 1450
Atlanta, GA 30305
(404) 240-1600

Fricks Group, The
2971 Flowers Rd. South, Suite 189
Atlanta, GA 30341
(770) 452-8560
Contact: L.C. Fricks

Interstate/Johnson Lane
945 E. Paces Ferry Rd.
Atlanta, GA 30339
(404) 240-5000

James, Raymond, & Associates
11 Piedmont Center, Suite 510
Atlanta, GA 30305
(404) 365-9712
Contact: Debbie Lokey

Jeffries & Co.
3414 Peachtree Rd., Suite 656
Atlanta, GA 30326
(404) 264-5050
Contact: E.T. Laird

Jones, Edward, & Co.
10892 Crabapple Rd.
Roswell, GA 30075
(770) 998-0902

Knox, W.L., & Co.
3340 Peachtree Rd., N.E.
Atlanta, GA 30326
(404) 231-4711
Contact: Don Bettencourt, Operation and
Compliance Manager

Lehman Brothers Division of Shearson Lehman/Hutton
3414 Peachtree Rd., N.E.
Atlanta, GA 30326
(404) 262-4800
Contact: Ann Pollard

Merrill, Lynch, Pierce, Fenner & Smith
3500 Piedmont Rd., N.E., Suite 600
Atlanta, GA 30305
(404) 231-2400
Contact: Martha Pollack

Morgan Keegan & Co.
3060 Peachtree Rd., N.W., Suite 1600
Atlanta, GA 30305
(404) 240-6700
Contact: Linda Green, Office Manager

Nuveen, John, & Co.
3060 Peachtree Rd., N.W.
Atlanta, GA 30305
(404) 233-6663
Contact: Jason Bach, Regional Manager

Olde Discount Brokers
5571 Chablee-Dunwoody Rd.
Dunwoody, GA 30338
(404) 523-6666
Contact: Geoffrey Centner, Regional
Manager
6 Atlanta locations

Oppenheimer & Co.
3414 Peachtree Rd., N.E., Suite 1200
Atlanta, GA 30326
(404) 262-5355
Contact: Will Lobb, Managing Director

Paine Webber
3399 Peachtree Rd., N.E.
Atlanta, GA 30326
(404) 262-3900

Prudential Securities
14 Piedmont Center, N.E., Suite 200
Atlanta, GA 30305
(404) 842-9000
Contact: Roxanne McDonald, Assistant
Manager

RAF Financial Corp.
3399 Peachtree Rd., Suite 1450
Atlanta, GA 30326
(404) 814-0288

Resource Securities
100 Norcross St.
Roswell, GA 30075
(770) 645-1651
Contact: Michelle Casler, Financial
Securities Administrator

Robinson-Humphrey Company, The
3300 Peachtree Rd.
Atlanta, GA 30326
(404) 266-6000
Contact: John Rhett, Branch Manager

Salomon Brothers
5000 Georgia-Pacific Center
Atlanta, GA 30303
(404) 827-7600
Contact: Herron Weems, Vice-President &
Regional Manager

Schwab, Charles, & Co.
3399 Peachtree Rd., N.E., Suite 150
Atlanta, GA 30326
(404) 231-1114

Seaboard Investment Corporation
3400 Peachtree Rd., N.E.
Atlanta, GA 30326
(404) 239-6270

Smith Barney
400 Perimeter Center Terrace, N.E., Suite
290
Atlanta, GA 30346
(770) 393-2000
Contact: Jackie Hines

Smith Barney Harris Upham & Co.
3399 Peachtree Rd., Suite 1800
Atlanta, GA 30326
(404) 266-0090
Contact: Juan Hamilton, Sales Manager

Southwick Investments
1000 Abernathy Rd., Suite 640
Atlanta, GA 30328
(770) 481-7450

Sterne, Agee & Leech
950 E. Paces Ferry Rd., Suite 1475
Atlanta, GA 30326
(404) 365-9630

Wadell & Reed
3003 Chamblee-Tucker Rd., Suite 142
Atlanta, GA 30341
(770) 452-0199
Contact: David Freeman, Account
Representative

Travel/Shipping/Transportation

WEB SITES:

http://www.earthlink.net/
~hotelanywhere/
links to travel-related industry sites.

http://www.slip.net/~jwithers/
tawww.html
is a site for professional travel agents.

http://www.yahoo.com/
Business_and_Economy/Companies/
Shipping
lists shipping companies on the Net.

http://iti.acns.nwu.edu/tran_res.html
links to transportation sites and
newsgroups.

http://www.itsonline.com/
is the Independent Forum for Intelligent
Transportation Systems.

PROFESSIONAL ORGANIZATIONS:

To learn more about the travel, shipping,
and transportation industries, you can
contact the following local professional
organizations listed in Chapter 5:
Georgia Freight Bureau
Georgia Hospitality & Travel Association
Georgia Motor Trucking Association

For more information, you can contact:

American Public Transit Association
1201 New York Ave., N.W., Suite 400
Washington, DC 20005
(202) 898-4000

American Trucking Association
200 Mill Rd.
Alexandria, VA 22314
(703) 838-1700

**Institute for Transportation and
Development Policy**
611 Broadway, Rm. 616
New York, NY 10012
(212) 260-8144

Institute of Transportation Engineers
525 School St., S.W.
Washington, DC 20024
(202) 554-8050

Travel Industry Association of America
1133 21st St., N.W.
Washington, DC 20036
(202) 293-1433

**United States Tour Operators Associa-
tion (USTA)**
211 E. 51st St., Suite 12B
New York, NY 10022
(212) 750-7371

PROFESSIONAL PUBLICATIONS:

Air Travel Journal
ASTA Travel News
Aviation Week and Space Technology
Business and Commercial Aviation
Daily Traffic World
Mass Transit
Passenger Transport
Tours and Resorts
Traffic Management Daily
Travel Agent
*Travel Trade: The Business Paper of the
  Travel Industry*
Travel Weekly
Trux
Urban Transport News

DIRECTORIES:

Aviation Directory (E.A. Brennan Co.,
  Garden Grove, CA)
Mass Transit: Consultants (PTN Publish-
  ing Corp., Melville, NY)
Moody's Transportation Manual (Moody's
  Travel Service, New York, NY)
*Official Directory of Industrial and
  Commercial Traffic Executives* (K-III
  Information Co., New York, NY)
Travel Weekly's World Travel Directory
  (Reed Travel Group, Secaucus, NJ)
*Worldwide Travel Information Contact
  Book* (Gale Research, Detroit, MI)

Employers, Travel:

AAA Auto Club South
1100 Spring St.
Atlanta, GA 30357
(404) 872-8222
Contact: Zana Clark, Office Manager

Adventure Travel
4920 Roswell Rd., Suite 13B
Atlanta, GA 30342
(404) 257-9600

Age of Travel
3500 Piedmont Rd., Suite 110
Atlanta, GA 30305
(404) 266-2900

American Express TRS Co.
200 Pinnacle Way
Norcross, GA 30071
(770) 417-3375

Amtrak
1688 Peachtree St.
Atlanta, GA 30309
(404) 881-3060
Contact: Personnel Dept.:
30th and Market
Philadelphia, PA 19104
(215) 557-1107

Atlantic Southeast Airlines
100 Hartsfield Center Parkway, Suite 800
Atlanta, GA 30354
(404) 766-1400

Boehm Travel Co.
1400 Indian Trail Rd.
Norcross, GA 30093
(770) 931-5500

BTI Americas
3350 Cumberland Circle, Suite 700
Atlanta, GA 30339
(770) 953-0027

Business Travel
5555 Oakbrook Parkway, Suite 650
Norcross, GA 30093
(770) 490-7462

Business Travel Consultants
1775 The Exchange, N.W., Suite 330
Atlanta, GA 30339
(770) 952-8181
Contact: Marcia Pelt, Manager

Carlson Wagonlit Travel
30 Perimeter Center E., Suite 220
Atlanta, GA 30346
(770) 353-2510

Century Travel
1100 Abernathy Rd., Suite 334
Atlanta, GA 30328
(770) 394-6606

Changing Places
2996 Grandview Ave., N.E.
Atlanta, GA 30305
(404) 261-8411
Contact: Jane Craig, Owner

Conway Travel
3230 Medlock Bridge Rd.
Norcross, GA 30092
(770) 263-2000
Contact: Jennifer Conway, Manager

Cook, Thomas, Travel
115 Perimeter Place, Suite 1060
Atlanta, GA 30346
(770) 604-3100
Contact: Kathy Kirby, Office Supervisor

Cruise Authority, The
1307 Powers Ferry Rd., S.E.
Marietta, GA 30067
(770) 952-8300
Contact: Howard Moses, Owner

Delta Air Lines
General Office Bldg. A-2
Hartsfield International Airport
Atlanta, GA 30320
(404) 715-2501
Contact: Employment office. Must pick
up application to send with resume

Discount Travel
2221 Peachtree St.
Atlanta, GA 30309
(404) 355-3229
Contact: Ruth Miller, Human Resources

First Travelcorp
1150 Lake Hearn Dr.
Atlanta, GA 30342
(404) 303-2966

Four Seasons Travel Service
1827 Powers Ferry Rd.
Bldg. 22, Suite 200
Atlanta, GA 30339
(770) 955-2572
Contact: Louise Lascik, President

Georgia International Travel
5447 Roswell Rd.
Atlanta, GA 30342
(404) 851-9166

Horizon Travel
2296 Henderson Mill Rd., Suite 109
Atlanta, GA 30345
(770) 491-8747
Contact: Mike Lipman, Owner

Japan Air Lines
245 Peachtree Center Ave., N.E., Suite 800
Atlanta, GA 30303
(404) 521-1616
Contact: Mr. Kyota, Administration
Manager

Japan Travel Service
5150 Buford Hwy.
Doraville, GA 30341
(770) 451-3607

Maritz Travel Co.
200 Ashford Center N., Suite 250
Atlanta, GA 30338
(770) 901-5070

Meridian Travel
5605 Glenridge Dr., Suite 310
Atlanta, GA 30342
(404) 250-9990
Contact: Linda Lynn, Manager

Midtown Travel Consultants
1830 Piedmont Rd., N.E., Suite F
Atlanta, GA 30324
(404) 872-8308

Park-N-Ticket Travel
3945 Conley St.
College Park, GA 30337
(404) 669-3800

Peachtree Travel Management
2 Concourse Parkway, Suite 250
Atlanta, GA 30328
(770) 901-8750

Rosenbluth International
1475 Peachtree St., Suite 1110
Atlanta, GA 30309
(404) 873-7800

Sabena Belgian World Airlines
3391 Peachtree Rd., N.E., Suite 220
Atlanta, GA 30326
(404) 814-6320
Contact: John Matthews, Regional
Manager

Sprayberry Travel
2440 Sandy Plains Rd., Bldg. 15
Marietta, GA 30066
(770) 977-0783

Teplis Travel Service
5885 Glenridge Dr., Suite 250
Atlanta, GA 30328
(404) 843-7460

Travel Desk, The
1117 Perimeter Center W., Suite 500E
Atlanta, GA 30338
(770)   392-3333

Travel Incorporated
3680 N. Peachtree Rd.
Atlanta, GA 30341
(770) 455-6575
Contact: Helen Morgan, Human
Resources

Travel Source, The
2550 Heritage Court, Suite 202
Atlanta, GA 30339
(770) 980-9500

Uniglobe Advisors in Travel
945 E. Paces Ferry Rd.
Atlanta, GA 30326
(404) 266-8228
Contact: Loyal Charles, Manager

Uniglobe Travel Southeast
400 Interstate North Parkway, Suite 530
Atlanta, GA 30339
(770) 955-2224

ValueJet
1800 Phoenix Blvd., Suite 126
Atlanta, GA 30349
(770) 907-2580
Airline service

Varig Brazilian Airlines
3384 Peachtree Rd., N.E., Suite 714
Atlanta, GA 30326
(404) 261-4846
Contact: Robert Lorenzo, Regional
Manager

Williamsburg Travel Management
210 Interstate North Parkway, Suite 110
Atlanta, GA 30339
(770) 952-0430

WorldTravel Partners
1055 Lenox Park Blvd., Suite 420
Atlanta, GA 30319
(404) 841-6600
Contact: Tim Severt or Wendy Friedland,
Human Resources

X-Ceed Motivation Atlanta
4200 Paces Ferry Rd., Suite 367
Atlanta, GA 30339
(770) 434-2400

Employers, Shipping/Transportation:

American Transport
5300 Oakbrook Parkway, Bldg. 300, Suite
370
Norcross, GA 30093
(404) 921-1113
Contact: Human Resources:
9487 Regency Square Blvd. W.
Jacksonville, FL 32203

Bennett, George, Motor Express
P.O. Box 569
McDonough, GA 30253
(770) 957-1866
Contact: Tom Draper, Leasing Manager
Nationwide motor freight

Commercial Transportation Services
1900 Century Place, Suite 340
Atlanta, GA 30345
(404) 634-4472
Contact: Kelly Johnson, Asst. to the
President
Transportation consultants

CSX/Sea-Land Intermodal
173 Boulevard, S.E., Suite 430
Atlanta, GA 30312
(404) 350-5168
Contact: Tom Ryan, Terminal Manager
Largest intermodal transportation facility
in Southeast

Evans Sand & Gravel
114 Rock Quarry Rd.
Stockbridge, GA 30281
(770) 474-3634
Contact: Chuck Evans, Owner
Heavy hauling

Florida East Coast Railway Company
2295 Parklake Dr., N.E., Suite 125
Atlanta, GA 30345-2812
(770) 934-7916
Contact: John McGahe, Regional Manager

Freight Direct
925 Ashby St., S.W.
Atlanta, GA 30318
(404) 753-2153
Contact: Robert Turner, Terminal
Manager
Local cartage

Industrial Transportation Consultants
P.O. Box 1319
Douglasville, GA 30133
(770) 942-1734
Contact: Diane Hall, Owner
Traffic management

Leaman Chemical Tank Lines
1251 Battle Creek Rd.
Jonesboro, GA 30236
(770) 471-4430
Contact: Ann Morton, District Service
Manager
Multi-chemical transporter

Lykes Bros. Steamship Co.
2000 Powers Ferry Rd., Suite 300
Atlanta, GA 30067
(770) 951-9476
Contact: George Vlahos, Area Sales
Manager

Malin Trucking Co.
3260 E. Bankhead Hwy.
Lithia Springs, GA 30057
(770) 739-0086
Contact: Jimmy Hickman, Safety Director
Petroleum product hauling, liquid asphalt,
sand, gravel

Metropolitan Atlanta Rapid Transit Authority (MARTA)
2424 Piedmont Rd., N.E.
Atlanta, GA 30324
(404) 848-5231

Sikes Transportation Services
450 Henry Ford II Ave.
Atlanta, GA 30354
(404) 763-4049
Contact: Marvin Sikes, General Manager
Private fleet management

Transportation Consultants
5605 Glendridge Dr., N.E., Suite 950
Atlanta, GA 30342
(404) 250-0100
Contact: Paul Gold, President
Private fleet management

United Parcel Service
Corporate Headquarters
55 Glen Lake Parkway, N.E.
Atlanta, GA 30328
(770) 828-7123
Contact: Leon Herron, Director of
Human Resources
Package delivery

Van Line Services
2679 Peachtree Square
Atlanta, GA 30360
(770) 452-1917

Utilities

WEB SITES:

**http://www.webfeats.com/preecs/mive/
resource.html**
is a comprehensive list of utility resources
on the Net; includes employment
opportunities.

http://www.energynet.com/
is a homepage for the public utilities
sector.

**http://home.ptd.net/~srjubin/
pubutil.html**
links to electric, natural gas, and water
utility sites.

PROFESSIONAL ORGANIZATIONS:

For networking in the utilities business,
check out the following local professional
organizations listed in Chapter 5:
Association of Energy Engineers
**Georgia Water and Pollution Control
   Association**

For more information about the utilities
industry, contact the following organizations. Also see **"Electronics/Telecommu-
nications"** for major phone and cellular
companies.

American Gas Association
1515 Wilson Blvd.
Arlington, VA 22209
(703) 841-8400

American Public Gas Association
11094 "D" Lee Hwy.
Fairfax, VA 22030
(703) 352-3890

American Public Power Association
2301 M St., N.W.
Washington, DC 20037
(202) 467-2900

Institute of Public Utilities
Michigan State University
410 Eppley Center
East Lansing, MI 48824
(517) 355-1876

United States Telephone Association
1401 H St., N.W., Suite 600
Washington, DC 20005
(202) 326-7300

PROFESSIONAL PUBLICATIONS:

Electric Light and Power
Public Power
Public Utilities
Public Utility Fortnightly
Telephone Engineering and Management
Telephony

DIRECTORIES:

APGA Directory of Municipal Gas Systems
   (American Public Gas Assoc., Fairfax, VA)
Brown's Directories of North American Gas
   Companies (Edgel Communications,
   Cleveland, OH)
Electrical World Directory of Electrical
   Utilities (McGraw-Hill, New York, NY)
Moody's Public Utility Manual (Moody's
   Investors Service, New York, NY)

Employers:

Atlanta Gas Light Company
Employment Office:
1219 Caroline St., N.E.
Atlanta, GA 30307
(404) 584-4705

City of Atlanta Water Bureau
68 Mitchell St., City Hill Tower
Atlanta, GA 30335
(404) 330-6000
Contact: Mary Ann Johnson, Director of
Human Resources

Clayton County Water Department
1600 Battle Creek Rd.
Morrow, GA 30260
(770) 961-2130
Contact: Angela Denicke, Director of
Human Resources

Cobb County Water & Sewer Department
680 S. Cobb Dr.
Marietta, GA 30090
(770) 419-6201
Do not send resume. Must complete
application in person.

DeKalb County Public Works—Water & Sewer Division
1300 Commerce Dr.
Decatur, GA 30030
(770) 621-7200

Douglas County Water & Sewer Authority
8763 Hospital Dr.
P.O. Box 1157
Douglasville, GA 30133
(770) 949-7617
Contact: Mara Williamson, General
Service Manager

Fayette County Water System
Board of Commissioners
245 McDonough Rd.
Fayetteville, GA 30214
(770) 461-1146
Contact: Personnel

Fulton County Department of Public Works—Water
141 Pryor St., S.W., Suite 4035
Atlanta, GA 30303
(404) 730-6833
Contact: Personnel

Georgia Power Company
333 Piedmont Ave., N.E.
Atlanta, GA 30308
(404) 526-6526
Contact: Human Resources
Employment office:
P.O. Box 4545

Atlanta, GA 30302
Electric service for metro area

Gwinnett County Public Utilities
75 Langley Dr.
Lawrenceville, GA 30245
(770) 822-7171
Contact: Personnel

Henry County Water & Sewer
533 Hampton Rd.
McDonough, GA 30253
(770) 957-6659
Contact: Helen Greer, Financial Officer

Oglethorpe Power Corp.
P.O. Box 1349
Tucker, GA 30085-1349
(770) 270-7600
Contact: Ann Ellison, Human Resources
Manager
Rural membership electric company

Rockdale County Public Works
981 Milstead Ave.
Conyers, GA 30207
(770) 929-4030
Contact: Mary Ann Miller, Director of
Personnel

Southern Co., The
270 Peachtree St.
Atlanta, GA 30303
(770) 393-0650
Electric utilities

Southern Bell Telephone & Telegraph Co.
2835 Brandywine Rd., Suite 408
Chamblee, GA 30341
(770) 780-2941
Employment office:
P.O. Box 54300
Atlanta, GA 30308
Local telephone service for metro area

Employers Index

General Index

Boldface indicates employer listings